MY LIFE
in
POLITICS

MY LIFE
in
POLITICS

JACQUES
CHIRAC

WITH JEAN-LUC BARRE

TRANSLATED BY CATHERINE SPENCER

palgrave
macmillan

MY LIFE IN POLITICS
Copyright © NiL Editions, 2009, 2011.
English-language translation copyright © 2012 by Catherine Spencer
All rights reserved.

First published in France as *Chacque pas doit être un but* and *Les temps présidentiel* by NiL Editions

First published in English in 2012 by PALGRAVE MACMILLAN® in the US—a division of St. Martin's Press LLC, 175 Fifth Avenue, New York, NY 10010.

Where this book is distributed in the UK, Europe, and the rest of the world, this is by Palgrave Macmillan, a division of Macmillan Publishers Limited, registered in England, company number 785998, of Houndmills, Basingstoke, Hampshire RG21 6XS.

Palgrave Macmillan is the global academic imprint of the above companies and has companies and representatives throughout the world.

Palgrave® and Macmillan® are registered trademarks in the United States, the United Kingdom, Europe, and other countries.

ISBN-13: 978-0-230-34088-6

Library of Congress Cataloging-in-Publication Data

Chirac, Jacques, 1932– [Mémoires. English]
  My life in politics / Jacques Chirac ; translated by Catherine Spencer.
    p. cm.
  1. Chirac, Jacques, 1932– 2. Presidents—France—Biography. 3. France—Politics and government—1958– I. Spencer, Catherine. II. Title.
DC424.C484413 2011
944.084'11092—dc23
[B]

2012018097

A catalogue record of the book is available from the British Library.

Design by Letra Libre

First edition: November 2012

10 9 8 7 6 5 4 3 2 1

Printed in the United States of America.

To my grandson Martin

CONTENTS

PART I
EACH STEP A GOAL

*It is not enough to take steps which may someday lead to a goal;
each step must be itself a goal and a step likewise.*

—Goethe, *Conversations with Eckermann*

1
BEGINNINGS

For many years I have kept with me a document depicting the main stages of the evolution of life, the earth, and the universe. This chronological table has accompanied me in both my personal and my political life, at the Élysée Palace or during my trips abroad. I would often get it out of my briefcase and study it in meetings that dragged on or got lost in futile discussion.

Reading this document gave me a comforting sense of the relativity of things and the detachment needed to understand people and events. It is still today one of my most valuable references in appreciating the importance of the issues our planet faces and in interpreting the psychologies of peoples and their leaders in light of the traditions and ways of life, being, and thinking that have fashioned them.

If I reflect on the reasons for my involvement in over forty years of public life, I inevitably come back to the conclusion that for me everything is linked to that passion for the human being, for everything that makes each person unique and the distinct quality—irreplaceable, in my view—of each race and each nation. Nothing, in fact, really predestined me for a career in politics. Surprising as it may seem, I did not grow up with an overriding obsession to one day attain the highest office in the land. For a long time, I had other aspirations and dreams, even if they still tended, one way or another, toward service of my country. After envisaging a career in the army at the time of the war in Algeria, for which I volunteered to fight, my sole ambition on graduating from the École Nationale d'Administration was to become head of the civil aviation authority or governor of the Bank of France, as my father hoped. It was only by chance, and virtually under orders, that I entered politics in 1967 at the age of thirty-five.

Appointed to Georges Pompidou's staff in December 1962, I was summoned by the prime minister one day in May or June 1966. "Chirac," he said, "you will run in Paris in the general election. That is how you will be of most use to me." Caught off guard, I replied that I did not think it was my vocation—having other ambitions, as he knew—but that, nonetheless, I would obey. However, I insisted on standing not in Paris as he asked but in Corrèze, a region in central France that was home to my ancestors and with which I felt more familiar. "Out of the question," Pompidou retorted. "The region is divided into three constituencies. The first is taken, the second is unwinnable at the moment, and the third is one of the hardest in France for us. Since the creation of the republic, the constituency of Ussel has never been out of the left's hands. And then there's the traveling—the roads are appalling. You'll wear yourself out and, when I need you, you will be no use for anything. Given all that," he insisted, "better to run in Paris." In the end, however—and not without difficulty—I won the battle. So that was how I was unwittingly born, if I can put it like that, into political life, at the heart of upper Corrèze, on the plateau of Mille-Sources, where human warmth makes up for the harshness of the climate. I was quickly fired up by the challenge.

Much more than a question of parties or ideologies, politics was from the first a question of people, personalities, and sensitivities for me. Instinctively and temperamentally drawn to other people, it was in this domain that I naturally found my true voice. Although the product of a family that fiercely defended secularism and authentically radical values—my four grandparents were all schoolteachers—I did not receive what might be called a political education from my father or mother. Neither of them had ever demonstrated any beliefs liable to influence me and even less to prepare me to become, one day, the member of Parliament for Corrèze. Were they rather more inclined to the left than to the right or vice versa? I never succeeded in finding out. Both of them, genuinely generous people, taught me the importance of sharing and of service to others, particularly the most deprived.

The only member of my family to have gone into politics was my paternal grandfather, Louis Chirac. I was barely five when he died in May 1937, but I still remember him quite clearly. He was an imposing character, in stature as well as character, being well over six feet tall. With his magnificent head of hair and his majestic voice, he terrified me as a child with an authority that none of his nearest and dearest dared challenge. In his presence, everyone knuckled under. He had only to enter a room and I would immediately flee or hide myself under a table. A teacher as much appreciated by his students as by his superiors, Louis Chirac ended his career as a principal of a school that is still called the Chirac school, so anchored was my grandfather in people's memories. I knew several of his previous pupils, whom he used to hit on the fingers with his ruler.

Well known as a Freemason, Louis Chirac became the venerable host of the local lodge. He was fervently anticlerical. An active member of the radical Socialist Party of Brive, Louis Chirac was involved in all the political battles between the two wars. In 1936, already president of the Popular University, vice president of the association of secular schools, and secretary of the local section of Pupils of the Nation, he took part in the convention of the French Union for Female Suffrage. A photograph that appeared in the newspapers shows Louis Chirac in the middle of a group of feminists under a banner proclaiming "Frenchwomen want the vote!" I was happy and proud of the role my grandfather played in the antifascist rallies held in Brive during the summer of 1936 to support Spanish republicans in the terrible civil war that pitted them against Franco's troops.

Although not as politically involved, my maternal grandfather, Jean Valette—who had been educated by the Jesuits—had, along with his wife, the same republican streak as well as the same principles of a rigorous, secular, and progressive radicalism. This humanistic spirit, which each of my ancestors had defended and enshrined in his or her own way, was an integral part of a family heritage with which I had always identified. It was not by chance that I became a fierce defender of secularism, convinced that a society should give its members the greatest freedom of conscience and conviction and that it was unacceptable to impose religious direction on anyone—although this commitment to secular society has never prevented me from being a believer or having a deep interest in spiritual matters and the history of all religions. My mother, a devout Catholic, took care of my Christian education. I was a choirboy before having briefly entered the scouts, where I was nicknamed—I don't know why—"selfish bison."

I was born in the Fifth Arrondissement of Paris on November 29, 1932. My father had settled there a decade earlier, leaving Corrèze to pursue his career in banking. He was at that time head of the National Bank for Business and Industry, a prestigious post that allowed him to forge close links with the aeronautical world. Like most men of his generation, my father had been deeply affected, emotionally as much as physically, by his experience of the Great War. Called up in 1917 at the age of nineteen, he was wounded in the chest by shell fire in May 1918 and left for dead. He had a three-month convalescence before returning to the front in August. The day after the armistice, he volunteered to fight in Poland against the

Red Army, where he earned a citation for courage and dedication to duty as part of the First Polish Tank Regiment.

My father returned to France in June 1920, worn out by his ordeal on the Russian front. He told me about his war experiences when I asked him, but without dwelling on them and trying not to betray his emotions. He obviously found it distasteful to return to a past that had wounded him on every level. My father had great natural authority. He was sure of himself, demanding, cold, and determined. I loved him very much, but our relationship conformed to the traditional father-son hierarchy, and it was my place to obey him. At the time, such a relationship was a matter of course. My parents were married in February 1921, and their young married life was immediately struck by a drama that traumatized them both: Their first child, a little girl, Jacqueline, was carried off by pneumonia barely two years after her birth. The tragedy probably explains why they waited nearly ten years before having another child.

My mother, born Marie-Louise Valette, was a woman of character, gifted and with a sharp sense of repartee and a frankness that could be disconcerting. Energetic, tenacious, and warm, she was attentive to others and extremely kind. She was also a wonderful housekeeper, reputed for her talents in the kitchen, and her priority was looking after my father and me, her only son, whom she showered with attention and went to extremes to protect. She catered to my every whim and satisfied the slightest of my desires. I adored my mother as much as she adored me. If my childhood was imbued with an atmosphere of certain authority, it was also extremely happy and fulfilling, despite the threat of a war of which I was only dimly conscious.

In the summer, I spent much of the holidays in Sainte-Féréole, the region of my ancestors, which soon became for me a symbol of freedom and exploration. I felt in every way more Corrézian than Parisian, attached to the people I encountered in Sainte-Féréole by ties that were more binding and authentic. In June 1940, when a military defeat unprecedented in our national history plunged France, in the space of a few days, into chaos and poverty, my mother decided to take refuge in Sainte-Féréole. An old family friend, Georges Basset, hurriedly came to pick us up from Paris. We threw a few suitcases into his Renault Vivaquatre and departed for the South like the thousands who were fleeing the capital in the midst of hopeless disorder. On the Parmain Bridge, our car was held up in a traffic jam. It was there that I witnessed a scene that I would never forget.

Georges Basset, a deeply patriotic veteran of the Great War, stopped an officer who was walking along the side of the road: "Captain, what is going on? What are you doing?" "I'm getting out of here. The Germans are just fifty kilometers away." "You mean you are not fighting?" replied an astonished Basset. I can still hear the officer's response: "You must realize, sir—they are shooting at us!" Such was, unfortunately, the mentality of some of my compatriots at that time.

At the time of the exodus, my father was in Canada, where he was on business for Henry Potez, who had recruited him in 1937 as managing director of his company. Potez and his friend Marcel Bloch had revolutionized the aeronautical industry with their development of the Éclair propeller during the war in 1914. Thus it was that during my childhood I always heard about aviation and secretly dreamed of one day making my career in it.

Potez had decided to transfer the headquarters of his company to Rayol, where we lived in a lovely house near Potez's property, where my father and he continued to work. In fact, they no longer had much to do, other than play bridge and discuss the news. Hostile to the collaboration, my father nonetheless had a certain respect for Marshal Pétain, like many men of his generation, united in veneration of the conqueror of Verdun. But over time he began to talk about Pétain with growing regret and a sort of despair while becoming more and more openly Gaullist. He would remain so until his death in 1968.

Every morning I went to the local school in Rayol, an hour's walk from our house. My best friend was Darius Zunino, the son of an Italian immigrant who worked as a farmhand. His family was Communist. Darius had the reputation of being a little hooligan, which I did not exactly object to. Together, we naturally got up to all sorts of mischief. After school, I spent almost all my time wandering about with Darius on the neighboring hills, running in the ravines, hunting birds and fishing, usually barefoot—to such an extent that I found it very difficult to get used to wearing shoes again when we went back to Paris. I have kept an enchanted memory of that period of my life, despite the arrival of the Germans in 1942.

After they invaded the free zone and came to the coast, we started seeing them everywhere, in the vineyards or on the beach roads. They communicated between themselves with field telephones. Kilometers of black wire, which they did not bury, ran through the fields. Darius and I had fun cutting these wires, little realizing the risks we were taking. We were not, of course, engaging in an act of resistance but merely procuring black wire, which had many uses for boys of our age.

On November 27, 1942, while I was walking in the hills of Rayol, I suddenly heard a huge explosion and saw the sky become a giant fireball before filling with smoke. I had just unknowingly witnessed my first historic event: the scuttling of the French fleet anchored in Toulon. When I got home, my father told me what had happened. He was very angry at the notion that France, or rather Vichy, had decided to destroy one of its last military assets. I too was instinctively shocked, feeling that something ignoble had just happened that should have been prevented. In a way, the Toulon crisis contributed to my political awakening.

Two years later, during the night of August 14–15, 1944, the first Allied commandos landed not far from our new residence. That was my other rendezvous with history in the making. Deceived by an abnormally calm sea, Captain Ducourneau's men came ashore not at the arranged place near Potez's beach but near the sheer cliffs of Cap Nègre, which they had to climb under fire from German batteries. Then, in the light of morning, we saw soldiers who spoke our language emerging from the water. Among them was an already legendary character, General Diego Brosset, head of the Free France First Division and one of the first soldiers to rally to General de Gaulle.

My parents put General Brosset up in their house the night following the landing. Awestruck, when I saw his two stars I called him Lieutenant, as I had been taught that lieutenants always had two stripes. The mistake tickled him. Afterward, he wrote me several letters that were always humorously signed "Lieutenant." Several months later, I learned that he had died when his car had fallen into a ravine. Stricken, I decided to pay him homage by christening the dirt road linking the coast to the main road in Rayol General Brosset Avenue, fashioning a simple sign myself. Thirty years later, when I was prime minister, the sign was still there. When the mayor of Rayol learned that I had made it, he asked me to come and install a more official plaque in honor of the hero of my adolescence. Which I duly did, in the presence General Brosset's two children.

Because of the war, it was a very particular childhood. It made me into a somewhat rebellious and provocative boy who was quick not to rise up against the established order but to follow his own inspiration, impulses, and curiosity. Those five years spent on the coast left me with an impression of freedom, a feeling of a kind of wild carefreeness and of being on a permanent summer holiday that did not incline me toward returning to the fold at an age when one should start taking studies seriously.

In 1945, I was enrolled in the Lycée Hoche in St. Cloud, where my parents had temporarily settled on their return to Paris. My stay there was brief, as I was expelled several months later for throwing balls of paper at my geography teacher. Despite my mother's insistence that I wear shoes, I could no longer bear them and walked barefoot whenever I could. Rather than argue about it, I would keep them on until I got outside the house.

The next year we left St. Cloud to live in the Eighth Arrondissement of Paris, where my father had succeeded, not without difficulty, in finding an apartment. I started attending the Lycée Carnot, where I made myself work just enough not to have to repeat the year again and risk spoiling my summer holidays by having to prepare for a re-entrance exam. Having nothing to do during the three months of the summer was my sole objective. I was often sent out of the classroom for unruliness and even decided, some days, to skip school altogether, preferring to stay in my room or wander the streets.

Other than the basic knowledge taught at school, most of what I knew at that time had been learned outdoors or acquired by myself. Around my fifteenth birthday, I began to construct a "secret garden" that I have endeavored since then to safeguard. With money from my mother, I secretly bought books of art or poetry. Why in secret? Due to fear of being misunderstood and a desire to be left to my own devices. As an adult, I continued to give nothing away about my private hobbies, to the extent that I was believed to be impervious to all culture. It is a mistaken belief that I have in fact carefully cultivated by letting people think that my only passions are detective stories and military music.

My interest in art and poetry dated from the time when my parents had just moved into the rue de Seine. I would spend long hours wandering along the banks of the river and the pavements of the Boulevard Saint Germain, fascinated and enchanted by all I was discovering in the booksellers' stalls or in the windows of bookshops and antique dealers. I was passionate about the poems of Aragon, Paul Éluard, and René Char; collected postcard reproductions of the paintings of Chirico, Balthus, Miró, and Kandinsky—who remains one of my favorite painters. It was at that time that I began, unbeknownst to all, stopping on my way to school to visit the Guimet Museum, an unparalleled place of initiation for a solitary boy attracted to the most ancient cultures and living a little out of time, indifferent to everything that was making the news, political or otherwise.

It was in the Guimet Museum that I encountered and learned to love Asia and discovered the genius and grandeur of the great civilizations that are too often placed into ethnographic or exotic straitjackets by the West. I admired the clash between graceful gods and titans on the lintels and pediments of Khmer temples, wondered at the enigmatic smile of magnificent Bodhisattvas, staring at these harmonious, calm figures and listening to their silent message of detachment and serenity. Like many visitors over the years, I meditated on the enlightenment of Prince Siddhartha and followed in imagination the long path of his teachings over the Silk Road. Before the Buddhas with the faces of Aphrodite or Ganymede excavated from Hadda, my mind dreamed of the awe-inspiring meeting between Alexander's lost soldiers and the horsemen of the steppes and the ascetics of India.

When I was about sixteen and considering a conversion to Hinduism, I got it into my head to study Sanskrit, one of the oldest languages in the world. I was told about a teacher by the name of Vladimir Belanovitch and lost no time in going to his little room at the end of a courtyard in the Fourteenth Arrondissement. He was a white Russian, a man in his sixties who managed to preserve a great elegance despite his rather wretched circumstances. A former diplomat forced into exile by the revolution, he had had—like many of his compatriots arriving in France—to try his hand at all sorts of jobs to survive. At first a worker for Renault, then a taxi driver, he made papier-mâché studies of human anatomy called *écorchés* for schools. When I met him, he also gave private language lessons. "M. Belanovitch" knew several languages, including Latin, Greek, and Sanskrit, which he attempted to teach me.

After several weeks, he advised me to give up: "First, you have no gift for it, and secondly, Sanskrit is no use. If you want to learn a language, it would be better to choose Russian." I agreed and, from then on, we were friends. I introduced him to my parents, who also took him to their hearts, even offering to have him stay at our house. He sometimes accompanied us on holiday to Corrèze, where this Russian-speaking Russian caused a stir in Sainte-Féréole.

M. Belanovitch introduced me not only to a language that I spoke almost fluently at seventeen but also to the history of his country, his people, and his literature. He made me read all of Tolstoy and revealed Pushkin and Dostoevsky to me. It was he who encouraged me to translate Pushkin's epic poem *Eugene Onegin* at the age of twenty, a translation that I would send in vain to a dozen publishers and that I still have in my desk. Vladimir Belanovitch represented for me an incomparable pathway to the Russian soul and to a nation to which I have remained deeply attached.

When I left Lycée Carnot at eighteen, my school-leaving certificate—awarded, to general surprise, with honors—under my belt, I had only one desire: to become an oceangoing sea captain. My only ambition since I had begun discovering other worlds and cultures was to travel the seas in every direction. My father, who nursed more serious ambitions for me, took command and enrolled me in advanced mathematics at Lycée Louis le Grand so that I could prepare for the Polytechnique entrance exam.

Notwithstanding, I was determined to follow my desire, and at the beginning of summer 1950, I decided to sign myself up secretly as an apprentice on a merchant marine ship. Heedless of everything but my desire to travel, I ran the risk involved in defying paternal authority. Perhaps it was because I felt confident, come what may, of my mother's unconditional protection.

Pretending that I had been invited to spend ten days with friends in Normandy, I went through all the procedures in Rouen to be taken on by a maritime company. I found a post in Dunkirk, on a 5,000-ton collier, the *Capitaine Saint-Martin,* owned by the Industrial and Maritime Union. Bound for Algiers, where it would offload coal, the ship would then go to Melilla in Spanish Morocco to fill up with iron ore, which it would bring back to Rouen. Before going aboard, I bought myself a pipe and a packet of black sailor's tobacco so as to be authentically maritime. And then there I was, ready to sail.

The captain of the boat was an old globetrotter. When it came alongside our boat, he would climb on to the stern, doubtless a little merry, put the loudspeaker to his lips, and scream "Whoops-a-daisy! There you are! Here we go!" I would later learn that he had overturned a barge going up the Seine and that the Industrial and Maritime Union had decided to divest themselves of his services.

In the Bay of Biscay, I was overtaken by seasickness. I should point out that I had been smoking the pipe continually, to make me seem more like a sea dog, and this naturally made me feel nauseous after a time. The bosun watched over me out of the corner of his eye. He had gone around Cape Horn when the navy still had sailing ships and had astonishing tales to tell about it. When he saw me in distress, bent over the ship's rail, he took me off to his cabin: "Come. You will see."

Conditions on board were hardly luxurious. We worked around the clock and had only one berth among three of us, which we occupied in turn. The bosun scrabbled around in his area, got out four tins of sardines in oil, and made me eat them. At first, I felt like I was going to die but he insisted: "More . . . more . . ." In fact, this remedy proved miraculous, and I was not sick again for the rest of the crossing.

At sea, I hatched plans. Resolved to give up my studies, I determined that when I got back I would take the competitive exam to become an oceangoing captain, with the aim of becoming a captain of a merchant ship, sailing the seas. I had only one desire: to leave Paris for as distant a destination as possible. If I had found a boat leaving for India, I would have jumped on it without hesitation.

Even before disembarking in Algiers, the sailors had spread the word. I was to be treated to the mating game. The bosun asked me if I was a virgin. I replied that I was. "Well, we'll take care of that, you'll see!" he said. It was very kind of him—it had to be done! He took me to the famous quarter of the Casbah where we spent the whole night. When I went back to the ship in the morning, inhaling the odors of disinfectant on the pavements, anisette liqueur, and exotic colonial products, I was a different man.

My adventure at sea lasted more than three months. It taught me more about life, men, and myself than any other experience I had ever had. It confirmed in me this taste for adventure, a love of open spaces that has never left me. When I returned to France, I felt in every way as if I had found my sea legs.

It was now October, and classes at Louis le Grand had begun without me, to the great fury of my father, who still had me down for the Polytechnique in his mind. When the *Capitaine Saint Martin* docked in Dunkirk, I spotted a familiar-looking tall silhouette on the quay and thought: "Here we go—trouble is starting!" In a somewhat brusque tone of voice, my father told me that the joke was over and it was time to come home. He barely let me get a word in. He took me back to Paris without giving me time to explain. It has to be said that, as my father was taller and more solidly built than I, the balance of power was clearly in his favor.

Farewell, then, Maritime and Industrial Union, and my career as a navigator of the high seas! I have kept my first salary slip as an apprentice. When I was appointed prime minister in 1974, the company published a copy of it in its newsletter, the only remaining trace of a life that might have been.

After studying advanced math without any real enthusiasm, I persuaded my parents to let me spend the following year at the famous political institute, Sciences-Po. If the experience proved no more conclusive, it was agreed that I would return to the Lycée Louis le Grand. I therefore entered Sciences-Po in October 1951. I was nineteen and still had the same yearning to travel. Full of an energy that sought occupation without really knowing how or where and conscious that the time had come to devote myself seriously to my studies, I remained a solitary, independent young man, still in search of myself.

Against all expectation, I quickly took to Sciences-Po, all the more easily because I had the benefit of marvelous teachers, whose classes I attended with interest and diligence. I soon formed a small group of friends to whom I have remained close. At the institute, I happily took up again with my friend from the Lycée Carnot, Jacques Friedmann. He would later work alongside me as an advisor and chief of staff in my ministerial offices and then as head of the government. He has been one of the most important people in my life.

It was also at Sciences-Po that I met my future wife, Bernadette de Courcel. A close bond soon developed between us, although we continued to use the formal "vous" to address each other, as was the custom in her family. I would be lying if I claimed that I immediately forsook the company of other young ladies at Sciences-Po, but a particular and deep affinity gradually made us inseparable. Harder working and more conscientious than I, Bernadette helped me prepare the book reports we had to hand in every week—when she did not read the books in my stead. Thanks to her help—the injustice of fate—I sometimes got better marks than she did.

We did not belong to the same social worlds. This was of little concern in my eyes, but I was not unaware that others found it important. It was with some suspicion and perplexity that Bernadette's parents watched a classmate from a humbler background getting so close to their daughter. I was not their natural choice as a match. Particularly as I was still young, jobless, and even thought to be left wing, even Communist . . . When they found out we were probably getting engaged, Bernadette's grandparents asked, "Is he at least baptized?" Bernadette was descended, on her mother's side, from a very old noble family, the Buisserets, whose arms have been featured on the keystone of Tunis Cathedral since the tenth century because of the part they played in the Crusades. Her paternal line of the Chodron de Courcels was a more recent aristocracy, but several of its members had had brilliant careers in diplomacy, the army, finance, and industry. However, the most famous of them, and the character who conferred a certain prestige on his family at that time, was her uncle Geoffroy de Courcel, General de Gaulle's aide-de-camp in London at the beginning of Free France in 1940.

The arrival of a presumed Communist militant in their midst was an understandable cause of alarm to my future in-laws. At eighteen, I had signed the Stockholm Appeal launched by the World Peace Council in 1950 calling for an absolute ban on nuclear weapons. This was in no way an ideological gesture on my part, for I recognized only one ideal at that time: that of nonviolence, as incarnated by my idol Mahatma Gandhi. I had heard of his assassination while listening to the radio in my room on January 31, 1948, and had been distraught. His death was one of the great shocks of my adolescence. Gandhi was one of those men whose teaching most contributed to the formation of my political philosophy.

Like many young people of my generation, horrified by the tragedy of Hiroshima, I was opposed to any further use of nuclear weapons. I knew that the people who urged me to sign the Stockholm Appeal were Communists—which, at first, did not bother me at all. Shortly afterward they invited me to attend one of their cell meetings. "If you want to belong to the Communist Party," they told me, "you will have to begin by selling *L'Humanité.*" Which I valiantly did for several Sundays, until I realized how I was being manipulated by Stalinist propaganda. Appalled by the sectarianism of my companions, I lost no time in distancing myself from them.

At Sciences-Po, I formed a friendship with a left-wing student named Michel Rocard, whose sparkling intelligence, sensitivity, and liveliness of mind I appreciated. He talked quickly, rode around on a moped, and smoked as much as I did. Constantly feverish, in a hurry, impatient, carting around with him a bag crammed with books and files, Michel was one of the organizers of the group of Socialist students. So deeply was I in agreement with his anticolonial, third-world views that I sometimes thought he was too moderate. One day, Michel told me it was time for me to join the French Section of the Workers' International (SFIO). After accompanying him to a section meeting, I replied that his party seemed to me too conservative, if not reactionary, and that it lacked dynamism. In short, the SFIO was not left wing enough for me. On this point, Michel and I were basically in agreement: We both took an unflattering view of the Socialist Party at the time.

How to separate out what was provocation and contrariness from genuine conviction in these first political forays of my youth? As with many of my fellow students, it was the rejection of a conformist and reactionary right, and even more so of the extreme right, that instinctively drew me to the left. But for all that, I would not join the Communist Party or the Socialist groups organized by Michel. As for Gaullism, for me it was synonymous with the Rassemblement pour la République (RPF) Party founded by General de Gaulle, which I also judged too conservative and to which I did not belong, contrary to what has since been asserted. In fact, my interest in politics was still very limited at that time. I was much more attracted to other experiences, primarily my still-unsatisfied desire for adventure and travel. At the end of my first year at Sciences-Po, I left for Scandinavia with a good friend. But the most memorable trip was the one I made to the United States in the summer of 1953. The American myth was more in vogue than ever, and it was in that period that I discovered the music of Sidney Bechet, Hemingway's novels, and the first films of Marlon Brando. Few students from Sciences-Po had ventured across the Atlantic, but I and two others managed to enroll in the summer session of Harvard Business School.

In October 1953, shortly after returning to France, I decided to get engaged to Bernadette de Courcel. Despite their initial reluctance, her parents had eventually given their consent, and in time my future mother-in-law became my greatest supporter. Our relationship was always founded on respect, openness, and mutual affection. Mme de Courcel, whom I called Mother, helped familiarize me with a world into which I managed, partly thanks to her, to integrate. In fact, I adapt quite easily to the different circumstances in which I find myself—but since that time I have always avoided every form of high society, refusing cocktail parties and dinners in town, where people, however intelligent and cultivated, rarely have anything interesting to say.

After three trouble-free years at Sciences-Po, I no longer had any doubt—even if I let myself be carried away by events to some extent—that my vocation was to serve the nation. In June 1954, after ranking third in my year, I decided to take part in the selective exam for the École Nationale d'Administration. In November, I was again in America when my father sent me a telegram to say that I had passed the written part of the exam and was to return to France as soon as possible to take the oral part.

The jury of the "Grand Oral" was composed of a dozen personalities, senior civil servants and university lecturers, and was presided over by Louis Joxe. After drawing a subject at random, candidates have half an hour—and not a second longer—to prepare a talk of ten minutes. It is a test of discipline and self-mastery. Unfortunately, that day I was suffering from flu and struggled to answer the questions I was asked. Joxe, who was a music lover, began talking to me about Bayreuth, the music festival. So I explained: "M. President, I prefer to tell you straight away that I am not a musician. Ask me about archeology, painting, sculpture, or poetry. Not about music." He said to me afterward: "The jury thought that was a good answer." It was again Joxe who asked me the last question: "Reference is often made to the philosophy of this doctor of the ancient world—you know who I mean, Mr. Chirac." My head was spinning more and more, and without pausing to think, I answered: "Yes, M. President, you are talking about Hypocrite." It was a slip of the tongue that plunged the panel into a fit of laughter but did not prevent me from being admitted to the ENA.

Before taking up my place, however, I had to fulfill my military obligations—this time during a war, which still dared not speak its name, that had just broken out in Algeria.

2

THE ALGERIAN PROBLEM

I was particularly sensitive to the Algerian problem because I fought in the mountains for over a year, from April 1956 to June 1957, before being appointed a civil servant to the seat of government in Algiers two years later.

Successive French governments might not have known what to do in regard to Algeria, but the orders we received on the ground were very precise. We carried them out without fuss, and my squadron performed well. We did not deserve to be beaten—indeed, we were not. For many of us, the most serious issue at stake was that we had given our word of honor, both personally and on behalf of France, to the people who had rallied to our cause that we would never desert them. And then we had, against our wishes and sick at heart, to abandon to the enemy those who had trusted us and who had often put themselves at risk on our behalf.

I had left Algeria by then, my military service over. However, I was able to measure the terrible consequences that policies dictated by Paris could have on the ground. Even if reason led me to support the actions of General de Gaulle, emotionally I felt closer to my comrades who demanded a French Algeria. I do not offer here any apology for that on the basis of my youth or political inexperience; if I were placed in the same circumstances today, I think I would feel the same dilemma and the same sentiment of being torn in different directions.

In March 1956, graduating eighth out of 118 from the officer training school in Saumur, I was completing my military service in Germany when

events came to a head on the other side of the Mediterranean. Parliament
had just granted the new head of government, Guy Mollet, "special powers" for Algeria, after having called in vain on the National Liberation
Front (FLN) for a cease-fire. He announced an increase in numbers to
500,000 men, the conscription of reserve soldiers, and the prolongation of
military service to twenty-seven months.

My squadron was called up. I was therefore preparing to leave when
I learned, to my fury and bemusement, that I had been designated to join
the French chief of staff in Berlin, where they needed an interpreter who
spoke Russian. I immediately said to my colonel that I could not possibly
accept such a comfortable and safe post at a time of war. He eventually
gave in to my insistence, as they needed officers in Algeria. It was there, and
only there, that I could be of use to my country, I believed. This did not,
however, prevent my decision from being very badly received by the highest
authorities. When I did not arrive in Berlin, the military police were alerted
and turned up in force at my parents' home to arrest me as a deserter. I was
already en route for Algeria. My colonel pleaded on my behalf, and the
matter was not taken any further.

My personal life was also disrupted. Shortly before leaving France, I
had married Bernadette; circumstances deprived us of a honeymoon and
condemned us to a separation of several months—a situation that was hard
for us both but even harder for Bernadette, who now had to get used to a
very untypical married life.

I arrived in Oran and took command of a platoon of thirty-two men
belonging to the Third Squadron of Chasseurs d'Afrique, the regiment of
France's army in Algeria. We were posted to the mountainous Souk el-
Arba, near the Moroccan border, a wild, desert area consisting of a handful
of cob houses perched on a promontory, from the top of which one could
survey the wadis to the south and the plains to the north. The region was
beginning to be taken over by groups of fellaghas, the Algerian rebels, when
we arrived, charged with the mission of maintaining order and protecting
the local people—who were torn between a desire to appease the colonial
power and not oppose the rebellion. We frequently arrested suspects, who
increased in number over the months.

Most of these suspected resistance fighters were transferred for inter-
rogation to our regiment's headquarters in Montagnac. Were some of them
tortured, as was increasingly alleged back in France? The only thing I can
say with certainty is that I never witnessed any such acts in the domain,
admittedly very limited, in which I found myself. Which does not mean that
such practices did not take place. In the area of my concern, I kept a strict

watch on ensuring that everyone in my platoon, without exception, treated the Algerian people with respect. The whip that was always with me was the best way of calling to order those tempted to behave disrespectfully to the indigenous people, particularly the women, or to give themselves over to all sorts of excesses. During my official visit to Algeria in 2003, President Bouteflika read an extract from a book written by a former maquis (resistance fighter): "There was a unit in the willaya commanded by a certain Chirac and I wish to pay this French officer homage. . . . Because he always behaved with total correctness toward people."

That said, the men under my command—many of whom were Polish volunteers—were in the main tough and resilient. For those who, like me, naturally sought contact with others, this was a rich human experience. It was one of the few moments of my existence in which I genuinely had the sense that I had a direct and immediate influence on the course of events and on the lives of those for whom I was responsible. We were not concerned with politics, which we were careful not to discuss, but with a brotherhood of arms that we experienced daily as we faced death in every ambush and every clash with an enemy that was ever more aggressive and elusive.

It would be improper for me to dwell on my war record, which was not particularly heroic. I will just mention the episode that earned me the military valor cross with the citation: "On January 12, 1957, at El Krarba, while a section of the platoon had just been assaulted by a rebel band, he brought out his platoon under enemy fire and led the attack at the head of his men. His action allowed the wounded to be evacuated and arms and equipment to be recuperated."

My most moving memory of that war, which was so bloody, was that of a young Muslim soldier, age barely fourteen or fifteen, who died in my arms after having jumped onto a mine right next to me. At first, I thought he had escaped miraculously unharmed from the explosion. He was not bleeding and had no visible wounds. When I opened his shirt, I saw a small red hole: An imperceptible piece of shell had gone through his chest and had lodged in his heart. Moments later, he closed his eyes, and I felt his body becoming heavier. Distraught and helpless, I tried vainly to resuscitate him. But it was already too late.

In April 1957, I assumed command of the Third Squadron for three months until the end of my prescribed time in Algeria. I left the army with sadness and even contemplated signing up for good. Back in France, I thought only of returning; were it not for the opposition of Bernadette and the principal of the École Nationale d'Administration, who reminded me of my commitment to serve not the army but the state, doubtless I would have chosen a life in the army—the career that seemed best to fit my aspirations.

What struck me on my return from Algeria, where I had lived for more than a year, practically cut off from everything, was the moral, political, and administrative collapse of our country, in which the bankruptcy of the government was combined with the apathy of public opinion. No one seemed angered or even surprised that, month after month, the French government was forced to go begging abroad to make ends meet. Having appealed to the Americans, now here we were forced to go to the Germans, twelve years after liberation. Politics at that time resembled a shadow theater in which interchangeable and disillusioned forms jostled about incoherently. I even wondered whether it was still useful, and even appropriate, for me to serve a state that was no longer worthy of the name. This period preceding the return to power of General de Gaulle had a profound effect on me; it was one of the rare times of disappointment and discouragement that I have known over the course of my life.

In 1959, I graduated sixteenth in my class from the ENA—a very average ranking that would still allow me to work for the Court of Auditors. At that time, thanks to General de Gaulle, serving the state had once more become an exalted task. De Gaulle! Before 1958, the general was a legendary figure for me, along the lines of Vercingetorix and Joan of Arc, a historical luminary as bright as Richelieu or Clemenceau. As for the Gaullists, they embodied for me the refusal to bow to fate and the capacity to stand up and say no—virtues that I believed more than ever laudable and necessary. But if in 1959 I felt close to those who had restored the state, I still did not see myself as part of their political family.

Politics was still not among my real preoccupations; I continued, even at a distance, to be interested in Algeria's destiny, in an instinctive, visceral reaction connected to people as people rather than to the ideas that might animate them. To demand a French Algeria when one has never been a mindless supporter of colonialism might seem contradictory, to say the least, but the strongest and best-constructed arguments often prove fragile when they face the test of realities that are themselves complex and paradoxical. I did not oppose the Algerians' right to independence and I was not unaware of the unjust treatment they had received, but I also understood the distress and even the anger of those who had been settled in that land of Algeria for generations and who were attached to the fruit of their labors and eager to safeguard it. In fact, reaching a compromise between the aspirations of the two communities would have been realistic if an extremist ideology had not swept both sides up in a more pragmatic vision of Algeria's future.

In June 1959, the students of my graduating year were sent to Algeria as "administrative reinforcements," with the exception of those who had already completed their military service. In theory, I was therefore exempted from returning—but I again volunteered to serve in Algeria and left France, this time accompanied by Bernadette and our little girl, Laurence. Appointed to the central government, my task was to ensure the application of the "Constantine plan." In the mind of General de Gaulle, already won over to the idea of self-determination for the Algerian people, this plan was a last chance. It involved the proposed redistribution of land in favor of Muslim farmers, something that had, unfortunately, been long refused by the great colonial landowners. Among my ex-classmates in Algeria, I was one of the few to believe that the Constantine plan still had a chance of success.

In the last week of January 1960, the so-called barricade riots, launched by a group of *pied noirs* who felt betrayed and abandoned by the mother country, marked a tragic turning point in relations between Paris and Algiers. Like many others, I was witness to the inconsistency, even collapse, of the authorities in charge of law and order on the ground. It was a disturbing sight.

At the time, the delegate general was Paul Delouvrier and the commander in chief General Challe. A superb pairing of a senior official of caliber and an authentic leader, respected by his men. At the end of the 1950s, Delouvrier had been the victim of a serious car accident after which a piece of steel had been placed in his leg, as a temporary measure. When he was appointed delegate general in December 1958, he did not have time to have it removed. In the days leading up to the Algerian uprising, Delouvrier had gone to Paris to be operated on. He had just come back and was walking around in slippers, leaning on two canes.

During the barricades affair, we witnessed an astonishing scene when Delouvrier and Challe appeared side by side. We were expecting to see the former limping and the latter proud and imposing. In fact, it was the exact opposite that occurred. Delouvrier, at the cost of a supreme effort, had put on his shoes and put his canes to one side and he walked, looking straight ahead, as upright as a ramrod. Challe, in the full uniform of an air force general, covered in medals won with great difficulty, shuffled along wearing enormous slippers: He was suffering from an illness affecting the soles of his feet.

The image of power embodied by these two men in Algiers, one doing all he could to save face, the other hiding nothing of his true state, was all the more poignant because their respective authority, over civilian administration and the army, was just as uncertain and shaky.

In my post, it was easy to observe the increasing disarray within the government. There were supposed to be fifteen deputies. How many remained in their posts? Two or three, at the most. The rest vanished into thin air. On the evening of January 24, after the bloodiest clash between the forces of order and demonstrators, one of the most eminent of these senior officials was discovered, terrified, hiding at the home of a friend. The others ran even farther. My boss, Jacques Pélissier, proved one of the strongest and most dignified, and perhaps the only one who was truly loyal. His example impressed me so deeply that, fourteen years later, I called on this courageous man to lead my cabinet in Matignon, the official residence of the prime minister.

Returning to France in April 1960, while General de Gaulle, through his firm grip and his eloquence, won a first victory over the uprising, I took up a post as auditor with the Court of Auditors. Nostalgic for what was, when all was said and done, the heady times I had spent in Algeria, I had nonetheless become convinced that the only way out of the crisis lay in a recognition of the right of Algerians to assume their own destiny. Such is the direction in which history moves, for them as for France.

In looking back at these events, however, I find it impossible not to shudder at the appalling fate inflicted on many of those who were our companions in arms, the harkis (Algerian fighters)—humiliated and massacred for having been unswervingly loyal to our cause. The suffering and the atrocities were, certainly, innumerable on both sides, but those experienced by the harkis who remained in Algeria after the cessation of hostilities can never be forgotten. We have a duty to remember them, a duty I have since aspired to fulfill.

3

APPRENTICE
TO POWER

When I think of the full, rich years I have lived, I also think of the harsh weight and the solitude of having to confront destiny alone. It is far more agreeable to have guidance and to be able to rely on experience, trust, and friendship. I had that good fortune for more than ten years, until Georges Pompidou's death, and indeed I would not be the person I am now if life had not blessed me with that encounter. Much more than a spiritual father, Georges Pompidou was for me a role model who never ceased to guide me especially when I found myself faced with the awesome responsibility of exercising power wisely.

Rare are those politicians who know how to disengage themselves from political ambition to become the embodiment of a nation's heart and destiny. Georges Pompidou was one such man. Working alongside him from 1962, I witnessed firsthand his transformation into the successor of General de Gaulle as president of the republic. In the beginning, Pompidou had not wanted power. He had refused when General de Gaulle had first offered him the post of prime minister in 1958. The second time, he felt it would have been unseemly again to refuse the honor that de Gaulle was offering him. It was not part of his career plan, as he had always made family life a priority; it also prevented him from enjoying the rather anarchic freedom he wanted to preserve. Nonetheless, he never lost his solid common sense. The general had observed him and had "chosen" him gradually, in the same way as ranchers groom bulls on their way to a bullfight. But Pompidou had not yet faced the test of the ring; that would come during what would be his rite of passage, the miners' strike of 1963, shortly after he was appointed head of the government.

Georges Pompidou counted more for me, personally and in terms of my political education, than the general because I knew him better. The man was exceptionally cultivated and had an unusual degree of moral integrity and intellectual rigor. To me, he symbolized France as much as de Gaulle. One aspect of his personality and of his qualities as a statesman particularly struck me: the humanity of his outlook, which sought to encompass diverse cultures and to facilitate the cultural cross-fertilization of contemporary society. This purebred Frenchman, the son of primary school teachers, prepared our country for the challenges of globalization and the difficult but necessary construction of Europe. To those who accused him of devoting himself too much to foreign affairs, Pompidou would remark—with a confidence that was clairvoyant—that internal problems increasingly found their solution in the international arena and one could no longer imagine peace without universal security or economic and social progress outside Europe.

The man gave the appearance of being secretive, wily, a little cunning— which he was, to a degree. However, it was primarily his intelligence, culture, and competence that conferred indisputable authority on him and commanded respect. I feel truly moved as I remember his untamed eyebrows, his penetrating, very kindly gaze, his perceptive smile, full of humor and mischievousness, his voice with its wonderful low, warm, gravelly tone, and a figure that was both powerful and elegant. Naturally reserved, little given to emotional outbursts, Pompidou did not forge very close ties with his colleagues. Whatever my feelings of affection or admiration toward him, I knew better than to express them too openly. Our relationship was never truly intimate, for that was not his style. In a way, I felt more at ease with General de Gaulle.

It was to a former classmate of Sciences-Po that I owed my entry into Matignon, the prime minister's headquarters, in December 1962. It was shortly after the birth of my second daughter, Claude. One of my former classmates' responsibilities was drafting reports of the interministerial councils; knowing that I had been treading water at the Court of Auditors since my return from Algeria, he proposed that I take over the task. I accepted without hesitation.

Six months later, after a reorganization of the functions in Matignon, I had become a member of the prime minister's office, where I was brought to the attention of the head of Georges Pompidou's cabinet, François-Xavier Ortoli, who offered me a post within his team at the lowest level, as a policy officer. One day in December 1962, he asked me to come at 6:00 P.M. to be introduced to the prime minister. I went with him into the office of Pompidou, who was signing correspondence. The room was barely lit. Absorbed in his task, he did not react to our arrival but continued to work in silence, not even according us a glance.

Embarrassed, a little anxious, I did not know what to do or say. Eventually, Pompidou lifted his head and then immediately lowered it. "Prime Minister," Ortoli said, "I want to introduce you to Jacques Chirac, a new member of your cabinet who comes from the Court of Auditors." Then he added: "He is very good." Pompidou replied, without giving me another glance: "I should hope so. If he wasn't very good, I don't think you would have taken him on." Realizing that this first meeting had come to an end, Ortoli gestured to me and we withdrew.

In Matignon, where I was quick to take on work and to resolve problems without worrying about conforming to a system that was often bogged down in tradition, I quickly acquired the reputation of a bulldozer. I was also suspected of never taking the time to reflect, of being overconfident and unaware of subtleties. In short, I was caricatured as a rather rough-and-ready, shallow go-getter. But the only thing that mattered to me was remaining faithful to the principle of serving my country.

Over the next five years, I served my political apprenticeship in Matignon, in the shadow of Georges Pompidou. The prime minister's entourage teemed with eminent people, who all left their mark on the simple policy officer I would remain until my direct entry into politics. All the other members of the cabinet managed to get appointments as technical advisors. Most of them had been determined to reach this grade, and, in hierarchies of this type, those who shout loudest are always the ones who end up being promoted. If I didn't become a technical advisor, it was simply because I did not ask for the position.

I was more preoccupied with the work I was assigned, particularly in regard to aeronautics and most of all the construction of Concorde, which I defended from the start. When the Labour Party came to power in Britain in 1966, it immediately decided to bring to a halt the two great Anglo-French projects that predecessors had initiated, Concorde and the channel tunnel; I was among those few who argued for France not to withdraw in its turn. Against the advice of the minister of finance, who was alarmed by the cost involved and who belonged to the group who wanted to abandon both projects, I fought for them, convinced of their industrial and economic benefits. In March 1969, General de Gaulle asked me to represent the government in Toulouse on the occasion of Concorde's maiden flight.

Back in Paris, he invited me to dinner to hear about it, as full of pride and enthusiasm as I was because France had been able to bring a project of this scope to successful completion.

Although I was not part of the prime minister's close circle, I often encountered him, despite the distance he wanted to keep from his entourage. Georges Pompidou and I did not need long conversations to create mutual understanding. The relationship that slowly grew between us was doubtless largely due to our similar backgrounds: We came from the same area of France and had been shaped by the same rural, provincial mold. We were both products of secular schools—and both lovers of good food and very fond of poetry.

My post enabled me to meet most of the important ministers of that period. The one with whom I dealt most often was without doubt André Malraux. I played an active role in one of the big decisions of his ministry: the creation, in January 1963, of the general inventory of France's monuments and artistic heritage. We often dined alone at his favorite restaurant, where our discussions about Asian art, about which he claimed to know much, often ended with one or the other of us raising our voices. I was not afraid to reproach him for the art trafficking he had engaged in as a youth while also challenging his supposed artistic knowledge. My criticisms exasperated him, plunging him into barely controlled anger, but for all that, he did not put a stop to our discussions. I could not help being fascinated by this character, whose mannerisms I would unconsciously copy on the days we met, and admire the author of *The Human Condition*, his political engagement against fascism and the colonial system, as well as his sense of justice and brotherhood.

For Malraux, with his flashes of genius, history became myth and political action a lyrical epic. With a lock of hair falling over his eyes, a bulging forehead, nervous hands, and staccato speech, Malraux tossed ideas, words, and images into the air like a magician, dazzling in his virtuosity without ever being completely taken in himself by the effect he sought to exert, and almost always produced, on others. In this way, he would paint me a portrait of the war in Spain that was both apocalyptic and intoxicating, full of lively shortcuts, vivid and unexpected metaphors in which the sublime competed with the paradoxical. Thanks to Malraux, I came to realize how romantic the political adventure could be.

In January 1965, I received a phone call from the prefecture of Brive-la-Gaillairde telling me that I was a candidate in the municipal elections of Sainte-Féréole. "You didn't know?" said the surprised voice. "You are on the list of the Republican Party. There aren't any others. You're sure to be elected." I immediately called the radical Socialist mayor, a man of Polish origin but the very archetype of a Corrézian. Lacking a town councilor to complete his list, he was adamant that he had approached me about it in writing. "You didn't answer me. I took that to mean you agreed." In fact, I had never received his letter. But that was of little consequence, since the affair was already under way. And that is how I made my first beginnings in politics: virtually against my wishes.

This first election did not have a direct consequence on the career I undertook, two years later. The constituency of Brive had been held since 1962 by a confirmed Gaullist, and I had no reason to try to infiltrate there. I obtained Georges Pompidou's agreement in principle ("No harm in trying") to stand for the constituency of Ussel, in Corrèze—a most unlikely one for a Rassemblement pour la République candidate as it was a radical Socialist stronghold in an area that had a significant Communist presence— and immediately set off for the fight. Politics is not war, but it resembles it. I took a liking to it, just as I had liked my all-too-brief experience as a soldier in Algeria. I would leave Matignon at the end of every Friday afternoon, driving fast for part of the night in my ancient Peugeot 403. After sleeping a couple of hours on my arrival in Ussel in the small public housing apartment I had rented not far from the station, which also served as my electoral base, I began to meet all those who, usually wanting to ask me to do something for them, were already queuing in the stairway. Then I went out into the constituency, usually accompanied by Bernadette, who was also actively campaigning for me.

My chances of success were, at first sight, very slim. Especially as I still did not possess any real political network apart from a small team of militant Gaullists, who were themselves doubtful that I could win. Among the few assets I possessed in a district that was rather hostile to the government was the fact that I belonged to the prime minister's cabinet. At that time, upper Corrèze was one of the most underdeveloped areas in France. Economically, it lagged significantly behind: Everything was lacking—roads, schools, telephones—and many of the young people wanted to leave, unable to find work. In a region so clearly neglected by the government, the electors, even those least favorable toward me, saw me as better placed than anyone else to mobilize the public authorities, get them the government grants they needed, help the farmers, and respond to families' expectations. A quick phone call to the minister concerned would sometimes get me a favorable answer in the ensuing days.

From the start of the campaign, I favored direct, personal contact over party considerations. I undertook to meet every elector, one by one, without distinction. My priority was to get to know them individually, find out what they were thinking, listen to their grievances—which I recorded on a little Dictaphone so they could be noted and if possible satisfied on my return to Paris. The local Communists often seemed surprised that I in no way shunned them, and they appreciated this unusual mark of respect from a candidate on the so-called right. With just one or two exceptions, I was well received everywhere. After several months, there were few houses where I had not gone at least once. The enthusiasm and energy that I displayed without forcing myself on people did not go unnoticed in this constituency in which the successful candidates, used to winning without even campaigning, limited themselves to a few public meetings. I also had the support in the local press of an influential force, the politician and entrepreneur Marcel Dassault; of several important local political figures; and of the mayor of Ussel, Dr. Henri Belcour, whose father had been head of the local Resistance. Their name was tremendously respected in upper Corrèze, where discretion, a sense of duty, and loyalty to the region were prized.

On March 12, 1967, I was narrowly elected member for Ussel by 18,522 votes against 17,985 for my Communist opponent. The next day, bubbling with excitement, I left for Paris and went to present myself at Matignon: "There you are! Mission accomplished." Georges Pompidou, who had come down to lend me his support in person during the campaign, seemed pleased. He advised me to go and declare myself in Parliament as soon as possible. The newly formed government had won by a single seat, and mine was one of the few seats, if not the only one, that it had managed to win from the opposition.

When I returned to Corrèze, I stopped off in Clermont Ferrand to see Francisque Fabre, a longtime Socialist who had given me much support during the campaign. We spoke. With him, I felt like a representative of the people, and when I left him, I was hungry—always a good sign with me. In the square, I spotted a large brasserie with the sign "All Day Choucroute." As I dined, I plunged into a newspaper story that went into great detail about my victory. I did not hear the voice that came through a loudspeaker: "M. Chirac is wanted on the telephone!" It took another announcement and the insistence of the visibly awed waiter: "It's for you. Hurry up. It's General de Gaulle!" to get me to respond. All eyes were fixed on me as I crossed the room to the telephone booth. If the owners of the brasserie had not seemed so genuinely agitated, I might have believed it was a hoax. I picked up the receiver. At the end of the line was the general's aide-de-camp: "The General is expecting you tomorrow at 11:00 A.M.," he announced. I went back to my seat and, to put an end to the spectacle, asked for the bill and left.

That morning in March 1967, at eleven o'clock, the day after my election in Corrèze, I met the head of state for the first time alone. During my five years in the cabinet of Georges Pompidou, I had glimpsed the general at every important occasion. Was that why I did not feel particularly intimidated, or even impressed, when I found myself alone with him? Certainly, any kind of familiarity with this man who already occupied a tremendous place in history was unthinkable. One spontaneously felt respect and admiration for such a monumental figure, who had always seemed to embody France itself. But what particularly struck me that day was his extreme courtesy and air of kindliness, so that he seemed extremely easy to approach. I said to myself that only great men manage to attain such simplicity.

The general was clearly very well informed about me—as a dossier on his desk testified—and he seemed to know everything about my career to date, my origins, my family, and my studies. Above all, he was interested in the young member of Parliament for Corrèze, having followed the election there with the same attention he gave the results for every constituency, monitoring what happened to them in successive elections. The high idea that the general had of France—the all-encompassing vision that he had of its destiny and its place in the world—was rooted in an intimate and detailed knowledge of its local idiosyncrasies, with its customs and habits, political, geographical, and even culinary. In the half hour interview he granted me, we spoke exclusively about the political and economic situation in Corrèze, on which he questioned me in detail, curious about every aspect, as if the future of the country was closely linked to what happened in every region of France—which he had taken the time to visit, one after another, since his return to power.

One evening in April 1967, I met Georges Pompidou on a stairway in Matignon. He had just come back from the Élysée Palace, where he had gone to propose the members of his new government to the general. He took me by the arm: "Jacques, don't say anything, but I have reserved a minor role for you." After a short silence, he looked at me, his eyes smiling. That was how I became secretary of state for employment. When my father-in-law heard the news, he said to his daughter: "Really, Bernadette, your husband does not know what he wants. . . . He has just been elected a member of Parliament and now he is resigning to do something else."

Indeed, I went into Parliament only twice as a member. Everything happened much more quickly than I could possibly have imagined.

4

MAY '68

Who can truly claim to have predicted the crisis of May 1968? It is always tempting to rewrite history after the event, but the truth is that we were all taken by surprise. No one, not even the general, foresaw the scope of the protest movement that seized hold of a youth more preoccupied with freedom of lifestyle than with a real political revolution.

However, a certain social malaise was perceptible, linked particularly to a level of unemployment that was beginning to cause concern. Georges Pompidou was one of the few to realize its importance and had taken the initiative of creating a department for employment. "You should realize," he said to me, when entrusting me with the task, "that employment will become a major problem in our country." My job was to help the unemployed find work while also protecting them. The first measures giving compensation to the unemployed were negotiated and put in place. This was followed by a job creation agency as well as a minimum rate payable to employees who were laid off.

These reforms gave our country one of the best systems of social protection in the world, one of the fairest and most needed even if it has regularly been criticized by the advocates of economic liberalism. Their vision can in part be blamed for the ravages and abuses felt so dramatically today. To his credit, Pompidou quickly discerned what action was needed and laid the essential groundwork for it, under the auspices of General de Gaulle.

The great lesson I learned from the general was how careful, exacting—even intransigent—he was in deciding government policy, not in terms of party position but in terms of what he judged France's best interest. One sensed that he was immovable on that issue, which conferred on the presidential role, as he embodied it, exceptional dignity and grandeur. Under his authority, the state seemed indestructible. Yet it took only a student move-ment to shake the power that he had held for a decade.

In May 1968, I saw politicians who had been preeminent in the Gaullist universe fall apart and fall away. The most terrified demanded, in the name of the good of Gaullism, the immediate resignation of the gen-eral. I often thought of him, this man of storms and solitude, who coun-seled others to walk the high peaks because one was certain not to meet anyone else up there. That formula had never been so relevant. Georges Pompidou, for his part, remained absolutely true to himself at the worst of the May crisis. I can still see him, in his office filled with people bustling about in agitated fashion while he stolidly carried on working, indifferent to the tumult.

In that period in which we were constantly on alert, I was struck by the calm with which Pompidou and his advisor Pierre Juillet, with cabinet member Pierre Somveille in the neighboring office, carried on their discus-sions in the small room in Matignon that we called the blue sitting room. They would occasionally take refuge there as if obeying some tacit agree-ment. Were they exchanging state secrets? Nothing of the sort. Pompidou and Juillet were following events minute by minute while discussing, quite simply, cigars . . . Both great cigar lovers, they analyzed the important ques-tions of how to preserve and smoke them.

If they disagreed on a problem, they would not leave each other un-til they had found resolution. Somveille would come rushing in asking "Should we charge? Should we destroy the barricades?" and Pompidou shifted, with astonishing suppleness, from one conversation to the other. He had the situation briefly summarized to him and gave his directions. The conversation about cigars served no other purpose than ensuring the detachment necessary for a measured reflection.

In politics as in war, a man's true character is revealed only under fire. While that test is not there, all hypotheses remain possible. One finds out who men really are when they are faced with danger, in that unstoppable moment in which every certainty is shaken.

I felt in no way hostile to the student rebellion as such, nor particularly shocked by the demands of a youth that wanted free morals. Desire for change is natural in the young, as I tried hard to make my government col-leagues understand. If I had been their age, I would doubtless have joined the '68 students. Like them, I had not felt blind submission or boundless gratitude to my teachers. Like them, I had felt ill at ease in my society and that adults did not understand me. However, the fact remained that I now found myself on the other side of the barricade, in the camp of the state, where I was working with all my might, alongside Georges Pompidou, to try to avoid a social explosion that was much more serious and uncontrollable.

"The unions must not come in now," Pompidou said to me the day after the great mass demonstration of May 13 that had sown terror in the government ranks. "I am counting on you to maintain contact with them." And thus I found myself in the front line in the more or less secret negotiations with the heads of the principal unions.

Everything began on May 20 in a somewhat fantastical manner. Having entreated General de Gaulle to engage in dialogue with the unions and obtained his agreement as well as that of Pompidou, I had a secret meeting with Henri Krasucki of the General Confederation of Labor (CGT) union. From experience, I knew that it was possible to find common ground with this determined, shrewd, and intelligent man who wanted to act for the general good. Discussions between government and unions were often crude, each side entrenched in its position, letting go only for tactical reasons. With Henri Krasucki, one could have a real exchange and go beyond the rather confined framework of traditional negotiations. Given the circumstances, however, our contact had to be clandestine; from now on, we even telephoned each other using code names, mine being "M. Walter."

Krasucki agreed to a meeting on a bench near the Place Pigalle. He did not come himself but sent one of his trusted men. I went alone. When I got there, I searched in vain for the meeting place, which seemed to have been replaced by a car park under construction. Was it a trap? A man approached me, smoking a pipe. He gave me the agreed password, then apologized for the misunderstanding; they had not known that the place had changed. I communicated the government position to him: We would open large-scale negotiations on pay, the minimum wage, and the national health care system. The man said he would pass on the message and disappeared. The next day, Pompidou ordered me to keep in close contact with the CGT from then on.

Three days later, another meeting, this time with Krasucki himself, in the same working-class area. On the advice of Pompidou, worried that I might be kidnapped, I carried a revolver, concealed in one of my jacket pockets. Two security men followed me at a distance with orders to intervene if I did not come back within three-quarters of an hour. Such precautions might seem ridiculous or excessive today, but in the climate of the time, they were in no way surprising.

Two CGT men took me to a small, untidy room on the third floor of a rather ordinary building, where Krasucki was waiting for me. This was the secret beginning of the negotiations that would officially start on May

25 and that would lead to the Grenelle agreements. Convinced like me that the only way out of the crisis was to reach an understanding with the CGT, led by Georges Séguy, and through it a Communist Party that was deeply resistant to the excesses of the left, Georges Pompidou also saw this as the best way of breaking the union stronghold.

It took two seemingly interminable and difficult days of negotiations before we reached a solution during the night of May 27. I regularly left the room in the ministerial department to go and talk in the corridor with Séguy and Krasucki; this was where the real bargaining in fact took place. The most contentious point was the increase in the minimum wage, on which we diverged sharply; eager to reach agreement, I took the initiative—with Pompidou's authorization, naturally—of offering, at four in the morning, the CGT leaders an increase of 35 percent in the minimum wage and an average salary increase of 10 percent. The deal was struck.

Although it was a decisive move, the Grenelle agreements did not immediately have the desired effect of calming the storm. Over the following days, the U-turns, desertions, not to speak of cowardice that I have mentioned were all the more in evidence, as much at the heart of the administration as in the government itself and extending even to my own staff. Fewer and fewer of us stuck by Pompidou. Which was why he had taken the general's sudden departure for Baden-Baden so hard; I later learned from his wife how deeply he had been wounded by it. This episode only fueled the war between the staffs of the Élysée and of Matignon and, by extension, between the president and his prime minister—a war in which I did not get involved, convinced as I was that (at the risk of seeming naive) one could remain in both camps.

On May 31, 1968, Pompidou reshuffled his cabinet. I was given the role of secretary of state for the budget. It was with a heavy heart that I left the Department of Employment, which had enabled me to forge close links with the trade unions. "You will make others," the prime minister laughingly comforted me. After the July election, Pompidou was forced to give way to Maurice Couve de Murville. Determined to resign in these new circumstances, I ran to the little office in the Boulevard de la Tour-Maubourg into which Pompidou had just moved and told him of my decision to leave the government and take my place beside him in Parliament. He dissuaded me, urging me to stay in my position. "It is a post that will train you. See what happens at the heart of government and keep me informed of movements in the French economy."

I was naturally saddened by the forced demotion of Pompidou, which seemed to me, as to all his friends, to have resulted from much ingratitude.

But I remember having said to Pierre Juillet at that time: "The best thing that could happen to him is being forced to leave. That way, it will be easier to prepare to take over the presidency." Juillet had replied that I was probably right—and events did not prove me wrong.

Pompidou's ejection hit me all the harder because it coincided with a painful event in my private life: the death of my father from a heart attack on June 30, 1968, the day before the general election. He died suddenly at the age of seventy, in perfect health, and I could not help thinking, amid my grief, that there was perhaps no more enviable way to go. He was buried in the cemetery at Sainte-Féréole, in our family crypt, where my mother and he now repose side by side.

5

POMPIDOU'S MAN

I never doubted that Georges Pompidou was the natural successor to General de Gaulle, based on the relationship of trust that had long existed between them. Whatever their differences in regard to May 1968 and the wounds and misunderstandings resulting from that time, the fact remained that the general and Georges Pompidou had for six years agreed on the basic decisions, principles, and approaches that had brought the country solid and stable institutions, strengthened the authority of the state, and restored France to its rightful place in the world.

When questioned about his concept of Gaullism, Pompidou invariably replied that it was "an attitude adopted in the face of adversity." For him, that was the real difference between Gaullists and centrists. The Gaullist, by temperament and conviction, refused to accept failure, misfortune, or resignation to one's fate. He was driven by an awareness of historical events, a man both demanding and loyal.

Pompidou was said to be conservative, but what struck me about him was, on the contrary, his sense of and taste for modernity. Having remained within the government at his request, my relationship with Pompidou after he left Matignon continued to be very close. During that period of his disgrace, in which many people distanced themselves from the former prime minister, I made no secret of my loyalty to him.

In the wake of May 1968, the French economy was in an alarming state. The Grenelle agreements, of which I had been one of the main negotiators, weighed heavily on the national budget that I now directed. The country's reserves had been bled dry, external trade was in a bad way, and the franc was on the point of collapse. In these circumstances, the worrying deficit in our public finances could no longer be addressed simply by plugging the gaps and limiting spending—the traditional task of a secretary of state for the budget. More radical measures seemed to me to be called for.

In November 1968, I again found myself isolated when I openly supported a devaluation of the franc, which I believed to be the only way of making business competitive again and of relaunching growth. Devaluation is a remedy to be used with caution but that can be advisable at the right time. Although he entirely recognized its necessity from an economic and financial viewpoint, General de Gaulle balked before a measure that seemed to him a moral and political affront to our national prestige. Most of his ministers eventually opposed the idea, and it was on the advice of Raymond Barre, vice president of the European Economic Commission and already crowned with a great reputation in his field, that the head of state finally decided against a devaluation that a few of us judged salutary for the country.

Contrary to what was written afterward, I did not take part in this battle at Pompidou's instigation, or even with his approval, but entirely from my own initiative—although I felt instinctively that Pompidou was not against it.

The former prime minister was much talked of in newspaper editing rooms and at dinners in town at that time in connection with the Markovic affair. Alain Delon's bodyguard had been found murdered in a rubbish dump in October 1968. Sordid rumors immediately began circulating, soon fueled by crudely fabricated photographs that attempted to implicate Pompidou and his wife in the murder. As I arrived at the Boulevard de la Tour-Maubourg one evening, a distressed-looking Pierre Juillet said that we must warn the prime minister of a "terrible story" against him. I advised him to do it as quickly as possible, but he hesitated, obviously fearing Pompidou's reaction. I insisted in vain and finally another member of the cabinet did so on Juillet's behest. Learning of the rumors circulating about his wife and himself, Pompidou took it very hard, to such an extent that he never forgave the bearer of the bad news, who was permanently expelled from his entourage.

Pompidou bore a similar grudge against those who had failed to warn him. Starting with General de Gaulle, who had told him nothing of the affair even though he had known all about it. In his book of memoirs, Pompidou expressed his surprise that the head of state had not rushed to his defense and that none of his ministers had had the courage to denounce the scandalous attacks of which the couple were victim. "The person who was the most loyal and devoted, and who truly helped me, was Jacques Chirac," he wrote. Pompidou considered his successor, Maurice Couve de

Murville, to have been one of the main instigators. My personal conviction, which I still hold today, is that the prime minister at the time had played a certain role in the affair, out of animosity and jealousy toward his predecessor. Whatever the case, the wound remained a deep one for Georges and Claude Pompidou.

After his Rome declaration on January 17, 1969, it must now have been common knowledge that Georges Pompidou would be a candidate, when the time came, to succeed General de Gaulle. I saw nothing shocking or open to misunderstanding in that announcement. Who could seriously doubt that Pompidou would, sooner or later, play a national role? It was the general's unexpected decision to hold a referendum on the creation of regional councils and the reform of the Senate that brought Pompidou into the limelight as a possible candidate if the referendum failed.

I became involved in the "yes" campaign, less from conviction than from loyalty to the general. One evening in March 1969, the general took me aside during an official dinner given in honor of an African head of state. "So, Chirac," he said to me, "how do you think the referendum is going?" I replied that, having just returned from campaigning in Corrèze, I was not very optimistic about the result of the ballot. He looked at me with a worried but not very surprised expression. When I said that everything would doubtless improve after his next television appearance, he replied: "No, Chirac, everything will not be better. It is clear I am going to lose the referendum."

I retain a memory of great sadness of that month of April 1969 when, disowned by the people, Charles de Gaulle immediately withdrew from power, as he had promised he would. Although it was very dignified, that ending of a reign took on a certain poignancy that overwhelmed us all.

In the days that followed, Georges Pompidou declared his candidacy for president of the republic. Success was far from assured in the face of his main challenger, Alain Poher, caretaker president since the departure of General de Gaulle. His good-natured manner appealed to the French, who seemed to want something more banal after the end of the great era of de Gaulle. In light of the opinion polls, which placed Pompidou ten points behind Poher, donors were reluctant to contribute funds. As a result, each of us had to make his own contribution; Pierre Juillet even remortgaged his house. What is more, Pompidou would not allow us to accept certain grants from what he felt were dubious sources and outlawed all money coming from abroad.

We therefore had to mount a campaign with limited funds and in a context that was not at the outset in our favor. It took several weeks for

Pompidou to climb in the polls. One evening Juillet said as I arrived at the Boulevard de la Tour-Maubourg that the prime minister was not in very good spirits and that we should take him out to dinner. I canceled my official dinner and off we went to the restaurant across the street. It was almost empty, and rather than taking our usual little table at the back, Pompidou decided to sit outside at a table, saying to us, "It's time to make ourselves known."

In fact, this refined, subtle man who knew as much about France as he did about the French possessed all the necessary qualities to gradually emerge as the likely winner and to impose his presence. On June 15, after an exemplary campaign, Georges Pompidou was elected president of the republic with 58.21 percent of the vote. A decisive victory.

One morning shortly before the formation of the new government, I received a phone call at my Paris home from the future minister of finance, Valéry Giscard d'Estaing. "I have just seen the president," he told me. "You will stay in Budget. That is what he wanted." Implication: He himself had not wanted it. I immediately said that having enjoyed a certain autonomy under his predecessor, I was eager to keep it. He appeared to acquiesce, but the message was clear: My staying on as secretary of state for the budget was not of his choosing, and Giscard was determined to limit my powers.

I had met Valéry Giscard d'Estaing in the early 1960s. Then a very young minister of finance under General de Gaulle, he was already quite noteworthy—and he did all he could to bolster that image. The man seemed to me exceptionally intelligent and impressive but with an obvious propensity to accord little importance to others, even though he wanted them to like him as much as he thought he deserved. It was doubtless a long time before he noticed me, and he really took account of my presence only when I was thought of as "Pompidou's man"—and when I can only have seemed troublesome to him. As the office of secretary of state for the budget had enjoyed relative independence since I had taken it over, it was inevitable that it would be regarded with suspicion by the minister of finance and his principal collaborators. And so, irritated by the independence with which I acted, members of his entourage were not slow to present me to Giscard as a public danger.

It is not exaggerating to say that Giscard could not bear the least intrusion into his territory, above all from someone who was thought of as one of the president's protégés. He began exhibiting his hierarchical superiority over me, which of course went hand in hand with the elevated notion he had of his intellectual superiority. I quickly understood that in his view of things, he was right at the top, then there was nothing, then me, very far below. Whenever our paths happen to cross today, I say to him "Hello, M. President," and he replies in the same way. We are now equals.

From the beginning of our relationship, Giscard was eager to remind me of everything that distinguished a minister of finance from a secretary of state for the budget. When he summoned me to his office one day, he asked me to come in not through the large door, as I had been used to do under his predecessor, but through that of his cabinet director, the customary entrance for occasional visitors. Another day, during a work meeting, he called the usher and asked him to bring him some tea, without bothering to find out whether I wanted something to drink. The scene was so comical that I could not help saying to him, amused: "Thank you, Minister, I never drink tea." Whether his attitude was natural or contrived, it is safe to say that at that time Giscard did nothing to make himself agreeable to me, as if he already foresaw in me a potential rival in his quest for power.

By responding to the referendum of April 1960 with an ambiguous "yes, but," at the very least, Valéry Giscard d'Estaing was one of the principal authors of the fall of General de Gaulle, bringing forward a presidential election from which he hoped to benefit as soon as possible. In November 1970, he commented on the death of the general in a telephone conversation to me with the revealing words: "A chapter has closed." Not exactly a phrase for posterity. But it was pure Giscard.

We were not, however, in fundamental disagreement about economic policy, and in the Council of Ministers or the National Assembly, we managed to appear more in harmony than we in fact were; it was even asserted that we were as one, united in our hostility for the head of the government, Jacques Chaban-Delmas. Now, my relationship with the prime minister was, until he left Matignon in July 1972, much better than was claimed.

In January 1971, my appointment to the ministry dealing with relations between the executive and the legislature arose out of a strategy that Georges Pompidou and his advisors had devised to take control of the Union of Democrats for the Republic (UDR), now under the leadership of René Tomasini, a declared opponent of Chaban-Delmas. Observers saw it as a simultaneous bid to destabilize the prime minister. In the centrist newspaper *L'Express,* Georges Suffert characterized me as "the man charged with watching over Parliament and the UDR."

Under the eloquent title "Chirac the climber," Suffert drew a portrait in his article of an ambitious man "without subtlety" who had "worked, traveled, and flattered" hard to achieve his own ends. "M. Chirac," he wrote, "is fascinated not by what is complicated but by what is simple. He is ambitious. End of story. His life, his work, his games, his money and his dreams, everything is geared to this one objective: to succeed. And as he is methodical, reasonably intelligent and has a liking for work, he walks his path with a determined tread. . . . It is the times that demand this. Young people who are not drawn to revolution are clearly drawn to efficiency at all costs." This was doubtless a rather shallow analysis of a "political ascent" that was less premeditated than was thought, by a man perhaps more complex than one imagined. Am I the man described here or someone else? The question is no longer even important; a politician propelled onto center stage has to resign himself to the stereotypes and misunderstandings of which he will immediately be the subject. That goes with the territory, and I got used to it, quickly ceasing to care what journalists wrote about me, good or bad.

It was without regret that I left my ministry at the beginning of the summer of 1972 during the government reshuffle that took place after the departure of Chaban-Delmas, replaced at Matignon by Pierre Mesmer. I then learned that Pompidou envisaged giving me the post of national education—a post for which I felt no better suited, however. With others' support, I set about trying to secure another one. I was offered a "big technical ministry," such as industry, but I knew that it gave almost no room for maneuver compared to that of finance. Better, in that case, agriculture . . . At the last minute, I was successful. And so I found myself at the head of this ministry in which I would spend some of the best years of my life.

6

THE CREATION
OF EUROPE

The Treaty of Rome that instituted the European Economic Community (EEC) was signed in 1957. Its goal was to create a "common market" between the six signatory countries (West Germany, the Netherlands, Luxembourg, Italy, Belgium, and France): in other words, the free circulation of goods and people within this area and the establishment of a single customs duty for people coming in from outside. It also proposed a common economic policy in regard to agricultural matters and general economic and financial cooperation. The principal authority envisaged for its functioning was the European Council, formed by representatives from the various governments but aided by an assembly of appointed members and a commission to deal with executive functions, as well as a court of justice.

The initiative was a bold one, but it was on the whole beneficial and reasonable; the governments of the Fourth Republic were to be congratulated on it. However, their leaders proved incapable of implementing the treaty because of the political, economic, and financial destitution of the regime. Without the recovery plan that was in place from 1958 under the Fifth Republic, France would not have been able to fulfill its obligations under the treaty or open its borders to competition. Without the will of General de Gaulle, this treaty would doubtless have gone unheeded, like so many others—certainly the common agricultural policy would never have seen the light of day. Our partners did not want it, and only the general would have been able to get them to consent to it. France had a great interest in it, without doubt. But it was also the first and for a long time the only common policy that had been implemented.

Without General de Gaulle, the Common Market would have soon fallen before the British offensive aimed at making it nothing more than a free trade zone. Unable to scuttle it at that point, Britain shortly afterward would try to destroy it from the inside. Without the veto of General de Gaulle, Britain would have become a member of the Community in 1962. If it had succeeded in joining, it would have been at a cost of so many exemptions that the organization would have collapsed. Fervent zealots of a united Europe at any cost criticized the general for his intransigence, but no one today could challenge the fact that his fears were well founded.

Through its gradual implementation of a very complex organization, the Community achieved undeniable results. It increased the revenue of French agriculture, in particular, and motivated the nation to increase productivity. This success was, however, tempered by several factors. As the parity of each national currency constantly varied, "compensatory sums" were introduced, weighing heavily on the Community budget and favoring countries with strong currencies, threatening to penalize our farmers. Community priority was discreetly ignored by several member countries, who were subject to external intervention, particularly from the United States, which meant that some of their products were removed from Community protection.

Other than that, the history of Europe at that time was nothing but a long series of failures and disappointments. There were many disappointments over the issue of monetary union, despite numerous attempts to reduce the fluctuations caused by international monetary chaos and by the variable inflation rates in each member state. There was no industrial policy worthy of the name. The divided Europeans let the United States smash, whenever it could, high-tech industries in the Community states. The aeronautical industry was, alas, the best example of that. When a number of European states wanted to modernize their air fleets and had to choose between a French plane and an American plane, we knew who would win this "sale of the century" and under what pressure. We knew how the Americans had welcomed Concorde and the hesitations of European companies about the Airbus. In sum, the Americans displayed a barely disguised desire to reduce the role of the only industry capable of rivaling theirs to a subcontractor—but several European states were indifferent to or colluded with this initiative to destroy. Without cultivating unwarranted anti-American sentiments or wanting Europe to assert itself by systematically opposing the United States, we can nevertheless aspire to a balanced cooperation between real partners. What will Europe mean and what status will it have if its industries have to depend entirely on the big American companies?

I have sometimes been wrongly accused of being a sort of reluctant convert, rallying to a cause in which I do not believe just through force of circumstance. The truth is that from the beginning I was a European, not from passion but from reason, desirous of defending French interests within the Union at the same time as striving to get it to adopt a more responsible and coherent means of operating—two aims that were often difficult to reconcile. But beyond the reservations and the warnings that I sometimes gave, the issue always seemed to me so important for the development of our country and for the stability of the continent that I never spared my efforts to boost the European Community as much as possible. In 1972, I came out in favor of the enlargement of the Europe of Six to add Great Britain, Ireland, and Denmark, in the referendum organized by Georges Pompidou to ratify their membership. Despite the possible complications, I saw more advantages than disadvantages to the entry of these three new members, principally Britain. How could we imagine a Europe from which it was permanently excluded, even if it was also easy to foresee that its integration into the Community would not be without all sorts of pitfalls and complications?

Aligned with the United States in this area, as in others, Britain was deeply hostile to the whole of agricultural Europe, which it saw as threatening its own interests. Nonetheless, after virtually constant negotiations and clashes, particularly with the French delegation, once it managed to accept the principle, Britain gradually came to accept it in practice. An anecdote will illustrate the climate of intense distrust that existed between our two countries. The tensions were so strong that no treaty could be accepted by the Nine without a Franco-British solution first having been found, necessitating long meetings with our British counterparts. I remember a British agriculture minister with whom I had a very fraught relationship, involving constant outbursts and altercations. This minister naturally refused to express himself in a language other than his own, feigning total ignorance of French until, with his party having lost the election, he was forced to leave Brussels. A dinner was organized in his honor by the other European agriculture ministers, as was the tradition when one of us was replaced. These meals were presided over by each minister in turn, and chance had it that the role fell on this occasion to the representative of France. At the end of dinner, I therefore got up to propose a toast, on behalf of everyone, to our departing British colleague. Imagine my surprise when he replied in flawless

French. He spoke our language perfectly and had taken care to hide the fact from me so that he could, unbeknownst to me, listen in on my conversations with my collaborators during our negotiations.

Britain was not the only partner with which we sometimes had an antagonistic relationship. The German agriculture minister, Josef Hertl, could be even tougher and more vindictive than his British counterpart. We had some spectacular clashes over the fixing of agricultural prices. One day Hertl even went as far as declaring to the German and French press that "Chirac is mad," advising me to get myself psychoanalyzed—a declaration that obviously made the front pages in both countries. That said, we were both equally attached to pursuing the Franco-German collaboration undertaken by General de Gaulle and Conrad Adenauer and therefore linked by a special relationship of trust. I remember my consternation when Hertl, taken ill during a meeting, was rushed to the hospital. We learned soon afterward that it was nothing serious, but I was as worried about him as if he had been my brother.

However intense they were, our arguments remained those of men who were conscious of the need, sooner or later, to reach agreement. Some agriculture marathons lasted two, even three days, almost without interruption. When I first arrived in Brussels, my principal private secretary had notified me of the two specific products for which I had to defend the price in a restricted meeting, and I was successful. However, I quickly understood that if the aim was indeed to guarantee the best prices for our farmers, the way to do so was not always through intransigence.

In a note on the situation of the common agricultural market of 1973, I warned against the danger of creating within the Community, as in the rest of the world, "a situation of nutritional dependence that could, in certain circumstances, prove critical." I opposed the notion that a country like France could be asked to give up its small family farming: "exploitations of this type can be useful to the environment, to the preservation of the earth and of landscapes, and to social and regional balance." In conclusion, I advocated the creation of "a kind of farming Organization of the Petroleum Exporting Countries" for agriculturally rich countries to impose their prices on the large consumer countries—the Soviet Union, China, and Japan—while also fulfilling the needs of the underdeveloped countries by allowing them to benefit from any excess production. This was something that involved, in my vision, "a change in the general perception of the food industry so that instead of leaving the market to a few competing companies, account was taken of this entirely new phenomenon of the world's growing population." Indeed, as the population was set to double by the year 2000, our objective should be to quadruple agricultural production in less than thirty years.

As I said in an article published in *Le Monde* in 2008, the planet faces the specter of great famines as it undergoes a dangerous financial crisis. The very delicate cohesion between the international community is doubly threatened, and this conjunction of dangers poses an unprecedented risk to the world. Without profound, urgent measures, I said that we would see increasingly violent riots, increasingly uncontrollable migratory movements, increasingly deadly conflicts, and increasing political instability. The ingredients for a major crisis were in place, and the situation could very quickly deteriorate.

Confronted with this danger, the international community has to assume its responsibilities, all its responsibilities, with complete cooperation between north and south. Europe and the United States finally announced the release of emergency aid for the world food program. I have no doubt that the other great powers, members of the G8, emerging countries, and OPEC countries that derive exceptional profits from the increase in oil prices will commit to playing a full role in this immediate act of support. But a real revolution in thinking and action is required. There was and is insufficient food in the world. I have fought ceaselessly against the freeze on production in Europe and for the agricultural development of poor countries. In the future, we will have to feed 9 billion people. Everyone has finally realized that humanity needs all its agricultural land to be producing. Food-producing agriculture needs to be reinstated and encouraged. It should be protected against the unbridled competition of imported products that will destabilize the economies of these countries and discourage local production. Investment must be made in both research, so as to develop production methods and varieties that are adapted to the new criteria of climate change and diminishing water sources, and the training and diffusion of agricultural techniques.

There is a massive need for long-term investment. State development aid must be maintained, with the objective of 0.7 percent of gross domestic product. Additional income must also be created by innovative financing. The tax on air tickets has enabled several hundred million euros to be given to create access to medicine. As the former president of the World Bank, Robert Zoellick, has proposed, part of the Bank's resources should also be directed to productive investments in Africa. Above all, in the face of the unprecedented current recession, we need to realize that the international community has no other choice but imagination and solidarity.

7

AN UNEASY
PARTNERSHIP

I refused to accept the obvious for a long time. Out of respect and affection for Georges Pompidou, I could not and did not want to believe that he was terminally ill. Certainly I noticed, like everyone else, his chronic fatigue, his unsteady walk, his repeated bouts of the flu. But I did not envisage the worst. Since his meeting in June 1973 with President Nixon in Reykjavik in Iceland, where his face had appeared swollen and his walk hesitant, rumors of cortisone treatment for a possible cancer rapidly spread as well as of his imminent death. I witnessed the indecent haste with which pretenders from all sides gathered in the wings, sometimes openly.

On March 1, 1974, I left the Ministry of Agriculture to take charge of the Ministry for Industry. Some saw this appointment as the sign that Georges Pompidou nursed great ambitions for me. "That way, your career will have covered all areas of government," he told me with his usual liking for the pithy saying. More than ever, the president needed people with unquestioned devotion, loyalty, and faithfulness—and he knew that, at times of great uncertainty, such men were usually thin on the ground.

On March 21, a communiqué from the Élysée Palace announced that the president had had to withdraw from an official dinner for medical reasons. Everyone now realized how serious the situation was. When I learned of his death, on the evening of April 2, I was overwhelmed by so intense a grief that I did not seek to hide it in private or in public. Although we had never been intimately close, the death of Georges Pompidou was to me as cruel as that of a family member. His colleagues and friends, who held him in admiration and affection, had lost a master—in spirit, wisdom, courage, and action. Above all, he was a man of the state. Rarely had our country undergone so much change as in the twelve years he was General de Gaulle's prime minister and then president of the republic. Those years, which we now call the Pompidou years, left a deep imprint in the collective memory of French people of a period of prosperity and full employment, happy years before the great oil crisis and the upheavals of globalization.

Georges Pompidou had a great talent for friendship. He made us want to be better people. That was the measure of the affection we bore him— and of our sorrow when he left us. His death, which came more quickly than expected, occurred before the government had had time to reach agreement on the question of his successor. Caught unaware, we faced a difficult situation in the shape of the leader of the left, François Mitterrand, an opponent all the more formidable because, in addition to the experience he had acquired over the years, age conferred a serene and reassuring air on him. The division was in our camp since it was presumed that Jacques Chaban-Delmas and Valéry Giscard d'Estaing would be rival candidates.

Having far outstripped Chaban-Delmas in the first round, Giscard defeated Mitterrand on May 19, 1974, with 50.8 percent of the vote—a much more moderate victory than that of Pompidou five years earlier. Two days later, the new president invited me to meet him. Without beating about the bush, he asked me to be his prime minister. To his astonishment, I greeted the offer without enthusiasm, seeing myself as badly placed to govern with such a limited majority. I asked for time to reflect.

In the following hours, I entered into a long discussion with Pierre Juillet as to whether I should accept such a responsibility in these circumstances. "If you don't," said Juillet, "I fear the Gaullists will disappear. We will be defunct." That was the decisive argument; the only one that could unequivocally convince me to accept Giscard d'Estaing's proposition.

Shortly after my appointment to Matignon, Claude Pompidou telephoned to invite Bernadette and me to dinner at her home that evening. "I need to see you, I need your affection," she said to me, inconsolable after the loss of her husband, as we all were. Perhaps that evening she wanted to give me to understand that in her eyes I had become the political heir to Georges Pompidou.

By agreeing to become prime minister, I thought that a different relationship with Giscard would be possible: the start of a new era, in a sense. It was an illusion that did not last long. He had never liked me, and he would not like me any more in the future. The exercise of power was also not conducive to an improvement in our relations.

Traditionally, the formation of the government was the responsibility of the prime minister. But I was barely consulted about the choice of ministers and even secretaries of state who would make up my team: The president saw fit only to indicate to me whom he wanted. Presented with a fait accompli, all I could do—if I wanted to avoid an immediate political crisis—was submit without a word or demand the minimum I could obtain. My only option, therefore, was to fight tooth and nail to prevent certain appointments that I thought unacceptable and to impose others that seemed to me necessary. Threatening to withdraw my support of this government, I asked the president to appoint as minister of health a woman who seemed to me worthy of the post on every level: Simone Veil, then secretary general of the Council for the Judiciary, who had long fought for women's rights. She was in my view someone exceptional, a courageous and indomitable woman with perfect moral and intellectual integrity. Giscard, who did not much like her and suspected her of having voted for Mitterrand during the presidential election, was frankly opposed to the idea. But faced with my insistence, he eventually gave in.

I also managed to save a project that was closer to my heart than any other: the national center for contemporary art planned for Beaubourg. Georges Pompidou had wanted this to be not so much a work of architecture as a sort of magnet that would, as in the 1920s, attract people to France from all over the world. At his death, all that existed of a museum that had been envisaged and planned under his personal impetus was the foundations. One day Giscard summoned me, in the presence of the secretary of state for culture, Michel Guy, to tell me of his great plans. "I am going to stop that monstrosity, the Beaubourg Center," he declared bluntly. I could not believe my ears. "M. President, that decision will also involve a change of prime minister. I will not agree to the abolition of M. Pompidou's last project."

I was counting on the support of Guy, a friend of the Pompidous to whom he owed his ministerial career and who had formerly campaigned for the project. However, anxious not to displease the new president, he took his side without worrying about the fact that he was betraying himself: "You are right," he assured Giscard in front of me. "In any case, I never thought it was a good idea." Angry at such cowardice, I did not refrain from telling Guy what I thought of him. I would not agree to see him again. Thanks to my intervention, the Georges Pompidou Center saw the light of day, becoming a shining success throughout France and the world.

Despite these initial snags, I have a good memory of that early period. We were at the dawn of the Giscardian era and, somewhat naively, I was

convinced that the president of the republic trusted me and would appreciate the work we would undertake together. The talk was only of innovation and reform. And then, quite quickly, the atmosphere changed. Valéry
Giscard d'Estaing was the first French president to institute another possible interpretation of the constitution, under which the president of the republic was no longer directly linked to the majority that supported him but
now placed himself in the position of an arbiter essentially responsible for
the institutions of which he was the elected head. This interpretation would
come into play not only in the event of an opposition victory but also in his
direct relationships with the existing government, dominated by a political
group not his own but that of his prime minister. It was this unprecedented
situation that caused most of the antagonism and misunderstandings that
would strain our relations and lead to my resignation in August 1976.

Nonetheless, in the months after Giscard was elected, I was ceaseless
in my efforts to regain control of a weakened, helpless Gaullist movement.
The task was all the more challenging because, in addition to the grievances
and resentments that were harbored against me within the ranks of the
Union of Democrats for the Republic, the Gaullists were little inclined to
accord trust to a president who, from his side, did nothing to woo or manage them. At the beginning of his seven-year term, I had tried to persuade
Giscard to make a gesture toward the UDR members of the Assembly and
the Senate. Accepting this in principle, he one day decided to invite them
all to dinner at the Élysée Palace. I was overjoyed at the news and called to
give him some advice to win them over: "It's very simple. You need to know
how to speak to their hearts. At the end of the dinner, get up and address a
few words to them along the lines of 'We are all united to win—I am counting on you!' That's all. Gaullists are always susceptible to being told that
they are being counted on."

On the appointed day, Giscard did exactly the opposite of what I had
recommended. Instead of the few words I had suggested, he decided to
launch into a forty-five-minute discourse on constitutional law at the end
of the meal. It was a veritable disaster. The guests wanted only to feel
loved; yet Giscard had been unable to resist the pleasure of making them
understand that he was cleverer than they were. The Gaullists went away
furious. From then on, the lack of understanding between them could only
worsen.

In 1974, I was the first government leader who truly recognized the
effects of the oil crisis of the previous year. I quickly realized that our economy faced a new era, at the threshold of an industrial and technical revolution that would transform the face of the planet more than any previous

one. A revolution in which we would be classed as victors or victims, great powers or minor ones, according to what was done. Nothing less than our place in the world of the future was at stake. In terms of energy, which was at the forefront of our concerns, no one can seriously think that the state has the initial and main responsibility for managing it; that is true even in a country as liberal as the United States. In addition, the role that nuclear energy has to play cannot be conceived of outside of state control. The same is true of industrial redevelopment.

It was in that spirit that, as head of the government, I prepared to confront the first economic recession our country had suffered since 1945. Initially, an austerity (or "cooling") plan was devised, principally designed to fight the inflation caused by the increase in the price of a barrel of oil. Its main features were the strict supervision of credit, an increase in taxation of companies, and the introduction of exceptional levies. These all were deflationary measures that would reduce the increase in prices and reduce the trade deficit, but to the detriment of the rate of investment, the drop in which would weaken industrial output even further.

Other than in exceptional circumstances—which these were, in a sense—I do not believe that austerity measures are a good response to a recession. In principle, I lean more toward those who want to kick-start the economy than those who want to curtail every initiative. My instinctive conviction is that it is better to do all one can to boost employment and purchasing power, because these are the very driving forces of an economy. In short, although I had to take on the package of measures desired by the president and the minister of finance, that did not mean that it corresponded to what I judged necessary and useful for the country. In July 1975, preoccupied by the risks of explosive social unrest linked to the rise in unemployment, I spoke up in a Council of Ministers to ask that the austerity measures, which I believed had not delivered the desired results, be abandoned. Against all expectation, several Giscardians wholeheartedly agreed with me. Caught unaware and visibly astounded, the president yielded some ground before announcing several days later "an important program to encourage economic growth," for which he would subsequently lose no opportunity to take credit.

My personal concern was also to protect employment and consumption by an increase in pensions, family allowances, and the minimum wage; a strengthening of the short-time working compensation scheme; the introduction of an additional allowance allowing those laid off to receive 90 percent of their previous gross salary; and the extension of the health care insurance scheme to all professions. This show of solidarity to those who were hit hardest by the economic recession corresponded with my notion of the essential responsibilities of the state and the demands of a humanitarian society. The same was true for two categories of the population who were at that time still very neglected: elderly people and the disabled, whose interests my government were one of the first to address. What greater destitution is there than that due to the incapacity, isolation, and vulnerability of old age? I have always been sensitive to the anxieties of elderly people and felt enormously beholden to the men and women who are so used to being overlooked. Helping them meet each other, find entertainment, maintain a social life through the creation of appropriate facilities, and lessen their material hardships was one of the "great work sites" of the two years that I would spend in Matignon.

Although foreign policy was, under the Fifth Republic, an area reserved for the president, the role of prime minister was not limited to home affairs. If it was France's duty to take part in the process of East–West détente, I pointed out in 1974, it was also to help accelerate the creation of Europe through monetary union, to strengthen its relations with China and its cooperation with the countries of the developing world, particularly in Africa. From 1974 to 1976, my trips abroad as head of the government were largely devoted to making French industry and technology better known outside our borders and allowing me to forge personal links with several foreign heads of state and to get closer to some of them during decisive moments in their own history.

One of these was the shah of Iran in June 1974. He was the first foreign leader to come to Paris after the election of Valéry Giscard d'Estaing. Relations between France and Iran had cooled after Georges Pompidou's refusal in 1971 to attend the grand celebrations commemorating the 2,500th anniversary of the Persian empire. However, the warm welcome accorded the shah in Paris three years later allowed, as they say in diplomatic language, ties between the two countries to be strengthened.

The shah hoped to exploit French technology to modernize his country. Some large armaments deals were made on this occasion, and a contract was awarded to French companies for the building of a subway in Tehran and the electrification of the railways. In December 1974, I went to Iran to negotiate deals that included the use of our color television system by Tehran. The sovereign welcomed me in a manner that reflected the powerful, majestic image he wanted to convey of his country and of his own person. Underneath the pomp and prestige, one glimpsed the reality of people more and more revolted by the gap between their way of life and the extravagant expenditures of an outdated monarchy. I would not be surprised by the dramatic events that ensued; a radical upheaval of that kind had seemed long overdue.

Through my mediation, France simultaneously negotiated energy and military cooperation treaties with Iraq. On that mission, I met with the country's ruler, Saddam Hussein, three times: in October 1974, during my first trip to Baghdad, then in September 1975 in Paris, on the occasion of the official visit of the Iraqi leader, and finally in January 1976, again in Baghdad, where I stopped over with the minister for external trade, Raymond Barre, on our way back from a visit to India. To understand the importance of these discussions, which took place in the middle of an energy crisis, it needs to be explained that France enjoyed a privileged position in terms of its oil supplies from Iraq. Acquired in the aftermath of the Great War, when the allies split the spoils of the Ottoman empire, its oil interests there had been preserved thanks to the Arab policy pursued by Pompidou. In June 1972, when the strongman of the regime, Saddam Hussein, had just—for the greater glory of his people—restored Iraq's oil independence by bringing an end to foreign concessions, the authorities in Baghdad made it known to the French government that they would not disrupt the existing agreements. In exchange, Iraq wanted to buy military equipment from France. It was in this context that in 1972 Saddam was officially received in Paris for the first time, by Pompidou. A treaty was signed, which largely satisfied the Iraqis while guaranteeing French oil interests for ten years.

From 1974, the industrial and military contacts between the two countries increased. In October, Saddam received me with open arms in Baghdad to negotiate new contracts. Although he had taken power in conditions that were, at the very least, brutal, the Iraqi leader—who at that time enjoyed great popularity in the Arab world—was not yet persona non grata with western governments. Anxious to free himself from the Soviet yoke, he was counting on France to help him strengthen his country's independence and pulled out all the stops to demonstrate friendship to me.

The man seemed to me intelligent, not devoid of humor, even rather nice. He received me at his home and treated me like a personal friend. The warmth of his hospitality did not go unnoticed, and our conversations were marked, on both sides, by great cordiality. I always had very easy contact with Arab leaders, perhaps because they displayed a frankness rarely found in their western counterparts. And then Iraq is a fascinating country that seemed to me destined to take the place it deserved among the great nations.

A year later, in September 1975, I welcomed Saddam to Paris. Together we visited the nuclear plants of Cadarache. As was traditional at that time, the trip ended with an official dinner in the Hall of Mirrors in the chateau of Versailles, during which I publicly confirmed to Saddam that France was ready to bring him "its men, its technology, its skills."

In 1978, after he had just expelled the Ayatollah Khomeini, who had been in exile in Iraq for several years, Saddam sent me a message through his ambassador in Paris advising that I ensure that Khomeini was not welcomed in France. As most of the big western countries had refused him, France was the only one likely to give him refuge. In his message, Saddam addressed the following warning to me: "Be very careful. Let him go to Libya because what he says in France will have international impact and what he says in Libya will go unheard." Even though I was no longer prime minister, I immediately forwarded this message to President Giscard d'Estaing, who took no account of it and did exactly the opposite of what the Iraqi leader recommended. The decision to let the Ayatollah Khomeini into France would have serious and irreparable consequences, as much for the future of Iran as for the stability of the world.

This was one of my last contacts with Saddam. I never again saw the man who at that time appeared not so much a despot as a fierce, determined patriot, possessed of a nationalistic pride and enthusiasm that seemed to reflect the great ambitions he nursed for his country. When I learned, years later, of the repressive madness that this dictator had disseminated, I cut off all personal contact with him. Nonetheless, I was still shocked by his ultimate destiny: a nighttime execution orchestrated with all the barbarity for which he had himself been condemned.

Among the meetings that punctuated those two years I spent in Matignon, the most striking for me was without doubt that with Deng Xiaoping during his official visit to France in May 1975, the first of a Chinese leader since the restoration of diplomatic relations between our two countries. After the catastrophic Cultural Revolution launched by Mao Zedong, Deng, who had become vice prime minister after a long period of disgrace, seemed to bring a new breath of fresh air to China. Under his Communist's clothes, I sensed the heart of immemorial China beating, the spirit of one of the most ancient cultures in the world that continued to inhabit a country shaped not by an ideology but by its centuries of rituals and traditions.

Deng Xiaoping is a man of much delicacy, subtlety, frankness, and warmth, the embodiment of all that is powerful and enduring in China. One evening when we were dining together, with an interpreter, I said to him, "You are in the middle of an enormous expansion of your agricultural output and soon you will have no arable land available. What are you going to do to feed your people?" He replied, with his mischievously twinkling eyes, punctuating his words, as was his habit, with an old Chinese expression, "Tseko," which he now repeated twice in succession: "Ah, Tseko, Tseko, Siberia is entirely empty." The communication between us was all the smoother because he knew the great personal interest I had in China and the admiration I felt for that age-old civilization that had given so much to the history of humanity, spirituality, literature, and artistic creation in all its forms.

We had long discussions about the history of his people, and Deng declared himself surprised that a western government leader seemed to know almost as much as he about this subject. On one occasion when we were talking about a particular period at the end of the fourteenth century, I said to him: "There were three emperors during that time." Deng quickly corrected me: "No, there were only two." I insisted that there had been three. Our friendly argument continued, neither of us willing to back down, until one day Deng, having done some research, had to admit that I was right, acknowledging it with his usual humor. There had indeed been three emperors in that period, including one who, age nine, had reigned for only six weeks. The anecdote has made the rounds in China.

I never had any conflict with him or any Chinese leader, even on the question of communism, convinced as I was that China used it not as an end in itself but as a means of achieving unity and of reasserting itself as a great power. Very well informed about international relations, Deng saw the relationship between Paris and Beijing as a cornerstone of Chinese policy that aimed at allowing his country to break with the policy of Communist bloc separation and the cold war.

Other than the statement that I issued announcing my decision, on August 25, 1976, to resign from my post of prime minister because I did not have the "necessary tools" to carry it out, I have never explained the real origins of a crisis unprecedented in the history of the Fifth Republic. Far from being a hasty decision, as might seem the case, it had been a long time in the making. It had forced itself on me only after I had done all I could to avoid a departure that was likely to be interpreted as a rupture. I believe that the time has come to outline the many warnings and suggestions that I addressed in vain to the president from February 1975 up until the last moment—when the conflict to which I was alerting him but that went unheard could be resolved only at the cost of a political crisis that involved serious consequences.

From the time of the formation of my government, it had clearly seemed to me, as I have said, that the president of the republic wanted to decide everything himself. From the outset, he attempted, more than any of his predecessors, to reduce and limit the role of the prime minister. General de Gaulle had immediately arrogated to himself the areas of national defense and foreign affairs. In the general's case, the advantage was that, by taking direct responsibility of what he considered essential, he delegated everything else to his prime minister. It was for the latter to conduct the affairs of government, with General de Gaulle not dictating how he did so. It would not have entered his head to discuss an issue that was the province of the head of the government with any of his ministers. He took charge of the state and respected the prerogatives of the prime minister to whom he had entrusted the responsibility of governing. Still affected by the events of 1968, the causes of which he had analyzed, Georges Pompidou had widened his exclusive domain by exercising tight control over economic and social problems; nonetheless, he gave his government a large amount of freedom in these areas.

With Valéry Giscard d'Estaing, everything changed. With a natural propensity to control everything and exercise his power even in the slightest details, he was in addition continually encouraged by his entourage to belittle—and, if need be, hurt—the prime minister. Knowing that they could, almost at any moment, interest the president of the republic in a topical issue, the cabinet members made sure they took over most cases, a practice that caused the prime minister to lose his prerogatives, one after the other, and therefore his decision-making power. I therefore sometimes learned, via one or another of my ministers or even by the press or the radio, of important decisions about which I had not even been consulted.

In February 1975, I wrote to the president about my concerns, suggesting that we find a common solution to the confusion that currently reigned. Despite the hand I was proffering him, Giscard did nothing to consolidate the position of his prime minister or to resolve the tensions between the different elements of the government. For their part, irritated by the repeated announcements of a "rebalancing" of the government, the UDR members were clearly more and more critical of certain of the president's unfortunate ideas. Elected with an extremely narrow majority and anxious to be accepted by and, even better, to please the whole of France, Giscard's priority was above all reconciliation and rapprochement; placatory gestures were distributed left and right and approval given for all new trends, practices, frustrations, and rebellions. He did not want to upset anyone or anything. He would never disagree with me outright on any question but would always, after our frank discussion, return to his own way of doing things, very different from mine.

In March 1976, the results of the by-elections, which demonstrated that the left was now the majority party in the country, rang out like a warning bell. The day after this first defeat, which heralded more serious ones if nothing was done, I insisted to the president that he take the situation in hand. Once again, I told him that I was ready, if he wished, to assume the role that belonged to the prime minister of coordinating the government—as long, of course, as he clearly and publicly entrusted me with the task.

Initially, Giscard minimized the consequences of what he called "local elections," refusing to rush into action. Then he allowed himself to be persuaded by Pierre Juillet, whose advice he sought, to give me the job of coordinating the majority parties, as he announced to the nation in a televised speech in which he came across as too stilted to be really convincing.

However, in the ensuing weeks, Giscard lost no time in reappropriating the responsibilities that he had unwillingly conceded to me—upon which the rivalries within the majority parties, deliberately encouraged by the presidential entourage, resumed with a vengeance. I was now facing so irresolvable a problem that I could see no other solution than to resign, unless the situation quickly changed. On May 31, 1976, it was in the hope of giving a salutary shock that I gave Valéry Giscard d'Estaing, during a private interview with him, a long handwritten letter setting out what I believed was necessary for the country.

After taking note of the admittedly risky solutions that had in my view become inescapable, the president told me that he wanted time to reflect. We would have the opportunity, he said, of speaking about it at the presidential summer residence of Brégançon, to which he invited me and my wife for the Whitsun holiday, in token of friendship and renewed unity.

However, far from opening the way to a trusting, harmonious communication—something that would in any case have amazed me—this brief trip together to Brégançon only underscored everything that divided me from a president so drunk on status that he could treat his guests, even his prime minister, with the offhandedness of a monarch. We were no longer surprised that Giscard was served first at table or offered his guests ordinary chairs while the presidential couple occupied two armchairs. What was most disturbing was the scene we witnessed on our second evening there, after an afternoon spent waiting in our room to be called. Giscard had summoned his ski instructor and his wife to dinner with us. The couple arrived, he wearing a polo shirt and she a short skirt, not having been told of the required dress: dress suit and evening gown. The situation was so embarrassing, even humiliating, for them that the poor woman spent the whole evening discreetly pulling on her skirt as if to lengthen it a few centimeters. I tried engaging her in conversation to distract her, but she barely responded, so stunned were she and her husband at finding themselves in such an awkward position before the president of the republic and his prime minister.

For his part, Giscard uttered not a word to ease the embarrassment of his guests or to diffuse the situation; on the contrary, he seemed to revel in it. I returned to Paris shocked by such a lack of respect and more determined than ever to get free as soon as I could. The episode confirmed my sense that I no longer had much in common with this president.

On July 15, without giving me any warning, Giscard canvassed opinion in the Council of Ministers on the question of elections to the European Parliament by universal suffrage—a subject that, as he knew, could only sow new divisions within the government. The procedure was now clearly not even to keep me informed of the order of business of government meetings—an omission on Giscard's part that, on such a sensitive subject, was in no way accidental, particularly as, two days earlier, I had communicated to him my reservations about the inclusion of three new countries, Greece, Spain, and Portugal, in the European Community. The addition of three extra partners to the existing Europe of Nine could only upset the existing economic balance.

The president chose to sidestep this debate, having already dodged the solutions I had recommended to end the political uncertainty that was badly viewed by public opinion, and tensions continued to mount between the majority parties. I decided that I now had no choice but to resign. On July 19, I informed Valéry Giscard d'Estaing, during a meeting that I had requested, of my wish to be relieved of my functions. He refused, assuring me that he understood the reasons for my discontent and irritation but saying that he saw no reason for such a premature departure. "We will talk about it after the summer," he said, asking me to wait until then. I was careful not to give him the least assurance in that direction, as I was fully resolved not to continue with a situation that could, in my view, only do a disservice to the country's interests.

On July 26, I handed my resignation letter to the president, saying that it was effective "from 3 August at the latest"—that is, after my official visit to Japan, which I agreed not to cancel. Himself due to go to Gabon, Giscard wanted me to wait until the next meeting of the Council of Ministers to make my decision public, the date of which he had fixed for August 25. At the end of this meeting—during which he said of my resignation, with calculated detachment, "when someone wants to go, you have to

let them"—I spoke to him in private. Before informing the French people
of my decision, I wanted him to read the text of the short announcement
that I was about to make to them. Its contents did not seem to surprise him;
at least, he made no objection to it, at the time. We then exchanged a few
words, in an almost relaxed atmosphere, before I went to Matignon, where
the television cameras were awaiting me.

When I saw him soon after my announcement, Giscard expressed his
surprise at the curt tone in which I had delivered it. I simply gave him to
understand that one does not abandon such an office without emotion,
which had perhaps led me to seem harder, perhaps more brutal even than
I had hoped. But I reaffirmed to him that my resolve to go was clear and
unambiguous.

Divested of all responsibility, I felt free, footloose, ready for action—a
feeling that was both exhilarating and demoralizing for a nature such as
mine. Not four days went by before I launched myself back into the fray.

Weakened by the failure of its candidate at the presidential election of
1974, the UDR was hardly strengthened by my departure from the government. Its future hung in the balance. The political force that it represented
in the country certainly remained considerable, but it needed a new impetus
to have a lasting effect against the Union for French Democracy (UDF),
which now united the centrist and Giscardian factions under the same banner and against the coalition of the left-wing parties.

To create this new impetus, it was not enough simply to rework the
existing structures. We needed to create, as soon as possible, a modern,
popular movement that would be the harbinger of a new kind of politics.
On August 29, 1976, I attended a decisive meeting held at the home of
Pierre Juillet, and the strategy for the creation of the Rassemblement pour
la République (RPR) was devised. It took its roots from deep within France
and brought together men and women of all social backgrounds and of
many different sensibilities. That was the very essence of Gaullism. Never
having been a man of the right in the strict sense of the word, or what one
could call conservative, I had no difficulty identifying with a political movement that sought to transcend the usual ideological boundaries.

The creation of the RPR was badly received by most of the "barons,"
who retained their intense hostility toward me, but it incited a great enthusiasm among the executive and the ranks of the UDR. On December
5, a huge crowd assembled in Versailles, whole carloads and trainloads of
people from every region of France: over 50,000 people united by the same
fervor, despite the icy temperatures that reigned over the capital. The UDR
gave way to the RPR, of which I was elected president with 96.52 percent

of the vote. It was for each of us one of those moments of communion and exhilaration in which one felt the soul of the Gaullist family vibrating, giving birth to a determination and a strength of will that was all its own.

As president of the RPR, as formerly when I was prime minister, I needed a second in command with whom I could work in harmony and whose word would be respected as my own. I had long been friends and associates with Jérôme Monod. We needed few words to understand each other and to know the transformations that needed to be made and the men who should be promoted to make the RPR into a modern political organization that looked to the future. It was Jérôme Monod who had introduced a young finance inspector to me when I was prime minister; a few minutes of interview had been enough for me to realize that Alain Juppé was a man of unusual culture and intelligence. I had immediately offered him a place on my team. After I left Matignon, Juppé, demonstrating a loyalty that would only increase over time, willingly agreed to stay with me. He joined the executive committee of the RPR in January 1977 and seemed already to promise great things.

If no hostile expression was made by our ranks toward the president, the same could not, unfortunately, be said of the presidential entourage toward us. The constant criticisms levied by my successor of my actions when I was in office and of the legacy, catastrophic in his eyes, that I had left him helped poison the relations between the government and the main constituent of its majority. Not a day went by that Raymond Barre did not imply—when he did not state it openly—that he had found the "coffers empty" when he took up his post; if this were true, it was a state of affairs that could not have been achieved without the consent of the president and was therefore a direct incrimination of the latter.

These attacks were all the more surprising in that my relations with Barre had, until then, never been bad—I barely knew him, in fact, on a personal level. Bringing with him a flattering reputation as a great economist, in January 1976, Giscard had, with my approval, appointed him minister for external trade. Seven months later, the choice to appoint him prime minister seemed to me just as sound, even though Barre had no experience of a political world that he prided himself on despising. Given the circumstances, our handover of power occurred in several minutes and without particular warmth. But I felt no hostility or acrimony toward my successor—on the contrary, I hoped that he would strive to appease the tensions within the ranks of the government.

Unfortunately, it was a very different attitude that Raymond Barre adopted toward me almost immediately by painting my period of office in the blackest color. The atmosphere of revolt and mistrust that soon developed between the RPR group and the new prime minister came as no surprise. It was with the greatest difficulty that, on certain occasions, I calmed down Gaullist members of Parliament who were so infuriated with the government that they were ready to abstain during the vote of confidence. My task was made more difficult by the deliberate provocations of the president as well as his lack of consideration toward us and the arrogance with which he treated all those who did not submit to his edicts. It was an attitude that would lead him to launch into an adventure as risky as that concerning the mayorship of Paris.

8

MAYOR OF PARIS

A law of December 31, 1975, provided for the election of a mayor of the capital, which had been administered directly by the government for more than a century. This mayor would be granted the same powers as those of mayors in other communes of France. Until then limited to a largely honorary role, the city council would regain its powers of initiative and decision making. Agreement had been reached within the government on the choice of the principal future candidate. At my instigation, and with the full agreement of the Élysée, Senator Pierre-Christian Taittinger had been designated as the candidate. Although a Giscardian, he had excellent relations with the Gaullist members of Parliament in the capital, who were in the majority in the existing council.

Unity therefore seemed guaranteed when, in November 1976, going against the pact that we had agreed to, Giscard announced—without consulting anyone, as was his wont—that Taittinger, whom he judged too consensual, was being dropped in favor of one of his followers, Michel d'Ornano, minister of industry and mayor of Deauville, reputed to be more anti-Gaullist. On November 12, the latter announced that he was going to run as a candidate, an announcement that was rightly seen as an act of aggression by the Parisian Gaullists, in particular their two leaders, who also now talked of becoming candidates.

Confronted with such a cacophony, from which the left was very likely to profit, it seemed to me more and more obvious over the coming weeks that I had no choice but to run myself. My entourage, seeing how advantageous such a political platform would be in the future, strongly encouraged me to do so. However, I feared adding to a division that was already well entrenched. That is, until Giscard intervened, on January 17, 1977;

preoccupied with easing tension, he held a decisive press conference in which he stated that, from then on, the government needed to be no longer uniform but "pluralist" and that each of the political movements that supported its actions should feel free to put forward its ideas. In short, this implied that there would be a plurality of candidates for the election. On January 19, I made a television announcement that I would be a candidate for the city council elections in Paris.

So off I went on my campaign! In other words, walking up and down every street, visiting each shop one after the other, greeting each passerby, and shaking every hand without distinction. Whether in Paris or in Corrèze, what better way to meet people, get known by them, and, in exchange, be able to appreciate them? All while being very careful not to utter the name of my opponent or even to acknowledge his existence! That was, for me, one of the golden rules of any electoral campaign. When people talked about Michel d'Ornano, I invariably replied "Who is that?" Years later, after a public meeting in Corrèze in which he had continually mentioned my name, I gave that same friendly advice to François Hollande: "Never mention your opponent's name. You don't want to give him free publicity!"

Strengthened by the Gaullist networks solidly established in most Parisian arrondisements and by crack campaign workers, our team was victorious on March 20, in the second round: fifty-four seats against fifteen for d'Ornano and forty-four for candidates from the left who, as a whole, had done very well. Five days later, I was elected mayor of Paris. The following day, the inhabitants of the capital flocked in great numbers to the Arc de Triomphe, where I had invited them to join us. It was a first success for the Rassemblement pour la République (RPR) and a humiliating defeat for Giscard. When I walked into the town hall as mayor, I was relieved to think that, for the first time in my life, I was not second in command to someone else.

As the minister of agriculture, I had never in two years taken a single decision that had not obtained the agreement of the four large farming organizations. I would sometimes be restlessly impatient with the seemingly endless negotiations—but, in the end, they saved so much time and avoided so many disappointments. As mayor of Paris, I intended to remain faithful to that method. As soon as I took office, I was required to settle the very controversial case of the urban motorway in the Fourteenth Arrondissement, the notorious Vercingétorix ring road, and immediately organized meetings between ecologists and engineers. The former quickly won out over the latter. For my part, when I went to look at it, I realized that however well designed it was, this road risked causing an unbearable concentration of cars in this part of the capital. I therefore decided not to go ahead with it, to the great dismay of the elected representatives of the area. This initial experience quickly led me to organize a system of consultation based on commissions that were as widely representative of the Parisian population as possible.

Placed under the supervision of the government since 1871, the capital now had a mayor and a municipal authority with the same powers as those of the other administrative departments of France. At the beginning of my first mandate, Paris was an aging city, in full demographic decline and with no real policies on housing, town planning, or the environment. In twenty years, Paris had lost a fifth of its population, most often to the suburbs. This demographic decrease, cause for concern because of its scope and persistence, was partly due to the property speculation that had undeniably contributed to dissuading the poorer sections of society from living there. But it was linked even more to the massive loss of industrial jobs that had not been made up for by the service sector. To this were added the situations of housing in the capital—too many families lived in unsanitary buildings; transport, with traffic flow and parking facilities totally unfit for modern life; town planning, a flagrant problem with whole areas having been razed to the ground in the name of renovation, to be replaced by a proliferation of often-uninspiring or revolting tower blocks. In addition, Paris no longer fulfilled its residents' aspirations in terms of green spaces, the cleanliness of the streets, treatment of household waste, or water quality.

The new mayor of Paris had considerable resources at his disposal: a budget of 5.5 billion francs and an administrative staff of 38,500. His powers were limited in just one sector: that of security, for which the sole police chief had responsibility. The new impetus that I intended to give in terms of management of the city could now depend on competent, efficient, and dynamic elected representatives. On December 12, 1977, during the first budget meeting, I announced my grand priorities for the beginning of my mandate: "to encourage social cohesion, sociological and professional balance of the people, and the national and international flowering of the capital."

Policies in favor of the elderly and the most disadvantaged people were naturally some of the closest to my heart. They consisted of three main areas: the improvement of guaranteed resources, the fight against isolation, and the development of collective facilities, with housing and hostels built for the most underprivileged. The second priority was the struggle against the increasing depopulation of the capital. It was particularly difficult for young people and families to live in Paris, and this made an active policy of government-subsidized housing more necessary than ever, based on a long-term program of renovating buildings and the purchase of vacant land. A little after my election, I gave out a strong signal in this direction with the auction of luxury buildings owned by the city in the Sixteenth Arrondissement to finance the construction of social housing. In 1980, 35 percent of the city's investment budget was devoted to the acquisition of property with this same aim.

Entrusted to the renowned composer and director of music Marcel Landowski, a friend of Georges and Claude Pompidou, cultural activity remained the best way of ensuring the prestige of Paris in France and abroad. To enable this activity to expand, the cultural budget for the capital would be doubled in the first two years of my mandate. Support was increased for prestigious events such as the Festival of the Marais, the Festival of Autumn, and the International Dance Festival. The renovation of the Châtelet Theater and of the Museum of Modern Art, the impetus given to large institutions such as the National Theater, the Orchestra of Paris—to be followed later by the creation of the Paris video library and the European photographic center—all demonstrated the same ambition of making Paris once more one of the foremost international cultural capitals. It was an ambition that went hand in hand with a policy of decentralization of cultural life that aimed at improved provision of artistic teaching in every arrondissement.

A mayor's most visible work is the image that he stamps on the face of his town. No sooner was I installed at the head of the Paris city council than I decided to abolish the town planning policy that had prevailed since the 1950s: large estates of high-rise and low-rise blocks, testament to a "bulldozer renovation" that was in complete disharmony with the capital's real physiognomy that had been shaped by history. Reconciling respect for cultural heritage and the traditional environment with the free expression of a more human contemporary architecture was the spirit of the new development policy that I wished to implement.

The most spectacular undertaking in this regard was that of the development of the Halles area in the very heart of the capital. Among the cases that I inherited when I became mayor of Paris, this was, by far, the hardest to disentangle. Since the transfer of the market at Les Halles to Rungis seven years earlier and the demolition of the Pavillons Baltard that had housed it, the area was no more than an immense wasteland, a huge, fenced-off excavation site more than thirty yards deep in water. Notoriously famous, the Halles hole had also become the symbol to Parisians of waste and impotence, because of the never-realized projects and abandoned work sites. I had to act quickly to limit the losses that had already been incurred and to give new life to an abandoned quarter.

The team of architects and engineers that I immediately organized slaved away to come up with a definitive project, along the lines of the general indications I had given them. Not a gargantuan project, this one was to remain human size, while respecting the identity of the quarter and validating its historical heritage. At the beginning of the 1980s, the Halles question was about to be settled, with the construction underground of the Réseau Express Régional (RER; Regional Express Network) station Châtelet–Les Halles and a center for shopping and leisure as well as the construction, aboveground, of a new development project that included a large pedestrian zone reaching as far as the Georges Pompidou Center as well as the creation of a garden designed to be a place for both walking and entertainment.

Despite the vicissitudes that the site would undergo over the course of time, the Halles project, fruit of exemplary collaboration between elected representatives and the population, was the result of a town planning concerned, for the first time, with both the environment and the inhabitants' quality of life. Just like the "Green Plan" launched at the same period, the "Clean Seine" project launched in 1977, and the modernization of household waste collection that was also organized at that time, the Halles development reflected my concern to make Paris, in every domain, a laboratory of ideas and projects likely to interest the whole country.

The same was true for international relations, which also reflect the preoccupations of the mayor of Paris and his political vision. Under my initiative, the Association des Ingénieurs des Villes de France (AIVF, Engineers Association of the Cities of France) was created and would form links with the other great capitals of the world. Each time I received a head of state or government became an opportunity to affirm the place and influence of Paris in the world. Tradition dictated that foreign leaders who were guests of France visited the city hall to greet the people of Paris and their representatives. This had always been an obligatory part of the program of their official visit. So it was until the day when, under I no longer remember what pretext, the president's advisors decided without warning to remove it from the program, declaring that it was no longer necessary. This did not prevent me from inviting to city hall those heads of state whom I believed should be welcomed there; few of them, even in that period, declined my invitation.

I attached great importance to most of these meetings. Beyond the element of protocol, they allowed the mayor of Paris not only to forge personal ties with most of those leaders but also to express his views on world affairs, particularly in regard to countries or continents that had long enjoyed particular links with Paris. In June 1978, the visit of the president of Senegal, Leopold Sedar Senghor, gave me the opportunity to celebrate one of the worthiest figures of the African continent and of humanity as a whole. He had initiated the great movement in the 1930s to restore a culture despised by the West. It was primarily to Africa that I sought to pay homage on behalf of Paris—that Africa whose soul had, like that of Asia, been revealed to me in my youth, not through politics but through art. Indeed, how better to discover the real history of a people than through the works of art that it had bequeathed posterity? From my late adolescence on, I felt the grandeur of the African people, a grandeur that probably derives from the fact, as I would later learn, that the first men on earth came from this part of the world. At the beginning of the 1950s, I occasionally went to the studio of the painter Ferdinand Léger, whose work was greatly inspired by Negro art. There I often heard about the culture of the Dogons of Mali, without yet realizing their real importance. This fascinating discovery of Africa carried on through the years, enabling me to realize the scope of all its richness, often plundered by the West. Today, when I go and admire the great wooden Djennenke statue in the Quai Branly Museum, I always reflect that this absolute masterpiece holds its own against the Venus de Milo.

In the speech that I delivered at the city hall in honor of Senghor, I paid homage to the genius of the man who, arriving in Paris in the aftermath of the Great War, where so many powerful and prophetic new ideas were percolating, had foreseen that European civilization would, for all its excellence, be no more than a mutilated society as long as it lacked the dormant energies of Africa and Asia. Senghor was one of the first people to recognize that two-thirds of humanity was not playing an active role in the world. "The miracle," I said to him, "is that in your fervent quest for Africanness, you have not rejected the importance of our ancient western civilization. You are a man of consensus. Your return to the sources of Africa and your refusal to turn away from Europe has given you a more accurate and relevant picture of what unites the heart of our two continents." I felt a deep communion of mind and heart with this poet and statesman who, transcending all barriers, highlighted all that was complementary in the characters of our respective peoples and civilizations—an attitude that, far from diminishing them, served to elevate the distinctive character of each.

In his reply, Senghor talked of the "Poetry Month" that I had just created with my friend Pierre Seghers and expressed, in several unforgettable phrases, his love of Paris, the "poetic city." It was with some emotion that

I heard this great voice of Africa declare that "the first poetry" he had discovered on first arriving in Paris had been "the concern to respect, in its particularity and its integrality, and to honor every man and woman of every race, every color, every country." His words seemed to echo those of Félix Houphouët-Boigny when he had welcomed me to Abidjan as prime minister: "Africa must be respected because of all it has given to the evolution of the world."

Houphouët, who became even more than a friend, a kind of father to me, had been very sensitive to the fact that I had chosen Africa as the destination of my first official visit abroad. The extremely warm welcome that I received from the Ivorian people, massed along the immense avenue that ran between the airport and the town, was an overwhelming testament of friendship toward and trust of France. What struck me that day was the indescribable enthusiasm of the young people who thronged around us, their joyous shouting as they saw Houphouët and me passing, standing in a magnificent open-topped car. Africans instinctively know whether they are loved or not. They are never wrong about it. And I think I can say that they never doubted the sincerity of my attachment to them, as demonstrated by the welcome that they give me whenever I have the opportunity to visit them.

It has always seemed obvious to me that development aid to Africa should be one of France's great causes. That is why I called in 1977 for our country and its European partners to implement, for the African continent, the same aid and support plan as that the United States had given thirty years earlier for the reconstruction of Europe. Nevertheless, the main question to be resolved, because it largely dictated all the others, was that of the political situation of each of the African states. It was a sensitive subject, so much did the very notions of power and authority still closely depend at that time on traditions and customs that sat uncomfortably with democracy.

Under what criteria should France cooperate with the head of the African states as they were? It would be hypocritical to deny that a decisive factor was its own interests on the continent. But it was equally important that these heads of state be, for their respective countries, lasting sources of political unity and stability. As was the case for almost forty years—however disparaged he was in certain Parisian circles—of the president of Gabon, Omar Bongo, whom I welcomed to the city hall for the first time in October 1980 and with whom I remained friends until his death.

What seemed to me more risky and debatable, at that moment, was the excessively complacent attitude of the French government toward another regime, that of the Central African Republic and its leader, General

Bokassa. He was a personality not unknown to me, even though I had always kept him at a distance. I had met him during his trip to Paris in 1968, in the office of the political advisor on African affairs, Jacques Foccart. I no longer remember why I was present at a meeting in which Foccart, shortly before the reception at the Élysée, had tried to dissuade Bokassa from calling General de Gaulle, as was his custom, "Papa" in his official speech. "You are being received by General de Gaulle as head of state," Foccart lectured him, "and you must therefore call him 'M. President.' If you call him 'Papa' in public, he will be very offended!" Bokassa promised, as he left, that he would toe the line. I was present at the ensuing dinner. After the general had delivered his words of welcome, Bokassa, getting up to reply to him, began his speech by saying, "M. President, you who are father of us all. . . ." It was an ingenious solution. Beneath his boorish air lay a man who was less rough and ready than he seemed, clever at playing with his interlocutors and, when all was said and done, only ever doing what he chose.

At the beginning of the 1980s, this anecdote came back to me when Bokassa had himself declared emperor in a masquerade judged degrading by most African leaders, who refused to attend. Bokassa managed to drag into his game the last country that would agree to deal with him: France, through its president. It was not difficult for me to predict which of them risked most being the dupe of the other and would not emerge unscathed from the Central African trap.

Sensitive to the problems of Africa, the mayor of Paris is no less concerned, of course, with those of the Asian continent, particularly China, where I went for the first time, with my wife, in 1978, at the invitation of the Chinese authorities. This trip served to reinforce the admiration and respect that I had long felt for the toughness and ingenuity of these people, heirs of an exceptional culture and history. The Great Wall is, even for the initiated, a remarkable sight, not only because of its immensity but for the incredible mobilization of techniques and manpower that it represents on every level. A military and political challenge on such a scale is without parallel in the history of humanity. I had the same vertiginous impression in Xian, for several centuries one of the most populous cities in the world and a prestigious intellectual and artistic center. The Great Tsin, the first emperor to unify China, to which he gave his name, is buried in Xian, along with all his army protecting his tomb. This mausoleum has never been opened, despite the many discussions that have been held on this subject. I am among those who have always argued that it should be left untouched, so as not to damage it. I understand that this mausoleum is, in fact, a sort of clay city, crossed by a river of mercury and surmounted by a celestial arch illustrating the knowledge held by the Chinese at that time, already more advanced than any other civilization in terms of astronomy.

The other highlight of this trip was my meeting in Beijing with Deng Xiaoping, who extended the warmest of welcomes to me. I remember the comment that he made during our talk: "Over the next twenty years, there will be no political problem between China and France. That is a certainty linked to history. On the other hand, if there is no economic problem today, there is the danger that there will be one in several years for trading is insufficient and that is where the two countries should be putting all their effort as a matter of priority. And if the economic relationship deteriorates, the political relationship will also worsen."

A year after this first trip, on October 16, 1979, I welcomed to the city hall Mao's successor, Hua Guofeng, on an official trip to France. I found in him neither the quicksilver lucidity nor the lively mind of Deng; nor, of course, was he the visionary genius of the "Great Helmsman." This apparatchik had apparently been chosen because of his ability to oversee peacefully the transition between the tumultuous Maoist reign and the advent of a new Chinese direction that was being minutely fine-tuned behind the scenes by Deng.

Confident of what China, powerful, active, and prosperous, could bring to the balance of world powers, I underlined in my welcoming speech the "exceptional convergence" of interests and duties between our two countries, with their common goal of affirming themselves independently of the two great Soviet and American blocs. In short, of inventing a new kind of world. At that time, China had nothing to fear from the dissolution that had occurred in the Soviet Union and the countries of the East of a Communist system that it alone had used to renew its energy and lift itself up once more among the first rank of the great nations.

I retained a very different impression from my contacts during the same period with the Romanian, Polish, and Hungarian leaders who came through Paris. Whether it was Nicolae Ceaușescu, Edward Gierek, or János Kádár, all of them seemed to me like the last vestiges of an outworn model and an ideology without a future. When I received them at the city hall, I was always at pains to highlight that all the European nations, without exception, belonged to the same civilization and that each of them drew their values from the same moral and spiritual sources.

We know how pivotal a role was played in the final toppling of the European Communist regimes by the election in October 1978 of a pope of Polish origin. The beginning of John Paul II's pontificate was marked by the resoundingly successful trip that he made to Poland. I immediately recognized its great significance, both for the church and for the whole of Europe. As I said in a speech given at that time: "After this visit, nothing can be the same again: The church and, with it, the values of man's freedom and dignity have just scored a resounding victory. This voice rising up amid our political quarrels was urgently needed, reminding us that Europe has existed for two millennia, unified by Christianity, and that the civilization it embodies remains, ultimately, profoundly spiritual."

It was the first time I had made such a strong testament to my personal attachment to the Catholic church. Out of concern for secularism, I had always believed that politicians should demonstrate a certain reserve or discretion in regard to their personal beliefs. For all that, I had never made a secret of my personal faith or of the respect I bore for all forms of belief. One of the most memorable times of my life was that which I spent on October 12, 1976, several weeks after I left Matignon, at the abbey of Solesmes. Overcome by the extraordinary beauty of the Gregorian chant, captivated by a wonderful liturgy, I did not cease to be fascinated by the atmosphere of this domed place entirely devoted to the study of the scriptures, silence, and contemplation.

I feel infinite respect and admiration for men and women who give their lives to prayer and contemplation. But I have to acknowledge that a vocation other than the monastic suits my own character and temperament better: that which achieves its goals through action, action not to amuse oneself but to give meaning to life and to realize ideals of justice, peace, and brotherhood. All politics involve a notion of man. And every notion of man has a religious basis, whether declared or not. Mine is the result of two thousand years of Christianity and is fed by precepts that were taught to me in my childhood. But this faith does not separate me from other believers, whatever their religion, or even from nonbelievers who share the same desire for a more just and peaceful world. A world that is to be built with our own hands.

Few men of God have impressed me as much as John Paul II. Besides the strength of his pastoral commitment, so striking for me as for all the Christians of the world, from his first trip to Poland what struck me most of all when I welcomed him to Paris in May 1980 was the intensity of his presence, his expression, the mixture of determination and extreme goodness that emanated from him as well as the message that he had undertaken to deliver, relentlessly, to his fellow man.

A little less than two years earlier, I had had, through the intermediary of my principal private secretary, Bernard Billaud, who was acquainted with Vatican authorities, a private meeting with Pope Paul VI in Rome, just a month before his death. Although already very frail, the pontiff—also impressive with his austere, reserved air and the firmness of his judgments—granted me a long interview, much longer than usual, according to his entourage. Seeming relaxed, Paul VI seemed happy to meet the mayor of a city that had remained dear to his heart ever since he had spent a summer there as a young priest, taking classes at the Alliance Française. After paying Paris the warmest homage, Paul VI turned to me and said, in a voice filled with emotion, a few words that I would never forget: "M. Mayor, we have been waiting for you so eagerly! We had given up hoping you would come back!"

In January 1980, when I learned that John Paul II was to come to France in the following months, I decided to pull out all the stops for him at city hall. I immediately asked Bernard Billaud to prepare for a new trip to Rome to meet the Holy Father, since the organizers of the pontiff's trip did not seem eager for him to go to the city hall of Paris, fearing that it would create a precedent in terms of other towns. In fact, this resistance was encouraged, if not directly inspired, by the president's office, as always hostile to the idea of the mayor of Paris being given too much attention. Confronted with this situation, I no longer had any choice but to go and plead the Parisians' cause directly with the pope. He met with me for twenty minutes on April 26 in an attentive and warm meeting, but without giving me any official assurances. After that, I did the rounds of the most influential cardinals. A week later, the papal nuncio telephoned to tell me that the pope had agreed to come to city hall and to address the people of Paris from there.

For the residents of the capital, this visit—the first since that of Pius VII almost two centuries earlier—immediately took on a historical dimension that was augmented by the immense popularity that the pope, nicknamed "the man in white," already enjoyed. Celebrities from every field, from the count of Paris to the general secretary of the Communist Party, Georges Marchais, asked to be introduced to this extraordinary pope who was changing the course of history. At city hall, everyone got busy, under the direction of Billaud, preparing the premises and the décor, down to the smallest organizational details, for a ceremony that was closely monitored by Monseigneur Marcinkus, who organized all the details of the pontiff's trips.

On May 30, 1980, as night was slowly descending on the capital, several tens of thousands of people thronged into the square in front of city hall. The middle of the building was covered with a white hanging onto which both the Vatican arms and those of the capital were projected. The papal cortege, arriving from the Notre Dame church, slowly crossed this human tide and stopped at the feet of the rostrum where I was waiting for the pontiff. When John Paul II appeared, an immense wave of applause rose up from the crowd. The pope spent a long time greeting the mass of the faithful who pressed around him. His face radiated a brotherly peace and joy. After exchanging a few words, we climbed the steps covered in red carpet side by side to the podium on which the papal throne had been installed.

An atmosphere of striking devotion and restraint now reigned in the square. Rarely had I been so awed by the presence of a foreign guest. In a slow voice, as though to contain my emotion, I expressed to the pope our great pride in welcoming him "to this place in which the greatest events in the history of our country took place and from where the noble ideas that inspired so many men in search of dignity, freedom, and honor spread to all four corners of the earth. Those who believe and those who do not believe have come to tell you of the hopes that we have in you, vigilant and untiring witness of conscience and mind."

When he spoke in his turn, John Paul II began by assuring the people of Paris and their elected representatives of his gratitude and affection: "In my country of origin, we know what we owe Paris." Then he highlighted the "concrete issues" of the present and of the "planned future." Speaking of the many organizational and planning problems that large cities experienced, the pope underlined that they were never devoid of a human element: "Paris above all consists of men and women, people swept along by the rapid pace of work in offices, research centers, shops, and factories: a youth in search of training and employment, and poor people who often live their financial difficulties, even their destitution, with moving dignity and whom we can never forget: an incessant ebb and flow of often rootless people, anonymous faces on which can be read the thirst for happiness, well-being, and, I also believe, a thirst for the spiritual, a thirst for God."

As I listened to the warm and vibrant voice of John Paul II, I thought of my own mission in service of the millions of Parisians about whom he was speaking and I felt comforted in the notion that the management of a town, like that of a country, should more than ever take into account its "human aspect." That evening, the deep truth of this admirable formula seemed to me particularly relevant.

9

IN OPPOSITION

On February 3, 1981, I announced my decision to stand for the next presidential election, due to take place two months later. It was alone, and against the advice of some of my entourage, that I had determined to engage in this new battle. I do not recall having hesitated for long over the decision, so inevitable did it seem to me. It seemed to me quite legitimate that the Gaullists, given the role they had played in our history, could once again aspire to lead the country. This aspiration was all the stronger because seven years after his election, Valéry Giscard d'Estaing had done nothing—despite my repeated appeals to him in that regard—to merit their support or win their sympathy. The reasons for my resigning as prime minister in August 1976 and then for the battle for the mayorship of Paris had led to many Rassemblement pour la République (RPR) voters and militants forming ranks against the president. Deeper disagreements were added to these causes for irritation. His relentless quest for the "happy medium," the timid project for slow growth, the insistent reminder of the numerical weakness of France and the French in the world were received by the Gaullists as attempts to destabilize them politically.

It was in vain that I issued warnings to Giscard, when I happened to meet him, along the lines of "It is better not to wound an animal. Kill it or stroke it." Or that I reminded him of an Arab proverb, which he did not take any more seriously: "Never push a cat into a corner." Communication between Giscard and me had always been difficult, before becoming virtually impossible at the end of his seven-year term, so hard did I find it to understand his reactions, behavior, and psychology. I had become aware of several disturbing aspects of his personality. Because one of his distant ancestors had taken part in the American war of independence, Giscard got it into his head to join, with all his family, the prestigious Society of the Cincinnati, the organization formed in 1783 by the officers in the Continental Army. After having moved heaven and earth to try to achieve this, he then asked me, as head of the government, to intervene with the association on his behalf. I carried out the request as best I could, but it resulted in a categorical refusal. After examining the application, the organization had decided that the applicant had not satisfactorily established, under the very strict rules of membership, that he was the descendant of one of the Sons of the Revolution. Giscard was deeply wounded by this, his pride and self-esteem jolted to a degree that seemed to me disproportionate.

This was not, however, the most serious setback that he experienced in the international arena. In May 1980, the president took one of his most controversial diplomatic initiatives in agreeing to go to Warsaw to meet Leonid Brezhnev, barely five months after the Soviet Union had invaded Afghanistan. Officially, this move, undertaken by the pressing demand of Polish authorities, was an attempt to protect Poland, then experiencing growing trade union agitation, from a Soviet intervention similar to that of twelve years earlier, when Moscow had taken tight control of Czechoslovakia. But a real meeting, in the context of the Afghan affair, could only be subject to caution, and its symbolic impact above all served the interests of the Soviet Union, seeming to let its leaders off the hook in exchange for a vague promise to withdraw Soviet troops from Kabul "when possible." That day, the spirit of Munich floated above Warsaw.

The other weak point in an evaluation of the presidency was in terms of his economic policy. The austerity plans devised and implemented by the Barre government were not enough, as I had always thought and stated, to prevent the rise in unemployment or even to control inflation, although it was the hobbyhorse of the prime minister. Our economy could be sorted out, in my view, only via a massive investment program. This had been, since 1975, one of my deepest and most constant sources of disagreement with Valéry Giscard d'Estaing. And one of the major reasons, six years later, why I ran for the presidency.

At that time, France had one of the highest rates of compulsory taxation, which risked damaging the expansion and competitiveness of businesses. I insisted on the need to "liberate" our economy—a formula that was immediately interpreted as an opportunistic conversion to the liberalism that had been in vogue in the United States since the election of Ronald Reagan. One of the U-turns to which, according to my detractors, I was accustomed. Yet they had only to read me to realize that what I was advocating in 1981 was in no way contradictory to the ideas I had put forward

three years earlier in my book *La Lueur de l'espérance* [The light of hope].
Although I stated that it was harmful and illusory to trust solely in liberalism, I nonetheless highlighted the "irreplaceable role of freedom and competition" that had been put at risk by the excess of bureaucracy. It was this
same plague that I denounced when I called, at the beginning of the 1980s,
for a liberalization of our economy while wishing that the nation would
remain faithful to its true goals, particularly in terms of employment and
social solidarity. It was the expression of a third way between a socialist
model and the project of an "advanced liberal society."

One day in October 1980, one of my close contacts in the Gaullist
movement suggested that I meet François Mitterrand at a dinner he was
organizing at the home of his friend Edith Cresson. I knew and liked her,
so I readily accepted the invitation—which was in no way, at any time,
at my initiative. Convinced of the contrary and eager to prove that I had
instigated the meeting, Giscard stated in one of his books that Mitterrand,
whom he claimed to have questioned in the last moments of his life, gave
him the confirmation that he sought in this regard. This probably explains
why Giscard never tried to question me, in turn, on the same subject. The
truth is that, summoned to dinner with the leader of the opposition, I
agreed without hesitation. Something, in my view, in no way abnormal or
shocking in a democracy. What would have been untoward would have
been to refuse such a meeting. Even if, due to the electoral context of the
time, I kept it secret for as long as possible to avoid giving rise to all sorts
of interpretations.

I did not know François Mitterrand personally. The impression I had
of him at that time was that of a man who feared neither man nor God;
fluid, ambiguous, and profoundly Machiavellian. Pompidou, who did not
like him, described him to me as an "opportunist," an expert in dirty
tricks. From a strictly political point of view, Mitterrand was above all
the incarnation of everything I was fighting against: not the humanist left
from which I never felt I had distanced myself but an ideological left, with
a program that was the opposite of everything I wished and hoped for our
country.

For all that, this difference of opinions—however extreme—did not
seem to me cause to ban all conversation between political leaders who
shared, above all, the same republican values. With the exception of extremists who did not respect such values, my rule had always been, whether
as the representative of Corrèze, as mayor of Paris, or as head of the government, to enter into dialogue with any of my opponents at every opportunity. There was therefore, in my eyes, nothing extraordinary or particularly

scandalous about meeting François Mitterrand in private, six months before a presidential election to which neither of us had yet declared ourselves a candidate. The meeting did occur, it is true, at a time when the disagreement between the RPR and the president had become such that I was led to declare, on October 22, 1980, that "if we want a change of policy, either we have to change the president or the president has to make the effort to change himself." This did not mean, as may seem the case, that I was thinking of Mitterrand as the possible successor to the outgoing president.

It was because there was nothing memorable about it that for a long time I refrained from talking about the dinner that took place shortly afterward at the home of Edith Cresson in the presence of Jean de Lipkowski. And I would probably never have spoken about it if the then president of the republic had not, twenty-six years later, published the supposed posthumous testimony of his successor, François Mitterrand, according to which I had declared to the latter that evening: "We must get rid of Giscard!" Shocked by this way of going about things, and indignant at the words that had been attributed to me, I could not stop myself reacting, this time by strongly refuting a version of the facts apparently inspired, as so often with Giscard, by nothing more than his resentment toward me.

The memory I have retained of this first meeting with François Mitterrand is of a courteous, relaxed conversation that was, however, without any real interest other than that of getting to know each other better and to size each other up, in search of possible points in common. I knew that he was a lover of Africa, but I knew nothing of his fascination for the Asian continent and China in particular—and he seemed no less surprised to discover the great interest I had for Chinese history. From the brief conversation we had on the subject, I got the impression of a man much more refined and subtle than the one who had been described to me and with a much broader culture than I had imagined. French politics was not a subject in which we had the most to learn from each other, so adept were we both at sticking to our respective opinions and to our opposing ambitions.

We both agreed to the suggestion of Cresson to meet after the dinner to discuss the situation of the country and the coming elections. The meeting lasted about an hour—not two, as has been claimed. The subject of the president naturally came up, and Mitterrand pointed out all the reasons, as it was in his interests to do so, that he believed I had to defeat him. In short, he believed that if Giscard were reelected, it would be "catastrophic" for the RPR as well as for France. Eager not to play his game, I limited myself to noting my own criticisms, which were already well known to everybody, of the actions of the president and his government. But I did not go as far as expressing to Mitterrand, who would not have failed to make good use of it, that we should "get rid of" you know who.

That is the true account of that dinner, which was in no way decisive and which did not deserve so much comment. The reasons for the defeat of May 1981 need to be sought elsewhere.

The RPR had not waited for the official announcement of my candidacy, on February 3, 1981, to mobilize forces. Programs, premises, posters, campaign committees, operational teams—everything had been ready for several months, under the leadership of Charles Pasqua. The campaign was soon in full swing, driven by the enthusiasm of hundreds of thousands of militants and sympathizers all across the country. I traveled the length and breadth of France, holding meetings in town after town and facilitating at every opportunity—as was my wont—direct contact with the people. On the ground, my chances of winning seemed more realistic every day.

To be elected, I knew that I had to appear the only credible alternative to the president, and therefore I had to eliminate Mitterrand in the first round. To achieve this objective, the whole Gaullist family would have to rally around me—but two other candidates from our ranks had decided to run as well as me. Between them they attracted barely 3 percent of the votes on the first round, but they weakened my own result by this amount. On April 26, I emerged third behind François Mitterrand and Valéry Giscard d'Estaing. The latter, with 28.3 percent of the vote against 25.84 percent for his challenger, had not achieved the result he had counted on to enter the second round in a position of strength. To win now, he would have to rally those RPR voters whom he had thought fit, for so long, to despise.

What struck me first on the evening of the first round was the disappointment that I saw all around me. Rare were those within my team who were ready to support a president whose policies they had not liked, any more than his behavior toward them. And the offer that was shortly after put out by the president's office to invite the RPR members of Parliament and officials to lunch was not guaranteed to put their minds at ease. Rather than expressing myself on my own account—which is what I did the following day by announcing that I would vote for Giscard d'Estaing—it was not for me to declare the position of the party without the approval of its members. Now, this was far from definitive, as was confirmed over the following days by the decision of the central committee to leave it up to our members how they wished to vote, while several Gaullist figures did not hesitate to declare themselves in favor of the left-wing candidate.

More than a political choice, this election was being decided on a question of trust—on whether the previous president was able to restore his credibility with the section of voters on whom his winning depended. Deep down, I feared that it was too late for Giscard to pull this off, so irredeemable did his bad relationship with the RPR seem. In any case, Giscard would not make any spectacular efforts between the two rounds to win over its leaders, whom he did not even try to meet, doubtless from fear of seeming to lower himself.

I did not want François Mitterrand to win, as I could not have made clearer in a text of May 6, 1981, calling on people to prevent the Socialist candidate from gaining power. But I no longer had any means of holding back the process, initiated long before, in which a minority of Gaullist militants openly rejected Giscard in favor of his opponent. Even had I managed to do so, it would not have been enough to reverse the course of events, as the results of the second round of the presidential election proved.

On the evening of May 10, the figures clearly showed that the president had swept the board of right-wing votes and even won 300,000 additional votes. It was therefore not the RPR voters who had created the gap of 1.2 million votes that separated Giscard from his Socialist challenger but the massive mobilization in favor of François Mitterrand by those who had abstained in the first round. It was proof that the arithmetic of such an election bypassed mere partisan logistics. I did not have the heart to rejoice in such a resounding failure. In politics, one does not build a victory on the defeat of one's own side. But how could responsibility for this defeat, which was also my own, not be laid at the door of a man who had set about, from the beginning of his seven-year term to the end, dividing his government instead of uniting it and governing without taking the slightest account of his allies' views? Giscard preferred to put the blame on others—me, in other words—by talking about "premeditated betrayals" when it would have been more honest at least to acknowledge that the fault was shared. From then on, he would continually rehash his grievances and designate me as the sole perpetrator of his exit from power. One day Giscard declared that he had "thrown all resentment into the river"—but the river must have been dry that day, so stubborn and seemingly inexhaustible was the resentment that he continued to harbor.

However negative it seemed in my eyes, the coming to power of the left did not mean the end of the republic or its institutions. At most it was the price of democracy, in which the defeat of a man is never, or rarely, an irreplaceable loss.

Out of power for the first time since 1958, the parties of the former government had to learn, overnight, to change roles and organize themselves as an opposition. On June 21, 1981, the results of the general election conformed to expectations: 269 seats for the Socialist Party versus 83 for the RPR and 61 for the Union for French Democracy (UDF). Once again, I had been elected on the first round as member of Parliament for Corrèze but just scraped past the 50 percent mark, running against a young Socialist candidate by the name of François Hollande.

It would have been a mistake to take refuge, while awaiting better days, in a systematic criticism of everything the Socialist government did. Believing that a change of power was in no way inherently tragic or irreversible, on several occasions during that time of tension I made a public appeal for more tolerance toward various figures in political life. No side paid much attention. Nonetheless, I remained convinced that it was not in the opposition's interests to rival the sectarianism of a government so quick to caricature the actions of its predecessors. As for my own judgment of the new government, it was not made in a doctrinaire spirit.

I felt concern about the economic and financial measures provided for in the "one hundred and ten proposals" of the Socialist program. It would take just a few months for the massive growth in public expenditures and the consequent rise in taxes as well as the nationalization, inopportune in every respect, of several large industrial groups and a large sector of the banking organizations to throw the country into an alarming situation. Foreign debt was higher than ever while deficits were growing and unemployment continually worsened. Neither the decrease in the working week to thirty-nine hours, with no decrease in salary, nor the introduction of a fifth week of paid holiday had the desired effect. On October 4, the Socialist experience was consolidated by a first devaluation followed by a second after the adoption, in June 1982, of an austerity plan that froze salaries and prices and attempted restrictions, albeit modest, on expenditures.

Inevitably, this ideological stranglehold led the victors of May 10 to launch into a dead-end program that brought new disillusionment for all those who dreamed of more efficient change. The country needed more flexibility and less bureaucracy in its economic organization, better judgment and rigor in the management of public money, and a new sharing of responsibilities between government and society, and the archaic policies now being implemented only increased the previous stagnation.

Nonetheless, I still approved of certain governmental initiatives promoting culture and research or endorsing the overall direction of the defense policy undertaken by members of the government, not all of whom were my enemies. From the prime minister himself, whom I believed to be a man of quality, to Michel Rocard, Charles Hernu, or Edith Cresson, who had become minister for agriculture, my personal relations with certain members of the government team were not dictated solely by partisan opposition.

As for the president, I was not among those in the opposition who denied the legitimacy of his position. "Are you going to contest my taking office?" he asked me when he received me at the Élysée Palace shortly after his inauguration. "Certainly not," I replied, "because I firmly intend to succeed you." Contrary to what may appear to be the case, and despite his long battling of them, Mitterrand in no way undermined the institutions of the Fifth Republic or sought, in however slight a way, to deprive himself of the powers they conferred on him.

On September 17, 1981, I was one of the sixteen opposition members who voted for the abolition of the death penalty. I had always been against the death penalty, believing that in no case did it constitute an act of justice. No one, I believe, has the right to take a human life. I was sorry that this reform had been delayed for so long, but it could come only from the president, the sole arbiter of whether a condemned prisoner should be reprieved or not. A poll published on September 17 indicated that 62 percent of the French people remained in favor of the death penalty, many of our voters among them. But I voted against it, independent of all electoral considerations and in accordance with my personal convictions.

From a strictly political point of view, the abolition of the death penalty was one of the few subjects of consensus with the government, as the left–right divide doubled in intensity during that period. Exasperated by our attempts to frustrate the adoption of their program, the Socialists went as far as to threaten to sanction all those who "opposed the popular will and the changes desired by the government." Eight months later, this threat was translated into a direct attack on the person who now seemed leader of the opposition: the mayor of Paris.

In February 1982, François Mitterrand summoned me to the Élysée to consult me about the "big projects" that he hoped to put in place in the capital. I gave him my agreement in principle. This ambitious program seemed to me in accordance with Parisians' concerns, even if, as I told him, the cost of it made me tremble somewhat, both as a taxpayer and a former prime minister. In the immediate term, we were talking about the project of La Villette initiated by Valéry Giscard d'Estaing and taken up and modified by his successor, and those of Opera Bastille, the Arch of La Défense, the Arab World Institute, and the transfer of the Ministry of Finance to Bercy to allow for the development of the Louvre, an idea I favored immediately. These big projects could not be realized without a perfect collaboration between government and city.

It was with stupefaction that I learned on June 30, 1982, of the decision of the minister of the interior to revoke the statute of Paris in the name of his decentralization policy. The goal was to create a fully autonomous town council at the level of each arrondissement. These town councils would then designate their representatives at the Council of Paris, which would then elect the mayor of the capital. The latter would be mayor in name only, his functions becoming those, at most, of a president of an urban community. On the morning of July 6, the first secretary of the Socialist Party, Lionel Jospin, issued a declaration that his party was the instigator of the project. The political maneuver could thus be in no more doubt.

The affair was all the more scandalous in that the statute of Paris, instituted five years earlier, had proved itself a success and enabled a more efficient management of the city in every sector. Finances were well handled, the city had little debt, and local taxes remained among the lowest of the big French administrative areas. My indignation in the face of so much cynical motivation was such that I refused all negotiation with the government members responsible, whom I publicly called "incompetent," "irresponsible," and "cheats." During a press conference organized, exceptionally, in the Tapestry Room of city hall, I called on Parisians to demand that the government hold a referendum on the issue. About 250,000 people responded to this appeal, as well as numerous associations reputedly supportive of the left.

A general protest was organized in the capital. This offensive would bear fruit. Forced to beat a retreat, the government eventually gave up on what was the essential objective of its reform: to remove all decision-making powers from the mayor of Paris. A law involving the three biggest French cities resulted in the creation of mayors in each Paris arrondissement but recognized the full authority of the mayor of the city in the overall management of city affairs. As far as Paris was concerned, this authority would be further strengthened the following year by our triumphant reelection in the local elections of March 1983. The existing team won the majority in all twenty arrondissements in the capital. Each of them, now wielding specific powers, would be administered by a mayor from our ranks.

After this affair, the issue of independent schools revived hostilities between the Socialist government and the opposition of which I had become the principal leader. Among the 110 electoral propositions of the left was the creation of "a large, unified and secular national education service"—a formula that contained an obvious threat for private education. At least that was how it was perceived by the French episcopate, which made public its concern and obtained from the minister of national education, after long consultations, a more acceptable revision of the text, until this apparent consensus was shot to pieces under the pressure of Socialist members of Parliament determined to limit financial aid to independent schools.

In short, the battle over schools, which had seemed definitively closed after so many years of quarreling and controversy, was reignited, thanks to the still-rampant anticlericalism of the new leaders of the country and the ambiguous motives of a president who was himself the product of a religious school. Educated in state schools, unlike François Mitterrand, and raised in respect for secularism, I was nonetheless attached to the preservation of independent establishments and, even more, to freedom of choice for families in matters of education.

Convinced that only a show of force could make the government withdraw, as I had seen two years earlier with the reform of the statute of Paris, I was skeptical that the more or less secret negotiations undertaken by the episcopate would be enough to resolve the problems and I warned Monsignor Vilnet, president of the bishops of France, and the archbishop of Paris, Monsignor Lustiger, against the illusion of a possible agreement with the government. Still persuaded to the contrary, my interlocutors asked me to do all I could to prevent the opposition taking over a debate that the Socialists had already greatly politicized.

The somewhat difficult relations that I experienced with Monsignor Lustiger date from this time. After suggesting to me that I go and meet Mitterrand to assure him of the pacific intentions of the RPR—which would help the president, according to him, calm things down with his party—the archbishop of Paris issued a second request to me, with no more success, in February 1984: not to participate in the large demonstration in Versailles on March 4 in support of independent schools. My absence from a march of some 800,000 people would have been all the more nonsensical and futile, given that the conflict had now taken on an overtly political character in the eyes of the French. I therefore decided to go to Versailles, as I would be present, on June 24, alongside the 2 million demonstrators marching through the streets of Paris.

On July 12, Mitterrand announced the withdrawal of the Savary Law, provoking the resignation of the minister responsible, followed five days later by that of the government leader Pierre Mauroy. Our fight had not been in vain—even if the Socialists did not intend to let their offensive against the opposition rest there.

The next step was the introduction of proportional representation on April 3, 1985. Another of the promises of the Socialist candidate, it also assisted in the emergence, four years later, of the National Front, which would obtain more than 10 percent of the vote in the European elections of

June 1984. I am opposed to a reform of the voting system, believing that it can only make it difficult for a real majority to emerge in Parliament. But this reform had in fact only one goal in Mitterrand's mind: to institutionalize the extreme right, enabling it to gain sufficient force to hamper the opposition. Which comes down to promoting racism and xenophobia strictly in the hope of electoral gain.

Used against us by the president, the National Front is one of the direct results of the policy followed since 1981. The decision taken by the government that year to regularize the status of clandestine workers had disastrous effects. Legalizing the presence in our country of 120,000 illegal immigrants risked not only unleashing a new wave of illegal immigration, in the context of a worsening employment crisis; it also provoked and fed virulent reactions in many of our compatriots in the face of this influx of foreigners. Reactions that were exploited ad infinitum by the National Front, to all the more advantage since the question of immigration, long banished from political debate, now resurfaced with resounding intensity.

I did not pay sufficient attention to it at the time, but the breakthrough made by the National Front occurred in autumn 1983 during the local elections in Dreux, Eure-et-Loir. That is how I allowed the local right-wing party to make an alliance with the candidate from Jean-Marie Le Pen's party in the second round, thereby winning the election. Only after the event did I realize the seriousness of what had just happened. I immediately cut short any notion of entering into a relationship or developing common strategy with the National Front, a party of hatred and rejection of others, in contradiction to all my beliefs. For me, patriotism was love of one's own people and nationalism was hatred of others. Determined not only to prohibit any future alliance with the National Front, but above all to denounce the ideas it propounded, I nonetheless found myself in a difficult political situation, caught in a pincer movement between the extreme right in full ascendancy and a left that had every interest in encouraging its growth at our expense and which did not hold back from doing so.

By introducing proportional representation, François Mitterrand and the leaders of the Socialist Party fashioned the destiny of the National Front with their own hands. The existence of the latter would be only a slight hindrance for the president while it helped him stay in power. Such was indeed his intention, whatever the results of elections to come.

From 1983, the opposition had begun to envisage the possibility of a power-sharing arrangement between the president of the republic and a prime minister from its party.

If it is hard to imagine de Gaulle sharing power, in the light of his personality, his place in history, and the concept he had of his legitimacy, it seemed to me likely that Pompidou would have agreed to stay in power even if he had been forced to appoint a prime minister from the opposing side. As for Giscard, he had prepared himself for it without even knowing whether the possibility would arise and seemed sorry that voters did not, in the end, impose it on him.

Contrary to what is sometimes stated, it was not Édouard Balladur who invented the idea of "cohabitation": At the most, he conceptualized it. And it is also not true that he converted me to the idea, even if we often talked about it in private meetings in my office at the Paris city hall, the Hôtel de Ville. No one could seriously doubt the determination of Mitterrand to continue, come what may, to the end of his term of office. The question was therefore openly posed from that time on, among the opposition, of a possible power sharing with the president.

Whether merely for appearance's sake as far as he was concerned, Giscard and I even began to enter into a public reconciliation. As for the question of the leadership, this was partly resolved after the televised debate between the prime minister, Laurent Fabius, and me on October 27, 1985. Arrogant, contemptuous, refusing to shake my hand, the prime minister inadvertently gave me the opportunity to appear the most credible candidate to succeed him.

The program on which the RPR and the UDF agreed on January 16, 1986, contained many projects for reform—denationalization of banks and large industrial groups; withdrawal of the wealth tax; introduction of free exchange, credit, and competition—which essentially aimed at reintroducing more flexibility and dynamism in the functioning of the national economy. Was it for all that a strictly liberal program similar to those implemented by Ronald Reagan in the United States and Margaret Thatcher in Great Britain? It must primarily be seen as the fruit of a synthesis between the aspirations of different currents of the opposition: Gaullist, centrist, and liberal. And, as in all syntheses, its implementation would not occur without concessions and adjustments from all sides.

The only worthwhile economic model had not changed in my eyes, whatever may seem the case. It was still that of a humanist economy that led to greater equilibrium between the duties of government and the responsibility of citizens. Humanism is founded on the conviction that nothing good or great can be achieved other than through man and on the total respect of individual freedoms and rights, freedoms and rights themselves justified by the duties incumbent on each person. This meant that the government should be a guarantor rather than a manager. Its role was not to replace civilian society but to respond to its aspirations in accordance with its recognized powers.

But the question that arose, on the eve of the general election of March 1986, was not just that of the policies we should embark on if we won but also that of how we would implement them in the hitherto unknown context of cohabitation.

10

SHARING POWER

The opposition won a very narrow victory in the second round of the general election on March 16, 1986. With just three seats more than the absolute majority, this was not the victory for which it had hoped. Proportional representation had borne its fruits. Introduced for this sole purpose, it enabled the National Front to enter into Parliament, gaining thirty-five seats. Enough to form its own group and fully exercise the power of obstruction for which it had been programmed. The Rassemblement pour la République (RPR) and the Union for French Democracy (UDF) certainly had the means to govern, but with far more limited room for maneuver than expected to take over the leadership of the country in the all the more difficult context of cohabitation.

In fact, the real winner of the vote of March 16 was none other than François Mitterrand, forsaken in the polling booths but assisted in his desire to remain in the presidency by the narrowness of the results. This was the paradox of the new political landscape, which the president had cleverly orchestrated to his advantage. Although he had lost, he had not done so by margins that would force him to resign, and although the new government had won, it had not done so with a majority sufficient to allow it to reign without sharing power.

What to do faced with such a situation other than adhere strictly to the constitution? This guaranteed the future prime minister control of the government and consequently allowed the government to implement its program. The president, meanwhile, retained his authority over defense and foreign affairs, sectors that were reserved, though not exclusively, for him. The fact that the executive was managed by two different parties obviously changed the picture, but I had seen in the past that the prime minister's freedom of action did not necessarily depend on the convictions he shared with the president.

In such circumstances, the choice of prime minister could not be left up to the mere wish of the president. If cohabitation were to function, it depended on the head of the most powerful majority party, or a member of his party of his choosing, being appointed. I agreed to take on the role of head of the government on condition that all the parties within it committed to participate in it, an agreement I obtained without difficulty. Given the small majority we had in Parliament, the stability of the next ministerial team required that all, without exception, be involved in the running of the country. It was up to the prime minister to take continual account of the aspirations of each of the groups that supported him.

On March 18, after having speculated about every hypothesis and letting doubt about his intentions take flight, Mitterrand officially made known his desire to meet me that same day, in the afternoon.

The interview lasted a little more than two hours. Citing the tradition that the representative of the largest party in Parliament be called on, as well as his personal wish, the president quickly announced his intention to appoint me prime minister. I responded that I was ready to accept his proposition, if he and I were in agreement that the constitution would be obeyed to the letter. The president assured me that "the government would govern, as stipulated in Article 20" and undertook to endorse all the laws voted by Parliament, including the edicts that would implement privatizations as rapidly as possible—if they were "in conformity with republican legality." This seemed to me scarcely in question, even if that detail was probably not devoid, for him, of ulterior motives, as I quickly verified. When I confirmed my intention of restoring, as quickly as possible, the first-past-the-post voting system, Mitterrand declared that he did not intend to oppose this, while feigning astonishment at my haste: "Why are you in such a hurry?" he asked. I replied that it was a matter of a commitment made to the French people: "If we don't do it now, we will never do it."

Then the president set out three conditions, which I had no reason to oppose: that the government would be respectful of him, that it would not revoke the abolition of the death penalty, and that it would allow him his right to control foreign policy and national defense. Which supposed, he added, that the ministers concerned "be people with whom I can speak in trust"—his way of reminding me that he would naturally have his opinion about the composition of the government.

I came out of this first meeting quite confident about the likelihood of sharing power with Mitterrand without too many upsets. Not that I underestimated the differences that could divide us or the attentiveness with which the president would scrutinize our slightest mistakes or the haste with which he would use them to his advantage. Since the affair of the mayoralty of Paris, I had learned to be wary of Mitterrand's pugnacity and skill at dissimulation. "Never let yourself be taken in by Mitterrand," Georges Pompidou had confided in me one day. "You should never believe what he says to you, whatever story he spins."

For my part, I felt in no way incapable of taking on such a partner and ensuring that he respected, in every instance, my prerogatives. But I did not doubt that our common interest would be to seek out, for as long as possible, the paths of appeasement and conciliation—even if cohabitation itself would be nothing but a permanent struggle for power.

As soon as I got back to the Hôtel de Ville, I addressed myself to the formation of my government. Édouard Balladur assisted me in the choice of the new ministerial team. He had become one of my closest advisors and appeared at my side, under what could be rather a deceptive guise, as a sage and thinker. I appreciated and respected his intelligence, his culture, and his great sense of government. If I had had to nominate someone else to Matignon in my stead, I would doubtless have thought first of him. I was probably wrong to have told him this at that time—it could only have put ideas in his head for later.

Skeptical by nature and liberal by conviction, Balladur was a cold calculator who hated bursts of enthusiasm or grand gestures as well as any form of open conflict. He gave me his assessment of men and situations with a sort of caustic refinement, rarely devoid of irony. Fully conscious of his intellectual value, he made no secret of the fact that he felt superior to all those who surrounded me or of his hope that, after long occupying secondary roles in the shadows, he would finally be granted the foremost position he thought he deserved.

The first Council of Ministers of the new legislature took place at the Élysée Palace on Saturday, March 22, 1986. As if to lose no time in pointing out all that separated him from the new government assembled around him—thirty-eight people who had been, until then, often fiercely critical political opponents—the president appeared before the television cameras at the start of the meeting with a tense, closed face, a fixed expression, as if he were being held captive by invincible enemies. But the reality of what had taken place that day was far from that dramatic.

The rules of the game having been fixed from our first interview, there had been nothing to fear, either for him or for us, from that inaugural meeting, destined above all to give an air of normalcy in public to relations between the two sides of the executive. What is more, there was no question in my mind of trying to hurt or humiliate, however slightly, the man who embodied the continuity of the government and who had displayed toward me, from the outset, more respect, consideration, and even friendliness than I had ever experienced with his predecessor. This would remain true of our personal relations until the end of the cohabitation, despite the turbulence that characterized it.

There was no doubt, for both François Mitterrand and me, that the cohabitation placed us in a delicate position in which, without being condemned to get along, we were nonetheless forced to act in concert for the good of the nation. During that period of mutual observation—"I will always be checking up on you," Mitterrand had told me in a playful tone during our first conversation—the most vulnerable was without doubt the one who assumed sole responsibility for the policies undertaken. For the first time since the creation of the Fifth Republic, this would be the exclusive domain of the prime minister—which did not mean that the president would be forced to remain in the shadows.

My government's aim was clear: to liberalize our economy with the principal objective of strengthening employment. While an upturn had been discernible all over the world since the mid-1980s, principally in the United States, the French economy had not followed suit. If inflation had decreased with us, as elsewhere, the gross domestic product had increased only slightly, foreign trade remained in deficit, despite the fall in the dollar, and the price of oil and investments remained inadequate, while youth unemployment was the highest in Europe with a quarter of young people looking for work.

All this was largely due to the fact that far from helping our companies become more competitive, as most countries had done by decreasing controls and regulations, the French government had taken the opposite route. It had continually increased the hold of government. Taxes and charges of all sorts had multiplied, control of prices and foreign trade had been maintained, and the power of bureaucracy had increased in proportion. The public sector, considerably strengthened since 1981, now employed almost a third of all workers, including the employees of nationalized companies.

I had to act quickly to remedy this situation. I was strongly encouraged in this by a faction of the government that was impatient to see the realization of what certain right-wing intellectuals called a "conservative revolution," in reference to the Reagan and Thatcher models. I always responded, for my part, that the emancipation of our economy should go hand in hand, during a period of recession, with the maintenance if not the reinforcement of our system of social protection and lead, as a priority, to a reduction of inequalities. This was doubtless not what the proponents of ultra-liberalism wanted to hear, but it was, globally, the direction of the policies that I had resolved to put in place as rapidly as possible.

The recourse to the use of statutory instruments, which first required that an enabling act be voted in Parliament, seemed imperative to us now as in all emergency cases. We were not the first, since the beginning of the Fifth Republic, to use this type of procedure. The last ones to use it had been the Socialists shortly after they came to power to speed up the implementation of their program of reforms, particularly nationalizations, which risked getting bogged down in parliamentary debate. These were the same reasons that led us to use the same methods—except that in our case the president did not intend to make the government's task easier.

Despite his promise, admittedly set about with several conditions, not to oppose statutory instruments that I might present to him, François Mitterrand lost no time in hampering the process. On March 26, he announced in the Council of Ministers his refusal to sign a first statutory instrument, revising the administrative procedure for redundancy introduced in 1975 by my previous government. Eleven years later, we needed to facilitate mobility of employment in a more difficult economic climate. It was one of the flagship measures, even though one of the least well accepted in public opinion, of the economic plan of action that we wished to implement. Since it could not be introduced by statutory instrument, this reform would be introduced by a law voted on on June 8, 1986.

After this first attempt at obstruction, Mitterrand made it known to the government, via the spokesperson of the Élysée, that he would agree to sign only a "limited number" of statutory instruments. It was henceforth clear that, if he was unable to prevent us from governing, the president was determined to do all he could to make things difficult for us.

On April 7, after I had presented him with the proposed privatization by statutory instrument of a great number of public companies and the amendment of the voting system, the president indicated to me in a letter sent the same day that he did not intend to support the revocation of nationalizations decreed by General de Gaulle after the liberation of France or those introduced since 1981 by the Mauroy government. As for the reform of electoral law, the president hoped that measures would be introduced in the National Assembly "to deliberate in good time on the rules for its own renewal."

The proposed privatizations concerned forty-two large banks and thirteen insurance companies, as well as large companies, such as the general electricity company and one of the three public TV channels. It was clearly one of the main projects of the new legislature, necessary both to straighten out the economy and to reduce the government deficit, which had increased fivefold between 1981 and 1985.

On April 23, Mitterrand denounced several so-called safety measures presented by the minister of the interior, Charles Pasqua. As safety had become a constant preoccupation of the French, I attached much importance to the government filling the duties incumbent on it in this domain. Our policies in this area were represented by a series of proposed laws designed to fight delinquency and criminality through improved application of penalties and of identity controls. They also provided for toughened immigration control with amended conditions for foreigners to enter and remain and restricted access to long-term residence rights.

Faced with an increase in terrorism, demonstrated shortly after I took office with the attack on a gallery in the Champs Élysées on March 20, I decided on the immediate creation of a national security council comprising officials of the ministries of the interior, justice, defense, and foreign affairs as well as various antiterrorist organizations. This coordinated effort was all the more urgent in that our country appeared defenseless and therefore vulnerable, lacking both sufficient intelligence on presumed terrorists and substantial international cooperation.

On all these subjects—privatizations, security, immigration, antiterrorist action—Mitterrand made known, on a daily basis, his criticisms, reservations, and changes of mood, thereby implementing a tactic of harassment aimed at marking out his territory in view of a likely renewed candidacy in the presidential election. Many members of the government were irritated at such behavior, which they thought intolerable. Some exhorted me to react or even to abandon ship without further ado. I left all of them to it, judging that it would be a fatal error to take responsibility for a rupture that, on his side, the president was taking great pains to provoke. I now knew Mitterrand well enough to know that he would not risk exceeding the boundaries he had fixed for himself—with the secret hope, naturally, that we would exceed them in his stead.

Paradoxically, I had fewer reasons to leave office in 1986 than I had had ten years earlier. Under the cohabitation, the means at my disposal for governing were far superior to those granted me earlier. The supremacy of the president was not, by the nature of things, the same even if he would not hear of ceding any of the authority conferred on him by the constitution. With or without the consent of the president, the work that had already been accomplished over the months following my appointment was considerable. My government had proceeded, one after the other, to abolish the wealth tax, to control prices, exchange, and credit, to remove tax on the revenues of 2 million lower-income taxpayers, and to launch an emergency plan in favor of youth employment, based on total or partial exoneration of social charges and the implementation of new arrangements giving employees participatory rights and stock options. We were also concerned with safeguarding and consolidating gains made in the social security system.

All this, and many other measures, was realized in the context of a cohabitation that was certainly eventful—it could not be otherwise, simply on political grounds—but that often functioned effectively. This period of power sharing with Mitterrand took place without heated outbursts and in an atmosphere in which our differences never prevented courteous and respectful dialogue.

Our most important meeting was the private one, lasting around an hour, that we had every Wednesday morning before the Council of Ministers. It was also the opportunity for informal exchanges, more useful than any others in terms of enabling the mutual understanding of two men whom circumstances did nothing to bring together. While people on the outside imagined us quarreling about political problems, our conversation frequently dwelt on more personal questions or on our common passions for art and poetry.

Unlike his predecessor, whose literary and artistic tastes barely went beyond the eighteenth century, Mitterrand proved curious about every domain of knowledge. Although he was principally interested in the traditional areas of French and European culture, he exhibited great interest in the history of other civilizations, such as that of the Far East or pre-Columbian America, with which he knew I was more familiar.

I am not unaware of the complexity of the character or the shadowy areas that fell across his career, but the man whom I discovered over the course of our meetings appeared to me one who had a finesse of judgment and a tactical intelligence that I had rarely encountered in the political world. His love for France was indisputable, and he would not allow the country to be brought down in any way. Our common values were those of two men from the provinces attached to traditions of the land and to ideals of the republic. And if, for the rest, our convictions seemed diametrically opposed, one was probably less to the left and the other less to the right than each respectively made out.

More than his ideas, cohabitation enabled me to admire the way in which François Mitterrand enacted them. "There's the artist!" I sometimes thought when witnessing one of his performances—and particularly the one that took place on July 14, 1986.

$\mathcal{A}$lthough the enabling act, fiercely contested by members of the left, was finally passed on July 2, it was increasingly probable that the president would refuse to sign the statutory instruments in regard to privatizations. I was not surprised, for the issue had a symbolic importance that it was in his interests to exploit against us. Since he could not block the denational-izations, he could at least delay them—thereby signaling to the public his dissension as well as his authority.

Determined to hold fast and also to tone down a quarrel that was in fact purely for show, I telephoned Mitterrand during the evening of July 14, the day before the traditional televised interview he gave, to propose a solution that would probably enable us to avoid all public confrontation: for him to be discharged, in a joint declaration of the presidents of the two parliamentary chambers, of all responsibility in the statutory instruments process. As I expected, he refused. But this last attempt at conciliation at least allowed me to test the president on his real intentions. "And so," I said to him, "you want to bring the cohabitation to an end." To which he replied that he "didn't want to go as far as that," knowing that it would do him no good to initiate a rupture that the overwhelming majority of the French did not want.

On July 14, Mitterrand declared, as predicted, that he would not sign the statutory instruments, provoking an intense protest among the govern-ment. From every side, I was pressed to respond. In what way? The most spectacular reaction would be to resign on the spot. But to whose advan-tage? Did this affair, dramatized to the extreme by Mitterrand, deserve that we too grant it such disproportionate importance? The real object of dispute, the privatizations, was in no way compromised by the presidential veto. If rupture is sometimes necessary, it should be in accordance with the general interest and not arise out of a mere fit of pique or a political calcula-tion designed to satisfy personal ambition.

On July 17, I announced to the Council of Ministers my decision to resort to parliamentary means to implement our program of privatizations. By these means, the essential issue was safeguarded and our task was ac-complished, above and beyond controversy.

11

A DIPLOMATIC DUET

*I*n a cohabitation, the idea of "reserved area" becomes a more relative notion. Although he remained head of the armed services and was in charge of negotiating and ratifying treaties, in conformity with the constitution, the president of the republic could not easily arrogate to himself the same powers in regard to foreign affairs and defense policy as in normal governmental practice. The prime minister automatically had greater responsibility in these matters. Two successive incidents that occurred in April 1986 would enable me to publicly demonstrate the role I intended to play in diplomacy and in every strategic decision, particularly that concerning nuclear deterrence.

The first incident involved the request of the United States for authorization to fly across our territory to go bomb the Libyan capital, Tripoli. Determined to exact justice on Colonel Gaddafi, who was believed to be behind terrorist attacks in Europe that had killed several of its citizens, the American government asked for the support of France in this reprisal action. On April 11, President Reagan telephoned me. "We are going to kill Gaddafi," he announced. "Our bombers need to be able to cross your territory." Shocked that France could be implicated in an operation about which it had not even been consulted, I immediately refused the American request. "France's involvement in this affair is completely out of the question," I said to Reagan. "Especially as you are very unlikely to get Gaddafi. . . . Such operations rarely succeed." Indeed, American planes, obliged to circumvent French territory, would bombard Tripoli and Benghazi in vain four days later, succeeding only in killing one of the daughters of the Libyan leader.

I informed François Mitterrand of the call I had received from Reagan and the refusal I had given him. The president told me that he had been solicited in his turn and had given the same response, without our having needed to speak about it. It was therefore natural that I should declare on television the day after that I had taken a decision "ratified by the president." Although we had made this decision jointly, the president lost no time in informing me that he alone was able to claim authorship of it. It was a way to remind me that what had been, up to now, his "reserved area" should remain, in fact, his private domain. Cohabitation, according to him, in no way changed this fact.

It would take a second incident to get him to reconsider his position. A summit involving the seven great world powers was planned in Tokyo at the beginning of May 1986, and I communicated to the president my wish to take part in it, especially as the fight against international terrorism was one of the items on the agenda. The president, who had planned on going to Japan with only the minister for foreign affairs, seemed surprised, if not irritated, that I was seeking to impose myself on a meeting for heads of state to which, according to him, I had no reason to be invited. This was not my opinion, given our status as cohabitants. Mitterrand, resigning himself to my presence, asked me to arrive in Tokyo after him and not before, as I had publicly announced I would, to meet with Reagan before the start of the conference. I consented, after getting him to agree that we would meet the American leader together.

Our joint presence in Tokyo did not go unnoticed; everyone understood that the president no longer had the same preeminence in the domain of diplomatic relations. And no one was surprised to see me attend the G7 in Venice the following year or take part in all the international meetings that took place in Paris until spring 1988.

Even if this diplomatic duet continued to bother Mitterrand, the important issue for me was that it ended up expressing just one voice: that of France. Especially in terms of confronting a problem as serious as that of terrorism.

Since the kidnapping of two French officials, Marcel Fontaine and Marcel Carton, in Beirut in March 1985, France had become the principal target of Islamist attacks. In May, two other compatriots, the sociologist Michel Seurat and the journalist Jean-Paul Kauffmann, were also taken hostage in the Lebanese capital. The following year, there were a series of attacks in our country; the first was perpetrated in two large Parisian department stores in December 1985 followed on March 17, 1986, by the explosion of a bomb in the Paris–Lyon high-speed train before the one, three days later, targeting a gallery in the Champs Élysées, killing two people and wounding twenty-eight others. A new wave of attacks took place at the end of the summer.

At the same time, the extremist group Action Directe claimed responsibility for several terrorist operations: the assassination of General Audran on January 25, 1985, the explosion of a bomb in the main police station in Paris on July 9, 1986, and finally the murder of the president of Renault, struck down in the middle of the street on November 17. Since the imprisonment in July 1980 of Anis Naccache, the commando chief who had tried to assassinate the Iranian former prime minister, Shapour Bakhtiar, in exile in Paris and whose release was demanded, via the Palestine Liberation Organization, by the Guardians of the Revolution in Tehran who threatened to propagate terror on our territory, the origins of the Parisian attacks were in no doubt for the French authorities. The Iranian government or its intermediaries tried for some time to cause a diversion by making out that these deadly operations were the work of a Lebanese revolutionary group whose leader, Georges Ibrahim Abdallah, was also imprisoned in France, accused of the assassination of two American and Israeli diplomats. But this manipulation was quickly exposed: From the first kidnapping of hostages, in March 1985, it was clear that these terrorist actions were closely linked to the ayatollah's regime.

Ruling out all direct contact with the Iranian power, Mitterrand had vainly counted on promises of intervention from Arab capitals and recourse to more or less official groups to obtain the release of the hostages. When I took office on March 20, 1986, I inherited a situation of total impasse. The attack on the Champs Élysées, which occurred the same day, confirmed to me the notion that it was futile to negotiate with terrorist organizations, which were, most of the time, nothing but stooges. It was a question both of morality and also of efficiency. Giving in to the demands of those who planted bombs could only result in the stakes being raised even higher.

That was why, in agreement with the president, I opposed any release of the two activists demanded by Tehran without an immediate counter-release. Unlike Mitterrand, who was convinced that there was nothing to hope for from the Iranian leaders, I believed we should speak to them without further ado.

I am not among those westerners who believe that we should forbid all dialogue with Iran, given the nature of the regime. A political regime is one thing. The history of a people, its culture and its traditions, is another, more important and influential thing. I believe that it is never, or rarely, in one's interests to place a country outside the arena of the international community. Instead of convincing them to toe the line, in general the reverse effect is achieved, with both sides closing off in radical positions. What is more, since it is a part of the world where all the issues are intertwined, none of them—whether the Israeli–Palestinian conflict, the Iran–Iraq war, or the Lebanese question—can be resolved without taking into account all the parties involved.

This was my notion of French policy toward all of the nations of the Near and Middle East. Without questioning France's military support of Iraq, everything should be attempted, in my view, to achieve a normalization of our relations with Iran. The same went for Syria, which everyone knew was capable of scuppering all political solutions in Lebanon. Which is why I called President Hafez al-Assad shortly after I came into office to express my wish that relations between our two countries be improved.

But the most important question remained that of the steps to be taken in regard to Tehran. In accordance with Iranian demands, it was agreed, on one hand, that the Mujahadeen, the main movement of resistance to the mullahs and their leader, Massoud Radjavi, would be expelled from France, and, on the other, that negotiations to resolve financial contentions be opened over the following weeks. From its side, the Iranian government committed to using its influence in Lebanon to obtain the release of the eight French hostages in exchange for Anis Naccache or of two hostages without any counteroffer. On June 20, the two journalists from the TV station Antenne 2 were back in France. Naccache therefore remained in prison.

On July 24, my diplomatic advisor, François Bujon de l'Estang, had a secret meeting in Geneva, at the request of the Iranian authorities, with Farhad-Nia, the man in charge of international affairs in the cabinet of Prime Minister Mir Hossein Mousavi. The report, drawn up at my request by François Bujon de l'Estang on his return to Paris, inspired me with cautious optimism although two obstacles had surfaced, despite our common desire to reach a political agreement as soon as possible: The first related to the financial disagreements and the second to a new Iranian demand that cooperation with France be resumed in every domain, including military. As for the six hostages still in captivity in Lebanon, the Iranian official proved rather evasive, speaking only of the possibility of persuading the group that held them to release two more.

Over the coming months, it became practically impossible to know who was making decisions in Tehran and at which door one should knock. The war of succession among the Iranian hierarchies was already under way, which made the exercise of power very complicated. The influence of Ayatollah Khomeini was certainly critical, but if he made the important decisions, he did not do so every day or on every subject. In March 1987, the arrest of a "combatant for the Islamic cause," Fouad Ali Saleh, a Tunisian who had been Khomeini's pupil and disciple, had the result of confirming the true identity of the authors of the attacks committed in France the previous year and of their instigator. The involvement of Tehran was clearly established, especially as the inquiry revealed certain connections between the commando and a foremost member of the Iranian embassy in Paris, Wahid Gordji, the presumed head of his country's secret services in Europe. From then on, the affair took an altogether different turn.

The judge in charge of the antiterrorist campaign decided to interview Gordji—who, having at first disappeared from Paris, came back at the beginning of July to hold a press conference at the Iranian embassy in which he made references that were threatening toward France. Eager to exploit the affair to put pressure on Tehran, the minister of the interior advocated taking strong measures by announcing that diplomatic relations with Iran were cut off. Mitterrand and I were of a single mind in rallying behind the idea, even though we were both ignorant of the exact charges—"damning" according to Charles Pasqua—against Gordji.

The blockade of the Iranian embassy in Paris bore its first fruits four months later with the liberation of two more hostages. As for the Gordji affair, it had the outcome one might expect: As convincing proof was lacking, the diplomat was released and allowed to return to his country. During the televised debate between François Mitterrand and me on April 28, 1988, this affair gave rise to a famed clash. Responding to criticisms that I had just made against him in regard to Action Directe, my opponent leveled the following accusation at me:

"I am obliged to say that I remember the way in which you sent M. Gordji back to Iran after having explained to me in my office that his case was damning and that his involvement in the bloody assassinations of Paris at the end of 1986 had been established."

To which I responded: "Can you say to me, M. Mitterrand, looking me straight in the eyes, that we had proof that Gordji was guilty of involvement or of actions in the previous acts? When I had always said to you that this affair was solely the province of the judge and that I did not know, as was to be expected given the separation of powers, what there was in this case and that it was consequently impossible for me to say if Gordji had truly been involved in this affair or not and that the judge, at the end of the journey, had said he was not. . . . Can you really challenge my vision of things looking me straight in the eyes?"

Mitterrand: "In the eyes, I challenge it. Because when Gordji was arrested and when that serious business of the blockade of the embassy began, with its consequences in Tehran, it was because the government had brought us what we thought had been sufficiently serious [proof] that he had been one of the instigators of the terrorism at the end of 1986. And that you know very well."

The president would acknowledge, after his reelection, that he had never heard me say that the Gordji case was "damning," a declaration that had come from the minister of the interior during a meeting held in his office during the summer of 1987, at which I was also present. But cohabitation could lend itself, it is true, to this kind of misunderstanding.

*I*t was in relation to Europe and questions of defense that Mitterrand and I had the most sensitive collaboration, often allowing us to speak with a single voice during international relations where we defended France's interests shoulder to shoulder.

Yet Europe was not, at first sight, the subject on which we could most easily agree. From when he was in opposition until he acceded to power, the first secretary of the Socialist Party had approved, without many caveats, France's European policy—a policy that I, as leader of the Rassemblement pour la République (RPR) and member of the government, had more often criticized over the recent years. Attached to the notion of a Europe consisting of distinct nations, my reference was the vision of General de Gaulle and Georges Pompidou. I had never made a secret of my reservations about the very functioning of the institution or of the enlargement of the Community to new countries that we were in no way ready, in my view, to welcome.

Whatever its disadvantages, however, a unified Europe had become not only a reality, more than thirty years after the signing of the Treaty of Rome, but also an asset for France, which seemed increasingly necessary to me in the light of developments in the world. Signed by the previous government and ratified by the new government on December 16, 1986, the Single European Act led the way to the realization of the free circulation of goods, services, capital, and people from then until the end of 1992. The most traditional Gaullist wing was opposed to it, but, after considered reflection, I decided to lend my wholehearted support to this decisive step in the construction of Europe, as I would do six years later for the ratification of the Maastricht Treaty.

My sole difference with Mitterrand was in regard to Spain's membership in the Common Market, which Spain acquired in principle but without all the problems arising from it having been resolved. I had retained such a bad memory of the rushed conditions in which Britain had entered the Common Market—being on the front lines at that time as minister for agriculture—that I feared a repetition of the problems. Spain's arrival posed many still-unresolved problems, principally for French farmers threatened by competition from Spanish products but also in regard to Basque terrorism.

I brought up this twofold concern with the president on several occasions, without ever obtaining a reassuring response from him. On March 11, 1987, I seized the occasion of the Franco–Spanish summit in Madrid at which we were both present to publicly decry, during a press conference, the lack of seriousness with which my Socialist predecessors had treated these issues. I announced that, for my part, I would show that I was as concerned with the defense of our economic interests as with the security of our territory by sanctioning as many extraditions of Basque militants suspected of terrorism as necessary. Stung to the quick, Mitterrand denounced my comments the following day, judging them ill-placed in the context of an international meeting held abroad and at which we were both representatives of France. But it would not have been honest to give the impression that day that we were speaking with one voice.

On this subject, as on the question of Community resources, I often found myself closer to the positions taken by my British counterpart, Margaret Thatcher, with her well-known passion and incisiveness. Our complicity was also a source of some irritation to Mitterrand, who took umbrage in November 1986 during a Franco–British summit at our long tête-à-tête, organized at the request of Thatcher, that took place outside the official meetings. I had already had the opportunity as mayor of Paris and president of the RPR to meet her after her accession to power in 1979. But it was the first time I had met her in my role as head of the government.

Her inflexible and intransigent positions had made her one of the most feared personalities on the international scene. Since the Falklands war in 1982, in which Thatcher had not shied away from military intervention against Argentina to win back territory over which her country claimed sovereignty, everyone knew that Margaret Thatcher would stand up to anything in defense of British interests. But what gave her stature in my eyes was primarily her force of conviction. I observed her during certain meetings that I attended in London with one or another of her ministers. She did not seek to impose her point of view from authority but employed all her energy in convincing others of the sound basis of her arguments and in transmitting her ideas; the fact that she never doubted she was right made her even more successful.

After years of dispute between Paris and London in regard to the common agricultural policy, to which Thatcher was long a fierce opponent, a more peaceful Franco–British relationship began to be established after my arrival in Matignon in March 1986. This honeymoon arose in large part out of the fact that our two governments shared the same anxiety about the laxity of the European Commission and its desire to make itself into a superstate as well as the same concern to reinforce budgetary discipline at a time when the countries of the South that were coming into the Community would seek, in Thatcher's view, to "get the maximum of money out of the countries of the North." While France was nonetheless prepared, according to Community logic, to make a big effort to help Spain and Portugal, Great Britain's prime minister declared that its own contribution would be far more restrained.

I remember Thatcher's fit of anger during a conversation in Matignon on July 29, 1987, on the subject of the financing of common agricultural expenditures. She took great exception that day to the attitude of the Germans, who according to her did not care about contributing more because the European agricultural policy was so beneficial to them. "The Community should adhere to budgetary discipline. Great Britain will insist forcefully on that point, again and always. The Community has taken difficult and courageous decisions on dairy products; it still needs to take such decisions on cereals. And we should be very concerned about the overproduction of vegetable fats. If the countries of the South don't want to hear reason, we just need to be firm, to refuse to pay, to say that the Community has no more money. They have to be reasonable and they must accept that prices will go down if production increases."

I pointed out that it was not so simple, that there was a document called the accession treaty and that its provisions should be observed, even if I had not failed to criticize them myself when I was in opposition, and that they allowed the countries of the South, in any event, to use the blocking minority power. Thatcher exclaimed that she couldn't care less: "Blocking minority or not, there are nine countries that take money, only three that pay and I no longer agree to put into the pot! The Germans will do it, you will do it but I will not pay! In any case, there is no more money."

Thatcher finished on a more moderate note, conceding that the common agricultural policy was not bad per se; it was the way in which it had been implemented that was reprehensible. There were certainly solutions, but we all had to agree on the strategy to follow. She nonetheless understood that the French political calendar did not lend itself to a thoroughgoing debate in the months to come. She did not want to create problems for the government that I led, but she wanted to "kick the ball into play" as often as necessary until the month of May 1988, the date of the next presidential election.

Much more than agricultural affairs, it was in regard to East–West relations and the question of disarmament that Germany's attitude seemed to me worrying. Not that the Franco–German understanding, the central pillar in the creation of Europe, was itself threatened. I had total confidence in the will of Chancellor Helmut Kohl to perpetuate the work of his long-ago predecessor Konrad Adenauer. Deeply German and attached to the idea of the reunification of his people, Kohl was equally deeply European and eager to preserve the agreement sealed between our two countries on September 22, 1984, when Mitterrand and he had presented an unforgettable image by posing hand in hand in front of the ossuary of Douaumont. But two years later, Paris and Bonn were no longer completely on the same wavelength, because of a continually thorny problem that arose between the two governments: that of the nuclear disarmament of the European continent, relaunched by the new master of the Kremlin, Mikhail Gorbachev, during his meeting with President Reagan in Reykjavik on October 12, 1986.

France had always been in favor of the "zero option" concerning the reduction in the nuclear arsenals of the two great powers and their allies—on the condition that this objective was not ultimately translated into the unilateral neutralization of Europe, which could be the result of Gorbachev's proposal, approved by Reagan, to withdraw all American and Soviet midrange nuclear weapons on the continent. It was a proposal that was well received by the German leaders and a German public opinion that was more and more given over to pacifist notions but that was met with great suspicion by France and England, which thought that it risked destabilizing Europe, to the advantage of the Soviet Union, which would, at the same time, maintain an overwhelming military superiority in terms of conventional weapons and of ballistic missiles. In the long run, the whole system of French and British dissuasive power could be threatened under pressure from Moscow and with the agreement of Washington, whose attitude in Reykjavik contained both weakness and ambiguity.

President Reagan—who, if his advisors had not stepped in to save the situation, would have consented to a generalized denuclearization in favor of a nonnuclear spatial defense, the SDI project (Strategic Defense Initiative), popularized under the name "star wars"—would do little to reassure his western allies. At the beginning of December 1986, the visit to Paris of Defense Secretary Caspar Weinberger dispelled certain misunderstandings, even if many uncertainties about American intentions persisted.

During our meeting in Matignon, I first took care to remind this fervent defender of the SDI project that since I had taken over as head of the government, France had adopted a new law on military equipment, which provided for a large increase in funding allocated to all elements of dissuasion. While awaiting the development of a new defense system, which could only occur in the long term, "we have only nuclear deterrence to maintain the peace," I said to my American interlocutor, insisting on the fact that "the French and British forces must not be taken into account in the general American–Soviet negotiations." I added that France, favorable to a reduction of 50 percent in strategic arsenals, judged that "to go above that would cause problems" and "disarmament efforts should progress at the same pace in every domain and not overlook the conventional and chemical threat."

Weinberger gave me a rather reassuring analysis of the Reykjavik conference in which, he said, "the Soviets had advanced a large number of proposals concerning the elimination of nuclear arms that seemed very important but which were, in fact, not very serious, to make the United States give up SDI. Which," he went on, "seemed to alarm Moscow as much as the Pershings some years ago." On its side, the United States would advance proposals in terms of disarmament only if these left the country, Weinberger said, "the means of effective deterrence" that did not involve an "uncoupling from Europe" and that, above all, contributed to "eliminating the most threatening Soviet arms." It was in this context that one had to consider, according to him, the negotiations taking place between Moscow and Washington on the simultaneous destruction of midrange nuclear weapons.

In fact, everything rested, in his eyes, on the degree of confidence that one could give to the new leader of the Soviet Union. I was less optimistic in that regard than was François Mitterrand, who was convinced that there was more to hope for than to fear from the intentions of Gorbachev. My own conviction, at that time, was that the latter did not intend to overthrow the Soviet system but to make it more modern and efficient and that in his foreign policy he was pursuing the same objective as that of all his predecessors: trying to ensure that Europe became the hostage of the Soviet Union.

I had a somewhat vigorous exchange with the leader of the Kremlin during my official visit to Moscow on May 15, 1987. Gorbachev became angry when I expressed my surprise to him that his primary objective was the reduction in the number of nuclear warheads in Europe. If his other objective, in putting a brake on the arms race, was to increase the resources available for the economic development of the Soviet Union, it remained no less true, according to me, that his goal was still to neutralize—to "Finlandize"—Europe so as better to dominate it. While other countries, Germany in particular, let themselves be somewhat maneuvered by Soviet diplomacy, it seemed to me salutary that France and Britain had decided to reinforce simultaneously their own defense.

This was again the position that I affirmed in Venice on June 6 during the meeting that Mitterrand and I had with Reagan on the occasion of the latest gathering of the G7. While the president of the republic was eager to point out that France unreservedly approved of the American efforts on disarmament and hoped that the negotiations with the Soviet Union would be successful, I underlined the need for caution: "There are today 12,000 nuclear warheads in the Soviet Union and around the same number in the United States and only 600 in Europe. Why, in these conditions, should the absolute priority be the nuclear disarmament of Europe? We cannot subscribe to such logic. France wants for its part to modernize its forces to be able to meet any eventuality. It is obviously worried that disarmament should primarily be conceived as involving Europe."

Reagan, who continually consulted the documents prepared by his advisors as he spoke to us, responded that there was no question of his country negotiating on behalf of third-party states: "French and British forces are not and will not be included in the negotiation. What is more, the Soviets have agreed to that and for the moment it is not a problem." To him, Gorbachev seemed "serious" in his desire to "eliminate certain weapons. But things cannot be easy for him," he added, "and he has to deal with a certain opposition."

In November 1987, one month before the treaty on midrange nuclear weapons was to be signed in Washington, Margaret Thatcher, on a visit to Paris, shared her concern with me about this new summit. Ronald Reagan did not seem capable to her, either intellectually or physically, of "undertaking a long negotiation." For her, the last year of his presidency "was going to be very dangerous for the security of the West"; "France and Britain should remain vigilant."

It was doubtless this common vigilance that meant that the Washington agreement, signed in the White House on December 8, did not operate to the detriment of Europe by attempting to restrain the military capacities of the sole two nations able to guarantee its stability.

This matter, perhaps more than any other, demanded that there be a seamless unity in the position expressed by the two halves of the French executive. This was the case, with the exception of several nuances. While

Mitterrand placed the greatest hopes in this first disarmament treaty, I remained convinced that, however positive it was, it should in no way lead us to lower our guard and that we needed to remain sufficiently dissuasive to prevent all future temptation on the part of the Soviets or any other foreign power. But this difference of analysis was not a factor for discord with the president. In short, there were very few subjects of foreign policy on which we were not in accord.

12

A SECOND FAILURE

*A*mong all the projects of reform proposed in our government program, that of the universities was obviously one of the riskiest. It touched on an extremely sensitive area and on a milieu that was always quick to ignite. No one, however, including the president, who was principally preoccupied with the business of statutory instruments, nor any student union, had taken particular notice of it when it was presented in the Council of Ministers on July 11, 1986. Devised under the authority of Alain Devaquet, a teacher of great renown and minister in charge of research and higher education, and René Monory, the minister for national education, its text provided for greater autonomy for universities and the introduction of greater selectiveness for entry to each establishment. It introduced so many changes to the university system that I was almost astonished to see it so little discussed.

It was only at the end of November that the opponents to the Devaquet law began to make themselves heard. I have no proof of it but am certain of the role played by the presidency in the delayed birth of this protest movement. The presence of political manipulation is in no doubt when one knows that the call to strike was launched by a Socialist student group in Paris. What is more, some of its members were shortly afterward officially received in the Élysée Palace by the president, who was always ready to declare support for anything that could contribute to destabilizing the government.

Already passed by the Senate, the Devaquet proposal was due to be presented to the National Assembly on November 27, when students marched en masse through the streets of Paris and other large cities to demand its withdrawal. They protested against the rise in fees, the fact that fees would vary according to establishment, and of course the very principle—believed to be sacrilegious—of selectiveness. From then on, the specter of May '68 began to haunt those around me who were least inclined to compromise.

Should I immediately withdraw a law that was objected to by not only the left, who rejected it en bloc, but also by a faction of the right? To my great surprise, Charles Pasqua was the first to advise me to back down in the face of student reaction. "We cannot keep to it; better leave it at once" was the substance of what he said to me. But what would happen, if we did so, to other reforms if we abandoned them the minute there was protest on the streets? That was the argument advanced by the two ministers concerned, Devaquet and Monory, who threatened to resign if their law was thrown out.

Although I was not unaware of the fears of Pasqua, who believed the worst course of action would be to cut off from young people by persisting with a law that seemed to run counter to their aspirations, I was no less attentive to the arguments of his colleagues, for whom giving in to the demands of the student unions would be to lose all credibility with the public. It was the dilemma that Georges Pompidou had faced in May '68 and that he had tried to resolve by maintaining as much balance as possible between dialogue and firmness.

From experience and from temperament, I was wary of all extremist attitudes in the management of social conflicts. I leaned more toward negotiation than confrontation. The desire for reform has little chance of success if it does not benefit from a minimum of consent and understanding. On November 30, during a televised interview, I declared myself ready to speak with the various protagonists of the crisis. Wrongly or rightly, I wanted to believe that there was still a chance of saving the reform by perhaps dropping its most controversial proposals. But this was a mistake on my part because our opponents in fact wanted only one thing: the wholesale withdrawal of the proposed law. The principal ministers and leaders of the government remained deeply divided, some urging me to finish with it as quickly as possible and others advising me to keep going. The latter position largely remained my own, given the impossibility of finding common ground with the student movement in the immediate future.

On December 5, I accompanied Mitterrand to the European summit in London, charging Édouard Balladur, as minister of state, to look after the Devaquet affair in my absence. While the clashes between the forces of order and the most radical demonstrators had been worsening since the previous day, particularly violent incidents broke out that night in the Latin Quarter. Around 1:30 A.M., a student, Malik Oussekine, was clubbed by three policemen. Already ill and receiving dialysis, the young man died of his injuries. Balladur informed me of the news during the night.

I immediately returned to Paris, shocked by what had happened and determined to accept the consequences. No reform was worth a man's death. Everyone who knows me knows that in that respect I have little in common with Margaret Thatcher, who preferred to let a dozen Irish militants die rather than give in to their demands. On December 8, I announced the withdrawal of the Devaquet project. "It's a wise decision," Mitterrand declared to me, having recommended it to me with all the magnanimity of someone who had no doubt of the benefit he would derive from it. "As you know, I myself gave up on a proposed law on education. As you know, I was fine about it!"

Naturally, I did not believe a word of it, knowing above all that some failures were more costly than others and that this one, because of the death of Malik Oussekine, risked permanently tarnishing the record of my government, however positive it might be otherwise. It would do no good to declare, figures at the ready, that the economic situation of the country was better after two years in power than when we had taken over; that results had been obtained, even if insufficient, in the fight against unemployment; and that progress had been achieved in matters of security as well as social policy; it was on other terms, moral and political, that we would ultimately be judged.

Mitterrand was under no illusions about that when, announcing his candidacy for the presidency on March 22, 1988, he presented himself as the guarantor of national unity, civic peace, and social cohesion, denouncing, with calculated virulence, the hold exerted over the country by "intolerant minds, people who want everything, clans and bands." These attacks angered me at the time, so unjust and excessive did they seem to me. However, today I must recognize that his criticisms of the Rassemblement pour la République government were not all unfounded and that I myself, without always realizing it, was trapped in an overly partisan mode of functioning and overly rigid ways of thinking. I do not attribute my electoral defeat to the cohabitation in itself, however perverse a system it was in many ways, but to the fact that I had become prisoner of a political image that did not in fact resemble me: that of a man of the right in the most limited sense of the word. In these conditions, it was easy for my opponent to present himself as a man of openness.

Declaring myself a candidate for the presidential election on January 16, 1988, and immediately embarking on the campaign, I benefited, it is true, from a party in working order and a network of members of

Parliament and activists who were as efficient as they were enthusiastic. But the entrance into the competition of Raymond Barre deprived me of a section of voters of the center; in addition, Le Pen was again a candidate, with the prospect of attracting a large number of votes. Despite pressure from some of my entourage and the manifest desire of some of our voters, I had always refused to consider any alliance or even the beginnings of a dialogue with the National Front since the deplorable affair of Dreux in 1983. From his side, Le Pen did all he could to attract me into his net, going as far as trapping me, one day in August 1987, to give credence to the idea that we were in contact. On vacation with my family in the Cap d'Antibes, I was coming back from the beach at the end of the morning along the little path that I customarily took when a man suddenly appeared in front of me and held out his hand with a loud, firm "Hello, M. Chirac!" As I was walking along with my head lowered, I did not at first recognize the man whose hand I was shaking. It was a smiling, hovering Le Pen, clearly delighted at having achieved his objective of forcing me to greet him.

This was in no way a chance meeting, as one might imagine. Having spotted me several days earlier and knowing my daily route, he had arranged to be discreetly followed by a photographer to "immortalize" the scene. I did not realize this at the time. I learned of it only on my return to Paris from the boss of the Sipa Press agency, who, having bought the photo, immediately came to see me in Matignon to give me the original. "These are scandalous methods," he said to me. "I acquired this photo because it was my duty. But there's no question of my using it. I give it back to you." I offered to reimburse him, but he refused. As Le Pen probably had kept a copy, the image came out in the press some time later, but without having the desired effect on public opinion.

It was only between the two rounds of the presidential election that I finally resigned myself to the idea of a secret meeting with the leader of the National Front. "You must see Le Pen," Pasqua continually repeated to me, convinced that my attitude was politically suicidal. But it was better to lose an election, in my view, than to sell one's soul. What was the good of talking to a man to whom, in fact, I had nothing to say, so much did I hate all that he represented?

In light of the results of the first round, which were, it has to be recognized, rather disappointing—I obtained a little less than 20 percent of the vote, followed by Raymond Barre with 16.6 percent and far behind François Mitterrand with 34 percent—Pasqua's pressure that I make a pact with Le Pen, whose 14.4 percent of the vote was far from negligible, became stronger. "You have to meet him," he insisted. "You can no longer ignore him totally." Pasqua was no longer the only one to be presenting such arguments. Many around me were now of the same view, the most unexpected of whom was Édouard Balladur, who came to explain to me, with his customary subtlety, that it was now essential that I come to an understanding, one way or another, with the National Front.

I persisted in ruling out any such eventuality but consented, despite everything, to attend a meeting that Pasqua proposed to arrange discreetly with Le Pen in an apartment belonging to one of his friends. Pasqua was there to welcome me before leaving me alone with Le Pen. The meeting was very brief, lasting barely a few minutes. Just long enough to confirm to Le Pen that I did not intend to make any concession to the ideas of the National Front or make the slightest alliance with him. Realizing that no agreement was possible between us, Le Pen replied that he had no reason, in that case, to make any appeal to me.

I was not surprised and felt relieved in a certain sense. The worst would have been if he had taken it into his head, despite everything, to lend me his support. On May 1, 1988, the leader of the National Front asked his electors not to vote for Mitterrand, leaving them free to choose between a protest vote and the candidate that he described as "residual." A lesser evil . . .

Barre backed my candidacy from April 24, the evening of the first round. I had planned to do the same for him if he had beaten me. I was conscious that I would not be able to free myself from my rather off-putting image as head of the party, man of order and conservatism: "Fascist Chirac," as some people had formerly liked to nickname me—the kind of label that one does not easily shake off.

The Caledonian affair, occurring right in the middle of the presidential campaign, in no way helped dispel that image. Based on the irrefutable fact that a majority of the inhabitants of this territory wanted to remain as part of the French Republic—as confirmed by 98 percent of the votes cast in the referendum on independence for New Caledonia, albeit boycotted by the independence movement—my government had introduced a new statute revising the illegitimate one set out by our predecessors that offered a mitigated independence. After several bloody clashes between activists on both sides, the tragedy we feared occurred on the little island of Ouvea on Friday, April 22, the day before the first round of the presidential election. The police station was attacked and taken by a Kanak commando: Four gendarmes were killed and twenty-three others taken hostage. I immediately decided that everything should be put in place to free them, if necessary by force. The president initially wanted to try to resolve the situation through negotiation; this proving unsuccessful, he eventually agreed, five days before the second round, for the armed forces to move into action. The operation ended with an appalling bloodbath: Two soldiers and nineteen Kanaks lost their lives. I was immediately suspected of having used force for electoral advantage—a despicable suspicion that I will not even bother to refute.

This massacre, which no one could have wished for, somewhat overshadowed news about which everyone could only rejoice: the release of the last Lebanese hostages, Marcel Carton, Marcel Fontaine, and Jean-Paul Kauffmann, which had been obtained the day before and, through it, the end in sight of the dispute with Iran. Before leaving my duties as prime minister on May 10, I was able to hand over to Mitterrand and my successor, Michel Rocard, the agenda fixed with Tehran for the reestablishment of diplomatic relations with France.

In an irony of fate, it was in regard to Iran that the decisive moment of the second-round campaign played out, to my detriment, during my televised debate with Mitterrand on April 28. I was expecting nothing good to come out of this head-to-head, never having been very comfortable, as was well known, on television. Was it a form of shyness on my part, or unconquerable stress? Whatever the case, I have never succeeded in being altogether natural or really amenable during this kind of exercise. But what worked against me, that evening, during the famous exchange about the Gordji affair was not any awkwardness on my part—on the contrary, I felt rather sure of myself at that moment—but the fact that the viewers were not able to witness the embarrassment of my opponent.

Mitterrand had, in fact, gotten an agreement that there would be no "cutaway shots" that allowed viewers to see the reactions of the other candidate. When I had asked him if he could refute my version of events "looking me straight in the eyes" and he had declared, appearing by himself in the screen to reply "in the eyes, I disagree," I was the only one able to see that Mitterrand had, in fact, turned his eyes away from me instead of looking at me, as I had asked. And so our confrontation had been aborted in a moment of truth that could have been decisive in my favor. Instead, it was the reverse that occurred.

On May 8, 1988, François Mitterrand was reelected president of the republic with a little more than 54 percent of the votes cast. My failure, the second after that of 1981, this time seemed decisive. Never did I think, however—either at that moment or afterward—that it would be permanent.

13

RECONQUEST

*A*s soon as I handed over my position as prime minister, I remember asking Maurice Ulrich in the car taking us back to city hall to organize a meeting the following week to prepare for the coming local elections. At fifty-six, I felt in no way ready to let go or even seriously to doubt my future.

The day after this defeat, was I as beaten down and helpless as some claim and as I probably appeared? It was a tough blow, and there is no point in denying that. But not to the extent that I slipped into that depression that was attributed to me, with so much insistence, at that time and afterward. I did end up going to consult my doctor and friend, Professor Steg, to find out if I was indeed in as precarious a mental state as was said. "Ady," as I called him, immediately reassured me. "I know," he replied, "that you are not subject to that kind of problem."

Whatever weariness or even bitterness I might feel after two long and difficult years of government and at the end of an exhausting campaign, it was not in my nature to give up or to complain about my fate. What is more, I belong to a generation of politicians who are not in the habit of displaying their moods for all to see. Nonetheless, this did not prevent me from questioning myself on the reasons, not only political but also personal, for the loss I had just undergone and the lessons I must draw from it. Why had the French people refused, for the second time, to give me their trust? What was it in me that worried or disturbed them? "The French do not like my husband" was Bernadette's affirmation at that time. Doubtless she was right, but I could not resign myself to believing it. It was not what I experienced when I rubbed shoulders with them. But perhaps I had not been able to find the right words to convince them, to embody an ambition for France that responded to their expectations, their hopes, and their concerns. . . . The election of a president of the republic, in General de Gaulle's conception of it, arose out of a particular alchemy that could not be pulled out of a hat. It was always, it was said, the mysterious encounter between a man, a people, and a moment of their history. And it was one that had not, clearly, taken place for me.

Never since the beginning of my political commitment had I questioned myself so critically as in the period following this missed opportunity of May 1988. It called me first to inner reflection, in the inevitable solitude of the days after the defeat. Deep down, I did not doubt my ability to jump back and to reach, the next time around, the destination I had set myself. But I also knew that I needed another route to do so: that of a man moving closer to his convictions, affirming himself as he was and expressing himself according to his heart, faithful to his values, his principles, his idea of France, and his vision of the world.

In March 1989, the voters of Paris massively confirmed their confidence in me by reelecting the existing majority, for the second time in a row, in every arrondissement in the capital. While several large towns in the provinces—Strasbourg, Dunkirk, Quimper, and Aix-en-Provence—fell to the left, Paris overwhelmingly resisted the Socialist advance. This victory comforted me in the sense that I was probably the last one, within the national opposition, still able to win future electoral battles. Unanimously reelected president of the Rassemblement pour la République (RPR) within the National Council, I was still free to continue at the same time affirming a personal commitment above partisan contingencies and in line with what I believed to be the interests of France—sometimes even positioning myself in opposition to my political party.

Major upheavals had taken place in the world since my departure from Matignon in May 1988. The dismantling of the Communist system in the Soviet Union, driven by Boris Yeltsin and despite the predictable reservations of Mikhail Gorbachev. The fall of the Berlin Wall in November 1989, which would lead the way, ten months later, to the reunification of Germany. The withdrawal in January 1990 of the Soviet troops from Hungary and Czechoslovakia and the simultaneous start of the Hungarian crisis. The unleashing, at the beginning of the following year, of the Gulf War, after Iraqi troops invaded Kuwait. And the first stirrings of the Rwandan tragedy, which would end with an ethnic genocide of terrifying proportions, adding to the curse that seemed to hang over the destiny of Africa.

To this end-of-century context in which the world was breaking down everywhere, so abundantly full of promise and so heavy with crisis and uncertainty, was added a topic of growing concern but to which the public and most political leaders as yet gave only halfhearted attention. It involved nothing more or less than the future of our planet and of the people who inhabit it. I published an article in *Le Monde* on June 16, 1992, the day after the United Nations conference on the environment and development, entitled "The Duty of Humanity"; it reflected the importance I attached, from that time, to that vital question that involved the fate of the whole of humanity. In the article I painted the picture of an alarming situation that, seventeen years later as I write this book, has unfortunately not lost any of its relevance, so slow have we been to react. I set out here the main points:

The issues at stake in the conference that has just finished were, in the etymological sense of the word, essential. At the heart of the debate figured the question of the compatibility of the demands of development with the great issue of ecological balance.

However, as one might have feared, the summit was often reduced to a polemic between the South and the North, obscuring the true priorities of the world as we approach the end of the century: the demographic explosion of developing countries with its corollary, the expansion of poverty and malnutrition, and the industrial assaults on the environment in rich countries that are mortgaging our future.

It is in no way surprising, therefore, that the commitments undertaken in Rio by the international community are clearly insufficient in the light of its initial ambitions. The convention on climate change, designed to limit the effects of greenhouse gases, is nothing more than a framework without precise goals or binding schedules.

The convention on biodiversity, aimed at protecting the diversity of animal and vegetable species, contains no concrete provisions and has not been signed by the United States. The declaration on forests is no more than a collection of promises without the slightest legal weight. Symbolically, the final compromise on funding leaves it open to rich countries to choose to reach or not the objective of 0.7% of their GNP given to foreign aid.

The relative failure of the Earth Summit cannot, for all that, lead to resignation. It must be the opportunity for a leap into action, so urgent is it to go beyond the stage of petitions of principle and general declarations to implement clear and realistic objectives.

First priority in my view: *the creation of a system of observation of ecological risks on a planetary scale, precisely evaluating the risks of damage to the environment, the influential factors and the causal links that maintain them. Such initiatives should be encouraged, in close liaison with the international scientific community, today insufficiently associated with the environmental combat. Its knowledge about the atmosphere, climates, forests, acid rain, the greenhouse effect, the use and recycling of waste and renewable energies are so precious for our common future that it would be an incredible collective irresponsibility not to exploit them.*

Second demand: *the control of demographic growth in the countries of the South. Six billion people today, more than 10 in 2050, with a large increase in the proportion of poor and disadvantaged people. These are not random extrapolations but certainties.*

Third imperative: *to put the economy of the market in the service of a better equilibrium between development and environment. The economy and the values of freedom and ownership on which it is based are in no way incompatible with respect for the environment. Just the opposite: everyone knows today to what extent communism generated pollution, dangerous industries and risks, notably nuclear, to world security. The liberal economy is better placed, because it rests on individual responsibility, to respect restraints.*

What is at stake is the right to exist on this earth of billions of people. What is required and is at the heart of our future is solidarity, in other words the political will finally to institute planetary solidarity. Until now, that has been lacking.

This challenge, like all those that the world confronts, ultimately convinces me that the response to the great problems of humanity lies in strong cooperation between nations based on a recognition of a common destiny. I believe that this is the benefit of building a united Europe and it is at the basis of my commitment toward an ever tighter cooperation between the countries and states that have chosen to join it. How can one not feel, more than ever, the need for such an undertaking at a time when the collapse of communism has put an end to the bipolar system in place since 1945, when Germany has been reunified, when the United States remains the last large world power, when Japan, the new industrial countries of the Pacific, and China itself are experiencing considerable expansion, and when the situation of Africa is continually deteriorating, at the very doors of our continent?

That was why I did not hesitate to support the ratification of the Maastricht Treaty, which allowed the creation of economic and monetary union beginning January 1, 1999. I publicly requested that President Mitterrand organize a referendum on the subject, despite the risks associated with this kind of consultation. Many in my party feared that the treaty would seriously threaten French independence and sovereignty, ending with the creation of a federal Europe or the bolstering of a purely bureaucratic authority. Now, the treaty should, in my view, have calmed their fears since it expressly excluded such a system and stipulated that the European Union "respect the national identity of its constituent countries." By increasing the powers of the European Parliament, the treaty also allowed for the restraint of the, rightly criticized, all-powerful Commission of Brussels. I have never been in favor of a Europe fabricated by unelected technocrats, as I have had occasion to say with a certain vehemence when this Commission did not seem to take France's interests sufficiently into account.

However, these arguments did not manage to convince all those within the RPR who had always been skeptical about Europe. The opponents to the Maastricht Treaty mobilized en masse under the joint leadership of Philippe Séguin and Charles Pasqua, who both endeavored to explain to me that if I came out in favor of "yes," I would be betraying Gaullist ideals. On July 4, Pierre Juillet and Marie-France Garaud tried in their turn, several hours before I was officially to declare myself in favor of the treaty, to bring me to reason by invoking, with all the necessary solemnity, my "historical responsibility" in the matter. "The result depends on you," insisted Juillet. "On you alone. For pity's sake, reflect!" I replied that "all reflection had been done" and that I would go to confirm my choice that very evening at a meeting of all the party executives.

That evening, it promised to be a rowdy reception. I had prepared myself for it, determined to let my opponents speak until they were tired before declaring in my turn that I would vote yes "in the interests of France, of peace, and of democracy." Booed during the entire first half of my speech— something that had never happened to me since the creation of the party—I managed to turn the situation around by the end of the session, receiving a standing ovation from a room that was, if not won over, at least eager to demonstrate its loyalty to me.

Nonetheless, success was still far from assured, and the yes vote won only narrowly on September 20, 1992, with 51.05 percent as against 48.95 percent of no votes. Doubtless the result would have been different if I had based my position on partisan considerations. I see no reason to regret that.

*I*n May 1991, on the occasion of the tenth anniversary of his accession to power, François Mitterrand chose a woman, Édith Cresson, to succeed Michel Rocard as prime minister. A wise choice, on first impression. I liked and respected Cresson, whom I had known for a long time. She lacked neither courage nor determination, qualities that would be extremely useful to her in her new post. But I could not help asking myself what real methods of government would be granted to her, especially as she would be, I was in no doubt, very closely monitored by the president.

A climate of doubt and bemusement soon set in around her, fueled by her own gaffes and with the surreptitious encouragement of some of her ministers. Nothing was done, it must be said, to make her task easier. In the face of growing problems—growing unemployment, social unrest, government deficits—rebellion little by little took over all organizations, from nurses to farmers. But the sharpest tensions were those that manifested in the suburbs, partly linked to the difficulties of integration experienced by a foreign population who were usually without jobs.

On May 27, 1991, the death of a young beur—a man of North African origin born in France—while in police custody in Mantes-la-Jolie caused an uproar in that small town near Paris, where lived many immigrants of North African origin. While the prime minister did not hesitate to threaten those who were in our country illegally with expulsion, if need be by means of "charters"—a proposal that the left had once heavily criticized Charles Pasqua for putting forward—it was the immigration debate, successfully exploited by the National Front, that shook up the French political class, reflecting the problems it brought up in a society undergoing deep change.

I have no intention of brushing over a debate that I am comfortable about participating in, having often expressed my attachment to a vision of a pluralist, multiracial France. That was one of the reasons behind my introduction in 1976 of a policy allowing immigrants already present in our country to bring their families to join them. But abuses of an uncontrolled immigration had become, fifteen years later, intolerable for many of our citizens, often the most disadvantaged, who were angered at seeing increasing numbers of foreign families benefiting in many cases from social welfare payments without even working or paying taxes. This downward spiral had become a real boon for the extremist and xenophobic beliefs against which I had always fought. From then on, it seemed to me futile to denounce extremist ideas without taking account of the problems that fueled them and deciding to tackle them.

It was this fight that led me on June 19, 1991, during a dinner debate in Orléans, to criticize the flaws of an immigration policy that now served only the interests of the National Front because it was so unpopular with public opinion. I spoke about the notion of "overdose" and the problems encountered by "French workers" living next door to certain immigrant families in a working-class quarter of Paris, added to which was the nuisance caused by the "noise and the smell"—an unfortunate, pointlessly provocative phrase that did not in any way reflect the real content of my thinking on the matter and that could only be wrongly interpreted.

It caused an uproar among those who wanted to see my words as an attempt to capture National Front votes. That was, however, neither the meaning nor the goal of my speech in Orléans. Nowhere was it in my mind to concede anything, for electoral reasons, in terms of the theories of a party with which I had refused all alliance three years earlier in terms that were, in my view, irreversible. I had wanted rather to lift a taboo about the very question of immigration as it was really experienced in the country and the solutions that were needed—the risk, indeed, of playing the National Front's game.

The political reconquest that I had fixed in my sights immediately after my defeat of May 1988 obviously did not involve the denial of my personal values. On the contrary, it rested on the desire to express in every area— Europe, the environment, unemployment, immigration, the situation of the most disadvantaged—convictions that were largely founded on my experience as an elected representative, in Paris as in Corrèze, as minister, and as head of the government who had twice confronted the social, economic, and cultural realities of a nation in the grip of a moral and political crisis worsened, in the last years of Mitterrand's second seven-year term, by crises and scandals that implicated even the authority of the state.

I will refrain from commenting here on the climate at the end of the presidency that had been marked by the suffering and illness of a man whom I had learned to respect and will not add to the remarks of certain of his friends who do not hesitate to reproach him for his past or point out his errors and inadequacies. It was not in a spirit of revenge or desire to cross swords personally with the president that I launched, at the beginning of 1993, into the electoral campaign that every indicator showed would lead to an overwhelming victory for the opposition. However, the results of the first round were so catastrophic for the previous government—the Socialist Party having gathered barely 17 percent of the vote—that I felt it was my duty to question publicly the legitimacy of a president so rebuffed by the country.

I recoiled from the possibility of another cohabitation when I declared on March 23, 1993, in the following declaration: "If the second round confirms the message of the first, the president of the republic should assume all the consequences of that. It would be in France's interest not to remain, in terms of our foreign partners, in certain ambiguity. Its interest would no doubt be served by M. Mitterrand resigning and our holding new presidential elections." Five days later, the left was defeated even more resoundingly than forecast, with 62 elected members versus 257 for the RPR and 215 for the Union for French Democracy. But this was not enough to convince the president to leave his post, as I had requested. It was one of the reasons why I decided not to assume the leadership of the new government as I had planned but to hand it over to a man whom I judged, in the circumstances, better qualified to lead.

I had confidence in Édouard Balladur. His appointment as prime minister reflected a desire that he himself had often expressed to me in private, without my realizing, or wanting to realize, for a long time that it was the sign of a rival ambition—although I had not been lacking in people on all sides warning me of such a risk. But a political agreement, which also had the value of a moral contract, was sealed between us for the two years to come. A distribution of tasks, as it were. Balladur would head the government while I prepared myself for the presidential election. And I did not think I had to doubt his word.

If I had wanted Balladur more than any other to occupy the post to which he aspired, it was not only because of his capacities and the prominent role he had played in drawing up and implementing the economic program during the first cohabitation but also because of links that had long since united us. One of my closest advisors at the end of 1980, Édouard Balladur had been obliged to recognize in me a political authority of which he was probably jealous. We were doubtless polar opposites in many areas, but there is nothing greater than the attraction of opposites. I appeared rather a country bumpkin next to this Parisian member of the upper middle class, with his stiff, distant manners. We had neither the same tastes in artistic matters nor, with a few exceptions, did we frequent the same circles in the capital. Other than the fact that we called each other by our first names, our relationship was devoid of all familiarity. For all that, we shared certain political views, and for a long time I had the feeling that we shared the same vision of our country's future. What inspired my confidence in Balladur, despite his excess of pride and certainty, was his deep intelligence, his culture, and what I thought was his loyalty toward me. I am not habitually suspicious of others.

In early April 1993, I learned from a television report of the definitive makeup of Balladur's team, even though we had telephoned each other several times on the subject over the previous few days. Very quickly, the prime minister was at pains to establish a certain distance with the president of the RPR. I took note of this desire for autonomy and did not feel, from that point on, any duty of solidarity with a governmental policy that I wanted to support without giving up all my freedom to criticize it.

Various sources soon began assuring me that the prime minister was betraying his commitments, but deep down I found it hard to believe. However, it began to be confirmed to me, and everyone else, during a television broadcast of August 12 when, questioned on the future presidential election and whether he still considered me the "natural candidate" for the RPR, the prime minister abstained from replying. Everything became clear to me on September 11 after a two-hour private meeting with him in Matignon. At the end of the interview, Balladur called me back: "Jacques . . ." I turned round and heard the following words: "Make no mistake. I will never be your prime minister." He had waited until the last moment to make that unexpected pronouncement. I was flabbergasted, but at least the message was clear.

It was in vain that we tried to make a good show of it two weeks later during the RPR party meeting that took place in La Rochelle beginning on September 26. Our respective entourages had instructions to save appearances and reassure our members. I played my part, insisting on my good relationship with the prime minister to an audience of our members of Parliament, saying that he was a friend of thirty years' standing with whom the rules of the game had long been established. But no one was fooled about what was happening, and everything came out in the open on the quays of La Rochelle, where we went to walk, some distance from each other, escorted by a pack of photographers and cameramen, without being able to speak to, or even look at, each other. We were supposed to be giving an official demonstration that we were still friends, but every photo opportunity has its limits.

I never had a heart-to-heart with Édouard Balladur about the situation. What is more, I did not seek one, as I judged that, since battle had been engaged, it need only follow its course. Inevitably, the ranks began to thin out around me. The first member of the Balladur government to distance himself was the budget minister, Nicolas Sarkozy. On October 24, asked by a journalist about the reasons for his increasingly frequent absences at meetings of my advisors, Sarkozy declared that he intended to devote himself exclusively, as the prime minister had requested, to his ministerial department without concerning himself with the future presidential election. But a month later, at the end of an RPR political meeting, he asked to speak to me alone. "I intend to support Balladur if he runs for the presidential election," he announced. "That's fine," I said, "but why come to tell me?" "I am a politician," he said. "I engage in politics and it is obvious that Balladur will be elected. So, I have decided to support him." I did not seek to dissuade him, recommending only that he rush nothing and not put all his eggs in one basket. I confirmed to him, before we left each other, that whatever happened, I would be a candidate.

I was not untouched by this first defection. Sarkozy is in my eyes much more than a simple collaborator. I had noticed him during one of our meetings in the mid-1970s. Having asked to speak for a few minutes, as a young Gaullist departmental delegate, he had expressed himself with panache for more than a quarter of an hour. He was barely twenty years old and displayed a promising political temperament. I had asked him to come and work for me, which he did straightaway, playing an efficient role in all my campaigns with that willingness, which has not left him, to become indispensable, to be always there, nervous, zealous, eager to act and distinguishing himself by an undeniable aptness for communication.

In 1983, I naturally lent him my support—even though he later disputed this—when he decided to run for the council elections of Neuilly-sur-Seine, becoming mayor of the town over Charles Pasqua, whom I had not been able to dissuade from running. Sarkozy's energy and enthusiasm did not let me down over the course of the next ten years, even if he was sometimes exasperated at not being able to exercise an exclusive influence over me.

On December 19, it was the turn of Simone Veil and François Léotard to rally behind Édouard Balladur, publicly declaring that they believed he had the necessary qualities to make a good candidate. I preferred not to react directly and left it to the assistant secretary general of the RPR, my friend Jean-Louis Debré, to express surprise at such a hasty step that could only sow discord within the government. But the person most irritated by this announcement, which he judged premature, was the president, already upset at the overly obvious intrusions of the prime minister into his reserved area and who had begun to make him the target of some of his customary jibes. The president was no less exasperated, I was told, by the insistence and solicitude with which the prime minister kept asking for news of his health.

I never believed that a lasting understanding between the two men was possible, knowing how little they had in common. The least one can say is that they did not have the same lifestyles. I felt closer in that regard to François Mitterrand. We could easily go for a walk together in the mud of the countryside, side by side, stamping our shoes clean from time to time without too much ceremony. If Édouard Balladur ventured out in such circumstances, he would have a much more distinguished way of proceeding.

This period in which I had to face myself alone, abandoned by many people but supported by several trustworthy friends and surrounded by those who were more supportive of me than ever, was one of the happiest of my life. Doubtless this trial proved salutary; it was perhaps to it that I owed, ultimately, that victory in which I never stopped believing but that had never seemed so improbable.

While some people around me faded into the background, others grew even closer to me. Bernadette had always been and remains essential to me; I know all that I owe her after thirty years of political commitment. She never stinted in her efforts to support me, from my first electoral campaign in Corrèze in which she accompanied me everywhere, to cafés and to farms, and then in Paris, where she helped me on the ground, staircase after staircase, to win the most difficult arrondissements before playing a big role in the social and cultural life of the city. And finally in Matignon, where she ceaselessly carried out the tasks, sometimes thankless, of wife of the prime minister.

Bernadette is outspoken and her views can be trenchant, sometimes overly so for my taste, particularly when they concern me. But her opinions, advice, and criticisms have often enlightened me as to the decisions I needed to take, the people I could trust, and those I should avoid. Her intuition, listening skills, and political sense as well as her experience in every milieu, from the poorest to the wealthiest, often led her to be right before everyone else, me included. For a long time she seemed limited to a behind-the-scenes role, but sometimes there is no one more important than the people one thinks are in the wings. In reality, Bernadette never was. We remained inseparable, partners embarked on the same voyage, and the ups and downs of the crossing changed nothing of that.

But one does not lead the type of career as I did without having had to sacrifice a large part of one's private life. Particularly in regard to what should be more important than anything else to a father: bringing up his children and helping them with their studies. I devoted far less time to it than I should have, leaving the task to Bernadette. But, like her, I tried to transmit to our two daughters the values that my parents had inculcated in me: tolerance, respect for others, refusal to submit to the powerful, and consideration for the most disadvantaged.

Laurence was a brilliant student, hardworking and advanced in many subjects, with a very strong character. At the age of fifteen, she was a very pretty, voluble, dynamic, and athletic girl with a strong sense of initiative. And then everything in her world collapsed, as it did in ours. . . . It is a drama that I long refused to speak about, from simple reserve and refusal to divulge any information about my private or family life. And because it does no good to exhibit one's suffering in public.

Laurence's illness began in July 1973. Bernadette was on vacation in Corsica with her mother and the two girls. I had stayed in Paris, overwhelmed as always by my ministerial functions. On her return from a regatta in which she had taken part, sailing being one of her passions, Laurence complained of a violent headache before being taken over by a raging temperature connected, according to one doctor, to an attack of lumbago. But the next day things had gotten worse. A second doctor diagnosed polio. Bernadette instantly alerted me, asking me to come as soon as possible. Meanwhile, a third doctor gave yet another diagnosis: According to him, Laurence was in fact suffering from meningitis. Not only could she not be treated where she was, but he believed that she could no longer be moved.

Having gotten the advice of competent people in Paris, I went to get Laurence in a hospital plane, equipped with a medical team, and took her to the Pitié-Salpêtrière Hospital in Paris. As soon as she arrived, she underwent a lumbar puncture that turned into a nightmare: The needle broke during the examination. I heard Laurence screaming with pain. We rushed to her bedside, while the nurses came running, panicking. I leave you to imagine the feelings of terror, helplessness, and outrage that one feels at such a moment. . . .

One misfortune following another, it was in the same period that my mother died. Suffering from successive cancers, she had faced illness with unshakable courage, without ever expressing a single complaint, either to me or to Bernadette, who took care of her until the last. Toward the end of the summer of 1973, her doctor warned us that her days were numbered. We decided to take her by ambulance to Corrèze so that she could end her life in our house in Bity that she loved so much. Bernadette accompanied her in a separate car with Laurence, who had just come out of the hospital, lying beside her. I went to join them shortly afterward.

My mother died several days later. I was not present, having had to go back to Paris after a whole night spent at her side. I did not expect the end to be so rapid, although I feared it. When Bernadette telephoned to tell me, just after my return to Paris, I could say nothing but "So soon!" I was incapable of adding anything, I was so overwhelmed and shocked. I had remained very close to my mother, and I felt immense sadness at her death.

It was in Bity over the following weeks that Laurence began to stop eating, giving the first signs of the illness from which she was suffering and that would be confirmed to us some time later: anorexia nervosa, provoked by the meningitis but the cause of which we were never able conclusively to establish. According to a professor whom we then consulted, Laurence's illness was of viral origin. The meningitis had destroyed her pituitary gland, which could not function normally again. But according to other specialists, this illness could be linked to frustration experienced by a child, from her earliest infancy, in the relationship with her father. Had I been insufficiently present for her? Had she suffered very much from this, without my realizing? Such were the questions that I inevitably asked myself. For a long time I strove to go home and have lunch with her every day to get her to eat. But it was in vain.

Laurence gradually began deteriorating, alternating suicide attempts and periods of hospitalization. She was taken into the care of one of the great French psychiatrists, Professor Louis Bertagna, who had looked after André Malraux and who was admirably patient with her. But that also came to nothing. On April 18, 1987, after we had just arrived in Thailand, Laurence jumped from the fourth floor of her apartment in Paris. Miraculously she escaped death, which did not prevent a sordid rumor, fueled by some unknown source, that she had in fact died and been secretly buried.

Letters of condolence began to flood in, some from long-standing friends who expressed their regret in all good faith. We did not reply to any of them. What could we do other than remain silent? Denials would have been worse than anything. It seemed unthinkable to me to issue a statement giving the reassurance that my daughter was still alive. And then, in a way, this crisis concerned nobody but ourselves, even if it helped me realize, in the sharpest way possible, the distress of families confronted with the disability of one of their members and made me more sensitive and more considerate than I had ever been toward all forms of human distress.

On July 19, 1979, Bernadette and I went to Roissy Airport to welcome, at the height of the exodus of the boat people, the 180 Vietnamese refugees from Pulau Bidong. Men and women whom we saw arrive in France, stripped of everything, without luggage, identity papers, or clothes other than the ones they wore. As mayor of Paris, when virtually nobody was looking after them, I had organized a plane to take them blankets and food before arranging for them to come and stay with host families.

That was when I noticed a young girl sitting in a corner, crying. She looked about fifteen, at the most. I went up to her and held out a tissue. She was called Anh-Dao and she was the only one without a place to go. Bernadette came over in her turn, took her in her arms, and tried to comfort her. As nobody was waiting for her, we agreed to take her home with us. Bernadette and I looked after her as if she were our own daughter, until her marriage, with almost no one knowing about it.

Her sister's illness and my feeling that I had not paid sufficient attention to her in her own life played a large part in my suggestion at the beginning of the 1980s that my younger daughter, Claude, join my communications team. One day we were driving across the Place de la Concorde when Claude confided that she didn't want to make a career in advertising, where she had begun her professional life. "Why don't you come and work with me?" I immediately proposed. At first she seemed astonished by my suggestion and then agreed to give it a try. That was how our collaboration began, at a time when Claude seemed to me in search of her identity and I felt, for my part, the need to redefine myself. I wanted to change the image that the French had of me. Who better than her could help me do so?

Lively, beautiful, sensitive, intuitive, and with a natural sense of calm and reserve—but quick, when need be, to assert herself—Claude shared with me the same reluctance to express our feelings and the same instinct to rebel in the face of all conformity, which meant that we were certain to get on well. Close to the Parisian show-biz, fashion, and cinema circles that I was little used to frequenting, and very *au fait* with developments in French society, Claude not only advised me on my choice of clothes or certain of my public appearances, so that I appeared "less political" and more "trendy," but above all she helped me move outside the confines of traditional political speeches by taking more account of new trends in opinion and the emergence of certain issues, giving me the benefit of her contacts in that regard. It was thanks to her, for example, that I was able to meet Nicolas Hulot, who would be the first to alert me to the urgency of environmental issues for the planet.

Contrary to what I have often heard said about our relationship, Claude's role is not to reassure me, even if she sometimes does so, but primarily to enlighten me about social realities and changes in thinking about which I am not sufficiently informed. Which meant that she played a decisive role in the presidential election campaign of May 1995.

The problem of exclusion and of what I would later call "social fracture" had been a central preoccupation for me since the end of the 1980s. It was then that I had seen the need to implement new structures to assist the most disadvantaged, a growing number of men and women condemned to live at the margins of society, "without fixed address," in an expression that became more and more widespread, and consigned to a seemingly hopeless future.

In 1989, the creation of the "Paris Santé" card by the city council, against the advice of the Socialist government of the time, gave several tens of thousands of people in great financial difficulty—130,000 in the capital in 1995—free access to medical care. It was a pioneering scheme that would be replicated on a national scale three years later. In November 1993, I decided to enlarge this social action by launching, on the advice of Xavier Emmanuelli and in collaboration with him, a free ambulance service. Emmanuelli, the embodiment of human dedication and generosity, was the medical director of the center for homeless people founded by Abbé Pierre in Nanterre in 1954 and was one of the founders of Médecins sans Frontières, or Doctors Without Borders. No one could be better informed about the increasingly worrying rise in social exclusion in our country.

Emmanuelli wanted to institute a more efficient system of assisting these new outcasts from society who very often lacked all means of subsistence and suffered from traumas and serious health problems that plunged them into irresolvable isolation. His project met with skepticism from the department of health and social security and from the Ministry of Health as if they were afraid of bringing a whole group of people whom they did not know how to deal with out from the shadows. That was when he asked to see me, at the city hall in Paris, in October 1993.

I freed a morning for him and listened as he set out his project at length. By the end of the meeting, I had made my decision. "Doctor," I said to him, "let's go! The powers that be will doubtless try to prevent us from doing this, but never mind. It's going to work!" And that was how the Paris charitable ambulance service was born.

One night in November 1993, we set off for the first time with a group of nurses and social workers in unmarked vehicles to seek out homeless people to whom we could, if need be, offer medical treatment. Most—I was struck by how young most of them were—were very wary when they saw us coming, thinking that we wanted to persuade them to stay in hostels. But all we wanted, as they quickly realized, was for them to be able to benefit from the same medical care as everyone else and for their dignity to be respected.

In February 1994, Emmanuelli gave me a first report: "We were expecting eight thousand calls. We've had fifteen thousand. They are calling us from all over. We're overwhelmed!" It was now clear just how much unrecognized poverty and distress there was in France: people alone in the city, people with disabilities left to their own devices, sick people without resources, drug addicts, poorly integrated immigrants, long-term unemployed, young people looking for work. . . . All, however different their situations, their pasts, and their prospects, were experiencing the same anxiety about the future and the same uncertainty and abandonment.

How many were there? Seven million, it was said, who would have to house themselves, feed themselves, dress themselves, and take care of themselves on less than 60 francs a day if social welfare did not exist. Every mayor was confronted with these difficulties which each had a human face and a story, often the same. It was a flood tide of marginalized existences. A future that once seemed certain had become a privilege. "Social insecurity" was everywhere.

However, from my experience as mayor, I became convinced that we could win this battle against exclusion. Every day I met volunteers, social workers, and organizations that overcame their disillusionment and successfully implemented their projects. We still had to succeed in breaking the cycle of isolation. Projects aimed at social reintegration, driven by courage and intelligence, flourished in suburbs with difficult reputations and in the most isolated rural areas. Listening to those who ran them, I often said to myself that their faith and enthusiasm enabled exclusion to be dealt with for what it was, a sickness of society that had to be prevented as well as fought on the ground.

Prevention primarily meant tackling unemployment, the primary cause of exclusion since in its wake could come loss of income, housing, identity, a sense of goals in life, and broken families. Preventing exclusion also involved amending our housing policy—in 1994, France was home to 2 million people in precarious housing situations—and re-creating normal lifestyles in areas filled with rootless, unemployed people who lacked social and educational opportunities and facilities and where the forces of law and order felt impotent and in which an underground drug economy flourished.

The crisis of exclusion was the subject of my book, entitled *Une nouvelle France* [A new France], which was published the following June, with considerable impact. It set out my convictions concerning not only the fundamental role of government in the maintenance of national cohesion and solidarity among citizens but also the implementation of a more direct democracy and the need to reconcile economic development and social integration more effectively. Fifteen years later, however, I am forced to the even harsher conclusion that a rupture has gradually taken place between the French and those who govern them.

An economic recession to which they see no end in sight has broken the link of trust binding many people to society. It is no longer a case of apathy or anxiety but of a real collective depression. It is an evil that is sometimes insidious and sometimes expressed as explosive anger when an area, a profession, or a generation feels neither heard nor understood. This rupture between citizens and politics leads a sector of our compatriots to live as if they are in exile within a democracy. Others see no solutions except simplistic ones of extremism or populism.

I advocate a new social contract founded on an absolute priority at a time when 5 million French people are without jobs: the fight against unemployment. My project for France is in no way pessimistic or fatalistic. It is based on our social model, which I believe arises out of a fundamental choice of justice and human solidarity. I have never considered social protection and economic initiative mutually exclusive. The two have always seemed to me reconcilable. The action I have taken in these two domains has always aimed at bringing out the best of a system—while also developing it—to which we in France are deeply attached and of which many countries are envious. It flows out of a long humanist tradition that all those who, like me, draw their inspiration from the philosophy of General de Gaulle have more than ever the duty and the mission to pursue.

On August 26, 1994, Paris celebrated the fiftieth anniversary of its liberation, in the presence of the president—who, the day before, had it communicated to me that he wanted, after his speech, to go to my office with me for a few minutes to sign the city's visitors' book. Such a gesture was in no way customary for a president of the republic during such a ceremony. But François Mitterrand had clearly decided to defy convention, for motives that were doubtless diverse and, as always with him, somewhat inscrutable.

A month earlier, the president had undergone a difficult operation connected to the cancer he had been fighting for several years; everyone knew about it, as well as what it implied in the short term. Seeing the state of exhaustion in which the president found himself during the Council of Ministers following his operation, Balladur had seen fit immediately to set up his campaign headquarters in anticipation of a presidential election.

An interview with the prime minister entitled "My Foreign Policy" was published at the same time, adding to the presidency's exasperation, which already had been perceptible for months.

Did François Mitterrand also want to come up to my office so as to rest for a few minutes at the end of the ceremony, as was initially indicated to me? Whatever the case, the moment had been minutely prepared since the day before—to such an extent that after the mayor of Paris and the president had spoken, the prime minister, who had no speaking function that day, was forced to wait for us both inside city hall in front of four thousand spectators and all the television cameras until our return a quarter of an hour later. It was a period of time that must have seemed interminable to him and that Mitterrand had apparently wanted to be publicly interpreted as a snub.

In fact, during the minutes we spent alone together, Mitterrand took no medicine and even seemed to me in rather good health. After having signed the visitors' book, as arranged, he let slip to me in confidence: "It's your turn. You will be elected." I don't know whether that is what he sincerely thought at that time, but Mitterrand had several messages of encouragement conveyed to me over the following months. I had the opportunity of meeting the president again during various official ceremonies, and our meetings were always warm. On January 5, 1995, while I was presenting the new year wishes of the mayoralty of Paris to the president, we were again alone for several minutes and the president declared: "Fourteen years of political combat is a long time. But it allowed me to get to know you."

The opinion polls in autumn 1994 remained favorable to the prime minister and allowed him to think that he was already elected. However, I was able to rely on sources of support that would prove decisive. First Alain Juppé, who had clearly shown himself to be one of the great foreign affairs ministers of the Fifth Republic. He had made no secret of his commitment to me, despite the pressure exerted by the other side. During this same period, thanks to Denis Tillinac, a man of heart who was also a long-standing friend, I had some fruitful encounters with several celebrated intellectuals, such as Régis Debray and Emmanuel Todd, who shared and enriched my own analyses on the state of French society.

On November 4, I announced my candidacy for the presidency. I did not do so merely to force my presumed opponent to reveal himself, as commentators immediately claimed, but above all to begin the dialogue with the French people that I believed was so necessary. But it would take another few weeks before public opinion started coming over to me, to such a degree that, noticing the lack of enthusiasm I was encountering while campaigning at the end of the year, I joked to Jean-Louis Debré: "If it all goes wrong, we'll open a travel agency together. You run it and I'll travel."

In the first days of 1995, my second book, *Une France pour tous* [A France for all] was published with, on the cover, an apple tree as the symbol of the vitality that I wanted to restore to our country. In addition to my program of reforms, which I sketched out, and the theme of "social fracture," it was my personal story, the history of nearly a third of a century of a political career and of the changes I had undergone after a long period of retreat and reflection, which I wanted to explain to the French whose only image of me—doubtless owing in large part to me—was a rather cursory and caricatured one.

When he announced his official support of my candidacy on January 19, 1995, Philippe Séguin described me as a man who had matured through the experiences he had had to live through and overcome over the past months and was now ready to assume the highest office. I still had to set the seal on that "encounter" with the French; that alone would determine how much they trusted me. That is why I resolved to establish the most direct relationship with them, on the ground—man to man, so to speak—away from all media presence, going to see them, listen to them, and speak to them day after day in their workplaces, neighborhoods, and homes, one to one or in small informal meetings that taught me more about the difficulties my compatriots faced than all the expert reports or knowledgeable analyses by top sociologists.

"Where have you disappeared to again? You're wasting your time— you must engage in politics. That's all that counts!" one of my main campaign organizers sometimes exclaimed over the phone, exasperated at seeing me devote entire weeks to visiting the most out-of-the-way corners of the country. The fact was that I really was not concerned with Parisian hustle and bustle or with what my competitors were getting up to, the latest sound bite put out by one or the latest little jockeying for position manufactured by another.

On February 17, a meeting of more than twenty thousand people held at the Porte de Versailles marked a decisive turning point in the presidential campaign. It confirmed that the great majority of Gaullist activists had remained loyal to me; the expected defection of Charles Pasqua, announced several weeks earlier, had in no way changed that. The movement that was growing in my favor was all the stronger because it emanated from the people and went beyond my own political party. It was what differentiated me from Édouard Balladur.

If social issues were at the heart of the dialogue I had entered into with the French, I did not forget that our country's destiny was also played out, now more than ever, on the international scene. On March 16, I set out my general policy directions in terms of foreign affairs; needless to say, they were based on the thinking of General de Gaulle. I have always believed that France occupies a particular role in the world because of its history, language, culture, and values. France is a country that counts in the eyes of other nations and whose voice is wanted and listened to. Repository of a humanist vision and ideals, it is called to transmit that heritage and to express an ambition that goes beyond its own interests alone.

That was why the general had held that the president should be invested with a preeminent responsibility in terms of foreign policy. Conducting France's foreign policy at the dawn of the twenty-first century meant to me affirming the particular personality of our country and preserving its full freedom of action. When it was a matter of its vital interests or of questions vital for its future, France should keep control of its decisions. Its political choices would not be dictated by anyone outside. This was the best possible attitude in a world that had become multipolar since the end of the cold war and in which nations had to find other ways of relating to each other: united by common values but also attached to their independence while conscious of the need to assume their responsibilities in the framework of close cooperation.

When the Berlin Wall fell, some believed that it marked the "end of history." Seeing the fall of totalitarianism and the collapse of the Communist model, they immediately drew the conclusion that humanity was entering a new golden age in which peace, democracy, and prosperity would triumph once and for all. This illusion was quickly dispelled in the face of the realities of the world. While it is true that a powerful movement, since the beginning of the 1990s, has spread democracy throughout every continent and that humanity is slowly moving toward an awareness of a common world destiny, it is no less true that, very quickly, the winds of history started blowing again, bringing storms and tempests in their wake. Very soon afterward we witnessed the unleashing of destructive forces that one might have thought had been permanently crushed—in Rwanda and the former Yugoslavia, for example, with Europe rediscovering the hideous face of barbarity. Confronted with the world as it is, France must remain faithful to the moral responsibility conferred on it in terms of other peoples.

On April 12, 1995, eleven days before the first-round vote, Édouard Balladur, whom I had neither seen nor met for several months, wrote to me urgently to ask me to debate with him before the French "in all openness" about "our opposing convictions," adding rather comically that democracy could not be satisfied "by a series of monologues all over France." I declined an opportunity that seemed to me totally inopportune. The only debate that I had the duty to accept was the one that put me in opposition to my opponent, whoever he was, on the assumption that I would be present in the second round.

On April 23, the results of the first-round vote placed me, with 20.84 percent of the vote, in second position behind the Socialist Party candidate, Lionel Jospin, who had a total of 23.30 percent of the vote. Édouard Balladur came in third, with 18.58 percent of the vote. He made it known to me that very evening that he was standing down in my favor.

I had fewer votes than expected but enough to hope that I could win. Encouraged by his leading margin, Jospin proved a tough and very determined opponent. But from 6:00 P.M. on May 7, 1995, the result was no longer in doubt. At 8:00 P.M. my victory was confirmed, with 52.7 percent of the vote against my opponent's 47.3 percent.

In my office at the city hall of Paris, I was putting the finishing touches on the declaration that I would shortly afterward make to the French, from the ceremonial room of the Hôtel de Ville. Outside, I could hear the echoes of the immense crowd of enthusiastic and ardent young people, making its way toward the Place de la Concorde. Bernadette joined me, controlling her emotions with difficulty.

I felt a mixture of inexpressible emotions, those of a man happy to have reached the goal he had set himself and also of a man who now had to embody the hopes of a whole nation and assume responsibility for its unity. Such was, in my eyes, the role and mission of a president under the Fifth Republic. Directly elected by the people, the president must not address this or that faction but every person in France. He must ensure that he guarantees national cohesion and continually seeks out those things that, in any domain, could strengthen it. Everything must be done to ease tensions in a country whose history shows that it sometimes tended toward arguments, antagonisms, and sudden eruptions. I wanted to be the president of a united France, rich in its differences, capable of enabling men and women of all origins to live together and be respectful of all the human elements of which it was composed.

I dedicated the victory that evening to the memory of my parents and to all "the simple, straightforward patriots" who had made France into a tolerant, fraternal, inventive, and victorious nation. One in which I had always believed.

PART II
PRESIDENCY

14

PRESIDENT

The day after my election, François Mitterrand and I attended the ceremony in the Champs Élysées in commemoration of the fiftieth anniversary of the victory of May 8, 1945. We sat side by side on the presidential rostrum, chatting in friendly, relaxed style and, without departing from his customary reserve, the president showed me a friendliness that was in no way false or ostentatious. Despite his official support of the Socialist candidate, he did not in fact seem unhappy that the French had made a choice different from the one he had advocated. Everything led me to think that he secretly preferred as his successor a man from outside his political family, with whom he would not have to squabble over an inheritance or leave a stocktaking list.

I had been Mitterrand's opponent before becoming his prime minister, and now I was his successor. Whatever our past disagreements, I was aware of the particular link that now bound us and that went beyond our personal relationship, however warm. This link was primarily based on the fundamental task that the French people had conferred on us of assuming the destiny of the nation, ensuring its unity, its place in history, and its influence in the world. Every new presidency carries with it a hope and legitimate desire for change, but it also has the duty of ensuring a necessary continuity and the preservation of the values, principles, and traditions that have forged our people's identity, and which remain the best guarantors of its unity. This is what confers a sacred and inalienable character on the office of president, as conceived and embodied by General de Gaulle. The general personified the state, in its strongest, most elevated, and most demanding characteristics. "Without the state there is no France," he reminded us shortly after his return to power—he who knew all that the destruction of its institutions had cost France in terms of defeat, suffering, and humiliation. The state had a veritable mystique for de Gaulle, and he served it in that spirit. If his example remained awe-inspiring and naturally inimitable, I had always believed it vital to take inspiration from it.

From President Pompidou I received, like all those who worked with him, an example of determination, dignity, rigor, and self-control that had been very influential in the high ideal I formed of the role and the responsibility incumbent on the head of state. As I observed him in his role as president, I continually observed how much tenacity, courage, and self-abnegation it required. Pompidou did not carry the weight of history on his shoulders, but his rootedness in the land of France, the humanism of which he was fashioned, and the vast and eclectic culture he acquired, allied to an exceptional intelligence, had allowed him to ensure the success of the difficult succession of the general while making his own mark on the functioning of institutions. A tolerant, moderate man, he demonstrated that these institutions were not just designed for times of heroism but also offered the country a lasting possibility of balance and stability.

Mitterrand had the wisdom and intelligence to adapt himself in his turn to an institutional system that—until his own accession to power—he had actually fought and relentlessly criticized. He understood that his legitimacy depended on his ability to transcend ideological divides, to represent France in all its diversity, and to bring together the French people in their entirety. Winning a presidential election was not in itself enough to impose oneself as "president of all the French," to use the common phrase. Acceding to it demanded at the very least a certain degree of personal growth, an awareness of a transformation that was necessary and even indispensable if one was to go beyond the simple status of head of the party. Carried by his indisputable sense of the nation and political intelligence, Mitterrand quickly identified himself with the sovereign authority granted him under the constitution. With him, the decision-making power went hand in hand with a mastery of timing and an art of detachment that are also the marks of an authentic head of state. From him I drew lessons in the best way of conducting affairs of state, even if my own character inclined me more to movement and rapid action.

When we met that May 8, 1995, Mitterrand said to me in private that he wanted to stay a few more days in the Élysée Palace before moving out. "Don't worry," he said to me, laughing. "I won't make you wait as long as Giscard made me wait after my election. But you know what it is: In fourteen years, one accumulates a lot of things. It takes time to pack boxes, and I am not so quick on my feet." I readily agreed to his request, knowing that he was indeed very tired. However, it was only when he handed over power that I would find out the real reason for his request.

While waiting to assume office on May 17, I took advantage of the transition period to prepare for that personal transformation I have outlined and that involves the acceptance of a new solitude. The office of president imposes a certain withdrawal, distance, and overview. Around me reigned the impatience and feverishness of the aftermath of victory. The media pressure was relentless. Rumors were already flying as to the choice of the future prime minister and the composition of the government. I did not intend to let myself be overwhelmed by the expectations and solicitations from all sides; having finally attained the goal I had set myself, I felt the need to distance myself from the tensions and political agitation of the last few months. This period of calm and clarification was very useful in enabling me to confront, with as much serenity as possible, the task I had before me. For me, it was like a rite of passage between my status as a candidate and that of president-elect.

Entrenched in my office at the Hôtel de Ville most of the time, I regularly received and consulted with those who had worked alongside me during the campaign and who would form part of the future government or my presidential office team. I was determined to act quickly, once installed at the helm, to implement the reforms the French were expecting. I therefore had to equip the country with a strong, coherent, and determined leadership team—and immediately appoint the prime minister who would share responsibility with me. He would have to be a man in whom I felt deep trust and with whom I was in close harmony, whose loyalty to me was long proven, not to mention his experience of government. For all these reasons, it did not take long for my choice to fall on Alain Juppé.

My relationship with Juppé needed no explanation. For more than twenty years he had been a faithful collaborator and advisor, then the faultlessly competent assistant and minister whom I could trust in all circumstances. His help had not failed me in those difficult periods when my presidential ambitions seemed to have come to a dead end. This loyalty of his had always gone along with great frankness, devoid of any hint of indulgence, in my regard. His opinions were always clear, direct, substantiated, and well argued, to the extent that others, who did not know him well, criticized him for a certain stiffness. In fact, beneath his sometimes-inflexible appearance, Alain Juppé was a man of deep sensibilities and extreme modesty who detested effusive displays of emotion as much as the slightest demagogy. He revealed little of himself. That was also one of our shared traits and without doubt one of the reasons for a mutual understanding that had never flagged. Rare in politics, our relationship had never undergone any power play. We had never been rivals and remained bound by our ambition to succeed in service of the same ideals and a similar vision of France. As I knew, the division of roles between the Élysée and Matignon could be a formidable task, but I had confidence in our duo, which had more than proven its strength over the years.

The first concern that preoccupied me in the days before I took office was to establish greater closeness between the state and its citizens, that fundamental link that gives our democracy all its meaning. It was for me one of the essential elements in that republican pact, the shared values that were at the basis of the republic, that I was now called on to safeguard. Above all, this meant closing the gap of mistrust and lack of understanding that had not ceased to widen between the people and those who, supposed to serve the republic's interests, had too often exhibited only inertia, powerlessness, and resignation. The president's primary duties were to be truthful, determined, and humble. Invested with a sovereign power, he remained no less a son of the republic, a citizen among others. However elevated my notion of the president's function, I do not believe in the monarchical character that it has come to be given.

This was the spirit of the institutions of government as they had been forged by General de Gaulle in reaction to the abdication of responsibility of the state and its leaders. To remedy this, the Fifth Republic was created to reconcile efficiency of action and democratic legitimacy on the basis of a fundamental notion: Everything begins with the people and emerges out of the people. Elected by universal suffrage, the head of state enshrines this principle, which notably imposes on him the duty to let the French have their say on the subjects they judge essential for the future of the country. This was why I had resolved to widen the field of referendums to include the great questions of society by submitting a law in that regard to Parliament. To consult the people is of course to take the risk of being challenged, and the result may not be exactly what one desires. Nonetheless, I see this procedure as the guarantor of a greater democratic vitality, in perfect harmony with the Gaullist tradition.

As the first president from this political family to be elected in twenty-one years, I felt it important on the day of my investiture to visit the tomb of General de Gaulle at Colombey-les-Deux-Églises. This trip, carried out in the greatest privacy, would become public only after my return to Paris, in order to preserve its personal character. At seven in the morning, my closest advisor, Maurice Ulrich, telephoned the mayor of Colombey, Jean Raullet, to tell him that the helicopter of the future president of the republic would touch down in the village meadow in less than half an hour's time. The mayor, who had rushed to the spot, drove me to the cemetery in his red Twingo. After having placed a wreath in the shape of a cross of Lorraine on the grave, I stood alone in the rain for several long moments, contemplating that modest stone tomb that bore the names of Charles, Yvonne, and Anne de Gaulle. The emotion I felt at being there in such circumstances was combined with a deep feeling of gratitude and admiration toward the statesman who had restored grandeur, dignity, and independence to our country on more than one occasion.

On my return from Colombey, I went to the Élysée Palace, where President Mitterrand welcomed me on the front steps, then invited me to accompany him into his office for the traditional transfer of power. Entering the room, I stopped in my tracks, astonished to see that the usual décor had changed. Mitterrand watched my reaction with his mischievous air. Unbeknownst to me, he had had the office rearranged to how it was when General de Gaulle had left office, with furniture of the period. That was why he had asked me to give him a few more days before he left the palace. Mitterrand had wanted to make me a gesture—and he had found the right one. I saw in his eyes that gleam of satisfaction that I had come to know well: that of the man who had succeeded in his little trick. But most of all he seemed happy that he had given me pleasure.

We spoke for almost an hour, in an atmosphere imbued with the same cordiality as usual. Contrary to what one might imagine, the transfer of power remains a highly formal exercise. Everything is perfectly set down and regulated in advance, and it is neither the place nor the time to exchange great state secrets, other than that of the nuclear code, itself a primarily symbolic act. The outgoing president communicates to his successor what is called his "will," but which is in fact nothing other than the list of his protégés whom he would like to see reappointed. Mitterrand gave me his list, which did not seem to me excessively long. I promised that all his colleagues would be given new appointments as soon as possible.

As far as he himself was directly concerned, I asked Mitterrand if he would let me know of any difficulties with which I might be able to help in some way. I was thinking, of course, of his health problems, the seriousness of which were now no secret to anyone. On May 8, during the official dinner given in honor of the heads of state who had come to attend the fiftieth-anniversary ceremonies, he had confided in my wife that he was impatient for us to arrive as he was in such "atrocious" pain and was now forced to wear a surgical collar to ease the pain. With his customary reserve, Mitterrand preferred to ask me to take care, above all, of the little mallards that he had introduced into the gardens. "I know that you have a Labrador," he said to me, worried about their fate. "Try to make sure that they aren't all eaten in two days." I reassured him that I would make sure they were protected.

The most important, and the least known, help I could give was the financial aid that the Élysée, under my presidency, donated to the François Mitterrand Institute. With the objective of defending the memory of the former president, this institute came into being thanks to the very substantial aid that I felt it right to grant it. Its mission was to clarify and explain not only the personality and destiny of François Mitterrand but the activities carried out during his two seven-year terms of office, which are now an integral part of our national history. Supporting it is in my view an act of public service as well as a mark of respect to my predecessor.

Our meeting over, Mitterrand simply wished me good luck. His emotions, although always carefully controlled, were perceptible when he left the office that had been his for fourteen years. Ignoring the protocol that we should bid each other farewell at the top of the steps, I accompanied him to the bottom. We shook each other's hands for a long time before going our separate ways. Thoughtfully, I watched his car slowly leaving the courtyard of the palace, go through the entrance, and disappear into the rue du Faubourg Saint Honoré, where the crowd gathered on the opposite pavement was demonstrably warmer than it had been during the departure of his predecessor, Valéry Giscard d'Estaing, in May 1981.

Then I went to the ceremonial room where the crowd of guests who had come to attend the investiture awaited me. Going into the room, I looked first at Bernadette. We exchanged a brief smile, containing affection and complicity in equal measure. The same expression of happiness and pride could be read in the eyes of my daughter Claude. Accompanied by her maternal grandmother, Laurence was also present, a little in the background, almost unnoticeable, so rare were her public appearances. She disappeared as soon as the ceremony came to an end.

I had the pleasure of hearing the president of the constitutional council, Roland Dumas, a friend and former minister of François Mitterrand, declare himself "favorably impressed by the way in which the presidential responsibilities had been transferred" and describing it as "a credit to our democracy." Never, in fact, since the creation of the Fifth Republic, had the handing over of power been carried out in such a natural and easy manner.

In my first speech as president, it was above all that spirit of tolerance and continuity that I wished to highlight when I declared that "the presidential election did not represent the victory of one France over another, or of one ideology over another, but the victory of a France that wanted to acquire the tools that would enable it to enter the third millennium a strong and unified nation." In light of what had just happened, everyone understood that this preliminary declaration was in no way mere artificial demagogy. Indeed, it was based on the conviction that one of the basic tasks of the president of the republic was to enhance national cohesion in every circumstance. A strong nation was also a united nation.

At sixty-two years old, a certain experience of power had immunized me against all forms of idealism or utopianism in the vision of the great problems that our society faced and, above all, of the ways in which we should try to resolve them. The vital factor in doing so remained the political will to succeed and the refusal to give in to those widespread evils of fatalism and resignation, both of which are foreign to my temperament and, even more, to my concept of our country.

The deleterious notion was spreading, among both the ordinary public and the elite, that France had become a minor power and was fated to inevitable decline. Many experts, intellectuals, and, unfortunately, leaders had come to doubt that France would be able to preserve its influence in the decades to come. The most pessimistic had already consigned the nation to a permanent withdrawal from history, in which it would henceforth play only a background role. At a time of globalization, according to this theory, the French could no longer claim to be anything other than second-class citizens in the planetary village.

Everything within me revolted against that state of mind. I had complete confidence in France's ability to take on any challenge it may face and to play a center-stage role in world affairs.

During the afternoon, as I went back up the Champs Élysées to the Place de l'Étoile, I noticed the presence of many young people among the crowd that was cheering the new president. Some of them were waving banners or signs proclaiming the event while others ran down the side streets chanting my name. This victory that they were celebrating with so much enthusiasm was above all theirs. I knew what it represented to them and the influential part they had played in it. It was the victory of a generation determined to free itself from all ideological dogma and to seize the wonderful opportunities I was offering it, in every domain. The world had never seemed so open and promising, even if it had lost none of its complexity.

The last French president of the twentieth century, I would above all be the man who had the exciting mission of accompanying our country into the third millennium, which looked set to be the harbinger of gigantic upheavals that would probably be the source of both progress and innovation as well as drama, crisis, conflict, and instability. We needed to create a universal civilization in the context of a globalization that needed to be more thoroughly mastered and humanized, and France needed to play the role of both pioneer and leader in the creation of this new world order. Which, if it were not to give way to a chaos that could prove fatal to the entire human race, demanded greater supportiveness, cooperation, and respect between peoples as well as greater equity in the division of resources and wealth.

Loyal to the regulations governing our institutions, under which the responsibility of governmental policy fell solely on the prime minister, I had also acquired the conviction, assisted by experience, that the president should be able to count on a man in Matignon who was strong enough to implement the former's directives and ensure the running of parliamentary government. In this respect, Valéry Giscard d'Estaing above all taught me, during our two years of collaboration, that curtailing the authority of the prime minister inevitably led to the president's own authority being weakened, and this is what must never occur. In reality, the two functions were inseparable.

Beyond the link of trust that should bind the two heads of the executive, the division of roles should be clear. It was for the president to ensure national cohesion, to be the driver and actor of international policy, and to fix a precise framework in which the government can act. I did not share Giscard's concept of a presidency looking after everything, solving everything, and deciding everything. That was not the task of the president of the republic, and the Élysée, unlike the White House, does not in any case have the financial and material means to do so. In France, such a concept can lead only to a confusion of powers, to the loss of governmental and administrative powers, and to inefficiency and immobility.

This was why one of the first instructions I gave my own team of advisors was to ensure that the prerogatives of each minister with whom they had to collaborate was respected so that they never encroached on a minister's area of responsibility. Outside the president's "reserved areas" of national defense and diplomacy, the presidency did not control the work of ministers. It should not be the place where "everything happened" but rather where the overall direction that determined the future of the nation was decided—although this too should not occur in isolation from the prime minister and his government but in close and permanent coordination with them.

By entrusting Dominique de Villepin with the function of secretary general of the Élysée, I knew that everything would be done to guarantee that this perfect liaison between the two poles of the executive was the backdrop of daily activities. The former principal private secretary to Alain Juppé at the Foreign Ministry, he seemed to me the best qualified to ensure the continual cooperation that I knew was fundamental to the good functioning of the nation. This was not the only reason I chose him. The most difficult task in the exercise of power is equipping oneself with staff who dare state their point of view to the man leading them without fear of displeasing him and without simply repeating whatever they think he wants to hear. The courtier mentality is inherent to the functioning of those who surround people in positions of power; it is an inescapable evil that could become fatal if one does not have strong safeguards in place to limit its effects. A man of character such as one rarely finds within the apparatus of government, inventive, spirited, stimulating, rich with an international experience acquired since his youth, he was little inclined to mask his convictions or moderate his judgments. Villepin was an excellent antidote to that courtier spirit in which servility always jostled for position with conformity.

I had known that I could count on his frankness and loyalty since that day at the very start of the 1980s when, as a young diplomat who was already part of my team of advisors at the Paris city hall, he had bluntly recommended that I abandon a speech on foreign policy about which I had asked his opinion. He sent it back to me with comments to the effect that if I gave it, I would risk looking like a nitwit on the international scene. I immediately summoned him to city hall for a private meeting in which I told him that I was in most need of this kind of advisor. I promised him that we would, sooner or later, be called on to work together in another capacity.

Dominique de Villepin had been, behind the scenes and without anyone knowing, one of my most efficient advisors during the presidential campaign. His responsibilities in the ministry of foreign affairs and his strategic position with Alain Juppé meant that he was better informed on most subjects than I myself was at that time. Through him I also had access to firsthand information on government affairs, the imminence of certain defections around me, and the intrigues against us brewing in my competitor's entourage.

Our political destinies became linked during this period that was teeming with all kinds of betrayals. Villepin rightly had a lofty idea of his position. He possessed culture, style, and idealism. Was he too inclined to be fired up, to let himself be carried away by his passions, as those who had a more lowly vision of France accused him? At least he was not guilty, like so many others, of lack of boldness, energy, and idealism. Such qualities were important in my eyes.

I wanted the hierarchy of the presidency to retain a collegial and diversified character. I have always needed to have that collective intelligence that is the best safeguard against the solitary exercise of power expressed freely around me. It is inconceivable in our modern democracies that the taking of decisions, the exclusive responsibility of the head of state, should not arise out of almost continual prior consultation. The confrontation of ideas, points of view, and analyses has become more necessary than ever for leaders faced with the increasing complexity of the problems they have to confront in every sector of national and international life. I had experimented with this method of working well before my arrival at the Élysée and intended to remain faithful to it in my new position. That was why I took care, shortly after my arrival, to set up a meeting room in the office next to that of the president. Curiously, the palace did not have anywhere devoted to meetings between the president and his staff. This reorganization was in no way spectacular, but it seemed to me quite symbolic of this new style of governing.

From the very start, I benefited from the support of an extremely motivated, efficient, and competent team who worked tirelessly for the success of our objectives. This group of deliberately limited numbers, consisting of barely more than thirty people, was mainly made up of new faces, with a few old-timers from the Hôtel de Ville with whom I had many long years of shared commitment. The presidential publicity office was officially placed under the responsibility of my daughter Claude, alongside Jacques Pilhan, who was the often-ingenious architect of my predecessor's media strategy. There has been much gossip about Claude's role and the influence she is said to have exerted. It is true that we share an unshakable bond, but our understanding is based on the expertise Claude acquired in her professional sphere, which was brilliantly proven during the presidential campaign. Today she has become a very good public relations professional, doubtless better placed than anyone to get me to take part, without too much reluctance, in an exercise that is little to my liking and in which I have never felt at ease.

While the media fills an essential role in terms of public opinion, it has never seemed to me vital to listen to it to know the real feelings of the French. A man in the public eye learns much more about that through direct contact with his compatriots than by relying on the judgment of commentators, however talented and perspicacious they may be. This is doubtless why, at the risk of being occasionally misunderstood, I was less eager than I probably should have been to "communicate" intensively over the twelve years of my presidency; I was more concerned with acting and implementing than with publicizing and explaining—and even less with making myself into a celebrity. Pilhan was of the same mind. For him, who had already implemented the same philosophy with François Mitterrand, the president should make sure that he was not overexposed, that his appearances in the press or on television were limited, and that he made himself sufficiently scarce so that his words, reserved for important circumstances, had all the more impact. The fact that this corresponded perfectly with my inner nature and the ideal that I held of my office made me even more inclined to accept it.

I deliberately did not appoint any political advisors to my staff. After considered reflection, I decided not to designate any one person to take care of a function that seemed to me of limited usefulness. The influence of a political advisor tends, in the nature of things, to become exclusive and then excessive, as I knew from experience, recalling several men or women who ended up assuming the role of mentor to the person they were meant to be serving. Better to surround oneself with multiple views than to encourage the hold of a single advisor to the exclusion of all others. As always, I took very seriously the views of Maurice Ulrich; even more than an advisor, he was for me a friend and confidant, the discreet sage in residence who gave me his point of view without ever trying to impose it. His presence was essential to me. It went without saying that Maurice should accompany me to the Élysée, just as he had accompanied me for fifteen years whether in Matignon or at the Hôtel de Ville. A relationship of certain and soothing trust had grown up between us, and this would doubtless be more necessary to me than ever in my new role.

From the first Council of Ministers, I indicated through various immediate measures the style that I intended for my presidency: a lightening of protocol, a simplifying of the security system, abolition of the traditional presidential hunts and the presidential air fleet. "Leaders must change the way they behave," I said to members of the government. "The French will not put up with pretentiousness anymore. They have had enough of interminable ministerial motorcades, with motorcycles and flashing lights, driving at all speeds without ever stopping at red lights. People have become understandably exasperated by all that. The republic and all who serve her should adopt modest behavior and set an example to others." Simplicity, proximity, and economy would be the key words at this start of the presidential term, words that would have considerable significance for the future of our country.

I was conscious of the little time at my disposal to implement the changes expected by the French, even if most of the fundamental reforms

I had committed to introducing could be accomplished only over a period exceeding the first hundred days. I also knew that the shock of reality would soon dissipate that honeymoon period that all new presidencies are supposed to enjoy. The exercise of power demands that one looks truth in the face, however brutal or disturbing, unless one decides to shy away from it with demagogy or short-term political calculation. I did not, for myself, choose to do so.

During the war in the seaside town of Rayol in the south of France.

The day of my first communion, with my parents François and Marie-Louise Chirac.

With the scouts (I am third from right), where I was known as "selfish bison."

With Bernadette on my wedding day, March 16, 1956, at the church of St. Clotilde, in Paris.

In Algeria, at the head of the Third Squadron of the Sixth RCA Regiment.

May 25, 1967: I had the honor to be part of Georges Pompidou's new government serving under General de Gaulle. © G. Caron/Gamma/Eyedea

With Georges Pompidou and Édouard Balladur at the time of the Grenelle agreements, May 1968. © Christian Boyer

In the eye of the storm; on May 20, 1968, I left the Élysée Palace after a meeting with General de Gaulle. I was at that time secretary of state for employment. © Keystone/Eyedea

At the table of the Council of Ministers in the Murat room at the Élysée. This was the last Council presided by Georges Pompidou. © Christian Boyer

As minister for agriculture, with Valéry Giscard d'Estaing, minister for economy and finance, and the prime minister, Pierre Messimer, on September 4, 1972, after a lunch with President Georges Pompidou. © A. Dejean/ Sygma Corbis

With my friend Simone Veil, minister for health, during a press conference at Matignon, the official residence of the prime minister, in 1974. © Keystone/Eyedea

1977, during the election campaign for mayor of Paris. © Bonnotte/Sipa Press

With President François Mitterrand. © Rue des Archives/AGIP

With Pope John Paul II. Cliché Atelier Photographique des Archives Nationales

Welcoming Deng Xiaoping to Paris, May 1975. © Mingam/ Sipa Press

Victory night, May 7, 1995. © Jobard/Sipa Press

Proceeding down the Champs Élysées in the open-topped Citroen "SM Opera" ordered by President Pompidou. As I greeted the French people there, I took full stock of the extent, and the elevated nature, of the task that was now mine. I was responsible for their destiny and for that of France. © Gamma

On June 14, 1995, on the occasion of the G7 summit in Halifax, Canada. © Swanson/ Sipa Press

At the Élysée, with Russian president Boris Yeltsin. © Service photo Élysée

I arranged the signing of the Dayton agreements by Serbian president Slobodan Milošević, Croatian president Franjo Tudjman, and Bosnian president Alija Izetbegović in Paris on December 14, 1995, on the occasion of the peace conference on ex-Yugoslavia. © Villard/Chesnot/Witt/Sipa Press

January 27, 2005: Sixtieth anniversary of the liberation of Auschwitz. © Service photo Élysée

With British prime minister Tony Blair in the Élysée gardens. © Service photo Élysée

With President Bill Clinton I enjoyed an open and friendly relationship based on mutual trust. © Service photo Élysée

Brazilian president Lula and I shared the vision of a more united and humane world. Together we conceived of innovative development funding, the first example of which was a tax on airplane tickets to benefit the fight against AIDS, tuberculosis, and malaria. © Service photo Élysée

In Ramallah, with Yasser Arafat, October 1996. © Witt/Sipa Press

Helicopter flight over the site of Ground Zero, two days after the September 11, 2001, attacks. © Patrick Kovarik/AFP

*With American president
George W. Bush in the Élysée.*
© Éric Lefeuvre

*With German chancellor Angela Merkel and Russian president Vladimir Putin during a
Franco-Russo-German summit in Compiègne, in 2006.* © Service photo Élysée

Welcoming Indian prime minister Manmohan Singh to the Élysée in 2006. © Service photo Élysée

Bernadette is the woman of my life. We have accomplished so much together. © Éric Lefeuvre

With Mahmoud Abbas, president of the Palestinian Authority. © Service photo Élysée

Welcoming the new Afghan president, Hamid Karzai, to the Élysée. © Service photo Élysée

With President Lula and alongside Bill Clinton at the official launch of Unitaid, giving those suffering from AIDS, malaria, or tuberculosis easier access to medicine, particularly in developing countries. United Nations headquarters, September 2006. © Éric Lefeuvre

It was with great emotion that on May 16, 2007, after twelve years as president of the Republic in the service of France and the French people, I took leave of the Élysée Palace, of all those who worked there, and of my staff. After the traditional transfer of power, my successor, Nicolas Sarkozy, accompanied me to my car. I gave him all my wishes for his success in an office and a task that I knew were demanding.
© Service photo Élysée

15

LESSONS FROM HISTORY

*T*radition dictates that as soon as French or German leaders take office, they immediately mark their adherence to the special relationship between the two countries in a symbolic act. The day after my inauguration, on May 18, I met Chancellor Helmut Kohl in Strasbourg for the first time in my role as president. This meeting was the opportunity for me, also the new president of the European Council, to unreservedly confirm that France intended to respect the commitments undertaken in the framework of the Maastricht Treaty, notably in regard to the single currency.

The chancellor needed reassurance on this subject. Various rumors, disseminated from Bonn as much as Paris, had upset the financial markets and had made him fear a possible revision of the agreements that France had signed on to and that I had clearly supported in the referendum of 1991. Kohl did not hide from me his worry that the constraints and upheavals imposed by the treaty, particularly the massive reduction in government deficits, would cause our country to withdraw its agreement to it. He declared that a strong commitment on the part of the French authorities was vital in convincing his own public. Ultimately, the very future of the construction of Europe was at stake; it could not have been realized or pursued without the shared vision and objectives of the Franco–German partnership.

"The Germans are worried about the disappearance of the Deutschmark," Kohl confided. "Principally older people and the middle class, who fear losing their assets, haunted by the memory of the 1920s recession in which my grandfather had to carry around millions of

Deutschmarks to buy the smallest item. . . . We have made every psychological mistake possible! The Germans will never accept this name of 'ecu' that is being proposed for the new currency. It makes us think of the word *Kuh*, which means 'cow' in German. It's laughable, isn't it? Why not call it the 'euro franc'? We absolutely have to find another name."

"I agree," I said to him. "'Ecu' is the invention of your friend VGE!" "Yes," he replied. "The invention of a technocrat." Kohl insisted on the need for our two countries to adhere strictly to the commitments made at Maastricht, and I confirmed that the new French government did intend to conduct policy in conformity with the criteria of the future economic and monetary union.

I saw in Kohl's perspective the emotion and anxious sensitivity of a generation for whom the reconciliation and alliance of our two nations remained the essential guarantee of lasting peace on the continent. For Kohl's successors, this would doubtless seem an irreversible given about which there was no more need to worry. But for this disciple of Conrad Adenauer, it was still something to be nurtured and constantly strengthened and consolidated.

There are decisive moments between nations, just as there are between people. In terms of the Franco–German alliance, no period had been more important than the end of the 1950s and the beginning of the 1960s, between Adenauer's first visit to de Gaulle in September 1958 and the signing of the Franco–German treaty in January 1963. In that period, the French president and the German chancellor had not only established a close personal relationship as well as a respect and trust that the two peoples would henceforward feel for each other; they had also defined the construction of Europe as the common goal of their alliance.

During the difficult postwar period, in which General de Gaulle had likened our two countries to exhausted wrestlers, we shared above all a similar weakness: Germany had emerged from the conflict physically and morally destroyed while France, even if in the winning camp, was no less marked by the terrible trials of defeat and occupation. Since then, our two countries had regained their self-esteem and asserted their place among the great nations. France had once more become a power open to the world and above all Europe, and Germany was no longer hesitant to assert its ideas as well as its interests. This singular alliance was not based principally on our common interests but in fact was based on the many contradictions that it was vitally important to each of us to overcome, knowing all too well from experience how destructive conflict between us could be.

At the time, the Franco–German relationship entered a new era with the fall of the Berlin Wall and the subsequent unification of Germany—an event that most western leaders regarded with fear but that I, for my part, immediately supported and favored. Paris and Bonn, their reconciliation assured, now faced a new and huge challenge: successfully navigating together the inevitable, necessary enlargement of Europe. That is why our special cooperation with Germany is more than ever a priority and the vital condition for a European Community capable of rivaling the United States, Russia, China, and the other emerging powers.

At the end of our first meeting, I suggested to Kohl that we wander through the old Strasbourg streets, on an outing that quickly changed from a friendly walk to a walkabout. Afterward, we dined together at Chez Yvonne, one of the most famous restaurants of the Alsace capital, with which we were both familiar. On the menu were snails, head cheese, saveloys, calves' head, plum tart . . . All washed down with beer, white wine, and pinot noir. Helmut Kohl and I hit it off, as they say. But I am aware that, beyond displays of friendship, it takes time for heads of state to build a real relationship of trust. We had known each other for a long time, through contacts established between our respective parties, but I understood that Kohl would have to get used to dealing with me after a long period of personal understanding forged with François Mitterrand.

During the meal, we spoke of the situation in the former Yugoslavia. Even if our analyses differed on the origins of the conflict and the responsibilities of the different protagonists, the chancellor was clearly as concerned as I was by this war without apparent solution. For my part, I felt it was indecent and intolerable that such a tragedy could unfold at the very heart of Europe without provoking an international reaction that would allow a just political solution to be found.

These founding values of European civilization—rejection of ethnic and religious hatred, respect for the other, the primacy of law over force, in short a rigorously humanist concept—were now being directly threatened by the intolerable Bosnian civil war. This tragedy that we were watching with a sort of resignation involved the return of barbarity to a continent that had already had cruel experience of it. Situated at the crossroads of the Latin and Byzantine worlds, of Christianity and Islam, Bosnia-Herzegovina also constituted a link between them, not just the place where they clashed. What was at stake in the region was not only the reconciliation of the European family but also the existence on our continent of an open, tolerant Islam.

In what was a failure to assume the full weight of their responsibilities, the great powers had from the beginning made the mistake of refusing to threaten a military intervention that probably would have been enough to dissuade the aggressors from all sides while there was still time. Instead, they limited themselves to exclusively humanitarian actions that, although doubtless vital, became the substitute for a real political strategy.

France, which under the auspices of UNPROFOR—the United Nations Protection Force—provided the largest contingent present in the country, was in February 1994, on the impetus of its foreign affairs minister, Alain Juppé, behind the first UN ultimatum delivered to the Serbian forces to attempt to force them, alas in vain, to put an end to the deadly encircling of Sarajevo. It was also the personal efforts of Juppé that led to the setting up of a contact group uniting France, the United States, Russia, Germany, Great Britain, and the UN to reach agreement on coordinated and balanced peace proposals. But these diplomatic efforts came to naught in the face of the three Serbian, Bosnian, and Muslim camps that were locked in pitiless conflict in Bosnia-Herzegovina—in fact, the Americans were touting a possible lifting of the embargo of arms to the region and the French authorities were envisioning, shortly before my election, the withdrawal of their own contingent. Two solutions that would only have led, one way or another, to the country being plunged into total chaos.

The worst attitude, in my reading, was for the international community to abdicate its responsibilities by leaving the terrain open to the various belligerents, most particularly the Bosno-Serbian forces of General Mladić. The atrocities committed by these men in the Muslim enclave of Tuzla in mid-May 1995 forced western governments out of their wait-and-see attitude. After an ultimatum that was ignored, Washington, London, and Paris came together to order NATO (North Atlantic Treaty Organization) raids on the Serbian ammunition depots near Pale on May 25. The following day I learned that Mladić's forces had taken more than a hundred peacekeeping soldiers, mainly French, hostage in Sarajevo. Our men were exhibited like war trophies, tied to posts and stripped of their uniforms.

Furious at seeing our soldiers humiliated in this way, I immediately decided to take personal charge of the affair. In the limited Council of Ministers meeting that took place afterward, I expressed my indignation to the chief of the Defense Staff, Admiral Lanxade: "This situation is unacceptable! I do not understand how you could have left our forces unable to defend themselves, and I hold you personally responsible for what happened!" The chief of the Defense Staff replied that he had not decided on the rules of engagement alone but under orders from the prime minister of the time, Édouard Balladur, and his government: "I even offered my resignation," he explained to me, "not being in agreement with what I was being asked to do." "That's all very well," I said to him, "but you are still there and you therefore have to shoulder the responsibility for it!" I gave Admiral Lanxade a firm warning that I would no longer tolerate a single position held by our men being ceded to any side in Bosnia and that I now wished our troops to react systematically to any attack.

Having served in its ranks during the Algerian war, I knew our army well and felt much admiration and respect for it. I believed that it was the duty of the president to engage his soldiers on the ground only after having judged their real chances of success and weighing the risks to their security. It would be even more irresponsible, however, to set them a mission in which they were exposed without the means to fight back or at the very least defend themselves.

I was determined to put an end to an anomaly that meant that these same missions did not operate according to their own rules but, as was the case in Yugoslavia, conformed to the objectives conceived by diplomats or inspired by intellectuals. Also, there could be no more question of depending on nothing more than the goodwill of a UN-based authority whose procrastinations had led to the dramatic consequences that had once again been seen in Sarajevo.

Circumstances would allow me to implement this radical change of method and orientation very quickly. During the night of May 26, 1995, soon after my election, Serbian soldiers passing themselves off as peacekeeping forces took the bridge of Vrbanja in Sarajevo, guarded by the French contingent. The following morning, on my instructions, the latter mobilized to regain control of the bridge. In the attack, which was successful, two of our men died and several were wounded, while the Serbian soldiers were thoroughly beaten. This French initiative put a decisive end to the conciliatory passivity that had been adopted until then and restored our soldiers' honor and dignity. In addition, it put France into a position of strength to enter into immediate negotiations with the Serbian leader of Bosnia, Radovan Karadžić, and to obtain the release of our hostages as quickly as possible; all of them were freed two weeks later.

Firmness was paying off. I no longer had any doubt that a rapid reaction force should be set up immediately in Bosnia with the role of guaranteeing the security of the peacekeeping forces and allowing UNPROFOR to ensure that the security zones and the free passage of humanitarian aid were respected. The British prime minister, John Major, gave me his agreement in principle to its deployment, but nothing could be done without the backing of the UN Security Council and therefore the support of the American government and Congress.

This was one of the main subjects that I intended to bring up with President Clinton in our meeting at the White House on June 14, shortly before leaving for the G7 meeting, the conference of the heads of industrialized countries that would take place in Halifax, Canada, the next day.

After meeting him briefly when he came to Paris in February 1994, I met Bill Clinton again in Washington in September of the same year, through the intermediary of his ambassador in Paris, Pamela Harriman. A devoted Francophile, Pamela Harriman is one of the most fascinating women I have ever known, dazzlingly cultivated, elegant, and distinguished. A close friend of the American president, she had wanted to accompany me to the White House to introduce us, as she was convinced almost before anyone else that I had a strong chance of becoming the next president of the French republic.

I found Clinton a warm, open, pleasant man, a great professional politician, firm in his convictions but probably clever enough to adapt to any situation. His behavior could sometimes appear flippant but his charisma was striking. He radiated pugnacity, enthusiasm, and youth.

Along with everyone else, I knew the essential role in his rise to power played by the woman who shared his life and his struggles, his wife Hillary, whom I also met at that time. I have to confess that it was she who made the stronger impression on me, so struck was I by her intellectual superiority, her listening and interpersonal skills, and the energy, determination, and courage with which she devoted herself wholeheartedly to the realization of their common ambition. We talked for almost two hours in her office, where she passionately set out to me her plan for the reform of the American health system—a plan that she would never succeed in getting adopted and that would have to wait for the election of a new Democratic president, Barack Obama, before it was finally, and not without difficulty, accepted.

When I met him at the White House on June 14, 1995, Bill Clinton gave me the warmest possible welcome. We had a long private discussion about the situation in Bosnia, in which he declared himself in favor of the project I put to him of a rapid reaction force. But he declared to me, with a little embarrassment, that this project ran every risk of being rejected if he personally defended it before a Congress dominated by his opponents. The best solution would be for me to go and present it myself to the leaders of the Republican majority in the Senate and in the House, Bob Dole and Newt Gingrich. I had no objection to that, as I determined to try anything to obtain if not a commitment, then at least the neutrality of the American authorities. The two representatives having said they were prepared to meet me, I immediately went to Capitol Hill to argue my case to them.

Fierce supporters of the Bosnian cause, these dyed-in-the-wool, tough and intransigent conservatives made their disagreement known to me from the outset: "Your thing stinks," Gingrich launched in unceremoniously. "You make no distinction between the aggressors and the victims. This is a fight between good and evil!" I explained to them that there was no question, of course, of mistaking the enemy but rather of preventing the Serbian forces from continuing to attack the UN contingents and the security zones that they had the mission of defending. The two men eventually agreed, anxious, they told me, not to "get in the way of your plan when many of your soldiers are there"—on condition, however, that the United States was not involved in any way, financial or military, in the creation of this force, for which France and Great Britain alone would assume the cost. A force that would be equipped with the means not to make war but to impose peace!

The next day, the draft Anglo–French proposal along these lines, developed in agreement with Bill Clinton and Helmut Kohl shortly before the opening of the Halifax summit, was immediately submitted to the Security Council, which adopted it over the course of the following night. I had every reason to be delighted, particularly because it was the first time that Europe had demonstrated, in an affair principally concerning itself, a proactive attitude.

In this context, my presence in Halifax did not go unnoticed. All lights were trained on this "bulldozer" president, as I was nicknamed in the American press, who did not hesitate to upset diplomatic conventions in the cause of justice and efficiency. In terms of the G7 itself, it seemed to me that the usefulness of this kind of summit, as it then functioned, should be questioned. In short, I found it shocking that what was designed in the beginning as an informal meeting between heads of state and government leaders should end by setting itself up as a sort of worldwide leader on behalf of other countries, notably the southern ones, which were not even represented.

This type of conference has no point unless it is first very well prepared. It was not a question of trying to obtain spectacular results but of returning to the original intention of a frank conversation between the leaders of the principal economies of the world about their management: how to improve things and avoid certain failures, how to enable each country to succeed on its home territory, how to help each other by drawing on individual experiences—that was the original objective, which excessive media hype had succeeded in reducing to some big-budget entertainment.

I requested that the agenda no longer be limited to monetary and commercial issues but widened to those of employment, which had obviously become one of our mutual preoccupations. I also insisted on the need for a debate concerning another crucial question: the maintenance by the big powers of an adequate level of development aid to the poorest countries, notably in Africa. At a time when this continent, torn apart by crises as tragic as that of Rwanda, tended to be increasingly marginalized, I noted with much concern the growing disengagement of our Anglo-Saxon partners in terms of government aid.

I openly broached this issue in Halifax in an attempt to raise consciousness, particularly with the American government, that one could not simultaneously want to be the dominant power and withdraw into oneself by neglecting the duty to provide what was a fundamental support. At that time, however, Bill Clinton did not seem any more worried about Africa than his predecessors, who barely knew where this continent was located on a map of the world. In short, it was France's role, here as elsewhere, to remind its American friends of certain realities.

The rapid reaction force would prove its worth during the reprisal operations undertaken against the Serbian troops in Sarajevo at the end of the summer of 1995. By responding categorically to a deadly attack perpetrated on August 28 on the city's market, its heavy artillery, supported by NATO planes, contributed to the opening up of the Bosnian capital as well as to the relaunching of negotiations with all the parties concerned, culminating in the agreements concluded at Dayton in the United States four months later and signed in Paris on December 14.

However, this success was not enough to wipe from my memory the images of one of the worst tragedies of this war: the massacres of Srebrenica in July 1995. Mladić's men gave themselves over to an appalling operation of ethnic cleansing against the Muslim population, and the international community did not mobilize in time to prevent it, despite France's appeals for immediate military intervention. Although it formed part of the security zones organized under the auspices of the United Nations, the enclave of Srebrenica was taken without a fight. After witnessing the Serbian offensive without reacting, part of the Dutch peacekeeping forces was taken prisoner before they surrendered.

The moment I found out what had just happened in Srebrenica remains imprinted in my mind. It occurred in Strasbourg on July 11, during a Franco–German defense and security council meeting, in the presence of Chancellor Kohl as we were discussing cooperation between our two countries. The German foreign affairs minister, Klaus Kinkel, was twice called to the phone. The first time he came back into the room and informed us of the situation in Srebrenica where the Dutch battalion had been subjected to strong pressure from the Serbian troops, which, he said, it was resisting. "According to the Dutch, there is no need for air intervention from NATO," he declared. We therefore carried on with our meeting, and, an hour later, he was called out again. This time he returned looking upset and announced the imminent fall of Srebrenica. He had had the news from his Dutch counterpart, who was still asking that NATO refrain from intervening, as it could have done, so as not to "provoke collateral damage" among the peacekeeping forces as well as among the population.

That was when I exploded with fury. Addressing the French and German military leaders, I said we could not continue working in that way and that it was intolerable to learn news of this importance through a telephone call. After the meeting was suspended, I asked Admiral Lanxade and the chief of staff attached to the presidency, General Quesnot, to come to agreement as quickly as possible with their German counterparts on the plan of action to counteract the Serbian offensive and to win Srebrenica back. Then Chancellor Kohl and I agreed on a mutual communiqué condemning this latest attack and demanding an emergency meeting of the Security Council.

The following day, on July 12, the Security Council unanimously adopted the resolution submitted by France demanding the withdrawal of Serbian troops and the protection of the Srebrenica enclave. Nothing, however, was decided in terms of the concrete means by which this zone was to be taken back.

France did not have the power to initiate the appropriate reaction alone, unless it decided on a separate intervention, which would have proven unrealistic on every level. The only choice remaining to me was to exhort the other western leaders to refuse to accept the fait accompli. On July 13, when news from Srebrenica left no doubt about the horror of the ethnic cleansing that had just occurred, I had multiple telephone conversations with my American, German, and British counterparts.

Bill Clinton told me that he appreciated "France's hard-line approach" before explaining that in fact there was nothing he could do. His military experts were skeptical about the possibility of an intervention in Srebrenica, which they judged too risky. I strove in vain to explain that we were facing the following alternative: either we undertook together, as rapidly as

possible, a limited operation aimed at stopping the offensive or we decided to withdraw and to lift the arms embargo, in which case the United
States would have to choose between a now-massive military intervention
on behalf of the government of Sarajevo or accept—which was morally difficult—the crushing of Bosnian forces.

At the end of the following day, I called John Major to warn him in his
turn of the extreme gravity of the situation and to encourage him not to
give in. "We claim to be the upholders of democracy and the defenders of
human rights," I said to the British prime minister. "We have sent soldiers
and formed the rapid reaction force together, and now we are powerlessly
watching our television screens and seeing ethnic cleansing in which thousands of women are going to be raped and thousands of men will have their
throats slit and then be thrown into communal graves! If I were Serbian,
I would be laughing as Hitler must have laughed in Munich when he met
Chamberlain and Daladier. We are in the same situation. We have lost our
honor, which demands that France, Great Britain, Germany, and the United
States take back Srebrenica for the Muslims. At the very least, we must all
come to the aid of Goražde to guarantee the security of a zone that it is
your responsibility to defend, before it is too late."

After a moment of silence, Major, whom I knew was himself furious at
what was happening in Bosnia and in whom I had a sure and determined
interlocutor, said that he thought we must "above all carry out an evaluation of the situation on the ground and envisage a discussion between the
French, British, and American chiefs of staff." According to his experts, the
Bosnian Serbs were preparing to attack Zepa, which, just as badly defended
as Srebrenica, could very soon suffer the same fate. "Their long-term goal,"
he added, "is to take Goražde, which is precisely where our soldiers are.
They will probably wage a fierce battle; but presuming that the Bosnian
forces offer strong resistance, it will take at least three weeks for the Serbs
to take possession of the Goražde enclave. We therefore have sufficient time
to have a meeting in which we can come to a very clear position and decide
whether or not to declare war on Serbia. That is why the French, American,
and British chiefs of staff should meet urgently to examine the military options and see what is feasible or not."

Major also proposed that the foreign affairs and defense ministers of
these countries meet in London on Friday, July 21, to examine from their
side the political options and consider the future role and objectives of
UNPROFOR in Bosnia-Herzegovina as well as urgent measures to be taken
in the humanitarian field. I accepted the idea of a meeting of the chiefs
of staff, even though they were speaking on the phone every day and we

already knew their opinion. "What we need today is above all political opinions," I said to Major. "Our weakness is political and not military. Either we undertake a military process for the enclaves, which could lead to a war with the Bosnian Serbs but which would save our honor, or we decide that it is too dangerous and we must therefore withdraw the UNPROFOR. Whatever happens, we cannot accept a situation in which genocide is taking place with impunity before our eyes."

As I have said, France was resolved to proceed to withdraw its troops if nothing were done to oppose the criminal actions of the Bosnian Serbs and to prevent the enclaves of Goražde and then Sarajevo suffering the fate of Srebrenica. This determination, clearly demonstrated that day to the prime minister of Great Britain, would bear fruit on July 21 at the London conference, which included all member countries of the contact group and the main suppliers of troops to Bosnia. It was on our initiative that the important decision was taken at this meeting to simplify the procedures relating to the initiation of air strikes, which could now take place without waiting for UN authorization. In the future, NATO forces alone could authorize them, which I believed would guarantee better protection of the security zones. Regarding Sarajevo, for which it was directly responsible, France succeeded in getting an agreement that eight hundred men from the rapid reaction force would be sent to reinforce Mount Igman. The transport of 155mm cannons to the heights of Sarajevo would take more than a month, and it was eventually agreed that an ultimatum would be issued the following day to the Bosnian Serb leaders to warn them in the clearest possible terms that if there were renewed attacks, their installations would be immediately bombed.

I noted with satisfaction the willingness of the American government to become more actively involved in both the military and political resolution of the conflict. Considerations of domestic politics probably partly motivated Clinton's concern to tackle the problem. Still under strong pressure from the majority of the Senate to lift the embargo on arms to Bosnia, which he courageously continued to veto, the U.S. president needed to find a negotiated solution as quickly as possible. Whatever the reasons for it, his initiative obviously seemed to me salutary.

During the first week of August, I received at the Élysée the diplomatic delegation urgently dispatched by Clinton to the main European capitals, headed by his security advisor, Anthony Lake. I was happy to discover that Washington had finally decided to favor a global approach to the Yugoslavian problem rather than one centered solely on the issue of the survival of Bosnia. And I could only add my weight to the notion of organizing without delay a conference among the Serbian, Croatian, and Bosnian presidents, Slobodan Milošević, Franjo Tudjman, and Alija Izetbegović, with the aim of a mutual recognition of the three states.

It was, however, the tragic events of Sarajevo that would precipitate the opening of negotiations several weeks later. As I had maintained for months, only the use of force would get the Serbian authorities to listen to reason. By bombarding the positions held by Mladić's troops in Sarajevo—Mostar, Goražde, and Tuzla—for two weeks, NATO aircraft would produce the desired result.

France took a very active part in this reprisal operation, which was christened "Deliberate Force." But on August 30, one of our planes was shot down in the region of Pale and its two pilots, who had managed to eject from the aircraft, were taken prisoner. Two days later, Milošević assured me on the telephone that he felt "responsible" for what happened to them. I was under no illusions, knowing what the word of the dictator of Belgrade was worth.

Shortly after my election, I received a delegation from the Representative Council of Jewish Institutions in France, led by its president, Henri Hajdenberg. The leaders of the RCJIF, whom I knew well, had come to ask me to preside over the commemorative ceremony of the fifty-third anniversary of the Vel' d'Hiv roundup on July 16.

My predecessor had attended this ceremony on several occasions, marking by his presence the homage that the nation paid to the victims of racist and anti-Semitic persecutions, but without agreeing to speak. François Mitterrand refused to recognize officially the responsibility of the French nation in the deportation of sixteen thousand Jews who never came back from the concentration camps. For him, neither the republic nor France had to apologize for these crimes, imputable to the illegitimate Vichy regime with which neither one nor the other should be confused, in accordance with the Gaullist creed of which Mitterrand here made himself interpreter and guardian.

The rationale and the need for this creed arose out of the national work of unification and recovery undertaken by General de Gaulle at the time of Free France and continued after the liberation and at his return to power in 1958. But because they had not been spoken about, certain wounds still remained open in our collective memory, and all those men and women who expected from the nation a just recognition of the crimes of which their loved ones had been victim continued to suffer from them. This was so for the French Jews, who had the legitimate hope that the truth of what had been inflicted on them would finally be given public recognition, as well as the men and the regime guilty of the crimes.

A nation needs to reconcile itself with its history if it is forge a sense of unity. Its cohesion, just like that of a family, cannot occur in the midst of taboos, lies, and misunderstandings. It is in assuming its past as it really was and imposing a duty of clear-sightedness on itself that a people can avoid making the same mistakes and can, above all, unite around the real values on which its identity is based. More than half a century after the Vel' d'Hiv roundup, I felt conscience-bound to break the silence of my predecessors. The moment had come to speak clearly about what had happened that day. The speech that I decided to give would address, through the Jews of France, the country as a whole, but it would be no less a mark of gratitude toward all that the genius of the Jewish community had brought to the world and to France in particular.

I had always felt much respect and admiration for these people who attach more importance to the transmission of knowledge than to rites and beliefs. When Jews settle somewhere, they create a school before building a synagogue; Catholics in a similar situation would begin by constructing a church. I like that sentence from the Talmud that the very world rests on the breath of a child in the schoolhouse. The Talmud also says: "Who is a wise man? He who learns from all men." That is a magnificent lesson in life. Judaism is inseparable from study and the conquest of knowledge. My Vel' d'Hiv speech was a way of expressing, in the name of the French people, our recognition of and our loyalty to those women and men who were so cruelly and unjustly tested by history.

After the meeting with the RCJIF delegation, I immediately asked Christine Albanel, who had attended it, to prepare the text of my speech, giving her very precise indications of what I wanted to say. She encouraged me, saying: "You should speak. You must absolutely do so." I can see us, her and me, standing in my office, deciding in a few minutes the broad outlines of the speech I had determined to give. As was my custom, once the content of the text was established, I spent a long time reworking it, word for word. "Do you think I've gone far enough?" I asked her. "Yes, it's already a lot," she replied.

On July 16, no one among the hundreds of people gathered on the site of the old Winter Velodrome expected to hear the new president of the republic declaring so openly that "the criminal folly of the occupier was backed up by the French and by the French nation." I saw as much emotion as recognition on the faces that surrounded me when I related, without oratorical flourishes and as soberly as possible, exactly what had happened here fifty-three years earlier:

> On July 16, 1942, four hundred and fifty French policemen and gendarmes, under the authority of their leaders, carried out the orders of the Nazis.
>
> On that day, in the capital and in the greater Paris region, almost ten thousand Jewish men, women, and children were arrested at home in the early hours of the morning and assembled in police stations.
>
> One saw atrocious scenes: families torn apart, mothers separated from their children, old people—some of whom, veterans of the Great War, had shed their blood for France—thrown unceremoniously into Paris buses and police vans.
>
> One also saw policemen turning a blind eye and allowing several people to escape.
>
> And so began the long and painful journey to hell for all these people. How many of them would never see their home again? And how many, at that moment, felt betrayed? What did their distress feel like?
>
> France, home of the Enlightenment and the rights of man, a land of welcome and asylum, committed the irreparable that day. Failing to live up to its word, it handed those whom it was meant to protect over to their oppressors.
>
> Taken to the Vélodrome d'Hiver, the victims had to wait several days in terrible conditions before being taken to the transit camps—Pithiviers or Beaune-la-Rolande—opened by the Vichy authorities.
>
> The horror, however, had only just begun and other roundups and arrests followed, in Paris and in the provinces. Seventy-four trains would leave for Auschwitz. Seventy-six thousand Jews deported from France would never come back.
>
> We still owe them an indescribable debt.

This description of one of the most tragic episodes of our national history has meaning only if it serves as a warning to us. It was this aspect that I wanted to stress in the second part of my speech, in which I pointed out that, far from having been eliminated, the same evil that had destroyed part of humanity half a century earlier had lost nothing of its virulence and was ready to strike again if we neglected to take it seriously:

> When the wind of hatred blows, here stirred up by fundamentalism, there fed by fear and exclusion, when, on our doorstep, right here, certain small groups, publications, teachings, and political parties have shown

themselves, more or less openly, to be the carriers of a racist, anti-Semitic ideology, the spirit of vigilance that drives you, that drives us, should manifest more strongly than ever.

In this regard, nothing is insignificant, trivial, or set apart. Racist crimes, the defense of revisionist arguments, and every kind of provocation—little phrases, jokes—are derived from the same sources.

Transmit the memory of the Jewish people, the suffering and the camps. Bear witness again and again. Acknowledge the mistakes of the past and the faults committed by the government. To hide nothing of the dark hours of our history is very simply to defend an idea of Man, his freedom and dignity. It is to wage a ceaseless fight against the forces of darkness.

This is both your and my unending combat.

I believe that this combat should above all be one of hope. A clear-sighted understanding of human nature can go hand in hand with the belief that man is capable of distancing himself from those destructive forces that are in him and around him. I reject, for my part, a pessimistic reading of history, confident, as I said in conclusion, in the example of the courage and dignity of other French people at a time when certain of our compatriots were drowning in ignominy.

I want to remind myself that that summer of 1942, which revealed the true face of the "collaboration"—the racist character of which, after the anti-Jewish laws of 1940, was no longer in doubt—would be, for many of our compatriots, the starting point of a huge resistance movement.

I want to remind myself of all the hunted Jewish families who were saved from the pitiless clutches of the occupier and the militia by the fraternal and heroic action of numerous French families. . . .

Certainly errors were made and we have a collective responsibility for that. But there is also a certain idea of France: honest, generous, loyal to its traditions and to its spirit. . . . It was present, single and indivisible, in the heart of those French men and women, those "Righteous among the nations" who, in the blackest moment of the suffering, saved, at the risk of their lives as Serge Klarsfeld wrote, three-quarters of the Jewish community living in France. . . .

Let us draw lessons from history and not let ourselves be the passive witnesses, or the accomplices, of the unacceptable.

The words of peace and reconciliation contained in this speech were well received by the French people as a whole and greeted with quasi-unanimity

by the various political groups. They would offend only the most ortho-
dox Gaullists, who came to the Élysée Palace to signal their discontent, reproaching me for having committed a kind of sacrilege against the Gaullian
myth. It was not the first time that I somewhat upset the "barons" in their
noble and respectable certainty of being the exclusive holders of the general's heritage. But is Gaullism anything other, in fact, than a demand for
truth in the service of the only worthy cause: that of France, its grandeur,
its unity, and the example of humanism that it has the duty to set for the
rest of the world? That is, in any case, the idea I have of it and that I strive
to set out, in my speeches as well as my actions, as the head of the country.

*T*uesday, July 25, 1995. A terrorist attack had just been perpetrated in
the lower level of the St. Michel metro station. I immediately rushed to
the spot, joined by the prime minister, the mayor of the capital, and the
Parisian chief of police. There, in the smoke of the explosion, was the atrocious and indescribable spectacle of dismembered corpses and wounded
people in a heap. An unbearable vision that filled me with horror and revulsion. Overwhelmed, helpless, I could only repeat "It's appalling," followed
by the same obsessive question: "Who could have done this?" It did not
escape me that the attack had happened on the feast day of St. James.

It was not the first time I had been confronted by ignoble, unjustifiable
terrorism that struck randomly at innocent civilians in places and circumstances intended to hit its anonymous targets and create a maximum number of victims. I would never forget the sight, during the attack on the rue
de Rennes in September 1986, of a woman lying on the pavement, her legs
in pieces, half her face torn off. A memory that I had relived nine years later
in the depths of the St. Michel metro, where the bombers had every chance
of causing even more damage.

Returning from a trip as soon as he heard the news, the minister for
the interior, Jean-Louis Debré, told me that he had no precise information
on either the origins or the real motives of the bombing. Various bits of
information had, however, come to us several weeks earlier, alerting us to
a certain agitation in Islamist circles. The threat of terrorist activity by a
commando of the Armed Islamic Group (GIA), the Islamist group fighting
against the Algerian authorities, in our country had led us, immediately after my election, to bring in eighty-four militants close to these networks for
preventive questioning. This had not prevented the assassination in Paris on
July 11 of Sheikh Sahraoui, cofounder of the Islamic Salvation Front (FIS),
whose commanders we had not managed to identify. Had this first transfer
of the domestic conflict in Algeria onto our soil been the work of the GIA,

as the victim had condemned acts of violence committed against foreigners, particularly the French? Or that of the Algerian Military Security, at a time when attempts to reopen dialogue between the FIS and the government were opposed by some in the ranks of the Algerian army? The first lead seemed the most likely. But it was difficult to dismiss the second, given that armed groups were often infiltrated and manipulated by this same Military Security in order to discredit the Islamists in the eyes of the population and the international community.

On Wednesday, July 26, the day after the bombing, I declared at the very start of the Council of Ministers meeting that this deadly action could be the first of a series, as in 1986, and that we needed to prepare to face that. Then I gave the floor to the minister of the interior, who set out the security measures that had been implemented immediately: mobilization of the police, increased patrols and identity controls in all public places, as well as the reintroduction of border surveillance under the safety clause in the Schengen treaty. Although I was in favor, in principle, of freedom of movement within the European Union, in the present circumstances, our priority had to be guaranteeing protection of our country.

I was haunted by the fear that similar action would recur during the summer of 1995. On August 17, the explosion of a parcel placed in a trash can near l'Étoile unfortunately confirmed my premonition. The French were concerned and angry, particularly as the inquiry launched after the St. Michel underground attack had not yielded, a month later, any tangible result. Criticism of Debré intensified, and detractors from all sides accused him, more or less openly, of inertia and weakness. I knew the untiring, painstaking work that the minister of the interior and his department were carrying out behind the scenes—in other words, away from the media hype—to try to identify the real perpetrators.

On August 26, a failed attack on the Paris–Lyon high-speed train allowed us to take fingerprints from the unexploded devices. These material clues gave investigators a first serious, credible lead: one Khaled Kelkal, known to the police because he had driven through a roadblock several weeks earlier and left fingerprints in his abandoned car after a shoot-out with the police. It appeared likely that the suspect, a delinquent of Algerian origin who lived in the Lyon suburbs, had links with Islamist networks. Every means was now put in place to find him. But Kelkal was still at large when a car bomb exploded on September 7 near the Jewish school of Villeurbanne, killing fourteen people. It seemed increasingly obvious that the terrorist problem we were facing was closely linked to an Algerian political situation that eluded us.

Since I had taken office, France had striven to clarify its ever complex relationship with Algeria. At the risk of upsetting both parties, I had made it clear that our country did not support either the government or the fundamentalists but simply the Algerian people, who benefited from the aid of France as well as that of the European Union, the United States, and the large financial institutions of the World Bank and the International Monetary Fund. My conviction was that being too close to the Algerian government, which was always inclined to suspect the French government of interference, would only play into the Islamists' hands. At the same time, I had over recent years made the decision to stop nonofficial contacts with armed Algerian groups via various intermediaries, which had led to the prime minister's decision to withdraw the authorization previously given to a leading FIS figure to come to Paris for a television program to commemorate Algeria's independence.

France wanted greater democracy established in Algeria—and the fact was that it could expect nothing in this regard from the fundamentalists who had come to power there. Was this refusal to back, directly or indirectly, the Islamist movement the basis for the attacks of that summer of 1995? There was no overt proof of that, even if the GIA would claim authorship in a nonauthenticated document, after having invited the French president in a first message of equally uncertain origin to convert to Islam to be "saved." I am a friend of Islam but not of an Islam that propagates hatred, violence, and oppression.

At the end of September 1995, Khaled Kelkal was found and killed by police. Shortly afterward, the members of his group were arrested as they were preparing to commit another terrorist act. Their responsibility in the attacks perpetrated since July 25 was in no doubt. Even if all the evidence pointed to Kelkal having been in large part exploited by the GIA, the background of most of its members, starting with its leader, led us to other sources, which now came under examination.

I wanted to expose the situation in our suburbs, those urban ghettoes in which the despair of a whole section of excluded youth served as a breeding ground for agents of political and religious fanaticism. And so, on October 13, during a visit to the Lyon area, I decided to go to Vaulx-en-Velin, the town where Khaled Kelkal had grown up and studied before becoming delinquent. A private meeting, which was not planned in my program, was held in a hotel there, in the presence of about fifteen people, including the Communist mayor of the town, the chief mufti of Lyon, and Father Christian Delorme. The latter had declared, at the young terrorist's funeral: "Only the president can say loud and clear: This youth is our youth and we love them." I had been affected by this message. Its meaning was that the role of the president, guardian of national unity, was not to excuse the worst crimes but at least to try to understand their causes. Also present was the writer Azouz Begag, whom I would have the pleasure of meeting again ten years later when he formed part of the Council of Ministers. Begag had assumed the role of spokesperson of this youth of North African origin who aspired to integration but suffered rejection and discrimination.

I had not gone there to set out my own arguments but, rather, listened in silence for more than two hours to the testimony of each participant. The description they gave me of the situation in a suburb like theirs was clear-sighted but not pessimistic. They all underlined the seriousness of the problem, but they all believed there were solutions if the authorities rallied themselves more effectively. This work was also the responsibility of the state, and therefore me.

16

A TEST OF TRUTH

*T*he state of public finances that the prime minister and I took over in May 1995 proved much worse than we had estimated over the previous months. We were inheriting, it has to be said, a calamitous situation that the previous government had carefully hidden from the country.

The accumulated deficits in the budgets of the government and the general health program exceeded all records, reaching 400 billion francs, or almost 6 percent of gross domestic product, and unfortunately gave credence to Alain Juppé when he painted the picture of a France that was "virtually bankrupt." The hole in the national health insurance system alone, which neared 250 billion francs, had become bottomless.

And so we were confronted, from the outset, with two possible options. Either we let ourselves drift along, with the risk of disastrous consequences for the country. Or we immediately resolve to set things right through measures that would necessarily be unpopular but that could only benefit the country's future. It was naturally the second option, the most reasonable if not the easiest, that Alain Juppé and I decided to adopt.

Convinced, as I had stated during the presidential campaign, that France was living beyond its means, I had long realized that a policy of austerity would sooner or later be necessary to stop the trend of excessive public spending that had occurred since the end of the 1980s. But the extent of the problem, set out with force and insistence by the finance minister as soon as we took office, had taken us by the throat and forced us to rush austerity measures into place.

For all that—and contrary to what has been incessantly affirmed and repeated since then—I never felt that, in putting order into public finances, I was turning my back on the other commitments I had made to the French people during the presidential campaign. It was in no way a U-turn. The reduction in social inequality truly remained one of the essential priorities of my presidential term of office. It never ceased to be. One cannot govern by pitting one Frenchman against the other. This antagonistic concept of social relationships is totally contrary to my notion of the state, whose role is not, in my view, to sow discord and misunderstanding between citizens of the same nation.

It would be a grave mistake not to do all we could to consolidate the tradition of solidarity that was at the basis of our republican pact, of which the national health insurance system had become one of its vital symbols. The fiftieth anniversary of its creation on October 4, 1995, gave me the opportunity to highlight the fact that the president is the primary guarantor of this model of protection, more valuable than ever in the face of rising unemployment and increasing marginalization. I also emphasized all that was exemplary about a system that was unequaled in the world.

Fifty years after its creation, the national health insurance system constituted the largest of our public services. Its scope was huge, involving 1.8 trillion francs and theoretically protecting all the residents of our country. Since 1945, the system had been part of the identity of France and the heritage of the French. It had its place in our history and in our daily life. It expressed our national spirit.

Neither the slowing of economic growth that had occurred from 1974 nor the inexorable growth in unemployment that had followed in its wake had impeded social progress. However, these difficulties, notably financial, had forced our national health insurance system to adapt and change. In 1945, the primary objective of the system was the health of the people— and, in 1995, never in our history had France's state of health been better. It was to the national health insurance system that we owed that; it had enabled the payment for treatment, encouraged prevention, created and managed health institutions. Each year we gained a quarter of a year in life expectancy. Thanks to medical progress, certainly—but what would that progress mean if the population in its entirety did not have access to it?

The organization of retirement pensions had experienced the same success. In 1962, a commission studying the problems of aging had issued an alarm signal: Retirees had been forgotten in the march toward social progress. Thirty years later, all the studies showed that the situation had improved.

These were unprecedented achievements. Yet the figures did not tell the whole story. They did not reveal to what extent the national health insurance system had become the cement of our national unity even while our

society was sick. With 3 million unemployed, 5 million victims of social exclusion, and 6.5 million people living in troubled neighborhoods, in 1995
society was more torn apart by exclusion than it had ever been. But amid
this great disorder there existed a reference point and a place of ultimate
protection: the national health insurance system.

However, this system was now in crisis—a crisis linked to the economic
situation and to the worsening in unemployment that had dried up the pro-
ceeds that funded the insurance system, essentially based on salaries, but
also due to increased life expectancy and the fact that there were more and
more retirees, to advances in medical techniques, and to the appearance of
new plagues, such as AIDS, with the expenses they entailed.

All that had a cost: a deficit in 1995 that had increased by 60 billion francs over three years, despite 110 billion francs of debt paid off by
the state. Eventually, this deficit, along with that in public services, would
threaten the whole of our system of protection and end up weighing on our
economy as a whole. Because its very survival was at stake, we now had to
adapt the functioning of the national health insurance system to these new
realities while remaining faithful to the republican pact. It was our duty of
responsibility.

On the occasion of this fiftieth anniversary, I announced the principal
objectives of the recovery plan that we wanted to put in place: the creation
of a general system of health insurance that would guarantee access to
treatment for all and especially the most deprived; the diversification of
sources of funding so as to replace salary contributions by fiscal contributions determined according to an individual's entire resources; the development of structural reforms that should allow better control of expenditures
in the hospital sector as in the doctors' sector; and the strengthening of the
role of Parliament in the financial control of the health insurance system.

This package of measures was a response to an observation that the
government was not alone in making and which that part of the press that
could be least suspected of indulgence toward us summed up in even more
categorical fashion: "The social security system has the choice between
thoroughgoing reform or bankruptcy," Robert Sole wrote in *Le Monde*.
"The situation will not be resolved by increasing payments for the ump-
teenth time. Its salvation will be found in radical innovations, involving
modernization of the medical system and new working practices." We
could not have said it better ourselves.

It was among the working population, not to mention the trade unions,
that reform came up against the strongest opposition. As predicted, the
dispute centered less on the reform per se than on one of its aspects that

eventually would skew the whole debate about the Juppé plan, as it was called. The reform of the special retirement plans, which aimed at extending the period of contribution for a retirement pension from 37.5 to 40 years and which focused on all public service workers, addressed an obvious concern for justice and fairness in terms of salaried employees in the private sector and the professions who, since the Balladur reform in 1993, had their contribution periods set at 40 years.

It was to be expected that the beneficiaries of such long-standing benefits would not want to give them up without protest. Their revolt was inevitable. I warned Juppé about the dangers of this kind of measure being rushed through; haste would provoke lack of understanding and conflict. I also understood the prime minister's desire to hide nothing of the problems posed by the state of our social security system. He did not want to postpone, from caution or political calculation, the announcement of part of his reform on the pretext that it would be unpopular. On November 15, he revealed his recovery plan in its entirety to the National Assembly.

Over the following weeks, we were confronted with the most intense strike movement that France had experienced since May 1968. First, public sector workers went on strike, particularly those of the RATP, the Parisian transport authority, and the SNCF, the nationalized railways, before the strike spread to private sector staff who wanted to express solidarity but also their own opposition to the austerity measures that we had been forced to put in place.

If the opinion polls were to be believed, my popularity and that of the prime minister took a spectacular nosedive. I took note of it without concerning myself unduly, as I am not in the habit of basing my decisions on polls. A leader is made not to be popular but rather to be respected. As president of the republic, I also knew that my role was to ensure that social tensions did not become so acrimonious that they compromised the already precarious equilibrium of a nation like ours.

Furthermore, the spread of a large-scale social movement, leading to the virtual paralysis of the country, risked killing the reform in its entirety and handicapping in the long term any other notion of evolution or change. I therefore began to think that it was better to defuse the conflict before it deteriorated and forced us to capitulate in the full flush of battle.

Little did it matter if we seemed to draw back for a time from a particular point if it meant that we preserved important advances in terms of the rest. On December 15, the government announced the deferral of reform of the retirement pensions in the civil service and that of the special retirement plans. They would be implemented by my government in 2003 for the great majority of civil servants and by my successor in 2008 for the special retirement plans. As for the other elements of the Juppé plan, far from having been abandoned, as we had wanted people to believe, they were adopted by Parliament on December 20 and put into force the following year.

It was our draconian measures, naturally poorly received by those who were seeing their advantages or their powers cut back, that would enable us to straighten out the accounts of the health insurance system and modernize it. Observing, fifteen years later, the difficulties that President Obama came up against in reforming the American health system, I could not help thinking of our own fight and the energy that we had had to expend to make the common good victorious over corporate or sectional interests. The obstacles were of another nature and the resistance less unremitting. Globally in agreement on the diagnosis, we differed on the remedies and on the scale of the shock treatment to be prescribed and implemented. But in both cases long-standing arrangements had to be upset. It is this kind of fight that proves the commitment of a man in the public eye.

*I*n the course of many meetings on the ground that taught me much about the wounds of our society, I had forged an unshakable conviction. The fight against social fracture was not only a financial question, although that was not off limits. Above all it arose out of a vision of man and of society. I reject intransigent individualism and liberalism just as much as I reject passively giving support to people in a way that enshrines poverty in statute. The social model that I wanted to make a reality—for it was a decisive element of our identity and the key to our future—had to go beyond the old thinking of treating nothing but the effects of social exclusion to a new approach that attacked the causes.

It was this determination that I expressed on October 17, 1995, at the Trocadero, on the occasion of the International Day for the Eradication of Poverty: "We must no longer treat social exclusion as an inevitable scourge. We must put the fight against social exclusion at the heart of all policy and all collective action. Employment, housing, access to schooling and medical care, aid to troubled neighborhoods: All these domains form a whole. They should give rise to a single policy in the service of man, with and for the most deprived."

Methodically and despite all resistance—the most open kind not always being the most dangerous—these policies were put in place from the time of my election. Employment was the first priority, for unemployment was at the root of all social exclusion. That was the urgent issue and the first mission that I conferred on the new government. From the first weeks, we therefore introduced a reduction in charges on low salaries in order to encourage the hiring of people with few qualifications and prevent the risks of layoffs in the most vulnerable sectors. At the same time, we created the employment initiative contract to combat long-term unemployment and facilitate hiring by companies, not just organizations or local groups. Very quickly, the facts validated the instincts on which these innovative policies were based and which ran counter to everything that had been tried up to then: Programs that facilitated employment in the commercial sector proved more efficient in terms of return to employment than other measures. It was not surprising that the tools put in place at that time remain today the main instruments of employment policy.

Housing was a problem that could be resolved only in the longer term, but here too we immediately undertook measures that were based on a new approach. Beyond an immediate plan to extend the amount of emergency housing and a relaunch of the policy of requisitioning empty buildings and properties belonging to banks or insurance companies, public housing was on the agenda. We needed to make up a considerable gap, which placed us in a situation similar to that denounced by the Abbé Pierre in 1954, in the worst of the housing crisis. Homeownership needed to become more accessible, to meet the desire of many of our fellow citizens. The zero-interest loan introduced to help with homeownership very quickly achieved the lasting success that I hoped for and considerably lightened the pressure on government-subsidized housing to the benefit of the most impoverished.

Employment and housing were essential levers of social cohesion, and they were our priority objectives in our action in extremely troubled neighborhoods. The separation of economic activity and housing constitutes, in my view, a major error of postwar town planning. It is, in great part, the origin of the problems in these areas, which suffered from record rates of unemployment. No improvement can be obtained if businesses were not reestablished there. The creation of urban free zones would allow companies that wanted to set up there to benefit from large reductions in charges and taxes. Here, too, this radically new step rapidly proved beneficial.

The difficult question of dependency required, in my view, the same effort of imagination in order to put an end to the silent social exclusion of so many elderly people whose progressive loss of independence left them relying on only the devotion of their families. I saw this as one of the greatest social challenges at the turn of the millennium. The collective answer could no longer wait, no matter what financial constraints it imposed on us. I believed it was vital that a first step be taken without delay; that is why we introduced the specific "dependency payment" while awaiting a larger-scale reform.

Undertaken in the first hundred days of my presidential term, these reforms foreshadowed the law combatting social exclusion presented to Parliament in 1997. Questions of social urgency would never cease to be one of my central concerns.

17

INCIDENTS IN

JERUSALEM

On October 20, 1996, I flew to Damascus, the first stage in a journey to the Middle East that would take me successively to Syria, Israel, the Palestinian autonomous area, Jordan, Lebanon, and Egypt. Few official trips had been so meticulously prepared, in light of the tensions that continued to rage in that part of the world and the various sensitive issues that needed careful handling. Aimed at marking the return of France to the region, this trip fulfilled twin ambitions. First, to restore a relationship of trust with Israel. Second, to relaunch our Arab and Mediterranean policy along the lines set out in the speech I made in Cairo in April of that year. These ambitions were doubtless difficult to reconcile, but they illustrated the specific mission incumbent on us in regard to peoples separated by decades of hatred and violence.

If France enjoyed guaranteed good credit with most Arab countries, its ties of friendship with Israel had worn thin over time. That was the impression I got in June 1995, shortly before my election, at a working lunch with Yitzhak Rabin at the Élysée. A reputedly difficult interlocutor, the Israeli prime minister did not seek to hide a certain suspiciousness toward France and Europe, perceiving its reservations or criticisms as so many marks of support for the cause of his adversaries. He preferred to rely on American diplomacy to accompany the peace process undertaken since the Oslo agreements, while France remained the largest contributor to the Palestinian Authority. My personal image remained "uneven" in Israel, where my Gaullist affiliation meant that I merited the same disapproving attitude as that adopted by the general toward Tel Aviv after the launch of the Six-Day War in 1967. The Israeli authorities had even noted, after the appointment of Alain Juppé, that for the first time in many years, a French government included no minister of the Jewish faith—something that was in no way premeditated but that was sufficient to fuel their distrust of us.

I expressed to Rabin my total support of the courageous peace policy that he was conducting toward the Palestinians against the wishes of a growing number of his citizens. I shared his conviction that no reasonable alternative existed other than the pursuit of these negotiations. Despite his austere, reserved appearance, Rabin seemed to me a man of heart as well as a clear-headed servant of the State of Israel, determined to reach reconciliation, whatever the cost.

Overcome when I heard of his assassination, I immediately decided to go to Jerusalem to attend the funeral on November 6, 1995, of Yitzhak Rabin, victim of the fanaticism of several of his compatriots, just as Anwar El Sadat had been fifteen years earlier. During the ceremony, before a crowd gripped by emotion and pain, I took the floor to salute the memory of this statesman who had sacrificed his own life for his ideals, then offered the Israeli people a message of friendship, solidarity, hope, and confidence.

I had every reason to be reassured by the choice as successor to the assassinated prime minister of my friend Shimon Peres, admirable symbol of justice and tolerance. I knew that for Peres, the reality of Israel's coexistence with the Arabs meant that they had to get to know each other, respect each other, and talk to each other. Constructing a better world necessitated the construction of a common history. The dream of Shimon Peres, which was not a utopia, was that of a State of Israel that could live in peace and security next to neighbors who were also living in the freedom and dignity of their sovereign state.

Since the Israeli–Palestinian agreement of Taba in September 1995, real progress had been made in this direction. But the good faith that seemed to predominate on both sides was soon marred by the renewed outbreak of fighting in southern Lebanon between Israel and the Lebanese Hezbollah, over which Syria certainly had a hold.

On March 3, 1996, the first of a long series of suicide attacks was perpetrated in a bus in Jerusalem, killing eighteen people. I called Peres the following day to assure him of France's support at that time of trial. The Israeli prime minister told me that this attack was a veritable tragedy for his country, likely to bring into question the peace process undertaken by Israel and continuously upheld by his government. He was quite severe in regard to Yasser Arafat, judging that he had acted "too late and too little" to prevent such acts, while he was in no doubt that the perpetrator of the attack came from the Occupied Territories. According to him, Arafat had not taken the necessary measures to ensure at least the control of these territories in time—the only thing that had been expressly asked of him not only by Israel but also by Egypt and Jordan. I therefore proposed to telephone the leader of the Palestinian Authority to urge him to demonstrate greater firmness; otherwise he risked being a victim of terrorism in his turn. Peres encouraged me in this: "Coming from you," he said, "that would be a very important step."

I did not have great hope, deep down, even if I had a good relationship with Arafat. The Israelis did not consider the Palestinian leader a reliable partner because he had shown himself incapable of carrying out what I called "the last gesture." In the markets of my home region of Corrèze, seller and buyer begin negotiating the price of a head of cattle in a discussion that can seem interminable. But when they finally reach agreement, they shake hands on the deal and, from that moment on, everything is settled. They do not even need to sign any piece of paper, so sure are they that the agreed sum will be paid.

Arafat's great weakness lay in the fact that he always wanted more, once an agreement was reached. "You don't know how to shake hands on a deal," I often said to him. "You always want to get a little bit more." The man was intelligent, devoted body and soul to the defense of his people, and worthy of respect on many levels, but it was in his nature not to know how to put an end to a debate or a demand and to want to come back again and again to demand more. Nothing with him was ever completely finished, whereas the Israelis had a very precise and even definitive idea of what they wanted and rarely budged from their position. That was what made their dialogue with Arafat often difficult and almost impossible, and prevented them from being able to trust him fully. Yasser Arafat had his own reasons, it is true, for remaining on his guard with his interlocutors who, from their side, were often guilty of excessive intransigence.

On April 11, 1996, exasperated by the incessant Hezbollah raids, Israel launched a reprisal operation known as Grapes of Wrath against the positions of the Shi'ite movement in southern Lebanon. Five weeks before the general elections, Peres had wanted to prove that he too could use every means to ensure the security of his country. But this demonstration of force ended in the massacre in Cana of more than a hundred Lebanese civilians, killed in a UN camp by Israeli shells. There was raw emotion worldwide, and I was particularly affected by this tragedy. France mobilized all the more actively to obtain a cease-fire because the Cana attack hit a country with which it had long-standing ties. On April 14, after having received the president of the Lebanese Council, Rafic Hariri, at the Élysée, I decided to dispatch the minister of foreign affairs, Hervé de Charette, to the area to try to put an end to the hostilities.

As I have said, the United States took this intervention very badly, seeing our mediation as a factor that disturbed its own diplomatic initiative with the Syrian authorities. But the fact is that the Syrian authorities preferred the French government as interlocutor, as Warren Christopher was quick to see when he arrived in the region at the same time. Appalled by this realization, the American secretary of state explained vehemently to our foreign affairs minister, during a stormy meeting in the Syrian capital, that neither Washington nor Tel Aviv needed France to resolve the crisis. This viewpoint ignored the Cana tragedy and its negative impact on Israel's international image and that of America in the Arab world. France's influence was thereby enhanced, and our intercession seemed vital in achieving the cease-fire of April 27, placed under the auspices of a committee that gave France equal status to the United States.

By becoming Lebanon's closest ally while strengthening its relations with Syria, France had already managed to restore much of its influence in the region, without this damaging Israel—as was demonstrated by the message of gratitude Peres wrote to me on June 5, 1996, shortly before he was succeeded by his opponent in the Likud, Benjamin Netanyahu: "Our cooperation," he wrote, "has been of vital importance and I wish to express my deep appreciation for your personal effort in the extraordinary advances towards peace that have taken place in the Middle East. Your friendship has been, in fact, of incalculable value."

Unfortunately, his successor was far from sharing this benevolent attitude. Elected on a program promising both peace and security, Netanyahu was hazy on the subject of his precise intentions. His inaugural speech, in which he called for negotiation "without prior conditions," seemed to me to augur well. However, the new Israeli prime minister also declared himself in favor of enlarging the settlements, and his governmental platform was based on a triple rejection: rejection of a Palestinian state, rejection of all retreat from Golan, and rejection of the least sharing of sovereignty over Jerusalem.

When I undertook, in October 1996, to go to Israel and most of the neighboring countries, the situation in the region had once again become untenable. The considerable progress accomplished between Israelis and Palestinians since the signing of the Oslo and Taba agreements seemed seriously undermined. The election of Benjamin Netanyahu did nothing but aggravate a climate that had already deteriorated because of the cordoning off of the Occupied Territories after the attacks of Hamas extremists in Israel. We had had to wait three months for the successor of Shimon Peres to agree, on September 4, to shake Yasser Arafat's hand. While he claimed to want to respect the signed agreements, no concrete gesture was made to confirm these apparent good intentions. The new prime minister gave priority, in fact, only to the policy of the fait accompli. In the last week of September 1996, the opening of the tunnel under the mosques in the old town of Jerusalem provoked violent clashes with the Palestinians. This explosion expressed the rising anger and frustration of a population that, after resigning themselves to recognizing their old enemies, felt they were humiliated in exchange. To the political disappointments were added the economic difficulties exacerbated by closing off the Occupied Territories, where almost half of the inhabitants were unemployed and living conditions were worsening day by day. Traffic blockades had become so draconian that ambulances transporting the wounded had even been stopped from passing through during the September riots.

In this context, France had no other choice than to ask Israel to respect the international agreements ratified by the Knesset—agreements that were meant to lead to the creation of a Palestinian state—and to encourage Yasser Arafat and his men to persist in the only worthwhile objectives: negotiation and peace. After our meeting in Paris on October 4, the leader of the Palestinian Authority had publicly expressed the hope that Europe and France be associated with a possible relaunch of negotiations, but this request had met with a flat refusal on the part of the Israeli government, which wanted to restrict France to goodwill missions in the Arab countries.

While readily criticizing France for its support of the Palestinians, its relations with Syria, and those—judged reprehensible—with countries like Iraq and Iran, the Israeli authorities did not hesitate to ask us to transmit messages to certain of these same interlocutors whom they judged beyond the pale. France remained suspect in their eyes, however, principally due to its refusal to commit itself unilaterally to Israel's side as the United States did so enthusiastically and almost unconditionally.

France's advocating that agreement be sought with Syria, which we considered a key factor in the peace process, made the new Israeli government even less disposed to accept our intervention. It was not by chance that I chose Damascus as the first stop on my tour of the Middle East, at the risk of upsetting the authorities in Tel Aviv a little more. In my mind, it was not just a matter of marking the reestablishment of Franco–Syrian relations; my goal was also to help Syria emerge from its isolation, in order to encourage it to renew dialogue with Israel and to loosen its hold over Lebanon.

Alain Juppé had renewed our contact with Damascus shortly after taking office as foreign affairs minister in 1993. Relations with Syria had been extremely strained since the assassination in September 1981 of our ambassador to Lebanon, Louis Delamare, followed by terrorist attacks whose authorship was no longer in doubt. By succeeding in getting the Syrian president, Hafez al-Assad, to participate alongside Israel in the Barcelona conference in 1995, aimed at establishing a real Euro–Mediterranean partnership, Juppé had enabled our diplomacy to turn a corner that I thought beneficial. During our numerous exchanges on the subject, my friend Rafic Hariri had finally convinced me that we were on a false trail by making the improvement of our relationship with Syria dependent on its withdrawal of troops from Lebanon. In his eyes, we should do the exact opposite: first establish a strong relationship with Damascus. Doing so necessitated the lifting of certain obstacles, such as the repayment of the debt that Syria had contracted with France but that had been ignored since the 1980s.

Shortly after my arrival at the Élysée, I charged the secretary of state for finance, Hervé Gaymard, an expert in Near and Middle Eastern affairs, with the mission of discreetly negotiating a treaty on this subject with the Syrian authorities. He had to arm himself with patience before achieving his goal fifteen months later, after several return trips to Damascus, slow and laborious wrangling with various envoys, and two long meetings with Hafez al-Assad, an expert in the art of subjecting his interlocutors to the test of time. The agreement seemed on the point of being concluded just before my official trip to Syria in October 1996, when everything was suddenly up in the air on our arrival. The exasperation displayed by Gaymard, who threatened to withdraw if the agreement was challenged again, enabled this last misunderstanding to be cleared up. France agreed to expunge 60 percent of Syria's debt, in order to encourage the economic development of a country that had had to live in virtual isolation in recent years. This financial aid was shared with Germany, which we had succeeded in enlisting to our side, when its own debt was far greater than that of France.

On Sunday, October 20, Assad welcomed me in person at the Damascus airport. There was no warmth to Assad, a thin, ascetic man with emaciated features and tough expression, evidence of all the harshness of twenty-six years of absolute power. The slightest gesture seemed to emerge from a meticulous and long-premeditated calculation on his part. This sphinx lived above all in shadows and secrecy. He rarely showed himself in public and traveled little, calling his colleagues himself since they were forbidden from entering into direct contact with him. The mystery that surrounded him, along with the fear or the terror that he inspired and knew how to spread, enabled Assad to reign supreme over a people of whom the Alawite community, from which he came, represented barely 10 percent of the population. It was said that his health was not good, and he did indeed seem to me physically weak, although I did not feel that he had lost any hold over the governance of the country or over his desire to assert Syria's ambitions in the region.

Despite the coldness that served as his protective shell and the oppressive atmosphere that reigned around him, Assad greeted me with friendliness, concerned that all should be done to establish a relationship of trust between us. He had organized a sumptuous dinner at the presidential palace in honor of the French delegation the very evening we arrived, during which he conferred on me the decoration of the great Order of Umayyad. The following day, we met alone for several hours. Our conversation was punctuated with the long monologues Assad was accustomed to giving, delivered in a monotone voice that did not allow for the expression of any emotion.

Assad was both worried and angered by the change in Israeli policy since Netanyahu's arrival in power. "It is necessary," he declared to me, "to base oneself on the resolutions of the Security Council and on the principle that peace should be based on the secession of the Occupied Territories. The new situation leads us to believe that Israel wishes to overturn these cornerstones. By doing so, they are issuing a challenge to the international community. The European Union and the Arab countries uphold the cornerstones of the peace process and hope that this process is pursued until its successful conclusion. Mr. Netanyahu wants to go back on all that. This can only result in misfortune, destruction, and blood for the entire world."

I confirmed to him that France wanted to see the whole process relaunched and to play a role in that effort, so as to rebalance the weight of the United States and its allies. "France could become a sort of cosponsor," I said to Assad, who did not seem unhappy with the formula. On the matter of the restitution of the Occupied Territories, which Syria rightly made the very basis of a lasting peace, I began by reminding him that France considered Syria's sovereignty over the Golan Heights, occupied by Israel, "indisputable." I added that it went without saying that if, in conformity with the demands of international law, France demanded that Israel unconditionally withdraw from southern Lebanon, the restoration of Lebanon's independence and territorial integrity also ultimately implied the withdrawal of Syrian troops. Assad limited himself to replying that he was himself favorable to a "fully independent and pluralist" Lebanon, in which every community could participate in politics. "The stability of Lebanon depends on national reconciliation," he insisted, as if to warn me—but how could I doubt it?—that nothing would be accomplished in this area without the backing of Syria.

I left Damascus for Tel Aviv during the afternoon of October 21, and it was already dark when our plane landed at Ben Gurion Airport. We were made to wait a long while on a taxiway before we could disembark. Through the window, I saw among the Israeli officials grouped at the foot of the steps the not-very-affable face of the head of protocol. "That woman hates us," I said to my entourage. "So I shall kiss her in greeting." Irritated by the fact that I had first gone to Syria, the Israeli government had sent only its foreign affairs minister to greet us.

The official dinner that followed, in the presidential palace of Jerusalem and in the presence of the president, Ezer Weizman, and Benjamin Netanyahu, took place in an atmosphere that was all the more relaxed because the prime minister's forty-seventh birthday was also being celebrated. However, the way in which certain of our hosts were looking at us, particularly the president of the Knesset, revealed just how deeply disturbing France's "Arab policy," and its reiterated support of the Palestinian cause, were.

A first problem had to be resolved even before we arrived, in regard to Orient House, the official headquarters of the Palestine Liberation Organization (PLO) in East Jerusalem. The French foreign affairs ministers, like most of their European colleagues, were in the habit of staying there, in an unofficial capacity, when they were in Jerusalem, despite Israeli pressure to dissuade them. This pressure had increased further since the change in prime minister. The latter clearly made it known to us after he took office that foreign visitors who persisted in going there would not be received in Israel. Given, above all, the risk of the building being permanently closed to the detriment of the Palestinians, I preferred to ask Hervé de Charette not to accompany me to Tel Aviv. In other words, I chose to adopt the least provocative solution in our hosts' eyes without, for all that, giving in to their demands. It was Hervé Gaymard, who had become secretary of state for health, who would stop over in his stead at Orient House.

This concession did not change anything, of course, in terms of the position of France and that of the European Union on the status of Jerusalem, which we held must take the Palestinian demands fully into account—a position that was translated, in practice, by the nonrecognition of Jerusalem as the unified capital of the State of Israel. However, if one was to avoid speaking about it as the "capital of Israel," the expression "government of Tel Aviv" was also to be banned if we were not to risk infuriating the Israeli authorities and public opinion. Likewise, it was preferable not to speak about "Palestine," since an independent Palestine did not yet exist, or about the "populating colonies," for which the strongly recommended term was "settlements"!

These linguistic precautions were not enough to prevent an incident that was to become memorable occurring on October 22, the day after my arrival. The Israelis had two obvious concerns, which they established without any fine shading, as was their wont. First, the laudable concern, even if it quickly became burdensome, to ensure my safety, and, second, that, more questionable and just as rapidly unbearable, to limit my contacts with the Palestinian people as much as possible. This would end up enraging me, causing me spontaneously to lose my temper: There was nothing deliberate or calculated about it. Impromptu reactions are generally the most sincere.

That day, I left the King David Hotel at nine in the morning, accompanied by some of my colleagues, for a visit of the old city of East Jerusalem. The itinerary had been established in agreement with the Israeli authorities and, contrary to what would subsequently be alleged, was scrupulously respected by us. The only unforeseen event came from the soldiers responsible for our security who, it quickly became apparent, had received orders to place extreme restrictions on our freedom of movement.

From the outset, I saw that the Israeli army was blocking off all the alleyways and all the surrounding shops. The soldiers were vigorously holding back the crowd of people who were trying, hands outstretched, to approach our retinue and to express their gratitude and friendship to France. I noticed shortly afterward that the policemen were trying to isolate me, this time from the journalists who were accompanying us, so that they were unable to do their work. Several of them alerted me to what was happening. Photographers and cameramen were unceremoniously pushed and shoved and their equipment taken from them, while invectives flew from all sides. The situation became intolerable. I tried to intervene but to no avail; the patrol that was supposed to be guaranteeing our protection was encircling us increasingly tightly as we walked, as best we could, in the middle of an indescribable swarm. After tolerating this situation for several hours and pushed past endurance, I finally shouted at the head of the Israeli security service, accusing him of "provocation" and threatening to return to Paris immediately if he did not stop what he was doing. Given the number of reporters present, this outburst immediately had spectacular impact through the entire world and notably the Arab countries.

Another incident blew up on our arrival at the Church of St. Anne in Jerusalem, owned by France since Napoleon III and therefore under French protection. Warned that the Israeli soldiers had already taken position inside the site, I demanded, as I was now on our own territory, that they leave the premises before I went in. They eventually did so, after I had waited more than ten minutes in front of the church door. When I spoke at the reception in the monastery for various religious and Palestinian figures in Jerusalem, I appealed for respect of the three religions, Christian, Jewish, and Muslim, that had fashioned the soul and the history of this sacred city.

It was 12:30 P.M. when I got back to the King David Hotel. Israeli prime minister Netanyahu, to whom I had addressed an official complaint, was waiting for me and asked to speak to me privately. He began by apologizing to me for the morning's incidents while trying to minimize them. According to him, they were due only to overzealousness on the part of an "overly active security" that had also bothered him during his own strolls. "Jacques, I am really sorry," he said, with a rather wily air, "but you know how 'they' treat me too. I am constantly getting digs in the ribs!"

Looking at him, I said to myself that he resembled one of those bodyguards who usually flank Israeli celebrities: square shoulders, short hair, a rapid and determined walk, peremptory tone . . . "Bibi," as his compatriots nicknamed him, had the appearance of a tough guy. His military air and his substantial physique expressed both self-confidence and a profound mistrust of those who did not resemble him. But Netanyahu was not an ideologue possessed by messianic convictions. His nationalist discourse was more that of a pragmatist whose sole preoccupation was to ensure the defense of Israel by deciding case by case on the best way of doing so. His references were taken primarily from the American model. Unlike most of his supporters, he was not a man frozen in his convictions or indifferent to the weight of international constraints. From the little I knew of him, I thought that he was prescient enough to understand that the peace process that was already under way could not stop with him and that he should not permanently close himself off in the inflexibility imposed on him by his partisans.

Netanyahu told me of his fear that Syria was organizing a surprise attack on the Golan Heights; Israel possessed serious information in this regard and was preparing itself for this eventuality. However, he explained in confidence, his government preferred to create the conditions for a dialogue with Damascus. I said to him that that was in the same spirit as the message that President Hafez al-Assad had asked me to transmit to him: "The territorial question is not negotiable in his view and he is prepared to do anything to get Golan back. However, if Israel sends him a positive signal, he is ready to envisage negotiations starting from scratch." Netanyahu asked if I would secretly make it known to the Syrian president that he did not wish, from his side, to use force but on the contrary wanted a "deescalation." "Only France," he acknowledged, "can help us get certain reasonable Israeli demands accepted by the Arab countries. I don't want to work only with the United States, but you will understand that I cannot say so publicly."

Then Netanyahu brought up, in an equally conciliatory tone, the question of the Israeli retreat from the town of Hebron. He complained that Yasser Arafat continually added new demands after agreements were already concluded and considered, for his part, that the redeployment of the Israeli troops was an affair that was already resolved. "If Arafat continues to procrastinate, he will play into the hands of the terrorists and we will end up with an irreparable catastrophe," he said, insistently requesting that I pass this message on to the leader of the PLO. I consented, insisting in turn that the cordoning off of the Palestinian territories would have equally catastrophic consequences. I reiterated my request for an agreement allowing the Gaza port project, financed by France and the European Union, to go ahead. The good diplomat, Netanyahu declared that he would take serious note of this request—but the fact that he failed to make the slightest commitment on the subject, as on that concerning the improvement of the Palestinians' living conditions, was enough to make me doubt that the intentions of the new Israeli prime minister were indeed peaceful.

When he announced several weeks later the extension of the settlements on the Golan Heights, Netanyahu risked killing a peace process that was already moribund. He was laying himself open to renewed violence with the Palestinians as well as to a freezing of the relations between Israel and the Arab countries that he assured me he wanted to reestablish. As for his continued opposition, under the pretext of security, to the construction of the port in Gaza, how could one not also see this as proof of his refusal to grant any new element of sovereignty to the Palestinians?

It was not surprising that, the day after the incidents in Jerusalem, a triumphant welcome accompanied my arrival in Ramallah on October 23. In the eyes of the Palestinian crowds, I was now a sort of providential hero, someone who had dared take on the all-powerful Israeli security and who now understood all the better, having experienced something of it myself, the humiliating constraints imposed on the Palestinians. It was also the first time that a western president had come to visit the West Bank since the establishment of its own freely elected legislative assembly—an assembly that I was the first foreign head of state to address. All the conditions were therefore in place to make me the representative of a friendly country, concerned about their fate and eager to defend their most legitimate rights and aspirations.

During the official welcome after we landed at the Ramallah heliport, our national anthem was played, clumsily and movingly, by a Palestinian orchestra in what was doubtless their first performance of it. Massed the length of the road that led to the Parliament building, thousands of men and women were waving French flags and banners in French that read "Chirac, Palestine's good friend" or wishing me welcome in Arabic: *Ahlan wa sahlan*. Others were holding aloft pictures of me and of their president. The most moving sight was that of Palestinian schoolchildren in their uniforms, waving in one hand tricolored pennants, as if France had become their second homeland, and in the other holding an olive branch.

Yasser Arafat's face was radiant. I sensed that he was throbbing with both joy and pride. More effusive than ever with his expressions of gratitude and friendship, he christened me "Dr. Chirac" because I had told him, during his last official visit to Paris, that he could call me at any time "in case of problems." Before the Palestinian parliamentarians, who had given me a long ovation as I entered the room of the legislative council, Arafat called me a real savior: "From the very bottom of my heart," he exclaimed, "I tell you that we need Dr. Chirac to give a new impetus to the peace process. We need you!" he concluded as he looked straight at me.

Everyone there knew France's commitment to the creation of a Palestinian state as well as the scope of its economic and financial support. Those present, who expected much more from me in this new hour of anxiety and uncertainty than a simple speech of solidarity, did not need to be reminded of the long-standing position of our country toward them. That was why I resolved to go further and to address, directly and concretely, the most crucial problems with which they were confronted:

> To make progress today, the signed agreements must first of all be respected, in letter as well as in spirit. The period of autonomy should allow the two parties to take account of what has been accomplished by both of them, to learn to live side by side and demonstrate that peace and neighborly relations are not utopian concepts.
>
> Settlement should stop immediately because the pursuit of this policy seriously threatens the chances of harmonious coexistence between Israelis and Palestinians. Changes to the status quo in Jerusalem, the destruction of houses, the expulsions, the construction and the use of reserved routes should cease if we want peace.

The unity of the Palestinian territories should be preserved. In conformity with the signed agreements, free passage should be assured in the interior of the West Bank and between there and the Gaza Strip. The Palestinians' right to economic development should also be ensured; peace will be an illusion if this right is not conferred. The construction of a port in Gaza, which France had decided to uphold with its European partners, is also an economic and political necessity.

Finally, there cannot be a peace that excludes "the city of peace," Jerusalem, as tragic events have recently proven. The whole of humanity turns its eyes toward Jerusalem, a thrice-holy city. I understand the passion that it excites. Its sacredness, for Muslims and Christians as for Jews, is inseparable from its life as a city. Its plurality must therefore be preserved so that it maintains its unique identity. Freedom of access for believers, all believers, must be guaranteed everywhere. But all notion of sovereignty, from wherever it originates, must be developed in the framework of the negotiated compromise provided by the Oslo agreements. This compromise must take account of the aspirations and rights of all the parties concerned.

It was planned that I would then go to Gaza to inaugurate a "Charles de Gaulle Street" together with Arafat. Ramallah was about sixty miles away from the coastal strip. Right up until the last minute, the choice of itinerary was the subject of intense negotiations with the Israeli authorities, who viewed this trip with suspicion and did all they could to complicate it. To top it all, my helicopter was not authorized to travel in a straight line, as I had hoped, but would be forced to take a large detour north in order to avoid flying over Jerusalem. In other words, no preferential treatment! The same kind that Yasser Arafat had to endure.

The reception in Gaza, as in Ramallah, was unforgettably warm and fervent. Everything was all the more moving because one felt here the heart of a nation that was still shackled, overwhelmed by insecurity and yet determined to assert itself by drawing all it could from the meager resources at its disposal. Friendship with France was part of that.

Along the length of the official route, bordered by a guard on horseback in national costume, I saw portraits of the general hanging from lampposts. Judging that the street that was supposed to bear the name of Charles de Gaulle was not prestigious enough, Arafat announced to me during the ride that he had decided to grant him one of the large avenues of the city. The ceremony over, we made our way to the site of the future port of Gaza, at that time still no more than a simple sandy beach. All that was needed to start work was the lifting of the Israeli veto. . . . But our presence there almost served as a starting point.

Shortly after my departure for Jordan, I learned that, due to fear of suicide attacks—according to the official version—the Israeli government had decided to tighten the cordon around the Palestinian territories.

𝒜cceding to the throne in 1952, King Hussein of Jordan was sixty-one years old and, after forty-seven years of uninterrupted rule, the longest-serving head of an Arab country. He was also one of the most respected leaders in the world. Having survived the worst trials—military defeats, conspiracies, terrorist attacks—he had succeeded in making his little country a central and influential actor in the history of the Middle East.

The geopolitical situation of Jordon was not the only reason he had been able to attain so much authority for it. This fragile, man-made kingdom would probably have shattered under the pressure of the Israeli–Palestinian conflict to which it was directly exposed if it had not had the courage, energy, and political intelligence of a particularly shrewd monarch. Small in stature, King Hussein did not impress with either his physique or his appearance. Yet what had always struck me when I observed him was the extraordinary charm that emanated from his person and the power that none of his visitors could fail to notice. Attentive to all that one said to him, Hussein of Jordan replied in an even, gentle—almost shy—voice that was also part of the very particular aura that surrounded him.

His openness of mind along with his great shrewdness led him to favor a pragmatic approach to problems. But this apparently conciliatory monarch could also prove inflexible if his country's interests warranted it. After successfully removing the various threats likely to jeopardize the survival of his kingdom, he was determined to ensure its stability, which he knew was inseparable from that of the Middle East as a whole. The peace treaty signed with Israel in October 1994 had no other rationale.

The king, who now received me in his palace in Amman, wished to speak about the possibilities of maintaining an agreement that he wanted, as I did, to be irreversible. He talked openly to me about his doubts and worries about the very continuation of the global peace process that had been forged over recent years. I replied that Jordan, which like France enjoyed good relations with all the parties concerned, was an irreplaceable asset in that regard. I added that his personal experience, moderation, and sense of compromise were qualities that would be more useful than ever in this new context. At the end of our interview, however, I wondered if his health would allow him to take on this ultimate challenge. I had not seen

King Hussein since August 1992, when we knew he was suffering from cancer of the kidney, for which he was operated on in an American clinic. The man seemed to be prematurely aged, far from that image of eternal youth that the portraits decorating all the public places of Jordan strove to perpetuate.

Beirut constituted the penultimate stage of my trip to the Middle East. I had already gone on an official visit there in April 1996, shortly before the Israelis launched their military operation against the Hezbollah stronghold in southern Lebanon. This second visit, of only twenty-four hours, was aimed primarily at demonstrating France's solidarity with and support for the Lebanese people in the new period of tensions it was undergoing.

Most of the Lebanese leaders I met confided that they had lost all hope of peace in the short term, believing that Benjamin Netanyahu's policy had led to an impasse. Their pessimism in this regard was all the greater because they were counting on the peace process to assist the vast project of rebuilding the country that their prime minister, Rafic Hariri, had masterminded.

Since his accession to power in October 1992, this businessman of jovial appearance had made his mark as a veritable statesman. Not without upsetting the traditional political milieu, he had, as a clever tactician, succeeded in uniting around him the multiple elements of a nation always quick to erupt into conflict because of its community divisions and power plays or under the influence of its powerful neighbors. While waiting to recover its independence and its sovereignty, Lebanon had found in Rafic Hariri the leader it had been lacking for so long, a modernizer who had put in the service of his country all the ambition and energy that had enabled him to build up his own commercial and financial empire.

As far as I recalled, we had met in Paris in the mid-1980s on the occasion of an exhibition on Saudi Arabia that Hariri, who, with the support of Crown Prince Fahd, had become one of the first entrepreneurs of the country, had been asked to organize. Hariri had come to present his project to me at the Hôtel de Ville, and we had quickly formed ties of friendship. I am not in the habit, in my day-to-day life, of socializing with heads of big companies, but I am particularly drawn to those who, coming from a background of nothing or almost nothing, have achieved success through their qualities of determination, intelligence, and drive. This was one of the reasons for my esteem and affection for Hariri and the indissoluble ties that were established between us and our respective families.

In terms of Lebanon, Hariri gave me a fairer and more complete vision of the social, religious, and cultural diversity out of which the real identity of this highly complex country arose. As a member of the Sunni community, he enabled me to better understand the need for France to take into account all attitudes, whether Christian or Muslim, and not just to gravitate toward those to whom it felt closest politically or spiritually. Hariri himself gave a fine example of tolerance before his accession to power by financing, through his own foundation, the studies of some 30,000 Lebanese students of all origins and faiths. He persuaded me to share this vision that he had of Lebanon.

On October 25, I stopped off at the Cairo airport to meet President Mubarak before returning to Paris. Several months after having laid down the foundations of France's new Arab and Mediterranean policy there, it was the Egyptian capital that I wanted to reserve as the last stop in this weeklong tour of the Middle East, the longest ever undertaken by a French president.

Hosni Mubarak had the great merit in my eyes of having upheld and pursued the peace process and openness with Israel that Anwar El Sadat had embarked on—a process that had become all the more difficult because it had to confront the rise of that radical Islamism of which his predecessor was the victim. At the same time, Egypt remained the only real support of Palestinians in the region. These were reasons enough for entente and concordance between our two countries, which had become, in a sense, much-needed intermediaries for the same cause and the same hope.

18
DISSOLUTION

For some time, an appalling atmosphere had set in within the government, mirroring a public opinion similarly overtaken by pessimism and gloom. Criticisms of the prime minister grew from all sides, despite the good results of his policies in spring 1996, particularly the reduction in the government deficit and the renewed rise in consumer activity. His detractors from his own camp gave him no quarter, some of them forgetting the disastrous financial situation he had inherited. The entry of four so-called Balladurien ministers into the government in the reshuffle of autumn 1995 was not nearly enough to appease the rancor, if not the hostility, of those who had still not forgiven us for the results of the presidential election. Philippe Séguin, president of the Parliament, was nursing a deep resentment at not having been appointed prime minister and began openly making life difficult for Alain Juppé, with the less and less disguised help of Gaullist members of Parliament. During our weekly meeting, he talked endlessly of his grievances against the prime minister. His continual desire to denigrate him exasperated me, although I could never get him to see reason. Finally, the sovereignists, led by Charles Pasqua, strove systematically to obstruct every one of our decisions on European policy. In short, everything indicated that the government no longer had the necessary political support to stay in power.

This situation was all the more worrying because we needed a stable, coherent parliamentary majority to implement the reforms we had undertaken, to pursue the policy of cleaning up public finances, and to keep our European commitments that would enable France to qualify for the single currency. Instead of which, a climate of rebellion and discord was being propagated through the ranks, restricting the government's room to maneuver. Contested by his peers, the prime minister saw his credit still further eroded with a public already plagued by doubt and worry.

The hopes for change that my election had raised had given way to a growing incomprehension among the French of the policies we had carried out and to a disappointment that was increasingly reflected in the opinion polls. Doubtless because we had been unable to explain the reasons and necessity for it, the austerity regime appeared to be the negation or even repudiation of my campaign promises to reduce the social fracture.

The launch of the initiative-employment contract, to combat long-term unemployment; the immediate increase in the minimum wage, the largest in fourteen years; the rescue of the national health insurance to the benefit of the most underprivileged: None of these was seen as a positive reform. The same was true of the powerful and totally innovative measures in regard to housing, through the creation of a zero-rate loan and the first action plan in regard to troubled areas that resulted in a relaunch package for cities and the law of November 1996 introducing urban free zones.

So many major reforms went almost unnoticed at the time or were eclipsed by those, more unpopular even though essential, that aimed at improving public finances. To the wind of dissent they had provoked were added the problems generated by the emergence of scandals in regard to the running of the Paris city hall, unleashed and exploited by certain members of the former government team to undermine the image of the new executive in the public eye.

No doubt we had made the mistake of excessive intransigence and haste in our determination to make up for accumulated delays in too many areas. The French expect immediate results from their governments but do not like to be rushed. We had not taken sufficient account of this contradictory aspect of our national character.

Some also accused the prime minister of a personal style that was too stiff and peremptory. It was true that Juppé could sometimes lack flexibility and openness in the exercise of power, which had led me to give him the friendly advice that he should be in less of a hurry when he shook people's hands, for example: "You don't look people in the eyes enough. You don't take the time. You have to know how to take your time." Occasionally I would call his parents, whom I knew well, to say to them: "Alain is not eating enough, he is really too thin!" To help with the problem, when I had the opportunity I would invite him to the best restaurants in the capital. At other times, conscious of the load weighing on his shoulders, I would telephone his principal private secretary to ask him to make sure that his boss's diary was not overfull.

That said, the image of the prime minister was not the only factor in the increasingly negative public opinion of us. I was also not spared, as evidenced in the fall in my own popularity. I was accused of being too removed from the real problems that concerned the French, of neglecting the commitments I had made to them, of abandoning the domestic scene in favor of global affairs—of preferring, in short, to mix with the big boys of the world rather than with my compatriots. A criticism that was naturally taken up, once again, by a considerable portion of the members of Parliament who were supposed to support us.

In my televised speech of July 14, 1996, when both the economic and employment situations were again deteriorating, I nonetheless strove to restore a climate of confidence to the country. After acknowledging the "profound anxiety" that was undermining the morale of the French, I urged my compatriots to rediscover "the spirit of conquest" that they had often displayed in the past. In regard to my frequent trips abroad, I underlined that they had had fruitful consequences for our economy with more than 100,000 jobs created entirely thanks to contracts concluded through my personal involvement. I confirmed my ambition to "get France moving again" while acknowledging that we needed "a little time to get things back on track." As for the government representatives, I made it clear to them that they would do well to demonstrate "a little more dynamism and optimism" and that their role was also to explain, to mobilize themselves, and to "set an example."

All to no avail. In September, the prime minister was confronted with a renewed barrage of criticism. A member of our own party thought it a good idea to appeal to his colleagues to cultivate their "difference." Juppé, clearly disheartened, told me it was time to bring order back to the government and asked me to speak with the president of the group in the National Assembly to this end. I immediately did so, but without, it seemed, great effect.

Shortly afterward, Juppé spoke candidly to me at one of our customary meetings before the Council of Ministers of his profound weariness and his desire to pass on the baton. "I've had enough, I can't take any more," he confided in me. "The economic situation is not improving and the political situation is just as alarming. I am so unpopular that it will eventually spill over onto you. I think the time has come for a change of prime minister. That is the only way you can embark on winning back public opinion. You need," he concluded, "another horse to hope to win the general election in 1998." I replied that this was out of the question and that I had no intention of appointing a new government leader: "That's not my concept of things. For me, a prime minister should accompany the president for the duration of his mandate, or at least for as long as possible. This was the case with Georges Pompidou and General de Gaulle, and France could only congratulate itself on the excellent relationship they enjoyed for six years. I want you to stay at my side!"

Juppé agreed to remain in his post, but the question of coming up with a powerful political gesture that would allow us to recover was still an urgent one. It was then that the idea began to form, initially without my knowledge, of calling the general election early—in short, of dissolving Parliament. When all was said and done, was it not the best solution to give the people their say once more? Could the government continue to act without a majority fully in agreement with the former's decisions? Was now not the time to do what I should doubtless have done immediately after my election in the interest of the country and despite my commitment not to dissolve Parliament? This debate would stir up some in my entourage as well as a growing number of members of Parliament.

When I was asked, in my television appearance on July 14, about the possibility of a dissolution of government, I replied that this should be used not "for the convenience of the president" but to "resolve a political crisis"—the existence of which I denied at that time. Several months later, I was forced to concede, as were most observers, that this political crisis had indeed become a reality, so severe had the climate between the government and the majority party become, although I was still not yet in favor of the idea of dissolving the National Assembly.

Who was the creator or the initiator of the idea? That was the question that has often been asked. I am not going to designate the likely suspect here, for if an error was made, I am solely responsible for it. The idea of dissolution has been unjustly attributed to the secretary general of the Élysée alone. In reality, launched and promoted by various leaders of the majority party, it had been in the air since the autumn of 1996, when Dominique de Villepin had come to speak to me, at the start of the following year, about this way of getting out of the political impasse in which we found ourselves. He then enumerated all the sources of support for it within Parliament and said that as far as he was concerned, it was the only option that could be envisaged. Other than a change of prime minister, which, as he knew, I refused to do. He told me that he had had several discussions on the subject with Juppé's principal private secretary and that they had both concluded that it was impossible to govern the country in such conditions until the elections of 1998, when the majority party was bound to lose, given its state of collapse. Only an early election could, according to them, allow us to avoid electoral disaster. Villepin therefore declared himself in favor of dissolution. My first reaction was, however, negative.

When the prime minister, who had clearly been persuaded by his principal advisor, came to speak to me in his turn, at the beginning of 1997, I gave him the same refusal: "It's pure madness. People will not understand." But from then on, I started to question myself about the advantages and disadvantages of renewing the National Assembly before the planned time. I remember a conversation, one Sunday afternoon, about this with Jean-Louis Debré, whom I wanted to consult as minister of the interior. I told him about my reservations, and I did not sense that he was any more enthusiastic. But his analysis seemed to me realistic: "It is obvious," he said to me, "that we risk losing a great many members of Parliament, since the state of grace is over. We are in the midst of a crisis, people are striking, the polls aren't good. But it will doubtless be worse next year. Early elections will have the advantage of taking the left by surprise. The government will probably be brought back, but with a reduced majority." Neither he nor I took sufficient account, at that moment, of the possibility that the National Front would continue into the second round, to our detriment, in a large number of constituencies—yet it was that factor alone that would make the difference several months later. My first mistake was to have underestimated it.

Many of the members of Parliament who marched into my office wanted to talk about only one thing: a dissolution, as quickly as possible. Their pressure increased from February 1997. Rare were those who put me on my guard against it or who openly condemned it; most representatives and many ministers declared themselves in favor, urging me to act quickly. To that was added the polls taken on the ground, in large administrative areas that were of differing political opinions. I consulted my own networks, as did Juppé. The conclusions that emerged from these various contacts were somewhat reassuring; our losses would, it seemed, be marginal. There was therefore little risk in going before the electorate. Less, at any rate, than I might have feared. . . .

In March 1997, given all these elements, I finally allowed myself to be persuaded in favor of dissolution. Above all, I saw it as a possibility of bringing the new Juppé government a fresh wind, to "relegitimize" it, in a sense, enabling it both to benefit from a recharged government and to have the time necessary to make decisions. After having widely consulted and long hesitated, I finally came to think it was the right solution. It remained to be seen whether the electorate would offer us a second chance.

On April 21, when I was getting ready to announce to the French that evening that the Assembly was to be dissolved, I telephoned Jean-Louis Debré, who was away in Strasbourg. After informing him of my final decision, I asked him about the last electoral forecasts gathered by his services. He confirmed the probability that we would win "but narrowly," this time emphasizing the only unknown element of the vote: the result of the National Front and the transfer of its votes on the second round. I sensed that Jean-Louis was suddenly less confident than before and even more worried than he dared admit to me. But the die was cast, and there was no question for me of retreating now.

In my television address, I talked of "the interest of the country" to justify my decision. "I have become convinced," I said, "that we must give the people their say, so that they can pronounce clearly on the scope and the rhythm of the changes to be undertaken over the next five years." I talked about the thoroughgoing reforms that were under way, in terms of social protection, the armed services and national service, higher education, fiscal prudence, and those that we still had to carry out concerning our educational system and justice. I also felt it important to remind people of the next great steps in the construction of Europe: the changeover to a single currency, vital if our continent wanted to assert itself as a major economic and political power; the reform of institutions to make them more democratic, the ambition to make Europe into a living social model. In addition to all that, I proposed to the French people that we "follow another path" that expressed more "the ideal of our republic": that of "increased social cohesion," "a modernized political life," and a France that was "at ease" and "respectful of each person's commitments."

The speech over, however, I was not pleased with it, feeling I had not been able to find the right words to convince my compatriots. Would this "other choice" and "new spirit" that I had talked about be enough to win their support? Should I not have made more of what was at stake in this election by emphasizing our European commitments more? And what sense would the French make of the fact that I wanted to renew a government when I had just praised their loyalty? Would they not have the feeling, in short, that the true political reasons for this dissolution were being hidden from them?

Indeed, as I had suspected, my message did not get through effectively. The public reaction was mixed, not to say negative. At the same time, the enthusiasm of the members of Parliament who had been most in favor of an early dissolution began to wane. The people in charge of organizing the campaign nationally could not manage to agree. Debré, who attended several of their meetings, emerged from them distraught. "Around the table," he reported to me, "are Balladurians, Séguinists, and friends of Juppé, and all these people are arguing. You can't hear a thing and no one is on the same wavelength. An electoral campaign can only work if there is a boss—but this is just a little private club of egos, vengeances, and hidden agendas."

Should I get more involved, take over as head of operations myself? Whether I liked it or not, my role dictated that I keep out of the fray. It is not appropriate for the president of the republic to become a party leader once more, even if it was the one from which he had emerged. It was not his role. Having decided, what is more, to keep Alain Juppé as prime minister, I had no other choice than to let him occupy the front line while making sure I called him daily to offer him support and encouragement.

On October 25, at the end of an overly long campaign that had allowed the opposition to unite and to assert itself while the majority party offered a spectacle of disorder and confusion, the results of the first round resulted in a crushing rejection of the latter. Right and center combined attracted barely 36 percent of the votes cast, the left 42 percent, and the National Front approaching 15 percent. Our fate was virtually sealed, since no alliance with the National Front could be envisaged.

That evening I met with my principal advisors, in the presence of the prime minister. Each one outlined the scope of the impending disaster if nothing was done to try to limit its effects, since it could not be totally avoided, as Juppé was the first to realize. Taking note of the situation with his customary dignity, he informed me of his intention to leave Matignon, whatever happened, the day after the second round.

We met again the following morning in my office, with Villepin in attendance. It was a difficult moment both for Juppé and for me, convinced as I still was that I had in him the best of prime ministers. Yet probably no other solution had a hope of winning other than the one he himself proposed. I unwillingly backed it, deep down already rather resigned to the probability of a defeat that Juppé's withdrawal, announced between the two rounds, would doubtless make more likely. Was it not to acknowledge in advance our mutual failure?

Calling on Philippe Séguin as the figurehead of our second-round campaign and possible successor of Alain Juppé ultimately turned out to be just as counterproductive. The National Front had decided to keep its candidates in almost eighty constituencies, so the fate of the election was now in no doubt. From then on, it would be futile to resign myself, as General de Gaulle did in April 1969, to the result that we all know about. That would be to run the risk of adding a political crisis to that already provoked by this failed dissolution. The institutions of which I was the guarantor did not in any way impose this decision on me.

On June 1, 1997, the parties of the left won the election with 320 members of Parliament, as opposed to 256 for those of the previous majority and 1 single member for the National Front. A decisive result. Deep down, I was not surprised. I had even had time, in a sense, to prepare myself for it—although that did not mean I rejoiced in the prospect of another cohabitation. Far from it.

Considering myself solely responsible for the dissolution and its failure, I refused to pick out any scapegoat who would give me a clear conscience or serve to appease my entourage. There was no lack, however, of people who urged me from all sides to immediately cut myself off from the man who was instantly designated as the evil genius, the fatal instigator of an operation that had gone so wrong. An advisor who was supposed to exercise such an overwhelming influence over me that I became virtually incapable of resisting him. . . .

Now that was not the true story behind the dissolution, and even less that of my relationship with Dominique de Villepin, who was obviously the man in question. If we needed to know who could have inspired such an unfortunate decision, let us say that this error of judgment was at the least a collective one. Villepin played his part in it, like so many others who, after the event, made sure they discreetly disappeared. However, it was incumbent on me alone, as president, to decide who was to blame.

And so when the secretary general of the Élysée, knowing he was incriminated by all and sundry, came to me on the day after this defeat to present me with his resignation, I saw no reason to accept it. He and I had other challenges to tackle together.

19

HOME AND ABROAD

What I knew of cohabitation I had learned first from François Mitterrand and then from my own experience. The former had revealed to me its vices and virtues, subtle games, and advantageous constraints. The latter had enlightened me as to the particular functioning of this two-headed power and enabled me to realize all its complexity.

I therefore did not feel unequipped to share power, this time as president, with a prime minister whose role I had previously occupied in a similar situation. Determined to abdicate none of my prerogatives, I also intended to let the new head of government fully enjoy his own powers under the strict framework of our constitution, which clearly conferred an irrefutable preeminence on the president.

Although he has the free choice of prime minister, the practice of cohabitation requires that the president of the republic call on the leader of the majority party to fill the role, unless the latter decides, as I did in 1993, to give way to one of his colleagues. The day after the election, I telephoned Lionel Jospin to confirm my intention to appoint him to Matignon. The leader of the Socialist Party did not seem surprised. We arranged to meet at the Élysée at the end of the morning.

I did not have the same personal relationship with Jospin that I enjoyed with other personalities of the left, such as Michel Rocard. We barely knew each other. He had been my opponent during the previous presidential election, and our televised debate, between the two rounds, had been as courteous as it was restrained. I congratulated him warmly when he arrived at the Élysée. He thanked me, with a rather tense air and with a cold smile, remaining on his guard—as he would give me the impression of doing during all our subsequent meetings. Doubtless he expected to find me rather bitter and disillusioned after having experienced such an electoral setback. But I am not a man who dwells on my failures. I took stock of what had just happened without overdramatizing it, changes in power being a frequent occurrence in our democratic life. Paradoxically, it was the man who had won out on this occasion who seemed the most strained in this first interview.

We had no difficulty in agreeing on the rules of cohabitation, the division of powers, and the recognition of those powers specific to the president in terms of defense and foreign policy. I insisted on one of the central conditions of our future relationship: the respect of our European commitments so that the aim of creating a single currency could be fulfilled. I knew the new prime minister was somewhat hesitant on this subject, but he assured me that he was determined to advance in the same direction as me. Then we agreed to meet again as soon as possible to examine together the composition of the future government team. Its appointment remains the exclusive responsibility of the president, but in a period of cohabitation, the president of the republic is particularly attentive to the choice of the two ministers whose functions touch on his reserved area.

When the prime minister came to submit to me, over the following days, the list of the members of his government, I asked him for a brief period of reflection before approving the appointment of Alain Richard as minister of defense—time, in fact, to find out about a man whom I barely knew. I did, however, declare myself immediately in favor of the choice of Hubert Védrine at foreign affairs. "One of the few positive things about this catastrophe is that you are there," I joked to him in our first meeting. No one seemed better qualified to me than the former diplomatic advisor to President Mitterrand, even if my friend Michel Rocard had discreetly applied to me for the post, which was not in my prerogative to give him.

For the rest, I posed no objection to the appointment of Jean-Pierre Chevènement as minister of the interior, Martine Aubry at social affairs, Dominique Strauss-Kahn at economy, Jack Lang at culture, Claude Allègre at national education, or Pierre Moscovici at European affairs. I liked some of them and waited to see the others at work before forming an opinion. In any event, I immediately committed to working with them all on good terms and to creating a courteous and harmonious relationship with them.

On June 17, I attended the European Council meeting in Amsterdam, accompanied by Jospin and Moscovici. We needed to prove, to our partners and particularly the German chancellor, that France was capable of speaking with a single voice to ratify the stability pact provided for in the Maastricht agreements. Despite the fierce criticisms that he had made of it during the electoral campaign, Jospin could not oppose it without bringing into question the planned schedule for the implementation of the single currency and imposing a considerable delay in this regard on the rest of Europe. A negative attitude would also be contrary to the work undertaken by Mitterrand in this area. The prime minister strove to place other conditions on the adoption of the stability pact but eventually, doubtless unwillingly, agreed with France's commitments.

Still a novice in the area, the minister for European affairs made a declaration at this meeting that was clumsy, to say the least. He asserted that France would decide whether to "move to the euro" in light of its public finances. One could not have done more to give our partners the feeling that the French government engaged in doublespeak. Observing the embarrassment of the young minister after this gaffe, which the Matignon spokesperson immediately tried to soothe, I came to his rescue and offered him several words of encouragement: "Never mind," I said, "you will make others!"

I had no difficulty agreeing with Hubert Védrine and Dominique Strauss-Kahn, during the G7 summit held in Denver in the third week of June, that we should express in a coherent and united manner France's concerns about climate change and our common rejection of "all liberalism" as an economic model. This brief trip to the United States served only to confirm the great human and professional qualities of Védrine. It also allowed me to discover in Strauss-Kahn a man of character and convictions, pragmatic in his judgments and already experienced enough to be conscious of the international realities that did not seem vital to most French political leaders.

In short, the most strained, not to say difficult, relationship was the one I had from the start with Lionel Jospin. "Cohabition is not fusion," he had warned me during one of our first public appearances, to prevent any form of complicity between us. "Nor is it fission," I retorted, without seeking to offend him. He made no effort to hide his suspicion toward me and clearly did not like me much. For my part, I tried to break the ice a little and ensure that our collaboration be as amicable as possible. It is not in my nature to be gratuitously unpleasant to my fellow politicians. But the truth in this particular case was that I was dealing with a person whose style and language seemed to me totally foreign. I felt I had nothing in common with a leader whose intellectual rigidity, black-and-white vision of society, and antagonistic concept of political relationships governed his behavior as well as his thinking—yet whose actions I could not predict. We were far from the finesse and subtlety of Mitterrand, who knew all about the complexity of human beings and knew well how to make light of political differences.

Faced with a prime minister who had all the advantages in terms of the media and parliament and who mastered most of the inner workings of political power, my own strength lay in the full and complete assertion of the institutional primacy over which he could not exercise any hold. I had only to continue to occupy my office, naturally, serenely, and in a sense physically, for my superior position in the hierarchy to impose itself on him. The all-powerfulness that he could display in public and in the carrying out of parliamentary affairs faded away the moment he entered the Élysée enclosure, where he found himself not in a position of inferiority but in his natural position in a role secondary to the president.

I observed this change of attitude in his custom of meticulously transcribing what I said to him during our weekly meetings. While I spoke, the prime minister usually applied himself to setting down the least of my words. He was not far from asking me to repeat what I had just said so as to be sure he had missed nothing. I pretended to notice nothing while secretly enjoying watching what he was doing. Of course, the prime minister was not scrupulously noting down my opinions just so that he could take greater note of them; it was above all a way for him to prepare himself on each of the subjects that were later likely to divide us.

The first clash occurred shortly after my televised address of July 14 in which I spoke of my wish for a "constructive cohabitation," on condition, of course, that the division of roles defined by the constitution be respected. I also reiterated that the constitution conferred a sort of "preeminence" on the president of the republic, giving him, in short, the "last word" on "everything that touched on France's place in the world" and on "European Union law" as well as on anything that touched on modernization and the "balance of our society." In addition, I spoke of that other characteristic of our institutions: "presidential time," which gave the incumbent, less involved in daily management particularly in a period of cohabitation, the freedom needed for "a certain reflection about the evolution of the world." Nothing in itself very original or controversial.

Two days later, Jospin abruptly cornered me in the weekly meeting of the Council of Ministers. After giving us a lecture on articles 5 and 20 of the constitution, he declared that I did not have the right to claim to have the "last word," a phrase that had clearly shocked him. He nonetheless wished to reassure me: I would always have the possibility, as a "man of politics," to "give an opinion" on the activities of his government. He could not have been more conciliatory.

At the time, I pretended not to pay attention to this astonishing call to order. Then, after the meeting, I made it publicly known through the Élysée spokesperson that I had every intention of continuing to tell the French, when I judged it useful, what I thought on the great questions that concerned the country's future.

Another subject of discord then arose: the new government's budgetary plans. The new team planned to implement new taxes immediately, primarily affecting companies and the middle classes. As often with Socialist leaders, they would end up taxing the economy and giving free rein to public expenditure. I addressed a warning on this subject to the prime minister while also expressing my concern to him about the large cuts that ministers intended to effect in the defense budget, at the risk of undermining future military programs.

In October 1997, I could only bemoan the fact that the Jospin government was, despite the reservations I had expressed, continuing to go down the wrong path. The government-assisted "youth employment" work contract, the so-called social modernization law aimed at complicating the layoff process, and finally the announcement of the reduction of the working week to thirty-five hours, promulgated without consultation . . . all popularity-seeking and erroneous measures that obliged me to emerge from the silence I had chosen to observe since the summer.

It was in regard to the thirty-five-hour workweek, a project strongly rejected by employers but also challenged, in veiled terms, by eminent Socialist figures, that my reaction was the most anticipated. On October 16, a long-planned visit to Clermont Ferrand to inaugurate a trade show for European company heads gave me the opportunity. I am obviously in favor of flexible working hours, conscious that this forms part of the evolution of society and is part of the legitimate aspirations of a great many citizens—but not in the violent and sudden manner that this had just been imposed on unions and management. I made an official declaration of my regret about the total absence of dialogue in the matter and asked the government to be sure that "the natural desire to work less is compatible with the good health of companies." In addition, I also called for the possibility of case-by-case negotiation within companies.

A veritable psychodrama was provoked by the memorandum on employment policy that I made public, before the icy glare of the prime minister, during a European summit held at Luxembourg on November 20. In this document, I denounced—not having been listened to on the subject—the "mirage of risky experiments" that were likely to impede the fight against unemployment. This earned me an immediate riposte from the prime minister, who did not hesitate to make ironic reference to another "risky" experiment—that, of course, of the dissolution. For all that, it was no less true that the reform of thirty-five hours, much as it was appreciated at the time by some of its beneficiaries, was based on an economic chimera, as would quickly become obvious.

Contrary to the assertions of the minister in charge of the project, I did not believe that it would automatically create half a million jobs. I was even persuaded of the opposite, fearing that the thirty-five-hour workweek would prove more destructive than beneficial to our economy. That was what I meant by talking about "risky" experiments. Fourteen years later, this reform continues to be controversial, even among those who initiated it—proof that, if nothing else, it was undertaken in a somewhat hasty, un-thought-out manner.

These first clashes did not prevent me from trying to create, in the interests of the country, a cohabitation that was constructive. Doubtless I would find the means to do so less easily on the domestic scene, where political passions are always the most intense, than on international matters, where the "presidential time" for which the president was solely responsible was best expressed.

On January 25, 1998, France was guest of honor in New Delhi at the celebrations of the fiftieth anniversary of the independence of India. I was there, accompanied by several members of the government—Strauss-Kahn, Védrine, and Allègre—as well as a large delegation of company heads. It was the first state visit undertaken by a French president for nearly a decade to a country I had already visited, on Indira Gandhi's invitation, twenty-two years earlier when I was prime minister.

I had never lost my youthful love and passion for India, cradle of a five-thousand-year-old civilization that had never ceased to fascinate me. India, like China, was in my eyes one of the best illustrations of the permanence of the great cultures of the world and of all that they have given to humanity in terms of intelligence, knowledge, wisdom, and spirituality. For half a century, India had also given the example of a successful parliamentary democracy and an economy in full expansion; its impressive economic performance made it one of the giants of Asia.

India shared France's attachment to the humanist values that were at the basis of our respective political systems. We also had in common the refusal to accept an unjust world order, source of confrontations and ideological conflicts, and the constant aspiration for a redistribution of power on the international scene. However, our political relationship remained weak and our economic cooperation insufficient. It was this realization that persuaded me to engage India in a real strategic dialogue. India could no longer remain in the background in terms of our foreign policy. The second-largest country in terms of demographics and the fourth largest in terms of economic power needed to build an ambitious partnership, in every sector. This needed to become one of France's diplomatic priorities, alongside its relationship with China and Japan.

My official trip, which took me to Mumbai to meet important heads of Indian businesses, then Delhi where I had a long meeting with President Narayanan before meeting the interim Prime Minister Inder Kumar Gujral and the foremost political personalities of the country, took place at a time when India confronted a major problem in sustaining its development. Although it possessed its own nuclear arsenal, India was unable to satisfy its huge needs in terms of energy. The second-largest producer of nuclear energy in the world, France was without doubt one of the countries, along with the United States, that could give India the most efficient help to overcome this handicap. But all such cooperation with India came up against another difficulty, hitherto judged irresolvable: its refusal to submit to the rules set down by the international community since the adoption of the nuclear nonproliferation treaty. It was a situation all the more paradoxical because India was also one of the countries most committed to disarmament.

This impasse arose out of the ambiguous policy practiced by India since its acquisition of a nuclear program for pacific ends. Fulfilling its ambitions for regional power, in the shadow of China, and for status on the international scene, India gained all the prestige that the mastering of complex technologies, until then exclusively reserved for the West, conferred on it. At the same time, its condemnation of nuclear arms allowed it to keep the role as leader of the nonaligned countries that it had held since the creation of the movement. Rejected by the recognized nuclear powers, it was in all the better position to denounce their duplicity; but with the disappearance of a bipolar world, this strategy was no longer beneficial to India's interests, even if it still refused to adapt to the new realities of life post–cold war.

Other than the fact that the isolation of a country of more than 900 million inhabitants constitutes a potential factor for instability, India's situation is worrying because of the likely deterioration of its electronuclear stock. Cut off from western technological advances, there could be risks of accidents with consequences disastrous for the development of civilian nuclear energy, both in India and in the rest of the world. To this were added the harmful ecological effects of using polluting energies such as coal.

This problem was obviously at the heart of my meetings with the Indian leaders. I did not hide from them the fact that I had limited room to maneuver in doing what they hoped and helping them unblock an apparently irresolvable situation. Restricted by its commitments toward the international community, France could not envisage wide-scale cooperation in the immediate future. I am nonetheless persuaded that a French initiative needed be taken on the occasion of my visit to set in motion a dialogue with India that another big power might eventually, sooner or later, take over, with all the political as well as economic benefits from that. In short, we needed to seize the opportunity of taking an important role in a play that otherwise risked being performed without us.

This strategic partnership would assume its full scope in 2002 when I would ask my new diplomatic advisor, Maurice Gourdault-Montagne, to take personal charge of the issue. We would need several years of negotiation to reach the cooperation agreements concluded in February 2006 during my second official visit to New Delhi. During that period, while campaigning to international institutions for India to have a recognized special status, France helped Indian authorities overcome numerous obstacles to allow the development of an atomic energy for strictly civilian ends. For its part, although it remained a nonsignatory of the nonproliferation treaty, India agreed to separate its civilian and military nuclear activities and authorize visits to the country from International Atomic Energy Agency inspectors.

The strategic agreement that India and France were thus able to establish assumed, in my view, a decisive importance above and beyond its financial and industrial implications. Above all, it was for me a means of establishing the primary role that India, by reason of its history, democratic choices, attachment to secularism, coexistence of different peoples, languages, and cultures, was called on to play in the aim of creating a more equally balanced world.

In the plane taking us to Abidjan on December 7, 1997, I gave the speech I was preparing to give at the African AIDS conference organized under the auspices of the United Nations, to the secretary of state for health, Bernard Kouchner, to read. In it I advocated the implementation of a worldwide strategy to fight, in a more coordinated fashion, against this planetary epidemic that had already killed 2 million men, women, and children in Africa.

During the flight, I confided to Kouchner that I had not mentioned in my speech the international fund that I hoped would be created within the United Nations because the government had not yet been consulted to unlock the necessary funds. Kouchner was well placed to evaluate the extreme seriousness of the health situation on the African continent. He encouraged

me to sidestep the usual procedures and to bring forward the announcement of a French decision in this regard. Assured of his support, I therefore
took the initiative, on our arrival in the capital of the Ivory Coast, to launch
in the name of France a world aid organization to provide medical help,
begun with an initial donation of 150 million euros. Here was one of the
finest possible examples of a "constructive cohabitation"! All we had to do
was to obtain a similar commitment from the other big industrialized nations. I would not cease in my efforts to achieve this during successive G7
or G8 summits before deciding in 2003 to call on other means of finance
than public funding.

The message that I brought to Abidjan that December 7, 1997, was
that France refused to remain apathetic and silent before the human cata-
clysm created by AIDS. It was also a message of commitment and solidarity toward the most underprivileged peoples who faced the spread of a
plague that richer countries had greater means of controlling, since the
implementation of multidrug therapy. "We do not have the right," I said
at the opening of the conference, "to accept that there are now two ways
of fighting against AIDS: treating the sick in developing countries while
merely preventing contamination in the South."

It was not the first time that I had protested against the idea, so widespread and so carefully maintained, of a degenerate Africa in which nothing but sickness, famine, and the most deadly conflicts thrived. It was true
that a kind of curse seemed to weigh on the fate of this continent, where
in recent years we had seen so many massacres and tragedies one after the
other, as if caught in some appalling spiral, in Rwanda and Zaire, not to
mention Burundi, Liberia, and Angola. But another Africa also existed,
which was not just that of dictators and military coups that France and the
other powers have too often tolerated—when they have not encouraged
them—for their own political strategies and interests. An Africa that, here
and there, was progressing, as much in terms of democracy and development as in the management of its public affairs. An Africa that was advanc-
ing at its own rhythm in the midst of innumerable difficulties, but that was
far from the apocalyptic state that had become for the West an easy pretext
for disengagement or indifference.

One man embodied, with strength and authenticity, this Africa that
was still so vulnerable but that displayed exemplary dignity in the face
of trials and whom I knew was capable of taking on gigantic challenges:
Nelson Mandela, who had become the hero of a whole continent since he
had succeeded, through pacific means, in bringing an end to apartheid. In
June 1998, it was with infinite joy and emotion that I met him in Pretoria

on the occasion of my first official visit to South Africa, where I had refused to go as long as racial segregation held sway.

I had met Mandela on several occasions when I was mayor of Paris and he had come to visit President Mitterrand. His first trip abroad after his release from prison was to France in June 1990, in an act of recognition for a country that had always fought for his liberation. I had myself worked on his behalf in the early 1970s, by participating in the financing of his political organization, the ANC, at the request of the king of Morocco. Hassan II had put together a network with this aim, to which I had discreetly donated in a personal capacity at a time when the South African authorities were putting great pressure on French ministers to agree to visit the country. Certain of them had consented. I was among those who had already declined the invitation, having fixed the principle that I would not accept it until Mandela was recognized as both a man and a citizen.

On July 14, 1996, I welcomed Nelson Mandela to Paris on the occasion of his first state visit to France since his election to the presidency of the republic of South Africa. I recall very clearly the moment he entered the grounds of the Élysée Palace: Everyone was at the windows to watch his arrival, overwhelmed at seeing this man who looked like a prince and who had sacrificed thirty years of his life to his ideals. As I looked at him, I thought only of that long period of silence and confinement he had had to undergo. At the same time, I was impressed by the fact that that terrible trial had in no way visibly affected the great serenity that emanated from him. His love of laughter and of life had both remained, unquenchable. The head of state I welcomed was much more than that; he was also the universal symbol of truth, justice, and tolerance. Indeed, I could judge his exceptional prestige all the more clearly from the emotional, enthusiastic welcome he received from the Parisian crowd during the July 14 procession, then by the overwhelming fervor of the thousands of young people who surrounded him during the reception at the Élysée.

The previous day I had gone to see him at the chateau of Rambouillet, where he was staying. Our private meeting went on for almost two hours. Mandela confided in me that the only real friends he had found, since his accession to power, were in the third world, whereas he and his people also aspired to play in the "big boys' playground," whose members had disappointed him. He had been given a rather cool reception by the Germans, he was wary of the British, he expected nothing from the Russians, he had nothing but difficulties with the Americans and no relationship with China . . . How better to give me to understand that he expected much from France: political recognition, advice, and economic aid to his country?

After its constitution was adopted on May 8, 1996, and the departure from government—something the ANC had not wanted—of the national party of the former president, Frederik de Klerk, on June 30, South Africa had completed its transition to democracy. But this phase of normalization was accompanied by much trouble and uncertainty. The level of crime and of political violence remained too high. The economy suffered from a lack of foreign investment and high unemployment. Everything, or almost everything, remained to be done to eradicate the huge divide that separated Blacks from Whites. Mandela was counting on France to support his reconstruction plan, help him realize his reform of the educational system, and implement the free trade agreement between South Africa and the European Union. I promised him I would do all I could so that our country would become one of his main partners, particularly as France had already been the principal European contributor to the development of South Africa.

"My dear friend, how are you?" he asked me in English in his gravelly voice, two years later when I arrived in Pretoria. Welcoming me in front of the Union Buildings, the government headquarters, he gave me a warm embrace as I got out of the car. At nearly eighty years old, Mandela continued to rule South Africa with the same peaceful, imposing authority. He had lost none of his charm or humor, but his fatigue was perceptible and he was said to be worried about his succession. While I helped him up the stairs that led to his office, he talked to me about the soccer World Cup and his country's elimination by France. He said jokingly that he expected me to apologize. I replied that a manager of the South African soccer team had come to say to us after the match: "You see, we are gracious people. We knew that you were going to South Africa and we wanted to be nice to you!"

Then, after rejoicing in the good, cooperative relationship that had been established between our two countries, Mandela opened up, in his simple, direct style, one of the main subjects that preoccupied him: the ravages of AIDS in South Africa and the rest of the continent. "AIDS kills those whom our society needs to cultivate the land, to work in the mines and factories, to make the schools and hospitals function. It creates new pockets of poverty everywhere. Today, the freedom, health, and well-being of each nation depends closely on those of others. That is even more true now in terms of AIDS." He knew my own fight to try to curb this catastrophe, principally in Africa, and suggested that we unite our energies in order to mobilize the international community all the more effectively.

In the encomium I paid him during the official dinner given in my honor on June 26, 1998, I saluted in Mandela the just and exemplary man who had been able to give his people their freedom and their dignity without ever departing from a spirit of brotherhood and reconciliation.

The construction of Europe is a slow and difficult enterprise, punctuated with pitfalls and too often bogged down in onerous, tiresome procedures. It also has its share of unpredictability—that is part of its charm!

The Anglo–French summit held in St. Malo on December 3 and 4, 1998, figured among those rare moments in which an unexpected position taken by a single man can precipitate, in spectacular fashion, advances that one thought would be subject to the most laborious negotiations. While our ministers and colleagues had never been able to agree on the issue, after a long meeting I managed to convince Tony Blair, the new British prime minister, to agree to commit to the European defense project. Blair's decision to bring Britain into a project, as France had long hoped, that had already begun with Germany was a considerable surprise for all those who were used, or rather resigned, to the idea of a Great Britain that was permanently hostile to all such developments. I was all the more pleased because the setting up of an autonomous military force could not take place without the approval and active support of the only two powers that had the logistical means to do so: Great Britain and us.

This U-turn in British diplomacy also owed much to the determination and convictions of a young government leader who wanted his country to root itself firmly in modernity and who was apparently resolved to free himself of the "special relationship" long established with the United States. Breaking with the Thatcher Euro-skepticism that reflected the great majority of public opinion that was deeply convinced that everything decided in Brussels could only negate its interests, Blair displayed a genuine passion for Europe. He wanted Great Britain to become an active part of a political and economic process that it no longer had the means, he felt, to do without. In a personal capacity, he favored its joining the single currency, but he realized that that would doubtless be demanding too much of his compatriots, who would make him pay for it dearly at the polls. Launching the European defense policy alongside us was for Blair a way of accomplishing a useful task without taking too many electoral risks.

Even if our relations subsequently became more difficult, I have to say that I got on well with Blair from the time of his election as prime minister in May 1997 at forty-four years old, the age at which I too was occupying the same post for the first time. He immediately struck me as a spirited, charismatic, and dynamic leader who was determined, after eighteen years of Conservative rule, to satisfy a whole generation's hopes for change without delay. I liked his quick, direct, pugnacious style. Blair had an easy friendliness, demonstrating much ease and naturalness in all circumstances. This spontaneity was disingenuous, of course, and in no way free of calculation—but it allowed him to express another way of governing, in complete contrast to the rigid stiffness of his predecessors.

Blair had another asset in my eyes. He loved France and, what was more, knew and appreciated the French character. I was touched by the fact that he had chosen our country as the location for his first vacation as government leader, in August 1997. During a telephone conversation at that time, he said he had wanted to highlight the new direction that Britain was taking in terms of European policy, which for him meant "a strengthening of the relationship with France" in every sector, principally that of security. These were the beginnings of our agreement at St. Malo at the end of the following year, a real turning point in the construction of a European defense force, an idea that until then had remained only embryonic.

The declared and defined objects set out in this summit were clear and unambiguous. We were equipping Europe with an autonomous defense capacity, relying on credible military forces that could be mobilized at a moment's notice to confront, in the terms of our joint communiqué, "factors of instability occurring on our continent or at its periphery." What I had advocated within the Atlantic Alliance, if nothing better had been forthcoming, now found an obviously more satisfying expression thanks to this unexpected Anglo–French agreement.

The decision to create a defense organization separate from NATO was not a contradictory position for France; the country had demonstrated a desire for independence for more than thirty years. It placed Great Britain, however, in a much more complex situation, particularly since Blair seemed to have taken his decision without consulting his American allies. The reaction of the United States would not be slow in coming, and it immediately saw in the St. Malo agreements "seeds of tension" between itself and the European Union. When I asked him in February 1999 what he thought of the Anglo–French initiative, Bill Clinton was careful to minimize its impact. He declared to me that he fully supported the collaboration between France and Britain while emphasizing that it must operate within the framework of NATO. He nonetheless conceded, during the fiftieth anniversary of NATO in April of that year, that the final statement issued at the NATO summit recognized that a European defense force could be useful to all concerned by it.

The crisis of Kosovo was one that an autonomous intervention force should have been able to resolve by itself, without necessarily having recourse to NATO. But we would have to wait for the European summits of Cologne and Helsinki, in June and December 1999, for the governments of the European Union to agree to equip themselves with a military capacity that would allow them to see through such operations alone. In the immediate term and despite the reservations of the U.S. administration, unwilling to reengage itself in this area, only NATO action could bring to an end the new ethnic cleansing operation launched by Milošević against Kosovo, barely three years after the end of the Bosnian conflict.

Everything had begun in 1989 when Serbia, which considered Kosovo an inseparable part of the Yugloslav federation, decided under Milošević's impetus to unilaterally withdraw the region's autonomous status. A resistance movement immediately formed, at first pacific but then increasingly violent until transforming, from 1996, into a full-blown war of independence. Milošević sent his troops into the province to try to tame the rebellion with a bloody repression. After his failure in Bosnia-Herzegovina, the loss of Kosovo would sound the death knell for his project of Greater Serbia. Hundreds of thousands of Muslim Kosovars of Albanian origin were killed or deported in the goal of radically modifying the demographic balance of the region in favor of the Serb minority. Engaged on a terrifying collision course to impose his plans and maintain himself in power, the intransigent Milošević relied yet again on the passivity or disunity of the international community.

A first proposal to resolve the conflict, presented by France and Germany in November 1997, did not succeed. The following year, in the face of the atrocities committed by Milošević's men, Great Britain set about increasing American awareness of this new humanitarian crisis. From my side, I invited Russia to put pressure on its Serbian ally to reach a long-overdue political agreement. In March 1998, the contact group, composed of France, Great Britain, Germany, Russia, and the United States, decided on sanctions against Serbia and issued an ultimatum to its leaders. Simultaneously, the UN Security Council voted a resolution putting an embargo on arms destined for the former Yugoslavia.

When, two months later, I welcomed to Paris the president of the Democratic League of Kosovo, Ibrahim Rugova, nicknamed the Gandhi of the Balkans because of his nonviolent resistance—a choice increasingly challenged by the radical wing of Kosovars—he did not hide the fact that the situation on the ground had become a tragedy after a new Serbian offensive. He told me how the repression had continually intensified after Milošević had ordered the closing of the "border" between Serbia and Kosovo on May 15, cutting short a negotiation that he had seemed to open that same day when they had met in Belgrade. Given the Serbs' military superiority and the intensified ethnic cleansing on which they had embarked, Rugova saw no other way out than direct intervention by NATO forces.

I replied that France was determined to adopt the same position of firmness toward Milošević as it had demonstrated in regard to Bosnia. But I also insisted on our adherence to two principles: a step-by-step approach that meant that the recourse to the use of the threat was credible, and political control, which in our view implied that all NATO action be approved and in a sense legitimized by Security Council mandate. In short, everything should be done to ensure that possible military intervention be based on a legal foundation. In this we differed from the American position. While most of our European partners also thought that authorization from the United Nations was necessary, the United States considered that such an agreement, while desirable, was not essential. It was precisely the same debate that would divide us five years later on the Iraqi affair.

Before getting to the stage of a military show of strength, France advocated doing as much as possible to achieve a negotiated settlement. A double policy of deterrence was put in place: diplomatic via the contact group and the Security Council, and military via NATO and the threat of air strikes on the Serbian positions. It was the former that would predominate for several months, until Milošević's intransigence justified the recourse to arms.

On September 12, 1998, the United Nations adopted Resolution 1199 demanding the resumption of dialogue between the warring parties. On October 13, NATO addressed a new ultimatum to the Serbian authorities, enjoining them to withdraw their forces from Kosovo and open negotiations with the Albanians. This twin pressure resulted, the next day, in the signing of a temporary agreement on a cessation to Serbia's operations and the return of refugees, whose safety was guaranteed. Far from ceasing, however, Milošević's crimes only intensified over the following weeks until the massacre, in mid-January 1999, of forty-five civilians in the little village of Račak. Faced with slaughter on such a scale, I decided to mobilize the international community in an ultimate diplomatic "forcing" in order to make Milošević understand that the threshold of tolerance had been exceeded and that signing a peace agreement was his last chance. On our initiative, a conference on Kosovo was organized in Rambouillet under French and British copresidency, Tony Blair proving as determined as I was to put an end to the Serbian leader's murderous folly.

Taking the floor at the opening session on February 6, I firmly exhorted the Serbian and Albanian representatives to find common ground between them and to seize this last chance of reconciliation before a more radical solution was imposed on them. After extremely hard negotiations, a partial agreement in principle was concluded on February 23. It set out the political framework for the future autonomy of Kosovo. But the second meeting organized in Paris from March 15 to 18 ended in failure. The Serbians refused to sign a document—which the Kosovars had already signed—that provided for a NATO contingent to ensure its implementation. Faced with this failure, NATO had to resolve to intervene to put a stop to the exactions and the ethnic cleansing in Kosovo and order air strikes on Serbia on March 24.

I immediately informed the French of the reasons why we were taking part in this operation, in a television address filmed at the venue of the European Council meeting being held in Berlin:

> *I wish to explain why NATO is going to carry out military action against the Serbian forces of President Milošević. I want to explain why I have decided, in full agreement with the government, that the French air force will participate in this action with all the other members of the Atlantic Alliance.*
>
> *For too long, the Serbian authorities have behaved unacceptably toward the Albanians of Kosovo, who represent 90 percent of the population of that province. The swarms of refugees, the destruction of villages, the assassinations, the massacres, all bear witness to that. And it cannot be tolerated.*
>
> *What is at stake today is peace on our land, peace in Europe, and also, for us, human rights.*
>
> *Britain and France, in agreement with their European, American, and Russian partners, initiated a peace conference. It was held, as you know, in Rambouillet and tangible results were obtained:*
>
> - *The Kosovars accepted a substantial autonomy over their province; they also accepted that their armed forces hand over their weapons.*
> - *On the other hand, the Serbians who initially gave the impression they accepted the political agreement, rejected it for no reason, just as they rejected the presence in Kosovo of a military forced charged with ensuring that the agreements were properly respected by both parties.*
>
> *In addition, in violation of commitments he had already made, the Serbian president amassed 40,000 men and more than 300 tanks in the province or at its frontiers.*

Everything has been done to facilitate a reasonable and a peaceful solution that is in accordance with human rights. Everything. Faced with the unjustifiable and incomprehensible obstinacy of President Milošević, the allies unanimously decided that there was no other choice than to intervene militarily against precisely targeted Serbian objectives in order to contain a tragedy that is gradually threatening the stability of the whole of the Balkans.

Because it is a question of peace on our continent and of human rights on our continent, I know that Frenchwomen and Frenchmen will understand that we have to act.

I wish to emphasize here the total concordance of views that prevailed between the prime minister and myself in terms of the decision to intervene and of the implementation of our military engagement in Kosovo, just as we totally agreed on the need to keep open the possibility of a diplomatic solution until the very end. The only divergence was expressed by the minister of the interior, Jean-Pierre Chevènement, who questioned, at the Council of Ministers meeting on March 31, the moral foundation of the NATO intervention with which France had associated itself.

Russia had threatened to use its right of veto against the employment of force in Kosovo, thereby depriving us of all chance of obtaining an explicit UN mandate to accomplish a mission that was strictly humanitarian, in accordance with the Security Council's previous resolutions on Kosovo. From then on, the question of the legitimacy of such an operation was posed. I naturally questioned myself deeply on this subject, given my own concern to see the Security Council's rules respected in every circumstance. Ultimately, however, it seemed to me inconceivable that in case of an intervention aimed solely at imposing peace, our country could refrain from taking part in the defense of its own values, flouted by a criminal regime within the continent of Europe.

Contrary to what certain of our friends in the world seemed to believe, our decision to proceed to joint combat was in no way dictated by a concern to follow in the steps of the United States; rather, it was we who had had to convince them to join us. It was merely the continuation of our common commitment to impose a definitive peace in the former Yugoslavia. Our country was not limited merely to active contribution to the air strikes launched on March 24 against the Serbian military positions but was closely involved in the conduct of operations as part of an informal directorate consisting of the heads of state or of government of America, France, Britain, and Germany.

In seventy-nine days of operations, not a single air strike was carried out without the agreement of France. The other participating countries could, had they wished, have exercised the same control—but they preferred, for their own reasons, to delegate their powers. Many of the planned actions never took place, at our request. Very lively discussions took place between General Clark, who commanded the NATO forces, and General Kelche, French chief of the Defense Staff, about the bridges of Belgrade, an important national symbol for the Serbian population. I protested against their planned mass destruction and also ensured that Montenegro was spared as much as possible, particularly in terms of its port facilities. I would add that none of the seventeen blunders attributed to NATO came from the French air force, even though we were heavily committed with a hundred or so planes, making our country the foremost European contributor to the war in Kosovo.

We also played an equally influential role in scrapping a project that would have had dramatic consequences if it had gone ahead. Conceived and launched by Tony Blair, it consisted of reinforcing the aerial bombardment with troops on the ground, on the pretext that the former would not be sufficient to have an immediately deterrent effect on Milošević. The British prime minister, who continually put pressure on the other allied leaders to get his idea accepted, categorically rejected my arguments. I tried to explain to him, in vain, that a land offensive would only worsen the conflict by giving the Serbs, who were seasoned soldiers, the opportunity of fierce resistance and would lead the two sides into an endless war that would be enormously costly in terms of human lives. He would not listen and launched into a veritable crusade to achieve his ends. Despite the stated opposition of France and Germany and the obvious reservations of the White House, Tony Blair refused to let go, counting on getting Bill Clinton on his side with Gerhard Schröder and me then presumably following suit. Far from convincing the president of the United States, however, Blair only dissuaded him when he sent him a message in May advocating the dispatch of 150,000 men, half of them European, into the former Yugoslavia.

Such insistence was even less justified at that time because the air strikes were beginning to produce the desired results. Coming on top of France's efforts to involve Russia and the Security Council in reaching a diplomatic solution, the NATO action ended on June 10 with Milošević's capitulation and the effective withdrawal of Serbian forces from Kosovo. The province was placed under UN administration while the international community had to confront the immense task of organizing the reconstruction of the region and the return of a million Kosovar refugees. An extraordinary movement of solidarity had developed in France, and our country played a full part in this humanitarian action through the engagement of its soldiers in the peace force on the ground and thanks to the work carried out by the nongovernmental organizations.

Our primary goal of putting an end to the barbarous practices that had once again threatened our continent was about to be realized. During this period, I had regularly informed the French in almost weekly televised addresses of the precise reasons why our country was taking part in the bombardment of another European nation. This mission would not truly be accomplished until the day when all those responsible for the war crimes committed in the former Yugoslavia had appeared before the international court. During my trip to Sarajevo in April 1998, I had already given an unequivocal message to the Serbian representative in the collective presidency of Bosnia, seen as one of the last devotees of Radovan Karadžić: "I am personally very attached to the fate of the war criminals," I had told him. "They belong in the Hague and nowhere else. Otherwise, the various communities will continue to distrust each other and we will never succeed in building a lasting peace. . . . If they do not give themselves up, they will be arrested!" For me, that demand for justice and truth remained as important as ever a year later. For as long as I was in office, it would be a determining factor in France's position toward Serbia and its possible integration into the European Union—which was unacceptable in my view as long as the authors of the slaughter of Srebrenica had not been arrested and taken before the International Criminal Tribunal (ICT) to answer for their actions.

On an official visit to Belgrade, in December 2001, in the aftermath of the fall of Milošević and the creation of a democratic government in Serbia, I praised the courageous decision of the new leaders of the country to pass the former dictator on to the ICT. I also urged the Yugoslav people to carry out their duty of remembering the past, however burdensome and difficult that may be. "It is not a question of an attack on sovereignty," I explained, "but, at the dawn of the twenty-first century, of strengthening respect for human dignity, founded on a system of law that no one can escape."

I draw two other lessons from the Kosovo affair.

The first concerns the capacity of the European Union to respond effectively to crises directly affecting it. In my view, Europe should consider the provision of an autonomous defense system one of its foremost priorities. This was the thrust of the plan of action that I submitted to our partners during the European Council meeting in Cologne in June 1999. A Europe that gradually took on its own political and military responsibilities, as it was preparing to do economically with the single currency, could only be a decisive factor for international stability, peace, and cooperation.

The second lesson touches on the reasons for our military engagement within NATO, which were sometimes badly interpreted, whether in Moscow, Beijing, or certain Arab or Latin American countries, and the suggestion that we were giving up our own vision of the world in favor of unconditional support of the United States. I was able to see this lack of comprehension for myself during my meeting with Boris Yeltsin in Moscow in May 1999. The Russian leader, politically vulnerable in a country that was economically and financially depleted, had expressed to me with his habitual forcefulness the feeling of humiliation and wounded national pride that he and his compatriots had experienced at the NATO intervention. He feared that the affair would undermine his country's position with the countries of the West, symbolized by the recent signing of an agreement between NATO and Russia. Yeltsin had fortunately made the right strategic choice in refusing all military engagement alongside Serbia, even though Russian Communists and nationalists had clamored for it, and by pursuing a dialogue with the allies and France in particular. As for the presumed risk of a French alignment with American policy, I set about depicting the reality to him: It was the Europeans who had brought the United States into Kosovo, not the other way around, and I intended to carry on underlining the fundamental role of the UN in international relations.

This was the same reassuring language that I planned on using with the Chinese leaders, who were all the more indignant about NATO's role in Kosovo because their embassy in Belgrade had been accidentally bombed. The visit to France in autumn 1999 of the president of the People's Republic of China, Jiang Zemin, was the opportunity for me to do so.

Three years earlier, I had begun the first leg of my first presidential trip to the Far East in Singapore. I wanted to pay homage to one of the greatest leaders of our time, Lee Kuan Yew, a sage and visionary who had made his city-state into a laboratory of Asian modernity. A longtime friend, Lee came to Paris shortly after my election, when France had the presidency of the European Union, to suggest that we organize together the first History Summit of our two continents. We immediately combined our efforts to realize this great idea of his, and it was decided that the first Asia–Europe meeting was to be held in Thailand in February 1996 after my visit to Singapore. I took advantage of this exceptional occasion to call for the creation of a real strategic agreement between world regions that I believed destined to get along with and understand each other. This would be the objective of the new French policy toward Asia that I wanted to put in place, a policy that also involved increased cooperation with Japan and a more ambitious relationship with China.

It was in fact Lee who had first alerted me to the fact that the West underestimated China's increasing power and that no western country had yet adopted a coherent strategy toward it. "Washington hesitates, Moscow is selling arms to Beijing for short-term profit, Tokyo is paralyzed, and the Europeans are absent," he said to me before suggesting that the Chinese question be added to the agenda of the G7 meeting in Lyon in June 1996. This was done.

In May the following year, shortly before the first round of the anticipated general election, I went on an official trip to Beijing, where Chinese leaders gave me an immensely warm and solicitous welcome, saluting me as a real friend of their country. Jiang Zemin, for his part, presented himself as an admirer of French culture—just like all his people. He told me that he had learned *La Marseillaise* when he was at secondary school and that his teachers, during the war against Japan, had made him read Alphonse Daudet as well as the novels of Victor Hugo. Later, the works of Alexandre Dumas—he particularly liked *The Count of Monte Cristo*—and of Romain Rolland had contributed to his education. Jiang gave me a gift of an eighth-century Chinese poem, which he said he had personally dedicated to me in calligraphy. In return, I gave him a unique document: the hiring paper of a worker named Deng Xiaoping at the Schneider factories in Creusot in the 1920s. A global partnership agreement was signed in Beijing on May 16, 1997, at the end of my visit.

During my fruitful exchanges with Chinese leaders, I had in no way brushed over the sensitive subjects of human rights and of Tibet. But, as always, I preferred to broach them in small meetings and far from all media attention, convinced that it would serve no purpose to lecture the Chinese in public on these issues or try to make them feel guilty, as the other western powers had done without great success. Far from seeming shocked or upset, Jiang displayed an openness of mind, particularly in terms of Tibet, that allowed me to think that the beginnings of dialogue between the two parties might be possible. On condition, of course, that one recognized, as France had always done, that Tibet was an integral part of Chinese territory. Having known the Dalai Lama for a long time, I proposed to Jiang that I act as intermediary.

Eighteen months later, in November 1998, I wrote to Jiang—having forgotten nothing of what he had said to me about Tibet—to tell him of the Dalai Lama's thinking as I perceived it: "I am now convinced that he is prepared to make a public declaration that, going further than his previous statements, would respond favorably to the conditions you have placed on any dialogue. In this public declaration, the Dalai Lama would notably recognize that Tibet is inseparable from China, which seems to me very important. I am well aware that serious difficulties remain, on both sides, before discussions on Tibet can be entered into. However, I have the impression that the Dalai Lama has a real determination to make progress."

When Jiang came to France in autumn 1999, I again spoke to him about Tibet and about the issue of human rights in his country in an equally frank and direct manner. Demonstrating that one can speak about these subjects freely and without taboo with Chinese leaders as long as they feel they are in a climate of mutual trust and respect, my guest opened up with an equal lack of diplomatic precautions. He confided his real thoughts, in a way that he had probably never done until then with a foreign counterpart.

This conversation took place on October 23, 1999, in Corrèze during the private party that Bernadette and I had organized in his honor in our house in Bity. It was the first time we had had a high-level foreign leader staying under our roof, and it had involved some work to the guest room on the first floor. I was perfectly well aware that this was an unusual gesture, and I made it deliberately to allow us to speak more freely. At the end of the dinner, I invited Jiang to come with me into the sitting room. We spent a long time that evening sitting near the fire, talking for more than three hours about the international situation, the question of Tibet and of human rights and public freedoms in a rapidly changing China.

Concerning Tibet, Jiang wanted first to give me his own version of the problem by going back to its origins: "Before 1950, Tibet was a theocracy that practiced serfdom," he said to me. "In 1959, we launched the democratic reforms to abolish that system. Mao and Zhou Enlai met with the Dalai Lama and the Panchen Lama, who both had important positions as vice presidents of the parliament of all China. We were very cautious about religious movements as a whole. In 1959, there was a revolt in Tibet and Mao said: 'Let the Dalai Lama leave.' In fact, we knew that that revolt was going to take place and we also knew that the Dalai Lama would try to leave. We let it happen, it was premeditated. At the time I was a chief engineer for the large car factory in Changchun.

"In 1990, shortly after I had become general secretary of the party," Jiang went on, "I went to Tibet, to Shigatse, where my friend the Panchen Lama had just been buried. I had often met him in his capacity as mayor of Shigatse and I wanted to pay him this homage. As for the Dalai Lama, he has exploited his people a lot. We have spent 100 million yuan on restoring the Potala palace in Lhasa and we have asked every province, even the poorest, to aid Tibet. I have received several messages from the Dalai Lama, looking for a way to come back. He has gone through different channels, including that of President Clinton. I placed two simple conditions: that the Dalai Lama recognizes that Tibet is part of China and, since he has gone to Taiwan, that he also recognizes that as a Chinese province. That is all. In fact, he has adopted ambiguous positions.

"During my visits abroad," the Chinese president continued, "I have faced various demonstrations, particularly in Switzerland, for the independence of Tibet. When we visited the United States in 1997, my wife noticed the presence of several monks and she said to me, 'I think some of them are shouting: Down with Jiang Zemin!' That started in Hawaii. I then said to Clinton, in the White House, that Hawaii had been a bit too noisy. . . . In fact, as I had learned how to play the ukelele in my youth, I began playing it and everyone clapped. In Williamsburg, the next stop, the atmosphere was already better, and when I arrived at the White House, I was able to say to President Clinton that it had been a very pleasant trip. President Clinton had wanted to make up for it."

Speaking in my turn, I again stressed to Jiang the need to find common ground with the Dalai Lama: "I don't want to judge what is an internal matter. Tibet is part of China, and no one can seriously contest that. But this question poses a serious international problem to your country. There are all sorts of Tibetans who feed a current of hostility in that regard. Is it inevitable or not, that is the problem. I think that it could be resolved and that it would constitute huge progress in terms of integrating China into the international community. I know the Dalai Lama and I think that one can obtain that double recognition you ask from him. If that operation succeeds, it should result in a meeting between the Dalai Lama and a senior-level Chinese personality. If there is unconditional agreement to those two statements, it should be possible to agree to a certain religious autonomy for Tibet. That would allow the resolution of a problem that is uselessly poisoning China's relations with a certain number of countries. Of course, no one should lose face. But secret negotiations would allow the question to be resolved."

"I have studied this problem," Jiang replied. "You have perhaps underestimated the Dalai Lama. He has sent lots of emissaries, including Dr. Wu Gongtan, the son of the president of the commission that presided over the reincarnation of the Dalai Lama. The Dalai Lama is not in good health. He thinks above all of his successor and wonders where his reincarnation will be born. I am an atheist; you are doubtless a believer, but some beliefs exceed all understanding. I think of those processions in Lhasa in which the Tibetans move forward by making full prostrations with each step. There are political reasons. Why those prostrations? Why?

"Do they want more religious freedom? We have already restored the monasteries. Practitioners enjoy the freedom to prostrate themselves. What they also want is political power. Tibet concerns the stability of a country of 1.25 billion inhabitants. The Himalayas are a natural defense. India, Great Britain, and the United States have tried to gain a foothold in it to get through, but our stability there is ensured by our correct handling of the policy on minorities.

"In fact, contact is very open," Jiang explained, returning to my suggestion. "There are no official channels, but the Dalai Lama can always transmit a message.

"I have never had such a frank conversation on this subject," he said contentedly. "Not with Clinton or Chancellor Kohl, or President Mitterrand. With friends, one can speak one's mind freely. We have a particular feeling for France because of its revolution, its leaders, and its independent foreign policy."

I congratulated him on the speech he had given in Lyon the previous day on the prospect of China's attainment of democracy. "It was a very interesting, far-reaching text. I have only one reservation, when you said that in 2050 China would be a 'civilized country.' That was not necessary because no one doubts that. China is going to be a great power, but that involves three necessary developments: ethnic, with Xinjiang and Tibet; national unity, with Taiwan; political, with human rights. These problems are not insurmountable, although they will not be resolved by external pressure but from the inside by the Chinese authorities.

"France's position on Taiwan has not changed for thirty-five years," I went on. "I hope only that reason will prevail and that the principle of 'one country, two systems' will triumph, as in Hong Kong. Xinjiang is a problem about which I have little knowledge. But I note that it is connected to a real danger that I do, however, know well: Islamic terrorism. The devotion of the Tibetans does not disturb me, but Islamic fundamentalism, which can lead to terrorism, worries me much more. It stems notably from the dangerous support that the United States gave Pakistan and then Afghanistan, from where terrorism can spread. And there we must act.

"On Tibet," I said to Jiang, "I continue to think that in terms of China's image in the world, the disadvantages of nonnegotiation are greater than the advantages. You fear the political power of monastics in Tibet but, in the modern world, that is not a problem. If the Dalai Lama is not in agreement, he will then be the one in the wrong. If you think that the Dalai Lama has a hidden agenda, catch him off guard. Force him to reveal himself. I understand your internal policy reasons but, in terms of the external world, it hurts China and I don't like that. I remain convinced that Tibet is a simple issue to resolve and that it presents no danger. We rely on a preconceived idea, which is constantly repeated but which does not correspond to reality. No one wants to take China from the rear, from the Himalayas. The Tibetan people do not want to demand independence. The independence of Tibet does not exist."

"Whatever the world says," responded Jiang, "what is important for us is the stability of Tibet. The Dalai Lama does not need to return, but if he accepts our two conditions, we could negotiate. In any case, China will not accept that Lhasa become a new Jerusalem. Tibet already benefits from autonomy. The only question is to know how to organize it. As for democracy, that is a relative notion that must confront reality. It is gradually being established with us. Even in Great Britain, democracy experiences problems. Look at Northern Ireland. It is a very complicated subject. We are poor, backward. Bit by bit we are getting richer, but we will never be a superpower."

I laughingly protested at this excessive humility while Jiang himself looked amused: "You are well aware that some people see China becoming a great power quite soon. It will be quicker than you think. But you cannot leave the issues we are talking about hanging. Your attainment of the status of world power means that you must resolve human rights issues. You say it yourself, progress toward the universality of human rights is necessary. You have already signed the two United Nations pacts of 1966. True, you have not yet ratified them but during my visit two years ago, President Qiao Shi told me that that would happen very soon. You say yourself that China's objective is to become a democracy. Of course, you have to advance step by step. I see the progress that can be made. Indeed, China must not be destabilized. But in ten, twenty, or thirty years, China should be a democratic country. If I say all that to you, it is because China has a special place in my heart."

"Are you thinking of a gradual independence for Tibet?" Jiang asked me. I confirmed to him that I was not thinking of that but rather of respect for Tibetan culture. I repeated that not engaging in dialogue with the Dalai Lama was counterproductive, at least outside China, and that gestures needed to be made on the question of human rights, which would not be settled in a day: ratifying, for example, the two United Nations pacts. I ended with the mischievous suggestion that we visit Tibet together on my next visit to China. "You go there, I've already been!" he replied in the same tone.

This free and meaningful exchange, on questions that were disturbing to him, was again proof that more is achieved through rigorous, constructive dialogue than through confrontation.

20

A NEW DEPARTURE

During the autumn of 1997, I remember having said to my friend Michèle Cotta, who had asked me how the cohabitation was going: "It's not an automatic deadlock. There are lots of subjects we can agree on. But it is true that a real ideological difference exists between the government and me. I think that most of the left's political choices are going to fail and then the left will be purged of its errors, as the right was in the last general election after the dissolution. After that, around the year 2000, everything will need to be rebuilt. The table will be clear for a new deal, and everything will be possible once more. But we have to go through this twin purge, of left and of right. In five years' time, the transformation will be complete and I can recover the lost ground."

Napoleon declared that in politics "one must never retreat and never retrace one's steps." My state of mind the day after the dissolution was not one of a man inclined to cultivate remorse or regrets. I was entirely focused on action and combat, as I had always been. Confronted with a political isolation similar to that which I had experienced after my defeat in the presidential election of 1988, I had the same impression of facing a new beginning where others in my own camp saw it rather as an ending. Like everyone else, I did not know exactly how long the cohabitation that was expected to last five years would continue, but I prepared myself for the notion of a long crossing, sensing that time would probably be my best ally in terms of public opinion as well as of all those who were already busying themselves, without bothering too much about hiding it, with preparing my succession.

After Alain Juppé's departure from Matignon, I had not succeeded in convincing him to remain as leader of the Rassemblement pour la

République, which would have assured me of a solid and loyal relationship with the main political force of opposition. On July 7, 1997, Philippe Séguin took the presidency of the RPR, seconded by Nicolas Sarkozy as secretary general, both of them determined to establish their independence from a president whom they believed discredited.

Séguin knew my reservations about the promotion of Sarkozy, which I considered premature, at the least. But he decided to disregard them by bringing into his team the former budget minister, Édouard Balladur, who, both before and after my election, had not spared his attacks on me or the government policy of Juppé, sometimes sparing nothing in his attempts to disturb us. From a concern to create unity, however, at the beginning of September I received the new secretary general of the RPR at the Élysée in order to discuss the immediate political situation with him, without reference to the past. It was time to bring an end to personal quarrels.

Faced with a government boosted by growth and that refrained from becoming unpopular by making courageous reforms, the opposition could not manage to overcome its divisions or even benefit from the revived popularity that I was personally experiencing. In vain I pleaded with the leaders of the RPR and Union for French Democracy (UDF) to agree on a common direction and make, as I did, a real effort at reconciliation. The tormented and tumultuous character of Séguin was not designed to pacify relations between the various personalities and the multiple currents of which the former majority was composed. His desire to stand for the RPR, if not the entire opposition, made it hard to envisage unity and lasting agreement with me or with his other colleagues. Séguin was probably right to declare that the RPR should not be the "Jacques Chirac supporters' club." But he was forgetting that it is in the nature of things for the political party from which the president emerges to support him.

Far from seeking consensus, as I urged, the leadership of the Gaullist movement closed itself off in a separatist wing. Then, two months before the vote, at the height of the campaign, Séguin decided suddenly to resign from his post. He was sickened by my refusal to denounce his centrist and separatist competitors while accusing me of having given in, with the Socialist government, to the "temptations of an emollient cohabitation." Sarkozy took over as interim head of the RPR.

It was now obvious that the political groupings of the opposition as a whole needed to be taken in hand. Three years away from the presidential election, my own chances of winning were at stake. The time had come to ensure the implementation of better coordination between the forces of the right and the center. I intended to proceed in stages, beginning with straightening out the RPR, whose next president should be directly elected by party members.

Sarkozy was the first to tell me of his candidacy. He assured me that he intended to commit himself to working alongside me and, as if to convince me all the more, spoke about a new pact he had just entered into with . . . Philippe Séguin, whom he was supporting in the latter's bid to become mayor of Paris. I found Sarkozy as I had known him several years earlier: nervous, impatient, spilling over with ambition, sure of everything—above all, himself. I had several reasons to doubt that he was the best placed to appease the tensions within the RPR and enable the movement to rediscover its unity. I advised him to bide his time and assume, when the moment was right, a higher office. I know that he would not be insensible to this argument, and I duly got him to agree to withdraw his candidacy.

Several aspiring candidates put themselves before the vote of party members, and, on December 4, 1999, it was Michèle Alliot-Marie who emerged victorious, after a hard-fought personal campaign. I had known her well for a long time, having had ties with her father, a former rugby referee. She had formed part of my second government in 1986 and was a woman of strong character, intelligent, generous, and methodical. No sooner was she elected than she began working for the sound objective of unifying the opposition around the president. Much remained to be done in this domain, however, and we needed more than a simple ad hoc agreement between the political parties of the former government. Why not bring the different elements together within a single organization? Others before me had talked of the "urgent need for an RPR–UDF alliance" but no one had really tackled the task.

And so, on the instigation of Maurice Ulrich, I decided to call on the man who had actively supported me twenty-five years earlier in the creation of the RPR: my friend Jérôme Monod. A meticulous and efficient organizer, a behind-the-scenes strategist who was an iron fist in a velvet glove, Jérôme had experience of the political world, even if he preferred that of business. He knew its weaknesses and its inadequacies but also knew how to appreciate its merits and qualities. I had every confidence in his judgment and did not doubt his power of conviction. Both directive and diplomatic, he was without question the man for the situation.

When I asked him in January 2000 to join me to draw up a unification plan for the parties of the opposition and thereby help me prepare for the future presidential election, he was initially hesitant. "I need," I told him, "a man who has proved himself in business and someone with whom I feel in harmony, whose words will be taken as my own." He was not thrilled by the idea of getting involved in politics again, but he was well aware of the importance of the mission I was offering him. "I have commitments until May 5," he eventually replied. "So, you can be there on the sixth?" I asked. Jérôme accepted on condition that he would not answer to anyone but me, which suited me very well, and on June 1 he set himself up in the "Silver Room" of the Élysée, which Bernadette had prepared for him.

Less than three months later, Jérôme gave me a fairly explicit analysis of the situation. "There are still no ideas, platforms, 'visions,' or programs. Everything is just starting," he wrote to me. "There is no coordination or shared knowledge about what each person is doing. Many external people want to be useful. They are little or badly welcomed by the members of Parliament, the parties, or the Élysée team because there is no distinct focus of activity." He told me about the internal organization that he planned, with a political coordination committee representing the various groups of the opposition. Concerning me directly, he thought I needed to devote more time to more direct and frequent political contacts and to meetings with people or "milieus" that I had hitherto wrongly neglected. Finally, he advised me to make better use of the confidence that the public had in Bernadette, convinced that her popularity would become an increasingly vital personal asset in the presidential election. An opinion that I shared.

In December, I invited Alain Juppé and his wife, Isabelle, to join Bernadette and me in Brégançon for the Christmas festivities. Those few days spent together, in the most relaxed and friendly atmosphere possible, allowed us to speak openly about the preparations under way within the opposition. It was the most frequent topic of conversation during our long walks on the path to the fort. Alain also thought that the time had come to modernize our political life and to end the old rivalry between the RPR and the UDF: in short, to bring them and the other existing parties together within a single group. For him, this was the only way I would win the presidential election of 2002. I encouraged him, particularly as he envisaged not the creation of a single party but rather gathering together distinct political families within a single organization; this formula seemed to me the most intelligent and in any case the only one that had any chance of success, given the likely internal resistances that would emerge here and there.

I already knew that Jean-Louis Debré, who led the RPR group in the National Assembly, opposed all notion of fusion, while François Bayrou was quite openly hostile to it. As for Michèle Alliot-Marie, I did not sense that she was in any way ready to give up the smallest part of the power she had just won. Others, such as Nicolas Sarkozy, distrusted an operation that they were unlikely to be able to control. Even if I did not share them, I understood the reservations and concerns that such a radical political change provoked. Even if I strongly urged them to adopt it, there was no question of my imposing it on them. That was not my role.

On June 17, 2001, Jérôme Monod announced that 335 members of Parliament had signed an agreement that would lead, in the following months, to the creation of an organization that united representatives of all strands of the opposition. An important step had been taken on the road to union, just as the cohabitation entered, less than a year before the presidential election, a phase of tension.

*I*t was my duty as president to make sure that relations between the two heads of the executive were as constructive as possible. Chosen by the French, the cohabitation needed to be accepted and worked with, on both sides, in a spirit of tolerance and dignity that was in conformity with our democratic rules. I was not afraid to display the harmonious and even cordial collaboration that I enjoyed with most members of the government; some on the opposition side reproached me for it, and some ministers were warned, by their leaders, against excessive friendliness toward me. However, it was essential for us all to ensure that the cohabitation did not harm the fundamental interests of the country.

This did not prevent me from expressing in public reservations or criticisms about policies conducted by the prime minister. As I had done in October 1997 on the law introducing a thirty-five-hour workweek, over the course of the ensuing year, I warned the government about the renewed escalation in national health insurance deficits. I also alerted the prime minister to a worrying political phenomenon: the political disaffection of a growing number of French people, translated in the most recent elections either by a record rate of abstention or by the rise of extremists. In this I saw the signs of a moral and political crisis that could have terrible consequences if nothing were done to check it. I had begun to be preoccupied with this question during the regional elections of March 1998, which had marked a spectacular breakthrough by the National Front while a majority of voters had turned away from government parties. It was not, in my view, a mere electoral blip. Political parties as a whole, whether in terms of the Republican right tempted in some regions to form alliances with Le Pen's party or the left, initially eager to take advantage of this situation, seemed to me to greatly underestimate the seriousness of the democratic challenge they now faced.

That was why, on March 23, 1998, in my television address on the eve of regional elections, I judged it vital to reject the tone of reserve requested by my office and call solemnly on the French to come to their senses and remain loyal to the ideals of our republican pact. Addressing representatives of the right and center, I asked them to respect "in letter and also in spirit" their commitments to accept no deals with the extreme right and to reject "those men or women who preferred political games to the voice of their conscience." I was just as firm in regard to the left-wing government, urging its representatives also to behave more responsibly and cease playing the game of the National Front, as it had done by adopting proportional representation. As for those voters who had chosen the extreme right, I invited them to consider the impact of a vote in favor of a political organization that was "racist and xenophobic in nature" and not to shut themselves off in a protest reaction.

Conscious of the extent of the discontent that was causing more and more French people to take refuge in abstaining from voting or in recourse to extremes, I argued for a profound overhaul of our democratic system, which I believed was no longer suited either to modern realities or to the expectations of our citizens. I then announced my decision to organize a study group on the question with opposition and government representatives, management and unions, organizations, and the most qualified people in the university world.

After this long period of dialogue and consultation, I was persuaded that systems should be put in place to give the French greater exercise of their rights and duties as citizens. Too many felt at the margins of public debate, distant from a political life that no longer concerned them but in which they wanted greater involvement. Women in particular should benefit from greater access to local and national responsibilities, and I wanted reform in this area. I also thought it vital that young people should play a more important role in our political life, which seemed to me ill-adapted to the profound changes that had taken place in French society.

These attempts to innovate required that more transparency and closeness be created in the relationship between state and citizen. Decentralization had become a priority for me. Decision making could no longer just come from on high. The time had come to introduce real local democracy; from every side, a growing need for autonomy, freedom, initiative, and individual engagement began to express itself.

It was in large part this need for a profound revision of our method of functioning that led to my own growth on a subject that concerned me even more directly: the duration of the presidential mandate. I had long been opposed to the idea of reducing it to a period of five years instead of the seven that had been adopted since the creation of the Fifth Republic. I feared that the five-year period, coinciding with the duration of the National Assembly, would lead to a sort of permanent cohabitation that would enmesh the government of the country in impotence or paralysis.

Georges Pompidou had envisioned the five-year term, though he had not managed to implement it; François Mitterrand had first advocated such a term before his election but then had not followed through with implementing it. Nonetheless, the idea remained current and resurfaced at the beginning of 2000 on the initiative of former president Valéry Giscard d'Estaing, with the implicit support of Prime Minister Lionel Jospin. However, it was not their combined influence that eventually persuaded me to espouse the idea, as was thought, but rather the fairly large consensus for it in the country. A five-year period, already instituted in most European countries, was seen by the majority of the French as the token of greater democratic vitality.

Although the constitution did not require it, I expressly wanted the possibility of a five-year period to be put to the public vote; it was the first time that such a reform had taken place under the Fifth Republic since 1962. The referendum on the election of the president of the republic took place on September 24, 2000. The "yes" vote won, with 73.21 percent of the votes cast—but the abstention rate of 69.81 percent of enrolled voters confirmed that much remained to be done to reconcile the French with a political life that they still judged too far removed from their real concerns.

This millennium year was also marked by a turning point in the history of the cohabitation, punctuated by increasingly intense clashes with the head of government. The deterioration had begun to show in February 2000, on the occasion of the official visit of Lionel Jospin to the Middle East. Eager to put his personal stamp on a foreign policy that had until then been consensual, the prime minister went to Israel without me—he was accompanied by Hubert Védrine—and talked about Hezbollah in a way that was, at the very least, unfortunate.

Describing the Hezbollah attacks against the Israeli army in southern Lebanon as "terrorist"—he would rectify the statement two days later by instead talking about "acts of war"—Jospin did not just choose the wrong word. He also took the risk of threatening the fragile regional equilibrium at a time when the new Israeli prime minister, Ehud Barak, was trying, despite the situation in southern Lebanon, to relaunch the peace process with the Palestinians.

Predictably, the Palestinians responded in the worst possible way to this unexpected challenge, which they took as a provocation, from the

French head of government. After a rather stormy meeting with Palestinian students in Birzeit University, near Ramallah, Jospin was violently taken to task by hundreds of demonstrators and forced to leave the premises hurriedly under a shower of insults and stones.

Learning that he had received a slight wound to the head during these incidents, I first inquired about the state of his health. Thankfully, the prime minister was fine. Then, as I had said to him immediately after his declarations, I asked to meet him as soon as he returned to France. On his arrival in Paris, however, Jospin preferred to spend the evening with friends, where I nonetheless managed to phone him. His voice was icy cold. Reproaching me for not having shown more support toward him, he refused to reply to what he took as a summons. His mood was not much better when I simply reminded him, during our weekly meeting before the Council of Ministers the following Wednesday, of the principles of French policy in the Middle East:

"The government assumes responsibility for what it does and I am a sort of scout," I said jokingly several months later, in my traditional televised address of July 14. "The president of the republic is not just an arbiter," I added. "He is also there to say to the people who have elected him how he sees things and how he anticipates the future. That is what I try to do both on the level of domestic policies and foreign policies but within a framework that respects the rules of cohabitation."

Questioned that day about the great reforms that remained to be carried out after three years of the Jospin government, I could only emphasize the delays and inadequacies observed in many sectors. Whether in terms of decentralization, security problems, the reform of pensions, the unequal sharing of the fruits of growth, or the weight of fiscal matters, I deplored the accumulated delays and blocks, imputing them to one of the major deficiencies of Socialist management: government inertia and excessive regulation.

The various "affairs" about which I was questioned between 1999 and 2001 were probably not designed to facilitate the exercise of the presidential mandate that the French conferred on me in May 1995. While wondering about their origin and agreeing to respond to them when I felt it necessary, I always greeted them with sangfroid, determined not to be affected or interrupted in the accomplishment of my task—until the time when, an ordinary citizen once again, I naturally made myself available to the justice system to answer the questions it wished to put to me.

All these affairs dealt, one way or another, with the question of the financing of political life as it was practiced, for each of its protagonists, at a period long before my election. In essence, they concerned the time when I was mayor of Paris or the president of the RPR. None of them implicated the president I became, at a moment in our national history when the activity of political parties was held in a framework of legal arrangements that did not previously exist. It might be useful in this regard to give a brief historical summary.

Until the beginning of the 1980s, political parties—like unions, organizations, or ministerial offices—largely functioned on the basis of practices that had evolved over time. In addition to the necessarily limited participation of its members, political groups called on multiple sources of aid: Individuals, whether activists or not, companies, and even public monies contributed to their running costs as well as to electoral campaigns through direct donations or the covering of various costs, the provision of staff, or the remuneration of permanent employees. This state of affairs was basically accepted by and known to everybody.

The first election of the president of the republic by universal suffrage in 1965 and the advent of two major ballots, European and regional, inevitably led to a change that was accelerated by vastly increased communication and publicity expenses. If they wanted to continue to be heard and to participate in the democratic debate, all parties without exception were obliged to mobilize funds out of all proportion to those they had formerly disposed of. The legal system had also modernized hidden practices that no one else had really expressed interest in before then.

People's thinking having moved on and the sums at stake being no longer the same, a profound change in the financing of political parties was needed. Over the space of a few years, therefore, we moved from a world of custom and practices to a regime that was clearly defined in law. In France, as in the United States, Germany, or Great Britain, political groups had to adapt to this new reality. All the major democracies experienced a difficult period before going from a lawless zone consisting of practices that had become obsolete and contestable to the fixing of clear and transparent legal rules.

In our country, seven years of experimentation and reflection were needed before a rigorous regulation was implemented. Three successive laws were passed in this regard between 1988 and 1995, two proposed by the right and one by the left, but all of them agreed on by a large majority of members of Parliament. In accordance with President Mitterrand, I adopted the first legislative text on the subject: the law of 1988, concerning the financing of electoral campaigns. The law of 1990, driven by Michel Rocard, strove to give greater control of the material aid given by businesses—but it was not until 1993 that we arrived, at the end of this long process, at what seemed to me the best solution: the prohibition of all financial aid of this kind.

None of these groups, of either the left or the right, was spared from scandals and legal problems linked to the ways in which it had fulfilled its financial needs over the previous decades. Contrary to the caricatures, the reality on both sides was that these cases had only very exceptionally been ones of personal enrichment—which were sanctioned, sometimes heavily. Most often they concerned the direct funding of the incriminated parties and the way in which—judged suspect and abnormal, even fraudulent, after the event—they had carried out their own financing at a time when this was neither regulated nor controlled and when this was, in a sense, a matter only for them.

Having myself contributed, in my role as prime minister, to this improvement that was rightly desired by our compatriots, I had every reason to be happy about a change that had already taken effect when I took charge of the country. However, this salutary overhaul of our political life did not prevent maneuvers aimed at exploiting past affairs involving certain leaders, and the president in particular, with the sole aim of discrediting us. It is obviously not a question of in any way challenging the work of the law in this area, but the methods I am talking about had quite another basis—in rumors, more or less orchestrated press campaigns, accusations fabricated without scruple to serve personal ambitions and tarnish the honor of people up to the highest level of the state.

In April 1999, a ruling was made by a judge in Nanterre against several former leaders of the RPR, including Alain Juppé, and myself as former mayor of the capital, on the subject of jobs, presumed to be fictitious, in the city of Paris. As far as I was concerned, the ruling hit up against the question of the criminal immunity of the president; despite a certain legal vagueness, it was clearly set out that only the High Court of Justice was empowered to prosecute a serving president of the republic and then only for acts of high treason committed during the exercise of his functions.

For all that, the largely political offensive against me did not stop. On September 21, 2000, several days before the referendum on the five-year presidential term, an evening paper published the contents of mysterious tapes in which a businessman, who had since died, accused me of having had a secret funding system via the HLM Office—the government-subsidized housing office of Paris—of which he had been both a participant and an observer. Questioned that same evening on television, I did not hide my indignation: "Today, we have had the report of an incredible story.

A man who died more than a year ago has been made to speak. Unlikely facts that supposedly took place more than fourteen years ago have been recounted. A recording made more than four years ago has been exhumed and the newspaper that published these words has itself described them as 'uncheckable' and 'without legal value.' All this, as though by chance, exactly three days before a referendum aimed at improving the way in which our democracy functions! These accusations are unworthy lies. That is why I ask that the facts be put into the hands of the law so that truth can sweep away the slander." At the same time, it was discovered that one of the foremost ministers of the Jospin government had been sent a copy of the tapes—embarrassment at Matignon was at its height, where people were beginning to realize the potential danger of tarnishing the image of the political world in this way.

On March 20, 2001, the supposed revelations concerning the HLM Office of Paris led one of the judges in charge of the case to send me a summons addressed to "Chirac Jacques"—the usual formula but pointlessly humiliating, whether in regard to the president of the republic or any other French citizen—to be heard as a witness the following April 4 at 3:00 P.M. This invitation to present myself in person to the judge's office was accompanied by the following warning: "If you do not appear or if you refuse to appear, you can be obliged to do so by the forces of law and order." While it was supposed to be known only to the judge and his clerk, the summons in question was immediately made public by the press, which cited a legal source, making a mockery of the secrecy of the case.

On March 28, I communicated my astonishment and disapproval at this malfunctioning of justice to the prime minister and asked him to launch an immediate inquiry into the affair. "The most serious aspect," I told him, "is that a judge can summon the president as a witness under the express threat of being obliged to do so by the forces of law and order. That is contrary to the principles of the separation of powers and the continuity of the state. The government must use all the legal means at its disposal to stop it." This the prime minister undertook to do.

In June of the same year, another affair surfaced, concerning the financing in cash of trips taken, here too, at a time preceding my election. On the twenty-second of that month, I learned that a ruling had been transmitted to the public prosecutor of Paris to investigate the origin of large sums of money in cash used to pay for air tickets for myself and several of my entourage. It was an additional opportunity to try to sow doubt among the public about my integrity. The televised address of July 14 allowed me to make some useful clarifications to the French. About the fact, for example, that not only private trips were involved, as had been alleged, but also professional ones. About the fact that the amounts declared bore no relationship to the reality. And about the fact that these payments had been made in a perfectly legal manner, since they had been marked on invoices and could not therefore have been hidden, as was claimed. As for the origin of the sums of money in question, a part of them, as I explained, came from personal allowances taken when I was prime minister, the other having been taken from secret funds.

It was the first time, to my knowledge, that a French president had talked in public and officially about the existence of these funds, which were in fact common knowledge and the most widely shared open secret of our republic. In fact, if the secret funds voted every year by Parliament essentially served to finance activities linked to the country's security, it was also known that a portion of these funds were traditionally used to facilitate the functioning of ministerial offices or make up the remuneration of members of the government and their staff. Finally, it was known that they had in the past been used to cover certain political expenses.

It was the uncertainty about this kind of use that could feed suspicion. That was why I accepted the proposal, put forward by the presidents of the opposition groups in the National Assembly, to freeze the part of the special funds that could not be officially traced by check payments or justified as special operations relating to state security. Questioned that July 14, I declared that I was shocked by the fact that people had gone as far as attacking my wife and my daughter Claude; the latter had been summoned by the judge and had been questioned about two trips, one a professional one she had taken with me that was in no way mysterious and the other to Kenya—where she had in fact never been. I did not hide the fact that I was deeply wounded by this.

During the summer of 2001, I learned through Dominique de Villepin that a former financial judge who had once belonged to the staff of a Socialist minister had investigated the presumed existence of a private account that I supposedly held in a Japanese bank, the Sowa Bank, until recently headed by its founder, Soichi Osada. I did indeed know him and had met him several times, but solely for reasons linked to industrial investment projects that he hoped to carry out in our country. This time, my heart missed a beat. Convinced that Jospin or his entourage likely had some involvement in this new affair, which had every appearance of being a contrived conspiracy against me, I sent the prime minister a letter in which I issued an extremely vigorous warning against this kind of procedure. He replied curtly that he knew nothing of such an investigation, although its existence would later be confirmed.

It was in this context that the Court of Appeals pronounced in its turn on the nature and the limits of the president's penal status. Its judgment, given on October 12, 2001, included the following: "Having been directly elected by the people precisely to ensure the proper functioning of public powers as well as the continuity of the state, the President of the Republic cannot during the course of his mandate be heard as a witness assisted by a lawyer or be indicted, summoned, or discharged for any infraction before a criminal jurisdiction." Finally, in regard to acts pertaining to the period before his election, it specifies that if the president benefits from absolute immunity during his mandate, the ban is only suspended during that period, which meant that he could be subject to legal process at the end of his term of office.

The situation was finally clarified, but I was still not completely satisfied. During the presidential campaign of 2002, I again took up the idea, formulated the previous year, of charging independent jurists with the task of objectively examining the question of the criminal responsibility of the president and to make proposals to reformulate once and for all Article 68 of the constitution. In July 2002, I entrusted this mission to Professor Avril and his commission; their proposals were eventually taken up in the constitutional law adopted by the congress on February 19, 2007. It was in this way that the criminal immunity and nonresponsibility of the president of the republic was confirmed, in terms of acts carried out during his mandate and of legal proceedings that could be entered into against him. Finally, in an important innovation, the possibility was henceforth open that a president could be impeached by Parliament sitting as the High Court in the event of a dereliction of duty manifestly incompatible with the exercise of his office.

Thanks to the adoption of this largely consensual text, I had the satisfaction of having preserved, for the benefit of my successors, their freedom of action as well as the continuity of the state.

21

THE CHALLENGES
OF A NEW
MILLENNIUM

*T*he accession to power of a new foreign partner necessitates a period of personal and political adaptation, which can prove long and difficult, before it leads to a lasting relationship of trust or transforms into permanent misunderstanding. The successive elections of Gerhard Schröder, who became chancellor of the Federal Republic of Germany in September 1998, of Vladimir Putin as president of the Russian Federation in March 2000, and of George W. Bush, who entered the White House in January 2001, were such experiences for me.

I had formed ties of friendship and solidarity, forged through shared trials, with Helmut Kohl, Boris Yeltsin, and Bill Clinton. Then I had to familiarize myself with new interlocutors whose political perspectives and vision of the world were not always those of their predecessors. In the case of the new German and Russian leaders, a real diplomatic continuity eventually developed, but in terms of my new American counterpart, our difference of view on the question of Iraq in particular would make it difficult to maintain the same quality of relationship between our two governments.

On December 18, 2000, the Europe–United States summit held in Washington allowed me to pay homage to Bill Clinton for the last time before he left the presidency. Preceded by a quiet meeting at the White House, the dinner that followed was, after five years of an intense and fruitful collaboration, more than ever imbued with warmth and friendship. The relationship between heads of state rarely escapes the tensions and the power plays inherent in the defense of their respective interests, and my relationship with Clinton had not always been an exception to this rule, having been punctuated with clashes and disagreements that could sometimes be stormy. But an immediate empathy, a shared love of life, allied to the same taste for action in the exercise of power, had always greatly facilitated our personal contacts. In regard to Bosnia and Kosovo, we had concurred without difficulty in the defense of principles and human values to which we were both attached. The bond that had also been established between our wives, united by a similar passion for public engagement, had also contributed to bringing us closer.

Like most of his peers, Bill Clinton did not always resist the temptation to emphasize to the other leaders of the planet how all-powerful America was—and sometimes this need for affirmation had a symbolic impact that could be both humorous and extravagant. At the G7 in Denver in 1997, for example, he decided to give his guests a cowboy outfit. The White House advisors procured all our clothing and shoe sizes. While Tony Blair, newly arrived in our midst, greeted the idea with juvenile enthusiasm, Helmut Kohl was dubious about dressing up like John Wayne and asked me what I thought about it. I supported him resolutely: "Helmut, I agree with you," I told him. "France will go along with Germany. . . . But to make Bill happy, I will at least put the boots on!" Unluckily, these were not the right size for me, and I had to make do with simply taking my tie off.

When the Monica Lewinsky affair, intensely exploited by his political opponents who desired his downfall, came crashing around Clinton in 1998, I immediately offered him my support. I called him several times a week to encourage him to keep going and not give up in the face of the baying hounds of his detractors, even fearing that he might put an end to his life through despair. I admired the courage and determination that he displayed at that time and I admired even more the strength of character with which Hillary Clinton confronted a trial that was humiliating for her, without ever wavering in the support she had immediately given her husband. Ever since I first met her, I knew that Hillary Clinton was an exceptional woman.

At that last moment spent in the White House on December 18, 2000, Bill told me about the foundation he wanted to create, and I promised him I would support it. It was hard to believe, seeing him still so young-looking and full of energy and enthusiasm, that he was preparing to leave power, although within his marriage it seemed that the baton had indeed been passed on: It was Hillary who would now, in her turn, launch into political battle, a goal she had always wanted and for which she was clearly destined.

I took advantage of being in Washington that day to meet the future president of the United States, George W. Bush. It was not customary for the newly elected leader to meet a foreign head of state before his inauguration but, knowing that he was there for a meeting, I nonetheless asked my new diplomatic advisor and our ambassador in the American capital to try to set up a meeting. Our ambassador had a good relationship with the diplomatic advisor of the next tenant of the White House, Condoleezza Rice, and through her a meeting was organized, though Bush's entourage required that it be as discreet and small in number as possible. It was fixed for the beginning of the evening of December 18 at the French ambassador's private residence.

As arranged, I made sure I did not attract the attention of journalists. For his part, George W. Bush arrived escorted by Condoleezza Rice and the future chief of staff of the White House, Andrew Card . . . and a bus filled with photographers! The French journalists resented the fact that I had not called on them, but at least I had kept my word. The president-elect and I exchanged a few courtesies and then began chatting, two men who for the moment knew nothing about each other and did not know exactly what subjects to tackle. Smiling, quite relaxed and self-confident, the new president of the United States did not seem to me to have the same warm and charismatic presence as his predecessor. Everything with him seemed under control, as if he were someone who had learned to be wary of himself.

He was not surprised when I mentioned the excellent relationship I had enjoyed with his father during his presidency, the friendship I felt for him, and the pleasure I experienced at meeting him during his trips to Paris. He was for me a great statesman, rational, moderate, cultivated, and full of humor. "He often talks about you, as well," his son told me, before asking me my opinion of several issues he would have to deal with when he arrived at the White House, particularly the situation in Iran since the reformers had come to power—"Can we trust these people?" he asked me, with the air of someone who did not—and the question of climate change, on which I felt he was equally skeptical when I talked of my concerns about it. We also spoke about energy problems, a subject about which he was visibly passionate. Curiously, he asked me no questions that evening about another issue that was just as pressing at that time: the disarmament of Iraq. In sum, I took away a largely favorable impression of this first contact, even if the opinion of the new president of the United States on most of the subjects that he chose to broach seemed to me already very fixed.

I had a first confirmation of this several months later, during the G8 summit held in Genoa from July 20 to 22, 2001, a meeting principally marked by the scale and the violence of the demonstrations it sparked in the streets of the city, with many people wounded in the clashes between the alter-globalists and the forces of law and order and one man tragically killed: "13,000 demonstrators, $130 million of destruction" was the summary the president of the Italian council, Silvio Berlusconi, gave us of this dramatic weekend at the end of our labors. Having warned my counterparts about this danger since the Lyon summit in 1996, I was not surprised by the rise in the protest movement against globalization. We had then seen it growing, with serious incidents already taking place outside the European Council meeting in Göteborg in June 2001. Yet I did not have great success when I asked them a month later to draw lessons from that experience and give all those involved in world affairs a greater voice in our deliberations; all we agreed was that we would not release the name of the city where the next summit would be held too early, for security reasons!

The other notable event of the Genoa meeting was the confirmation of George W. Bush's refusal to recognize the protocol of Kyoto—backed up by Russian and Japanese reservations about it—despite the fact that his predecessor had agreed to it. In a telephone conversation in April 2001, Bush had already indicated to me that he considered the current treaty "stillborn." He thought it was "unjust" because, according to him, it did not impose obligations on developing countries but would be "extremely costly for the American economy." The fact is that more than half the reduction goals set out in the protocol concerned the United States, the largest producer of greenhouse gases in the world.

For my part, I believed that there was no credible alternative to this text and that everything must be done to ratify and implement it by 2002 at the latest, the date of the Johannesburg conference and of the celebration of the tenth anniversary of the Rio summit, where the great powers had discussed environmental concerns for the first time. It was a question of our credibility in the eyes of the rest of the world. I firmly underscored this point of view at the Genoa G8 when I expressed the hope that all our positions would be clarified once and for all in terms of world public opinion. "We should not declare ourselves in disagreement in public," Bush said to me. "Otherwise, they will point the finger at us. There is a possibility that we will come to agreement at some time. We must not exclude that possibility. Do not place me, and the others around this table, in a difficult position." Rejecting this hypocrisy, I confirmed that I would not sign, for my part, any text that did not recognize our differences, each of us having to assume our responsibilities fully. This observation would indeed figure in the final communiqué, accompanied by a purely diplomatic phrase asserting that the signatories were "determined to work together to reach their common objectives." You never knew.

The only issue on which George W. Bush and I had any real agreement during this summit was on the fight against AIDS, to which we were both strongly committed. In May 2001, the U.S. president had announced that the United States was donating $200 million to the solidarity fund against the pandemic created on the initiative of France in Abidjan in 1997 with the principal aim of allowing AIDS victims of the countries of the South to benefit from care and treatment, obviously at a more affordable cost. Renamed the World Health Fund, it was officially launched in Genoa in July 2001 with the immediate financial participation of France, Great Britain, Japan, and the United States with sums that reached $1.8 billion. Private foundations such as that of Bill Gates also contributed.

Another meeting with Bush was planned in Washington during a trip to the United States from September 18 to 20 to attend a UN conference on children's rights in New York. A week before this trip, on September 11, I was in Rennes, where I was to give a speech at a business university. On my arrival, I was informed by journalists of the attacks that had just occurred in New York. Dominique de Villepin confirmed the news to me, and I immediately decided to return to Paris. Before leaving, I mounted the stage to announce my immediate return to Paris to the audience, who had also heard the news, expressing in a few words my reaction of horror and revulsion: "It is with immense emotion that France has just learned of the monstrous—there is no other word—attacks in the United States. In these terrible circumstances, the French people as a whole stand alongside the American people, expressing their friendship and support in this tragedy. I naturally assure President George W. Bush of my total support. France, as you know, has always condemned terrorism unreservedly and maintains that every means must be used to fight it."

Back in Paris, I had the flags at the Élysée flown at half-staff and immediately summoned a restricted ministerial council of the prime minister, the foreign affairs and defense ministers, the secretary general of the Élysée, and my personal chief of staff. We needed to decide on the security measures to be implemented without delay to protect our own territory against possible similar air attacks. To my stupefaction, I heard Lionel Jospin telling me unceremoniously that everything relating to air defense was, "under the order of 1975, the exclusive responsibility of the prime minister." I was obliged to remind him forcefully that under the constitution, the president of the republic was the sole head of the armed services and that I consequently wanted not only to be kept informed of the decisions taken but also to give my opinion and my agreement. I learned shortly afterward that the "Vigipirate" security plan had been reactivated by the government without my having been in any way consulted. However, I refrained from reacting, judging that in such circumstances, the only thing that mattered was national unity.

At the end of the restricted council meeting, I made contact with Tony Blair and Gerhard Schröder and with staff of George W. Bush in the White House. Then at the end of the afternoon I called our ambassador to the United Nations and asked him to propose a Security Council resolution to our allies that likened acts of terrorism to acts of war and acknowledged that states that were victim to them had a right of legitimate defense. This resolution, of French origin, was adopted the following day, on September 12.

Terrorism was nothing new in the West, even if it had now revealed a more sinister face than ever before. From G7 to G8, the great powers had continually condemned it, whatever its motivation, and emphasized the need to reinforce international cooperation in this domain and to draw up preventive strategies—an objective that was far from having been realized, to judge by what had just occurred. But the principal lesson I drew from the tragedy of September 11 was that the world was now confronted with acts of aggression that did not arise from an isolated phenomenon but from a new type of conflict that justified the use of force as a legitimate defense.

When I managed to reach President Bush on the phone on September 12, it was first to assure him personally of France's total support in this terrible trial: "I am your friend!" I told him. I then asked him if he thought it opportune, given the responsibilities he doubtless faced since the attacks, for me to continue with the official trip that had been planned in the following days. "It is not for terrorists to dictate the agenda of democracies," he immediately replied. "Come as arranged. I need to talk with you about what we should do."

And so it was, by the chance of my agenda and with the full agreement of the American president, that I was the first foreign head of state present in New York, barely a week after the attacks.

On my arrival in Washington on September 18, I immediately went to the White House accompanied by Hubert Védrine, where we were received by Bush, flanked by Vice President Dick Cheney and his principal advisors and cabinet members, including Colin Powell, Donald Rumsfeld, and Condoleezza Rice. The president seemed to me extraordinarily calm, very much in command of himself, as if inhabited by a cold and determined awareness of his duty and the mission incumbent on him. "We are going to flush out these criminals and drag them before the justice system," he declared to us in a tone that was both serene and emphatic. He was specifically talking about bin Laden and the Taliban. Obviously appreciative of the fact that we had come so rapidly, he said to me several times during this meeting, and then at the subsequent dinner, that he had been sincerely grateful for the expression of friendship and compassion that I had made to him in the name of France and on my own behalf. The atmosphere between us could not have been friendlier.

The following day I went to New York to visit the location of the tragedy. On our arrival, the mayor of the city, Rudolph Giuliani, suggested that I go up in a helicopter with him over Ground Zero, the site of the Twin Towers that were now reduced to a gigantic jumble of ruins and dust. He said that this was the only way one could get a sense of the enormity of the event. We went by ourselves, without ministers or advisors. The sight of the devastation I glimpsed through the helicopter windows was indescribable, as I thought of the thousands of human lives that were swallowed up there in the space of a few minutes, of the horror that these women and men had endured, searching in vain for a way out of the trap that was closing in on them before enduring an atrocious death. Thinking of that, a lump in my throat, I said to myself that there was never any valid reason or any possible justification for such blind destruction and killing.

During our meeting at the White House, I had made it clear to President Bush that France was ready and willing to cooperate with the United States and all our allies in the fight against terrorism. Al-Qaeda and its leader Osama bin Laden having claimed responsibility for the attacks, it was Afghanistan, the operational base of the radical Islamist organization, that was more than ever in the American government's sights. Western governments were all aware of the danger the Taliban regime posed to world security. Meeting in Rome in mid-July 2001, foreign affairs ministers had reaffirmed their "concern in the face of the growing terrorist threat" that this regime represented and condemned the barbarity that held sway in that country, particularly toward women. But, two months before the September 11 attacks, the big powers had above all been thinking of humanitarian action in favor of the Afghan people or of political negotiations aimed at establishing a multiethnic government in Afghanistan. Now the objective was altogether different.

Before the project of military intervention was even officially confirmed, I had taken care to make it clear to Bush, during this same meeting of September 18, that there could be no question of France automatically taking part in an operation to which it had not given its prior agreement. I had also expressed my rejection of all attempts to lump together fundamentalist groups and Arab and Muslim peoples. In other words, I warned him against the danger of falling into the trap of an ideological war that could only play into the terrorists' hands. But the American president, in agreement with my first observation, was more evasive about the second.

At the end of September, the Pentagon, which had just informed us of its plan of action in terms of Afghanistan, solicited our passive military support more than our direct participation in the operation christened "Enduring Freedom," which would be launched on October 7. In essence, it was a question of putting our bases at the disposal of American planes en route to Kabul and of contributing our own planes to air raids carried out from the aircraft carrier *Charles de Gaulle,* which would be dispatched in the Indian Ocean. I was immediately in favor, particularly as our commitment would be limited and as what was involved was an official peace mission carried out under the orders of the UN. In Paris, however, I once again faced a negative reaction from the prime minister.

One Sunday afternoon, I was in my office in the Élysée, discussing various cases with my own chief of staff when I received a phone call from Lionel Jospin: "You have seen, as I have, M. President, the request for authorization from the American authorities to fly over our territory so that their planes can go and bomb Afghanistan. I am opposed to that!" he declared. I let him develop his argument and set out his fears, principally that France would be accused of complicity if this bombing claimed victims among the civilian population. Then I responded as follows: "M. Prime Minister, are you aware of the fact that the Americans have just suffered, for their part, the loss of six thousand* of the civilians you are talking about? It is obviously not a question of creating an equal number in Afghanistan. But do you realize the trauma there would be in France if just two hundred of our compatriots were killed in an attack of this kind? I do not understand your attitude."

Probably under pressure from a faction of the left hostile to all military intervention in Afghanistan, the prime minister had not insisted. But I had enormous difficulty in getting his government to agree to the minimum of

---

* The number of victims presumed at that time.

operational support asked of us on the ground. For my part, I held to the two basic principles that underlay my "doctrine" toward Afghanistan: the duty of support toward our allies and concern that our participation be as limited as possible. For as long as I was in office, the French contingent remained fewer than 1,500 men, and only a few planes were involved in an operation that, as far as we were concerned, had no goal other than the protection of the Afghan authorities and the supervision of their army, both of which were in my mind temporary functions. In addition, our troops would be exclusively billeted around Kabul until 2003, when I agreed that our special forces be sent to the harshest and most sensitive mountain areas for one-time missions under American command. Nothing more or less— so as not to be caught in a potentially extremely dangerous spiral. In fact, I never believed that a military victory in Afghanistan was possible.

While I am in favor of the use of force in the name of a legitimate fight against terrorism, I reject with equal force all ideas of a conflict that aimed at stigmatizing a religion, a way of life, and a vision of the world that were different from western values, ways of thinking, and criteria of judgment. In sum, by associating France with an operation to eradicate a barbarous, deadly plague, I was not for my part thereby sanctioning the argument increasingly prized by the American government of a "clash of civilizations." This notion was in no way one I shared; indeed, it was even the very opposite of all I believed. The notion that the September 11 attacks resulted from the clash of two incompatible worlds seemed to me absurd and nefarious as well as serving the interests of extremists of all sides. I was firmly persuaded that the worst reaction to fanaticism was to feed hatred and rejection of the other in our turn and, under the pretext of curbing it, adopting an attitude that was equally radical, violent, and passionate. In my view, one should in fact do the exact opposite: first, reflect on the origins of the resentment on which extremism feeds, and then counter all arguments based on contempt, arrogance, and exclusion with ones based on respect, exchange, and dialogue between cultures, alongside the clear, unequivocal affirmation of the values and ideals that constitute the identity of all peoples and all civilizations.

But there can be neither dialogue between cultures nor respect for their diversity if one does not look at the real reasons for the lack of understanding and growing gap between North and South and if nothing is done to reduce the increasing divide between the poor countries that represent more than a third of humanity and the wealthy countries that do not adequately fulfill their responsibilities in terms of development aid. This demand for justice should go hand in hand with a willingness to look at ourselves honestly. While every nation, every religion, and every civilization can be proud of what it has accomplished and given to the world, its duty is also to take stock of its shadowy areas, criticize itself, and have the courage to face up to its own past. Much remains to be done in this area, even if the prevailing logic on both sides remains that of finding a scapegoat to make into the sole guilty party.

I strove to warn Bush against this logic and all that it implied in international relations when I met him once more during a short visit to Washington on November 6 and 7, 2001. Although he did not yet set out to me his next objectives, beyond Afghanistan, it was not hard to imagine what they were. On January 29, 2002, in his traditional State of the Union address, the American president denounced an "axis of evil" that was likely to "attack our allies or attempt to blackmail the United States." Among the targeted countries, other than Iran and North Korea, it was his words about Iraq and the regime of Saddam Hussein that were the most threatening.

22

THE IRAQ WAR

*J*érôme Monod's unifying efforts had borne fruit. At the beginning of 2002, the opposition was more united than it had ever been, even if several pockets of resistance still existed here and there.

On February 11, I announced my candidacy for the next presidential election. Having been invited to take part in a meeting of business leaders, I secretly decided to take advantage of the occasion to announce my intentions, taking everyone by surprise. "M. President, are you a candidate?" asked the mayor of Avignon, whom I had just taken into my confidence. I replied that yes, of course I was, feeling more emotion than I displayed. I never doubted, deep down, that I would again run for president at the end of a seven-year mandate that had been marked by five long years of cohabitation. The feeling of frustration I had sometimes experienced at not having greater influence on the management of the country and the difficulty of coexisting with a prime minister with whom I felt no particular affinity had considerably spoiled, I have to acknowledge, the pleasure of the ride.

Prisoner of his ideological convictions, the governing team and its leader in particular had not been able to meet what was a twin aspiration on the part of the French: first, to see the government fulfilling its fundamental objectives, principally in terms of security and justice, and second, that of greater involvement in the decisions that concerned them most directly. The fact is that a profound feeling of insecurity had taken hold in the country, fed by the rise in violence, delinquency, and antisocial behavior. This was an increasingly worrying phenomenon that did not just involve areas reputed to be difficult. It was not rare to hear that teachers had been attacked by their pupils in school, where drug trafficking and gangs often operated with impunity. The growing discouragement, weariness, and exasperation of our citizens were incitements for many to turn away from political parties toward extremists, even to the point of seeming to sanction openly xenophobic and discriminatory ideas.

One of the most eloquent symbols of this deterioration in the social climate was the France versus Algeria soccer match at the Stade de France on October 6, 2001, when the French national anthem was drowned out by the sound of whistles blown by thousands of young French people, some of whom were of Algerian origin. Present at the match, the prime minister, surrounded by several members of the government, had not seen fit to react or mark disapproval in any way. They all remained in their place as if nothing were amiss. These television images had upset millions of French people. I was myself deeply shocked by them, not without wondering about the real reasons behind such incidents. The people who had booed our national anthem had doubtless wanted to demonstrate the unease and distress they felt at living in a society that ignored them and deprived them of hope.

I was thinking of what had happened at the Stade de France, five months earlier, when I resolved to visit the area of Val Fourré near Paris on March 4, 2002. Nobody dared set foot there anymore, and it had become one of those no-go, lawless zones into which even the police hesitated to venture. By deciding to visit it, against the advice of some of my entourage, I first wished to affirm that the republic belonged to everyone in the national territory and to signal my rejection, as I would declare on the spot, of a world in which "rules and reference points have been erased." To the prime minister's resigned argument that this insecurity was caused not by a lack of political will but by the natural violence of society, I countered my conviction that "there was nothing inevitable about people being attacked."

My visit was deeply appreciated by the inhabitants of the area, who thanked me and pressed warmly around me. I did not, however, want anyone to interpret it as a provocation; its aim was not to set one France against another but rather to mark the fact that this fracturing of social mores had become in my view an unacceptable reality. As I was going back to my car, I was insulted by a handful of young people from the area. One of them even spat on me, although I did not realize it at the time; I only learned about it later, when I did not get unduly upset about it. I had experienced far worse, and far more underhanded, attacks in my political career. Indeed, the electoral campaign that was just beginning probably contained a few more in store for me.

While it was generally held that I was still struggling, a month after the declaration of my candidacy, to rediscover the wind and inspiration of my victorious campaign of 1995, my main opponent, always somewhat aggressive toward me and no longer seeking to hide his feelings, gave himself free rein on March 10 when he described me to journalists as virtually bedridden: "Chirac has lost a lot of his energy and strength. He is tired, old, the victim of a certain erosion of power. He is marked by a certain passivity now." How to raise the dead, or the presumed dead . . .

I didn't take offense, suspecting that power was indeed on my side, although the choice of words seemed to me somewhat inappropriate from a man who aspired to the highest office. Was the choice of future president going to be decided by the candidates' age and physique? Was debate going to be replaced by arrogance and contempt? Lionel Jospin found himself, it is true, in the always uncertain position that I had often experienced myself of having to justify a record, whereas mine now consisted essentially of offering the French a different vision of the future.

I had delayed entering the campaign, but everything now urged me to engage fully in a combat that I knew to be vital for the future of the country. I wished to focus on defending a new humanism, in the name of the values to which I was the most attached and that I had always defended, a humanism based on justice, security, order, tolerance, freedom, and responsibility. Eager to restore the authority of the state in order to guarantee the protection and well-being of our citizens as a whole, I also wished to introduce a new power sharing and to encourage the spirit of enterprise and innovation within a society that aspired to more dialogue, autonomy, and dynamism.

On Sunday, April 21, late in the afternoon, I was in a meeting in my office with the principal figures of the Rassemblement pour la République (RPR) and the Union for French Democracy (UDF) to prepare their contributions on various television channels when Dominique de Villepin came to give me the first results from a dozen test polling stations. All of them had the candidate of the left in third position behind the leader of the extreme right. I refused to put my trust in partial estimates that probably did not reflect the vote of the French, and we tried to continue our discussion as if nothing had happened. But I quickly realized that most of those around me had their minds elsewhere. They seemed flabbergasted, overwhelmed. Although striving to seem unperturbed, I too found it just as difficult to remain focused on the subjects we were dealing with. In the space of minutes, the atmosphere had become strange and unreal, as if we were obstinately insisting on talking about a situation that was already null and void to cover over one that seemed to us increasingly likely. The sense of shock was brutal for me, as it was for most of us.

When I was finally forced to face what was staring us in the face, a profound sense of unease overtook me, in which bewilderment mingled with sadness and incomprehension. If I was sad, it was primarily for France, for what it was and what it represented. Even if there was no longer hardly any doubt about my chances of winning, I did not have the heart to celebrate. In my view, it was not just the Socialist candidate who had been censured but all political parties. I probably had my share of responsibility in the confusion and exasperation that had led a portion of our compatriots to reject the traditional parties, equally blamed after five years of cohabitation. After all, although I had emerged on top, my own result, with less than 20 percent of the votes cast, had nothing satisfying about it. For all these reasons I refused to crack open the champagne that evening.

I now had the duty of addressing the French people to call on them to unite around my candidacy and the republican values that I was now alone in defending and embodying, faced with the representative of the extreme right. The fight that was now unfolding was of a very different kind; it was no longer that which I had been preparing to wage against an opponent who was in a sense a natural one, the spokesperson of a political party whose convictions had always seemed respectable to me even if I did not share them. Above and beyond our differences, it was now a fight that involved all those who shared the same idea of human beings and their rights and dignity and the same attachment to the traditions of freedom, fraternity, respect, and tolerance that were at the basis of our republican pact.

More than ever that April 21, 2002, I felt at one with myself and the ideas that I had always defended. Faced with the party of hatred, racism, and discrimination, I had always thought that no compromise, transaction, or even debate was possible with them. Two days later, I announced my refusal to participate in any televised debates with Le Pen. Indeed, the fact that I had remained unswervingly faithful to my rejection of the National Front, several times taking the risk of paying the electoral price for that, no doubt conferred on me the legitimacy that the French of all parties, who now declared themselves ready to unite around me, judged necessary.

Why, when an unprecedented republican mobilization was under way in every area of France, in reaction to the traumatic events of April 21, and when thousands of voters who had never voted for me recognized me as their sole possible candidate, did I not immediately envisage the formation of a government of national unity? Many people were disappointed, I knew, that I seemed to turn my back on them rather than turning to face them, as it would have seemed logical and desirable to do. Today I say to myself, on reflection, that I should doubtless have put together a governing team more representative of the 82 percent of voters who gave me their vote on May 4, 2002. I did not do so, and that was probably an error in terms of the national unity of which I was the guarantor. It was primarily from a concern, at the end of a long cohabitation, for greater clarity and efficiency in government. A new political compromise between the leaders of various strands of opinion on most of the big subjects would probably have resulted in those same stalemates that the results of April 21 had, in a sense, rejected.

It also held an obvious danger for our democracy: that of seeming to make the National Front the only lasting opposition that faced a coalition of the traditional parties, parties that nothing or almost nothing distinguished in the public's eyes.

The upsetting of the political landscape and the circumstances of my reelection gave me an even sharper awareness of the duties and responsibilities incumbent on me for the next five years. Just as I argued, at a crucial moment in the history of humanity, for a dialogue between peoples and cultures, I wanted more than ever to be the president of a France united around its ideals and knowing how to make an advantage out of its differences. A France that was faithful to its principles of equality, justice, and solidarity and open to the diversity of the world. My role would be to give it greater protection against all that could divide, isolate, or reduce it or turn it away from its real identity. This would be one of the great ambitions of my second mandate.

I began to reflect on my choice of prime minister the day after the first round of the presidential election. On the morning of April 22, I called to the Élysée the administrative staff of the new UMP party that had been launched two months earlier on the instigation of Alain Juppé and Jérôme Monod. I wished to inform our compatriots that a major change had taken place in our political life and the problem that now confronted me was to appoint the government leader who would best embody that. I had several names in mind, including Nicolas Sarkozy and Jean-Pierre Raffarin.

Sarkozy seemed the best prepared to take on the role, if only because he himself was so convinced of this—to such an extent, I discovered, that he had already started choosing his ministers. I did not underestimate his qualities: his capacity for work, his energy, his tactical sense, and his media talent, which made him, in my view, one of the most gifted politicians of his generation. Other arguments in his favor were his government experience, his dynamism, and his insatiable appetite for action. Certain members of my entourage, such as Villepin, wanted him to be appointed, believing that it would allow him to prove himself. Others, more numerous, advised me against it, saying that Sarkozy could not be relied on to create the loyal and totally transparent relationship that a president of the republic, in the spirit of our institutions, had the right to expect with his prime minister. Indeed, the risk was that I would very soon find myself confronted with a government leader quick to assert his autonomy, even to lay claim to my own prerogatives without making any secret of the fact that he had already set his sights on succeeding me. In short, undergoing all the inconvenience of a new cohabitation. . . .

The fact was that I needed a prime minister with whom I felt in complete harmony and on whom I could lean with complete trust. There remained too many shadowy areas and misunderstandings between Sarkozy and me for these conditions to be fully met. In addition, and this was probably the most important factor, we probably did not share the same vision of France. The choice of Jean-Pierre Raffarin seemed to me in every way more in keeping with my notion of how government should work. Still relatively unknown by the French, he would be seen as a new man. Elected from the heart of France, from the countryside with its strong sense of land, he represented that "republic of neighborhoods" that he had often talked to me about, disdained by the Parisian elite and aspiring to be heard and recognized. Calm, patient, tenacious, shrewd, skilled at gathering support around him and organizing networks, Raffarin knew how to advance without pushing himself forward or seeming to upset anyone. He was not a man of brilliant flashes or political arrogance but one of methodical work, sure determination, and balanced pragmatism. His arrival in Matignon would signal the return of common sense and of a just and well-reflected order. He exemplified the victory of humility over pretension and modesty over vanity.

On May 6, Villepin called him to ask him to come and see me at the Élysée as quickly as possible. "I have decided to appoint you prime minister," I told him as soon as he arrived. "And now we're going to call your mother to tell her the good news." I told him of my intention to give the ministry of foreign affairs to Dominique de Villepin and defense to Michèle Alliot-Marie. We agreed that we would offer Nicolas Sarkozy the post, as he seemed to wish, of minister of the interior. Then Raffarin set to work to decide the composition of his "government with a mission," announced the following day.

On May 27, 2002, in an exceptional event in the history of his country, the president of the United States celebrated Memorial Day on French rather than American soil. This annual ceremony honors the memory of American soldiers killed in combat since independence. George W. Bush had chosen to be in Normandy on that day to pay homage to the thousands of American soldiers killed in June 1944 on the landing beaches in the fight against the Nazi scourge. A symbolic gesture with which he wanted to mark his determination to get rid of a similar scourge, that of terrorism. "Today we defend our freedoms against people who can't stand freedom," he declared in the cemetery of Colleville-sur-Mer, "and this defense will require the sacrifice of our forefathers." When I spoke, I also emphasized the need to "get rid of terrorist barbarism" but also pointed out that this shared combat should have the goal of challenging not only fanaticism but also "exclusion of people who are different from us, racism and xenophobia"—in short, all forms of intolerance. Which was perhaps not exactly the meaning that my guest gave to his very personal commitment to fight a certain "axis of evil."

In our meeting at the Élysée the day before, Bush had confirmed to me that he considered Saddam Hussein a serious threat to world peace and stability. "I don't have a war plan on my desk," he told me, although he did not deny that his government was in favor of a change of regime in Baghdad as rapidly as possible. Our conversation had taken place in a relaxed and friendly atmosphere, as the U.S. president had himself wanted subsequently to emphasize to journalists, asserting that he had "no stronger or more solid ally than Jacques Chirac" and that he considered me a "personal friend" and a real friend of the United States.

Friendship being based on mutual honesty and loyalty, I gave Bush a strong warning against the risks of a possible military intervention in Iraq, even if I agreed with him about the danger that Saddam represented. "This is exactly what will happen," I said to him in private. "Initially, you will succeed in taking Baghdad without too much difficulty. Everything will be resolved in two or three weeks. But it is afterward that the problems will begin. You will be confronted with the beginnings of a civil war between Shi'ites, Kurds, and Sunnis. The Shi'ites are in the majority, and so sooner or later you will be obliged to give them power in the name of democracy, thereby strengthening Iran's position in the region and eventually destabilizing countries with a Sunni majority, such as Saudi Arabia and several others. This civil war will cause Iraq, which has never been held without a strong authority from its origins, to fall apart on every side. From then on, you will be able to control nothing. Nothing. With all the consequences that that will have for the balance of the Middle East." Bush listened to me without interrupting or making the slightest comment. At the most he gave a small, slightly ironic smile. And that was the end of our conversation on the subject.

I did not have access at that time to precise information about the imminence of conflict. But there was no doubt that the attacks of September 11, 2001, and the state of mind of the new American government, determined to avenge the humiliation suffered that day by every means, as well as the neoconservative notions then in vogue, had exacerbated a mistrust and hostility about Saddam that he himself had fed since the end of the Gulf War. Held to be one of the probable supporters or initiators of al-Qaeda's terrorist activities and more than ever seen as the sworn enemy of the United States, the Iraqi dictator was very strongly suspected of holding arms of mass destruction that posed an additional threat to the security of the United States. The American authorities were even more convinced of this because various reports emanating from their intelligence services signaled the existence in Iraq of a powerful arsenal of chemical, biological, and even nuclear weapons, secretly developed by Saddam over recent years, in defiance of UN Security Council Resolution 687, adopted in 1991 at the end of the Gulf War as part of the cease-fire agreement, ordering Iraq to destroy such weapons and to submit to a strict UN monitoring program. Forced to accept these demands, Baghdad had constantly maneuvered so as not to abide by its commitments, so impeding the work of the inspectors that they had been forced to leave at the end of 1998. After this, Iraq had conformed only sporadically and unwillingly to limited inspections, which no longer allowed the international community to have an idea of what its real means of defense were.

Over the course of 1998, I was personally involved, with the authorities in Baghdad as well as the members of the Security Council, in trying to find a diplomatic solution. However, it was another approach that ended up holding sway, in the face of Saddam's persistent about-faces and provocations of the UN, despite the incessant mediation efforts of UN Secretary General Kofi Annan, a man of peace, wisdom, and reconciliation if ever there was one. In August 1998, Saddam decided to suspend all cooperation with the UN Special Commission and International Atomic Energy Agency (IAEA) inspectors, thereby succeeding in convincing the powers most hostile to him that only force would make him see reason. Condemnation of this headstrong act—real or calculated, it was not known—was unanimous. While I pulled our representative out of Baghdad, the intransigence of Saddam led the United States and Great Britain in December 1998 to launch massive air strikes against Iraq.

Without disapproving of it in principle, France refrained from participating in this operation christened "Desert Fox." If a new bombing campaign could incontestably weaken the Iraqi nuclear potential, it also risked, in my view, permanently blocking all new cooperation with Baghdad on what should remain our primary objective: the control of nuclear, chemical, and bacteriological weapons that Saddam might possess. I also feared that the military option alone and the continued embargo would continue penalizing Iraqi civilian society without weakening the government or decreasing the popularity of its leader in Arab public opinion.

This was why France, in agreement with China and Russia, had striven between 1999 and 2001 to advocate a solution that would get Iraq to respect its international obligations without taking the country to a state of human and economic collapse that the regime could use as propaganda to exploit the West. The objective of the United States was already more radical, aiming at overthrowing Saddam and facilitating the emergence of a democratic government in Baghdad, under the terms of the Iraq Liberation Act, adopted by Congress in October 1998 with a large majority and promulgated by President Clinton but not followed up with action. In my view, this touched on another debate that could not be resolved in a unilateral manner and that required that the procedures of the United Nations, the only legitimate body that could resolve such a problem, be followed. In a letter addressed to Kofi Annan on September 30, 1999, I expressed the hope that the millennium summit to be held at the United Nations in the following year would be the occasion to reaffirm the seven vital principles of the new international order that we should have the ambition of creating. These principles were:

The principle of collective responsibility, outlawing the temptation of unilateral action and leading to a collective management of the global risks and threats that weigh on our peoples.

The principle of equity, so that the mechanisms of regulating globalization and the management of global risks act to the benefit of the greatest number and contribute to a fair division of responsibilities.

The principle of solidarity, to fight against the exclusion of people or nations.

The principle of diversity, to preserve the cultural, linguistic, and biological wealth of the world confronted with the risks of uniformity created by globalization.

The principle of caution, which should be applied well beyond the domain of the environment to deliver intact to generations to come the earth that belongs to them.

The principle of freedom, to ensure democracy everywhere and respect of the universal declaration of human rights.

Finally, the principle of necessity, for the new international rules should be implemented at a regional and world level only when they are essential.

It was these principles, which in my view could not be separated, that would dictate France's position throughout the Iraqi crisis. They sum up the fundamental reasons for our difference of opinion in this matter with the United States and its allies, engaged in a violent clash that would lead them, in the name of freedom alone, to lose sight of the very first principle, equally essential in my eyes: that of collective responsibility, exercised within the framework of the United Nations.

During the summer of 2002, signs that America was preparing for war began to be apparent.

On August 5, I received a confidential note from my private chief of staff, in whom I had total confidence. He informed me of various factors that indicated that a military operation against Iraq could be launched before the end of the year. First, the fact that Saddam himself seemed to be preparing for such an eventuality by redeploying his military systems and by trying to procure nonconventional weapons, principally from North Korea. Then the gradual implementation by the United States, with British and Australian support, of prepositioning around Iraq. Finally, the noticeable increase of their forces currently deployed in the region. However, the Pentagon did not seem to have decided on a definitive strategy. Four options were being studied: a large-scale land operation of 250,000 men including 30,000 British soldiers; a massive air strike combined with a land action; an operation of Iraqi resistance supported by 5,000 American soldiers and precision strikes; and a rapid taking of Baghdad and strategic points. According to my chief of staff, Washington was currently favoring the third option of an internal conspiracy carried out by members of the Republican Guard, with whom contact was under way, followed by an American land operation launched immediately after the fall of Saddam. Whichever option was chosen, the prospect of an armed conflict no longer seemed out of the question, even if I refused to acknowledge that publicly.

I was not the only one to take the possibility of an American attack very seriously from that time on. On September 2, Nelson Mandela expressed the same worry to me when I went to talk with him during the world summit on sustainable development being held in Johannesburg. He suddenly seized hold of my wrists and said to me, looking me straight in the eyes: "You should do all you can to stop Bush going into Iraq!"

The following day, I addressed a double warning to the parties present. First, I reminded them that the international community's foremost objective was that of an "unconditional return" of the UN inspectors to Iraq, thereby inviting the authorities in Baghdad to submit to this without delay. I then underlined, for the benefit of the United States, that if Iraq continued to resist this, "only the Security Council is authorized to take the decisions that might then be required," adding in conclusion: "I am not in favor, as you know, of 'unilateralism' from any quarter."

This was the position I would continually assert over the following months, with the aim of arriving at a solution to the Iraqi problem that was in conformity, on both sides, with the demands of international law. This solution did not envisage the option of force as inevitable but did not exclude it, within the conditions that I placed, should Saddam continue to refuse to cooperate. In my mind, it did not have the sole objective of bringing the existing power in Baghdad to an end, come what may, whatever our opinion of it.

"We have no confidence in the Iraqi regime, which has amply demonstrated its capacity for harm in the past, including toward its own people," I said to Tony Blair, who telephoned me on the subject on September 6. "But we remain convinced that the most efficient way of ascertaining that he is not producing weapons of mass destruction is for the UN inspectors to return there. As for the measures that could be taken if Iraq still refuses to listen to reason, I do not rule any out in principle. We must discuss it. But it is essential for France that the legitimacy of international action be guaranteed and the stability of the region maintained."

Blair had wanted to talk to me before he left for the United States, where he was to meet Bush the following day. He made no secret to me of the fact that he felt very close to the American point of view, in the sense that he also thought that the best way of ensuring world peace was to get rid, one way or another, of leaders like Saddam Hussein. Nonetheless, Blair declared that he wanted to act within the framework of the United Nations and that he was in favor of a new Security Council resolution to finally force Saddam to disarm.

Although I was disappointed by his rallying behind the ideological position of the White House, it did not surprise me. Britain traditionally had its eyes riveted on the other side of the Atlantic. Having tried, on coming to office, to free himself from the control of Washington, Blair had not been long in bowing down to it. What saddened and angered me, to be frank, was that he did not make greater use of the former experience that his country had of the Middle East and of Iraq in particular. By immediately rallying to the American side, Blair unfortunately deprived himself of any real ability to influence the analysis made by the American government of a regional situation that it knew less well than Britain. He was taking on a heavy responsibility from the point of view of history.

That same day, at the end of the afternoon, Bush called me in his turn, wanting, he said, to "inform a certain number of leader friends" of his position on Iraq, "conscious that it was the subject of concern in the world and even in the United States." He was probably alluding to the debate that pitted the hard-line advocates of "preemptive war" in his close team, such as Vice President Dick Cheney and Defense Secretary Donald Rumsfeld, against more legalistic advisors, such as Secretary of State Colin Powell. According to the information from our embassy in Washington, President Bush had not definitively chosen his camp, despite the extremely belligerent words he had delivered against Iraq at West Point Military Academy the previous June.

"Beyond our differences on Iraq," went on Bush, "there are two points on which we can agree: first, that Saddam Hussein constitutes a threat. Second, that he continues to defy the international community." He announced that he had decided to send experts into certain countries, without specifying which ones, to evaluate the extent of this threat. After which he would put measures designed to tackle it to the United Nations on September 9. "Contrary to the speculations emerging from all over, no decision has been taken on the subject in Washington," he assured me for the second time since our meeting on May 26 at the Élysée. I confirmed to him that I hoped, for my part, that Saddam would see reason and again emphasized that "military intervention would constitute a difficult and dangerous option." In any event, I told him at the end of our conversation, France remained open to debate.

The following day, in Hanover, I was the guest of Gerhard Schröder for an informal dinner at his home. Among other subjects, we had a long discussion about the question of Iraq. Our points of view easily coalesced, as the chancellor shortly afterward informed journalists at a joint press conference: "On the four points I shall now outline, we are in agreement. First, we are clearly and resolutely opposed to all unilateral action. Second, we believe that the UN inspectors should be able to return to Iraq unconditionally. Third, we are in agreement that the United Nations should have a vital role to play in terms of Iraq. Fourth, we are in agreement that the objectives that have been set out should not be changed. These objectives are and remain the return of UN inspectors to Iraq without this being imposed through military means." The chancellor ended by affirming that Germany, for its part, ruled out all participation in any armed intervention. That was the only difference between us because I did not exclude this eventuality for France so categorically.

I felt comforted by the fact that France and Germany had the same understanding of the Iraqi problem, its exact details, and the best way of resolving it. This alliance could be decisive in convincing the United States to give up the idea of all hasty action in favor of a more gradual and balanced approach.

A year after the attacks on the World Trade Center and several days before the speech George W. Bush was to give to the United Nations, I decided to make France's position publicly known by giving a long interview to the *New York Times,* which was published on September 9. Questioned about the doctrine of the "preemptive war" advocated by Bush and the most radical of his entourage, I firmly rejected the concept: "From the moment a nation gives itself the right to act preemptively, other nations will naturally do the same. That is, I believe, an extraordinarily dangerous doctrine and one that could have dramatic consequences. A preemptive action could be undertaken if it seems necessary, but only by the international community, which is today the Security Council of the United Nations."

Responding to another question about the right way to proceed in Iraq to be certain that Saddam was not developing weapons of mass destruction, I obviously condemned him and declared that I hoped to see the establishment of democracy in Baghdad. But I also pointed out that I did not, at that time, have any proof of the existence of such weapons in Iraq and that our sole objective should be to ascertain that Saddam did not possess them. "What is in question today is not a change of the Iraqi regime. We can want that, we do obviously want it, but we need a little order to manage the affairs of the world, we need several principles and a little order. . . . The Security Council had never been asked to discuss a determination to change the regime in Iraq. Because there are so many countries where one would like to see other regimes—but if we start down that road, where will it end up?"

I then warned the United States against the danger of exacerbating the rejection of the West that I sensed swelling up on all sides in poor and developing countries. This growing feeling of injustice and frustration worried me because it risked undermining the large coalition we had succeeded in organizing against terrorism. I took advantage of the opportunity to emphasize the urgency of a second coalition, "a coalition against poverty, a coalition for the environment—for ecology is headed in a dangerous direction—a coalition that would resolve the problems, crises, and conflicts that exist all over the world and to which we could find solutions if we were a little more generous or engaged. It would also be a very efficient way of fighting against terrorism and proving ourselves worthy of our human duty."

Finally, I set out my own strategy concerning the solution of the Iraqi problem. A plan that combined firmness and respect of law and presented an alternative to the plans of the American government.

Three days later, the speech of George W. Bush did not help dispel—quite the contrary—the threat of preemptive military action in Iraq. The president of the United States had justified it from the outset, in a tone that was both solemn and categorical: "Today we turn to the duty of protecting . . . lives without illusion and without fear." However, after having set out his demands in this regard, the U.S. president had ended by asking, as Tony Blair wished and under the obvious pressure of Colin Powell, that they be the subject of one or several "necessary resolutions" of the United Nations. In reality, his objective was above all to make the United Nations face its responsibilities and demand that it finally prove its efficacy, as he quite openly declared in asking, not without irony: "Are Security Council resolutions to be honored and enforced or cast aside without consequence? Will the United Nations serve the purpose of its founding or will it be irrelevant?"

Even if he satisfied part of my own requests in locating his action within the context of the United Nations, this speech left me few illusions about the real goal of the White House and Bush's determination to achieve it by any means possible. It was evidently both an ultimatum to Iraq and a formal notice addressed to the Security Council. In these circumstances, it was more imperative than ever to ensure that the future resolution desired by the United States be sufficiently explicit to oblige Iraq to submit to renewed inspections. This was the only way of achieving peaceful disarmament and therefore avoiding a military confrontation without legitimizing in advance an automatic, inevitable intervention. In other words, recourse to the use of force could only be decided later by the Security Council and only if the work of the inspectors was blocked or following the conclusions of their reports.

After I had sent him a message urging this approach, after full consultation with Kofi Annan, Saddam agreed on September 16 to the resumption of inspections. We obviously did not simply take his word for it and did not reduce our pressure to make him fall into line once and for all, without going much beyond the obligations that had long since been set out under the various UN resolutions. To strengthen them too much would be to provide Saddam with a new pretext for rejecting them, thereby playing into the hands of those most determined to procure his downfall. I was convinced that one of the ways of making this new resolution more efficient would be if it were unanimously voted.

France was in the front line of what were long and difficult negotiations with Great Britain and the United States but also all the other members of the Security Council, until Resolution 1441 was adopted on November 8, 2002. I followed the issue closely, engaging in many discussions with President Bush and a great number of my foreign counterparts, particularly German, Chinese, and Russian. My overall strategy about the Iraqi affair was prepared, deliberated, and instigated with the foreign affairs minister, Dominique de Villepin, with whom I worked in the most trusting and amicable collaboration, with the permanent support of a small team of senior diplomats.

On September 26, I was informed about the proposed Anglo-American resolution, which I judged unacceptable. As I was expecting, this resolution imposed considerably tougher demands on the Iraqi regime and above all provided for an automatic recourse to the use of force. Its announcement was heralded by a public statement by Tony Blair, two days before, affirming that he had overwhelming proof against Saddam. He stated: "The intelligence picture . . . is extensive, detailed, and authoritative" and, according to him, clearly showed that "Iraq developed chemical and biological weapons, acquired missiles allowing it to attack neighboring countries with these weapons, and persistently tried to develop a nuclear bomb." For the British prime minister, all this demonstrated that the "current regime" in Baghdad was "uniquely dangerous."

I responded to him on the same day that in my eyes, it was another reason to want the quickest possible resumption of inspections in Iraq and to wait for their results to be duly given. There could be no question, in the meantime, of going further in the ultimatum that the international community was preparing to issue to Saddam, and that was why I categorically rejected the proposed resolution that London and Washington were trying to impose on us.

George W. Bush called me to discuss the issue the following day, September 27. He began by thanking me for the help that the French army had just given to Americans in the Ivory Coast. Then he strove to convince me of the necessity of a resolution very different from the previous resolutions and that included the possibility of automatic recourse to the use of force, without which this ultimate injunction would not, yet again, be taken seriously by Saddam. I replied that France was also persuaded that we needed to exert extreme pressure on Saddam but that our resolution should not be perceived as a pretext to cause Iraqis to make a false move. I noted that we fundamentally diverged on the type of approach that should be taken in their regard. According to us, it should comprise two stages: first, the inspections, and then the possibility of military intervention. "It is a serious matter," I told him, "because it involves war." And I again warned Bush against the danger of provoking an eruption of violence in Iraq by precipitating, at all costs, the downfall of Saddam Hussein, in a regional context in which antiwestern sentiments were already virulent. The president of the United States still did not seem persuaded by my analysis, but we naturally agreed to continue the cooperation between our two countries.

I later had successive telephone conversations with Vladimir Putin and the Chinese prime minister, Zhu Rongji. The president of the Russian Federation told me that strong pressure was being exerted on him by the American and British leaders to obtain his support. After asking my opinion of the text, he declared that the clause on automatic intervention seemed to him just as unacceptable and that if it was put forward and if France supported Putin's position, he was ready to veto it. For his part, the Chinese prime minister declared himself no less favorable to the line I was advocating. He assured me that his country was prepared, if necessary, to take a position alongside France and Russia within the Security Council.

This alliance was to prove decisive in the course of our negotiations with the American government. On October 11, Congress overwhelmingly passed the proposed resolution from the White House. The situation seemed so deadlocked at that time that our representative in Washington began, whether from weariness or conviction, recommending that we prioritize the search for a compromise with the United States. He feared that it would ultimately renounce all UN agreements in order to realize its goal. But I refused to allow the slightest negotiation on the most contentious aspects of the proposed resolution: that would be to open a can of worms much more serious than a passing quarrel with our American friends.

The weeks that followed confirmed that I had been right to give in to nothing and to hold fast. On October 25, nine delegations out of the fifteen that made up the Security Council brought into question several clauses, notably that relating to automatic intervention. Mexico, Ireland, Mauritius, Guinea, Cameroon, and Norway seemed on the point of supporting the position of France, Russia, and China, even if certain nations were more vulnerable than others to possible Anglo-American pressure. Increasingly frequent contact between Colin Powell and Dominique de Villepin allowed us to arrive, at the beginning of November and after amendments and counterpropositions between our respective negotiators, at an agreement that seemed to me reasonable.

On November 8, 2002, Resolution 1441 was unanimously voted, after I had personally convinced Syria, the sole Arab nation that was a member of the Security Council, to agree to it. The text stipulated that in the case of "patent violation" of its obligations, Iraq should assume "serious consequences," which met the concern of the Security Council to put Saddam Hussein on the spot and make him understand, in an extremely firm manner, that he had no choice other than to cooperate. As we had hoped, the new resolution set down the regime of inspections in a way that was certainly more rigorous but also realistic. The chairman of the UN inspection commission, Hans Blix, and the director general of the IAEA, Mohamed ElBaradei, should have unhindered and permanent access to all the sites but without more binding conditions being imposed on Iraq. Above all, we had obtained consensus that there be no mention of the possibility of automatic and unilateral military intervention: In the case of Iraq's noncompliance with its obligations, the Security Council would meet on the basis of an inspectors' report and not at the instigation of one government. And so the Security Council alone would be called on, as France had always wished, to decide on the consequences that should ensue, thereby safeguarding the principle of collective responsibility.

The interpretation that the United States, firmly resolved in any case to fight with Iraq, would make of this resolution remained to be seen; it imposed certain limits on the nation that it would not necessarily feel bound to respect.

A month later, on December 8, Iraq's declaration on the real state of its armaments, required under Resolution 1441 within thirty days, was far from adequate to lift the presumptive evidence against it. The report submitted by Saddam Hussein to the Security Council was voluminous but contained few new elements in terms of the questions not resolved by the UN Special Commission and IAEA inspectors. For all that, no one had proof of the Iraqi omissions, which justified all the more our reliance on the results of the inspections. That alone could allow us to determine, as a last resort, the attitude that needed to be adopted toward Saddam. It was fairly quickly confirmed, however, that these inspections had meaning and interest for Washington only if they proved to be sufficiently damning for the Iraqi dictator—if they provided, in other words, Great Britain and the United States with the pretext they were looking for to launch the military operation that they had resolved on.

I had never, for my part, ruled out the possibility of France coming alongside the United States, as it had previously done in Bosnia or Kosovo, if military intervention again turned out to be legitimate. So as not to be caught short if such an eventuality presented itself more rapidly than foreseen, in December 2002, I asked the new chief of defense staff and my private chief of staff to make the necessary contact with their American counterparts. Immediately dispatched to the United States, the deputy head of operations at the army high command received a courteous and attentive welcome, but the powers that be at the Pentagon quickly gave him to understand that they were in the midst of finalizing their plans and the more time passed, the more impossible it became to reserve spaces for French forces. Which therefore supposed that we had to become involved now in the preparations if we did not want to be left out when the time came. When the chief of defense staff asked me, in a note sent on January 6, 2003, if it was "still too soon" to "take the risk of signaling a possible French involvement," I replied with an unhesitating yes.

At that time, even though the inspections by the UN teams had been carried out since November 27, 2002, without incident and at regular intervals, the impression prevailed on all sides that the United States and Great Britain, which were obviously trying to direct the work of the inspectors through their respective intelligence services, were fully engaged in preparing for combat. On January 9, 2003, Hans Blix and Mohamed ElBaradei addressed a first report to the members of the Security Council on the current inspections. They both emphasized the value of the inspections, not only because they prevented Saddam from opening new sites but because they also helped prevent the resumption or development of prohibited programs. They did not signal any outright obstruction on the part of the Iraqis, even if the latter were not always sufficiently cooperative. They nonetheless believed that the process already under way should continue indefinitely so that truly conclusive results could be obtained. In other words, the principal obstacle in their view would be the imposition of a time limit—which Resolution 1441 did not set down. But this was a debate that could now be held only with the United States, which wished to be the only one in control of timing, as the deployment of its forces, which was accelerating in the region, proved.

Since the beginning of the winter, the United States had already stationed more than 100,000 men in the Gulf, mobilized 20,000 reservists, and gathered considerable logistical resources. All obvious signs of an imminent war. On January 13, I sent diplomatic advisor Maurice Gourdault-Montagne to Washington to meet Condoleezza Rice and other influential presidential staff. I had scarcely any doubts about the reality of American intentions, but I wanted to be sure.

After describing the Iraqi declaration of December 8 as "a joke," Rice had summed up her opinion in these terms: "Saddam Hussein is not cooperating. He is deceiving the world. He is hiding weapons. If the next inspection report is not more substantial than the one of January 9, as in all likelihood it will not be, a final phase will begin. The credibility of the United States is at stake. Everyone knows that Saddam Hussein cheats and hides. If we do not act, the countries of the region and of the whole world will note our weakness. We do not want to renew the experience of the eleven years since the Gulf War. The American people will not accept it. The question is to know how we, Americans and French together, will manage this decisive period. We refuse to postpone the inevitable. So is it not better to confront it together?" For Rice, the only way of avoiding war would be the immediate departure of Saddam and all his team followed, shortly afterward, by the establishment of a democratic government. "There has to be a change of government," she insisted. "After a while, we can lift the sanctions."

My diplomatic advisor then met the assistant of Donald Rumsfeld, Paul Wolfowitz, one of the most outspoken proponents of the neoconservative group. He had proved to be as tough as we had expected, violently sweeping away France's arguments before speaking sarcastically about the trust we placed in the chief UN inspector: "Why put your foreign policy in the hands of a Swedish diplomat with fewer men than the police of a provincial French town? France's voice counts more than that of Mr. Blix!"

The die therefore seemed cast. Nonetheless, I did not resign myself to the idea that war had now become an inevitable prospect. War is always an admission of failure and the worst solution, as I publicly stated during the visit to Paris, on January 17, of Blix and ElBaradei. Ten days before the presentation of their second report, I assured the two chief inspectors of the unreserved trust and support of our country. I knew that their task was a formidable one and that they had to carry it out in the most difficult conditions, caught between apparently irreconcilable interests and issues. They both told me that Iraqi cooperation was good but that it remained essentially passive: "They are opening doors for us," they said, "and letting us carry out our inspections but we do not always have the cooperation we need. We need a certain amount of proof that there are no weapons of mass destruction: certain documents that we wish to see on bacteriological or chemical weapons, for example. We want to be able to interview Iraqi experts in private to be sure that we do indeed have the information we need. Nonetheless, Resolution 1441 has given more power to the inspectors to carry out their investigations."

This was exactly what they would write in their official report, presented on January 27 to the members of the Security Council. In it they noted that their collaboration with the Iraqi authorities was still too restricted to be able to give the international community, in a short time frame, all the answers they expected and demanded from Saddam. At this stage of their inquiry, it is true that the results obtained remained disappointing. But what counted in my eyes was their confirmation that the inspections were likely to lead to better results, given time.

The conclusion of the British and American leaders was, of course, quite different. For them, there was no more doubt that Saddam, with his still-uncooperative attitude, had now "violated Resolution 1441." The following day, the American president made a State of the Union speech in which he attacked Iraq in an extremely virulent manner and announced that Colin Powell would present to the Security Council on February 5 irrefutable "proof" that the country held weapons of mass destruction. In the meantime, he met with Tony Blair, who had come to New York to see him. It was during this meeting, as I was immediately informed by our diplomatic services, that the idea was born—insistently advocated by the British prime minister—of a new resolution maintaining that Iraq had not fulfilled its commitments and that we consequently were required to act.

We now entered the second phase of the Iraqi affair in which two opposing visions of the world and of the role of the international community would crystallize, as well as two concepts of the relations between nations and the principles that should inspire them. On one side, a multilateral and legalistic approach. On the other, a dominating and Manichean logic that favored force over law. This fault line over the issue of Iraq became more obvious every day between nations such as France, Germany, Russia, China, and the great majority of African and Latin American countries, which wanted to find a peaceful solution in accordance with the demands of the Security Council, and a minority of countries grouped around Great Britain and the United States, for which recourse to armed intervention was the sole option, or at least the most efficient one faced with an immediate risk of world destabilization.

On January 30, the British, Danish, Spanish, Italian, and Portuguese leaders, together with their Hungarian, Czech, and Polish counterparts, published in *The Times* (London) a call to consolidate the "transatlantic bond" in the face of the Iraqi threat and the fact that Saddam Hussein could not be allowed to "systematically violate" UN resolutions. It was a breakaway from the unanimous European position expressed several days earlier by European foreign affairs ministers and an unconditional rallying to the American position, combined with a no less obvious attempt to counter the French, German, and Russian resistance. To top it all, American defense secretary Donald Rumsfeld ridiculed the attitude of what he called "old Europe."

I denounced these diplomatic maneuvers as they deserved, but in a tone that was probably misplaced when I said that their authors, notably the ones who had most recently joined the European Union, would have done better to remain silent. But this was not the only kind of pressure that now began to be exerted on us in a bid to change the position of France and its allies. In the case of the United States, it would go as far as very specific threats to restrict our supply of armaments. At home, however, the position I had adopted and unwaveringly defended since the beginning of the crisis benefited from a massive and quasi-unanimous support from the French people, united as it always was in the major events of its history.

It was among the elite, or presumed elite, however, that the most discordant voices were to be heard. Among some of our diplomats a veiled but perceptible worry spread about the risk of France becoming isolated. Certain business organizations and leading businesses sent me more insistent messages in which they urged me to show greater flexibility toward the United States so as not to lose important markets for our companies. I remember Baron Sellière coming to plead with me on behalf of some of his peers. The most pro-NATO strands within both the government and the opposition parties were not to be left out and denounced, more or less openly, my obstinacy in seeming to defy the Americans.

I listened to these comments without being overly affected by them, given the great principles at stake with the war in Iraq. The same criticisms had been leveled at General de Gaulle when he made France's voice heard in a way that was judged too disturbing. Whatever people thought, and buoyed by the agreement of my compatriots, I was determined to stay the course. There was obviously no question for me of undermining, however slightly, the friendship that linked us to the American people, but our political and diplomatic relationship with the United States needed more than ever to abide by the principle that had been its basis since 1958: solidarity within a framework of independence.

On February 5, Colin Powell's statement—announced as definitive—to the Security Council did not present any new facts that could justify, directly or indirectly, a preemptive war. The "proof" that he offered, essentially based on accounts of telephone taps provided by his intelligence services, did not in any way constitute incontrovertible proof. Designed to legitimize an imminent military intervention, his indictment of Iraq consisted of a series of suspicions and presumptions that, as he would honestly admit several years later, were based, though he did not realize it at the time, on data that was erroneous, if not fabricated.

Far from provoking the effect expected by the White House, Powell's speech instead confirmed the majority of the members of the Council in their rejection of the war, as I found out the following day when I telephoned first Vladimir Putin, then Vicente Fox, the president of Mexico; Ricardo Lagos, the president of Chile; as well as the Syrian and Cameroonian leaders, Bashar al-Assad and Paul Biya. Several days later, the new president of Brazil, Lula da Silva, confirmed the unconditional support that he had already expressed to me on his official visit to Paris in January for the cause defended by France.

I took the initiative, without great hope of success, of renewing contact with George W. Bush on February 7. "I am phoning you as a friend, and as a friend of the United States," I said to him. "We have two analyses, which lead to war or to peace. It is a moral problem. You take one position and we take another. It involves two different visions of the world and we have to accept that—but it should not stop us talking to each other." I added that I was not a pacifist but that I was not in favor of war when it was not necessary. That too was immoral. "I appreciate your consistency and your compassion," the president of the United States replied. "I do not like war either. I know, like every head of state, the responsibility borne by the person who decides to send soldiers into combat. Nonetheless, we differ on one thing: I think that Saddam Hussein constitutes a threat to the security of the American people. That is why I have a different approach in terms of timing."

The tone of the conversation was, on both sides, courteous, calm, and considered, as it had in fact always been. But our dialogue was now just that of two men who had used up all their arguments. I acknowledged his determination to enter into combat with Iraq, come what may, and to go to the very end of what was almost a historical and quasi-mystical mission that he felt was incumbent on him. He acknowledged my conviction that the possibility of arriving at a peaceful solution should be kept open for as long as possible and that the conflict that was being prepared was both

unjust and futile. Before ending the conversation, we nonetheless talked of
the possibility of a future cooperation, once the war was over, to help Iraq
rebuild itself and relaunch the peace process in the region. This would be
our last exchange before the opening of hostilities on March 20, 2003, and
the end of Operation Iraqi Freedom less than a month later.

Although I was under no more illusions about the sequence of events,
at no time until the fateful hour had arrived was I resigned to the notion that we had lost all chance of dissuading London and Washington
from launching into such an affair. A renewed chance of avoiding the worst
presented itself on February 14 when Blix and ElBaradei presented their
third report to the Security Council in which was set out conclusive information transmitted by the Iraqi government that marked clear progress
in Saddam's desire to cooperate. In the ballistic sector, the inspectors had
been given precise information about the prohibited weapons held by Iraq,
enabling their destruction. In terms of chemical and biological weapons,
the inspectors had been able to obtain more enlightening documents from
Baghdad while the IAEA seemed in a position over the following months
to proceed to the dismantling of the nuclear program that was under way.
In addition, aerial reconnaissance planes would begin flying over Iraq on
February 17, and several private interviews had taken place with Iraqi sci-
entists. The inspections were therefore bearing fruit—yet this fact had no
effect on the representatives of the Anglo-American coalition, joined by
Spain and Bulgaria, the latter having been subjected to a kind of blackmail
in regard to its entry into NATO.

In a clear demonstration of the importance the members of the Security
Council gave this crucial meeting, the foreign affairs ministers of each country went to New York to attend this meeting and comment on the report of
the two chief inspectors. Deliberately minimizing the progress mentioned
in it, Colin Powell maintained his position. For him, the "broken promises" and "duplicity" of the Iraqi authorities had never been so flagrant. He
invited the Council to reflect on the "serious consequences of a refusal to
assume its responsibilities" and insisted on the dramatic risks posed by the
"emerging alliance" between Iraq and international terrorism. The weapons of mass destruction still held, according to him, by Saddam could cause
"hundreds of thousands of deaths if they fell into the wrong hands." His
British counterpart, Jack Straw, continued in the same vein.

At my request, Dominique de Villepin had gone to defend France's
point of view. The speech he had prepared, and which we had carefully
reread together before his departure for New York, was one fitting for the
historical moment the world was experiencing. Villepin delivered it with

a sense of nobility, energy, and all the appropriate sensitivity of the "old country" that we are, tested by history and having itself had the experience of wars, occupation, and barbarity. This impassioned plea in favor of peace and the responsibility of nations faced with their collective destiny was the expression of an ideal that gave meaning to our shared commitment. The standing ovation he received in the UN chamber gave me a sense of happiness and pride in our country.

The reaction of the Americans was, needless to say, less enthusiastic; they were as irritated by Villepin's speech as they were, shortly afterward, by the interview I gave to *Time* magazine. Eager to explain France's position to the American public, I had set out my own plan of action to achieve the necessary disarmament of Iraq. Above all, I was worried about the repercussions of a conflict on Arab and Muslim public opinion, fearing that a multitude of mini–bin Ladens would be created. Vice President Cheney was particularly stirred up against us. In a meeting with our ambassador in Washington over the following days, he did not hesitate to accuse France of the "unforgivable crime" of putting the security of America at risk by our rejection of war at the very moment when America was preparing to "get rid of the evil."

We tried to warn the British about the risk, in such a context, of putting forward a new resolution authorizing recourse to the use of force, but in vain. Such a resolution could only crystallize the differences within the Security Council and lead to a major division within the international community, which was in nobody's interests. The question of whether to go to war should not be decided by a simple vote. What is more, what use would such a resolution serve for Great Britain and the United States, determined as they were to go to war with or without the mandate of the United Nations, other than exposing them to probable rejection by the majority of the members of the Council? Despite this, Tony Blair remained obstinately attached to the principle of an agreement from the United Nations that would help protect him morally and politically in terms of British public opinion, which was largely hostile to the war. The White House eventually resigned itself to a UN vote and, indeed, declared its total confidence that the results of the vote would be in its favor.

According to the information put out by Washington, the United States maintained that it was certain to get nine votes out of the fifteen, with the abstention of China and Russia. France had to decide whether it would veto this resolution and assume all the responsibility for doing so. So here we were, designated in advance as the ones solely responsible for the resolution's failure.

On February 24, 2003, I was informed of the proposed resolution presented by Great Britain and sponsored by Spain and the United States. It was a text full of subtexts that nowhere stated its real objective directly. Despite the results already obtained by the inspectors, it repeated in veiled terms, under the guise of apparently factual and inoffensive phrases and through allusions and circumlocutions, the same accusations that Iraq was not respecting its obligations as set out in Resolution 1441. It included, on the other hand, a barely disguised authorization of recourse to the use of force.

I immediately instructed our representative at the UN to put everything in place to rally the majority of the nonpermanent members of the Council—on whom the result of the vote would probably depend—to our cause. We needed to concentrate our efforts on them, as the opposing side would also not fail to do. I had every confidence in the tactical intelligence and fine analytical skills of our ambassador, whose total support I appreciated. However, I also realized the need for both me and Dominique to make unstinted efforts of our own with our respective counterparts. It was first a question of pointing out that this new resolution had only one goal, hidden but nonetheless real: getting the Security Council to legitimize a military operation that most of its members did not want unless the inspectors themselves judged it essential. For that, we had to lose no time in intensifying our information campaign with the governments thought to be undecided or hesitant voters, such as Chile, Mexico, Pakistan, Guinea, Cameroon, or Angola, as well as the countries held to be "influential": India, Brazil, South Africa, Indonesia, Japan, Iran, Turkey, and the Gulf states.

The "resistance movement," of which France seemed more than ever the leader, took support from the memorandum signed on February 10 with Germany and Russia and accepted by China. I knew I could count on the total commitment of Vladimir Putin, Gerhard Schröder, and Jiang Zemin, despite the pressure—principally financial and economic—that Russia and Germany, at least, continued to experience. I admired the courage and tenacity with which those who had given us the most constant support since the beginning of the crisis had stood fast against the attempts to intimidate them. On the other hand, I deplored the unconditional support that the Spanish leader José María Aznar gave the Anglo-American arguments and the extremely critical judgments that he continually made of France. We would have a particularly stormy debate about this when he passed through Paris on February 26.

My first telephone contact with the Chilean president, Ricardo Lagos, seemed to me on the whole positive. Although he was in the middle of negotiating a free trade agreement between his country and the United States—understandably, given their geographical proximity—he wanted to confirm his country's opposition to the war and his preference for the solution we were advocating. He also expressed to me his worry, which he said he had also shared with the other nonpermanent members, about having to bear the responsibility for a negative vote against Washington and a section of the Security Council. I feared that both he and his Mexican counterpart, Vicente Fox, would eventually choose to give priority to economic interests with the United States. However, both of them seemed reassured by France's determination to go as far as vetoing the resolution, if need be, to stop it being adopted; certain rumors, emanating from Washington, had cast doubt on that. At the end of our conversations, they both affirmed to me that they shared our convictions and would abstain from voting on the proposed resolution if I confirmed my negative vote as well as that of China, Germany, and Russia.

At the same time, British and American emissaries trooped through all the capital cities concerned while Tony Blair and George W. Bush busied themselves phoning the other leaders. At the beginning of March, Henry Kissinger and several envoys went to Mexico, shortly before the arrival of Colin Powell. Pakistan, Angola, and Guinea were subject to equally insistent diplomatic maneuvers, and Condoleezza Rice was also brought into play, being sent to Moscow in the following days.

This campaign convinced me that I should intensify our own efforts at explanation. On the tenth of that month, Dominique de Villepin undertook a lightning tour of the three African states that had a seat on the Security Council: Angola, Cameroon, and Guinea. Curiously, the American government considered this an "unfriendly" action, seeing it as proof of a desire for systemic obstruction, whereas we had only given a warning about the risks of war and the existence of an alternative solution.

On March 7, the presentation of the inspectors' fourth report confirmed our position. Blix and ElBaradei declared that they were convinced that the now-active cooperation of the Iraqis could lead to real disarmament, as conclusively and visibly demonstrated by the destruction of their prohibited missiles. Yet this obvious progress did not stop Great Britain, Spain, and the United States from hardening their proposed resolution, that same day, by adding an ultimatum to Saddam Hussein with a deadline of March 17.

After proposing that the heads of state and government leaders be present that day at the United Nations to directly assume responsibility for their votes—an invitation immediately declined by President Bush—I confirmed publicly on March 10, in a televised address, that France would vote "no," however much support the resolution gained. In the unlikely event of the resolution obtaining a majority, France would still make use of its right of veto, which meant that, under UN rules, the resolution no longer had any chance of being adopted. Eager to have France's position understood by American public opinion, or at least for the truth not to be distorted, I gave an interview several days later with CNN and CBS. I also needed to reaffirm our position publicly in order to reassure the Chilean and Mexican presidents, whom I knew were still subject to strong pressure from the American government and businesses and who needed our guarantee that we would not give in.

I was aware of the seriousness of this decision and the responsibility that it implied. I also knew, in this critical moment, that two other permanent members of the Council, Russia and China, would commit themselves along the same lines and were equally prepared to go to the ultimate step of a veto. Vladimir Putin also confirmed to me his determination to vote with France in a private meeting on February 10.

On March 17, having discussed the matter in the Azores the previous day in a meeting chaired by the Portuguese prime minister, José Manuel Barroso, the partisans of war realized the impasse they were in and decided to withdraw their proposed resolution, directly accusing France of being responsible. We were their scapegoats. Nothing and nobody could now stop them from going to the very end of their own logic. On the eighteenth, the United States issued its ultimatum to Saddam Hussein and demanded that he give up power within forty-eight hours. I then made a solemn statement reminding each country of its responsibility. At dawn on March 20, the coalition began military operations in Iraq. That same day, I addressed the following message to the French:

> My dear compatriots:
>
> Military operations have just begun in Iraq. France regrets this action, entered into without the endorsement of the United Nations. I hope that these operations will be as rapid as possible with as few fatalities as possible and that they will not lead to a humanitarian crisis.
>
> Up until the end, France, with many other countries, strove to argue that the necessary disarmament of Iraq could be obtained by peaceful means.
>
> Those efforts did not succeed. Whatever the duration of the conflict, it will have heavy consequences for the future.

However, France will continue, faithful to its principles—the primacy of law, justice, dialogue between peoples, and respect for others—to strive to ensure that crises that threaten to pull the world into bloody conflicts find just and durable solutions within collective action. In other words, within the framework of the United Nations, the sole legitimate framework for building peace, in Iraq as elsewhere.

That is why we now have to unite, with our allies and with the whole of the international community, to take on together the challenges that await us.

While Iraq was plunged into a war that I had not managed to prevent, it seemed to me the moment had come to organize that other alliance, the urgency of which I had emphasized several months earlier in the *New York Times:* the coalition of peoples and states eager to preserve the natural balance of our planet, to achieve a better division of our wealth and resources in favor of the most vulnerable continents, to fight against poverty and the plague of great pandemics, to defend throughout the world the cause of peace, security, and cooperation. I wanted France again to be at the forefront of this vital fight for the future of humanity.

23

PROGRESS AND
SETBACKS

While I was working for a better world government and fighting for more responsible economic markets, increased aid to underprivileged countries, a revision of our modes of production and consumption, a strengthening of the fight against terrorism, and a global relaunch of growth, it was primarily the future of France and of the French that was on my mind. In arguing for peace and stability, the diversity of cultures, and the respect of peoples within Europe as everywhere else, I was defending the cause of our own security and identity. Even if many of my compatriots were still inclined to deny it, the growth of globalization meant that a country's internal politics were inseparable from its international politics. The world had become our shared territory, and everything that happened in it determined our individual and collective existence to such an extent that we could no longer remain simple spectators.

A stock market or banking crisis on a worldwide scale could have devastating effects, as we know, on the economic life of each country. Leaving an entire continent to rot away in distress and misery was to run the risk of a mass immigration that was likely to become rapidly uncontrollable for nations perceived as the wealthiest. Not to react to climate change was to be exposed to equally dramatic repercussions on our quality of life. All of this, as has been amply confirmed since then, gave meaning and coherence to the actions I had carried out on every front since coming to power. After the vast gathering of support I had been given on the second round of the presidential election, I was aware of the equally huge expectations of my compatriots, their desire for reform, their pressing demands in terms of employment, security, environment, and decentralization.

Bringing a new lease to life with him, the government chosen by Jean-Pierre Raffarin bore witness to our desire for action and innovation. As soon as he was installed in Matignon and without waiting for the results of the elections the following month, he announced the first measures taken by what I hoped would be a "government with a mission": the establishment of an internal security council, the setting up of special operations police groups, the launching of a new economic policy through the scheduled reduction of income tax for millions of households. . . . The French liked the modest, direct, and consensual style of the new prime minister, and on June 16, voters demonstrated massive confidence in the new UMP majority, which won 364 of the 577 seats in the National Assembly, thereby validating the political program I had proposed during the presidential campaign.

On July 14, I had my usual annual meeting with the French. It was only at the end of the procession down the Champs Élysées that I heard about the attempted attack on me. I had not noticed anything at the time other than the sound of a firecracker to which I had not paid any attention. "What happens, happens," I had often said to my entourage when they worried about seeing me diving into the crowd. The man who had fired the shot was a young extreme right-wing militant. Above all, I tried to understand the reason behind his act; it was not me personally who had been targeted but what I represented. People who feel rejected by society sometimes want to attack its highest symbol.

Interviewed by journalists that day, I began by acknowledging the presence on the Champs Élysées of West Point cadets and firemen from New York who had displayed such extraordinary courage in the attacks of September 11, 2001. Then, after setting out the course on which I wanted to steer the country over the next five years, I presented the three "great projects" to which I asked the government to bring a particular effort to bear: the integration of disabled people into society, road safety, and the fight against cancer. Three great priorities that touched on the integrity of the person and that concerned the French at the very heart of their daily lives.

I wanted there to be a rethinking of the place of disabled people in our society and a reaffirmation of their citizenship. School should become obligatory for disabled children, and the access of disabled people to towns, public transport, and buildings should be encouraged—as should their access to employment, leisure facilities, and cultural activities. In short, they should freely enjoy all the aspects of a rich social life. To my thinking, it was for organizations and environments to adapt to them, not the other way around. From 2002, this priority was reflected by the implementation of a national program of support for people with multiple disabilities and aging people with mental disabilities. Three years later, under the law of February 11, 2005, which recognized "equality of rights and opportunities" for people with disabilities, the latter benefited from guaranteed allowances while their status within companies was considerably improved.

The second great project, road safety, concerned one of the major scourges of the contemporary world, particularly in France. Our roads at that time were considered the most dangerous in Europe, and there was a record-breaking number of victims: more than eight thousand deaths a year. Over time, society seemed to become used, or rather resigned, to paying a price that was felt to be inevitable, in the absence of adequate measures to prevent it. The government needed to react if it was not to allow these killing fields, greater every year, to continue. To break the wall of silence, egoism, and indifference, I resolved to make this question into a political one, in the best sense of the word. Road deaths ruined lives, shattered families, and often affected young people. They were all the more scandalous because we had the means to prevent them. I believed that it was my responsibility, and that of public authorities, to signal the change and give a firm sense of direction. The police and gendarmes were brought into play more actively than ever before, and major prevention and information campaigns were launched.

A more punitive, or at least sufficiently deterrent, approach was inescapable if we truly wanted to reduce the number of accidents on the roads. The principal causes were well known: alcohol, speed, and failure to wear a seat belt. The law of June 12, 2003, provided for tougher penalties while controls were increased through the immediate installation of more than a thousand automatic radars on the most dangerous sections of road. From 2006, the effect of these measures proved spectacular, with a 43 percent decrease in annual deaths recorded, meaning that more than ten thousand deaths were prevented during this period.

The third of the great projects was the fight against cancer. Everyone knows someone in their family or their circle who is affected, and every year more than 350,000 people get cancer. Despite this, or perhaps because of it, a certain law of silence persists. We still avoid calling cancer by its name and often hear about a neighbor or acquaintance who has died "after a long and painful illness." This silence hides the difficulties, crises, and anguish endured by the patients, those close to them, and those who treat them. We need to change our view of cancer and make society more humane and more supportive in response to it. While it causes more and more devastation, it still seems to be a cause that is somewhat neglected by the public authorities. Research is making rapid progress, but an immense task in terms of prevention and detection remains.

The idea of launching an action plan against cancer owes much to my meeting one of our leading oncologists, Professor David Khayat, during the signing of the charter of Paris against cancer in 2000. Shortly afterward, I invited him to dinner. I wanted to know everything about this illness: how it developed and methods of treatment. Professor Khayat spoke to me for a long time about his consultations at the hospital where he worked and the suffering and anxiety of his patients, sometimes very young, and their desire to live. "One day, if I can, I will organize a national campaign," I said to him that evening. At my request, in July 2001, Professor Khayat drew up a charter project of health policies that I planned to submit to my G8 partners in Genoa. This project contained a dozen new propositions for "the universal promotion of health, the eradication of human suffering, and the protection of patients' value and dignity." The agenda of the summit already contained a debate on infectious diseases and AIDS, however, and I decided not to present it on that occasion.

Shortly after my reelection in May 2002, I called Professor Khayat to talk about the "cancer plan" I had promised him I would create, and which was eventually launched in March 2003 for a duration of five years. The government awarded it half a billion euros to help improve the treatment of patients and ensure that treatment was more evenly provided over the whole of the country. It enabled the immediate funding of new research programs, the launch of an antismoking campaign, and the widespread provision of breast cancer screening before launching research into the early detection of other forms of the illness. There too I was convinced that political will could prove a decisive factor. We needed to implement an unprecedented campaign involving all parties to improve prevention, screening, research, and treatment. We also needed to fight against all the discrimination that people suffering from cancer can face in the world of work or in access to credit.

The creation of the national cancer institute, charged with piloting the plan and its application, obviously did not put an end to the illness. But the positive effects of this policy were not slow in manifesting themselves: Almost 2 million people stopped smoking; from 2005, 7 million women were invited to have a free breast cancer screening; the treatment of pain was improved and more palliative care offered; magnetic resonance imaging equipment and scanners were provided and cancer centers established.

At the beginning of the summer of 2002, the essential components of the new economic and social policies were already under way. For twenty years, priority had been given to public spending as the means of sustaining growth, but it was the opposite logic that Rafarrin and I had decided to adopt in supporting purchasing power and the work ethic. Priority would now be given to training, long-term employment, and business creation over assisted employment, social payments, and overtaxation. This was the surest means of energizing our economy and creating the conditions for renewed growth.

*I*t all started at a middle school in Creil in September 1989. The head teacher asked three girls to leave the establishment because they refused to remove their head scarves during lessons. This provoked an outcry among antiracism groups, who protested against what they believed to be discrimination. This was the first in a multitude of similar cases. Under pressure from teachers, the wearing of the Muslim head scarf became the subject of a real public debate. Many called on the president, guarantor of the equality of all before the law of the republic, to arbitrate. It was clear that the decision implemented by Lionel Jospin when he was minister of national education, giving heads of establishments the responsibility of outlawing the head scarf on a case-by-case basis, no longer constituted an adequate response to the situation.

On May 22, 2003, the sixtieth anniversary of CRIF, the French Jewish council, gave me the opportunity of making a public statement reminding people that the principle of secularism remained "the mainstay of our unity and cohesion" and that it was a principle on which I would not waver. I then asked my staff to reflect on a more coherent solution to the issue. As I had done the previous year for the charter on the environment, I decided at the same time to set up a commission, chaired by my friend Bernard Stasi, ombudsman of the republic, and composed of many highly qualified figures, to study the possibility of a law on the subject. Rightly believing that it was also his duty to open a debate with the entire body of Parliament, the president of the National Assembly, Jean-Louis Debré, then set up a working group with a similar responsibility. This study was all the more vital because a certain skepticism, if not outright opposition, still prevailed on the issue of the need for a law. The majority of the members of the Stasi commission were themselves, it seems, not in favor of that from the outset, and equally strong reservations were expressed in the National Assembly and the Senate, on both the government and opposition benches.

For my part, I was convinced that we had to reaffirm our commitment both to respect for all religious faiths and to the strict neutrality of public services on spiritual and political issues. Schools, above all, should stick to their essential function of enabling the acquisition and transmission of the values we all shared, republican sanctuaries in which the citizens of tomorrow are trained in criticism, dialogue, and freedom of thought. It was not a question of making them into places of uniformity in which faith and religious belief were outlawed, but likewise they were not to become forums for the expression of the most diverse beliefs and opinions. Ultimately, it was the very functioning and teaching of schools that was being threatened.

My notion of secularism, forged by my parents, who were both the products of generations of schoolteachers, was not, as far as I was concerned, anticlerical or antireligious. In the exercise of my responsibilities as mayor of Paris, I actively supported the creation of Jewish schools. In the same way, I gave financial aid to the Grand Mosque in Paris and supported the activities of its rector, Si Hamza Boubakeur, the father of Dalil Boubakeur, the current rector. I also fought for private schools, Catholic and Protestant, to benefit from state financial support. With me, however, this concern to allow every religious body free expression of its faith had always gone hand in hand with that of guaranteeing the strict neutrality of public establishments in which no distinction should exist between pupils of Jewish, Christian, or Muslim faiths.

On December 11, 2003, the Stasi commission presented me with its report. Its virtually unanimous—minus one vote—conclusion was in favor of prohibiting the wearing of visible signs of religion in school and the institution of holidays for Muslims in accordance with their religious feast days. "Freedom of conscience, equality before the law, and the neutrality of public authorities," underlined the authors, "should benefit everyone, whatever their spiritual choices. But the state also needs to reaffirm strict rules to safeguard coexistence in a pluralistic society. French secularism today involves validating the principles on which it is founded, consolidating of the position of public services, and ensuring the respect of spiritual diversity. For that, the state has the duty of reminding public authorities of their obligations in terms of prohibiting discriminatory public practices and of adopting strong, clear rules in the framework of a law on secularism."

After considered reflection, I addressed the French people on December 17 to announce my decision to them. I began by asking all the citizens of our country to remember, and defend, the fundamental principles on which our national unity had been built for centuries: freedom, guaranteed by the primacy of the law over particular interests; equality between women and men in terms of opportunities, rights, and duties; fraternity of French people of all backgrounds and all origins. I underlined that it was these values that made France an open nation, welcoming and respectful of all beliefs, that on this ancient Christian land, a Jewish tradition going back almost two thousand years had also taken root, before the Protestant tradition had found its place in its turn, and that the Muslim tradition was now also becoming an integral part of our national history. I added that it was this whole structure that now seemed to me threatened, under the pressure of demands linked to the apparently contradictory development of a world in which the removal of frontiers and increased exchanges between countries was combined with the increasing tendency for people to shut themselves off in their own identity and for differences to be stressed.

I warned the French against this danger. I did not wish to minimize the tensions that existed in France, as in most western societies, but in fact sought to recognize them without ceasing to be faithful to what we were. This was what underpinned the policies implemented by the government to combat the true origins of an identity crisis that risked endangering our own national balance—policies such as our urban regeneration project that destroyed the ghetto apartment blocks and aimed to bring security, employment, and peace to no-go areas governed by the law of the survival of the fittest. Another example was the welcome and integration contract implemented at my request to enable foreigners legally entering and settling in our country to receive training in French citizenship and to commit, in return, to abide strictly by its rules and values—primary among which was the principle of secularism.

Following the recommendation of the Stasi commission as well as those, even more categorical, of the parliamentary working group, I announced that I was definitively in favor of a law prohibiting outward marks of religious faith in all public primary and secondary schools and asked that, once adopted by Parliament, it be implemented from the next school year. I decided not to add new holidays to the already numerous ones of the school calendar but expressed the wish that all pupils who wished it be granted an absence for large religious festivals, such as Yom Kippur or Aïd el-Kebir, on condition that the establishment receive advance notification. I concluded my address by affirming that the republic, determined to oppose "everything that separated, isolated, or excluded people," would also ensure that equality between the sexes and the dignity of women was preserved.

This stand did little, however, to calm matters. Within the majority party, voices clamored for the law to be abandoned. Some of them, admiring the British model, thought that the acceptance of communitarianism constituted a greater safeguard of harmony than our republican model. Others said that they feared that a limited right to religious expression would be to the disadvantage of the Catholic church—which also declared itself opposed to all legislative measures, although the representatives of the Jewish community, notably those within the Stasi commission, eventually approved it. Our ambassador to the Holy See informed me of the "real concern" of the Vatican, where people were worried, rumor had it, about my supposed Masonic affiliation. For other reasons, harder to decipher, the ecology movement and the parties of the extreme left also stigmatized my desire to enshrine in law the respect of a principle to which, moreover, they declared themselves in favor.

The most virulent opposition came from radical Muslim organizations like the Union of Islamic Organizations of France, which based its arguments on its own interpretation of religious freedom in our country. Demonstrations of young women wearing head scarves took place in Paris and Strasbourg, among other places, and bore witness to a resistance fueled by the equally intense criticisms of France expressed in the Arab world that would even serve as one of the pretexts, several months later, for the kidnapping in Iraq of two French journalists by a group claiming affiliation to al-Qaeda. From that point, many people, including some members of the government, worried that the situation risked becoming incendiary.

I, for my part, made sure that I kept my composure. I believed that I had nothing to fear from the Muslim community of France, whom I knew well. The moderate position adopted by the French Muslim Council and its president, Dalil Boubakeur, helped confirm that conviction. It was not the first time that the rector of the Grand Mosque of Paris had shown evidence of his clear-sightedness and integrity. In March 2004, the demonstrations stopped.

On February 10, the law was passed in the National Assembly, with a greater majority than expected, gaining 494 votes against 36 and with 31 abstentions. This consensus could not have been obtained without the responsible attitude of the Socialist Party and that of its general secretary, François Hollande, who behaved that day like an exemplary statesman. The law was definitively adopted by Parliament on March 15, 2004, and applied in the time frame I had set down. It amply fulfilled its goal of pacifying the situation within public schools.

Eager to restore social ties, I did not stop there. In my message to the French people of December 17, 2003, I urged that we "break the wall of silence and indifference that surrounds the reality of discrimination today." I called for an awareness and an energetic response to this intolerable situation affecting not only young French people whose parents were immigrants but also our compatriots in overseas territories who suffered discrimination because of the color of their skin, a large number of women and men discriminated against because of their sexual orientation, and people afflicted by a physical or mental disability. The government needed to assume its responsibilities in this new fight, with the aid of an independent authority that it set up with the mission of opposing all forms of discrimination.

Created on my personal initiative, the HALDE, an organization to fight discrimination and promote equality, was officially inaugurated in June 2005. Its task was to help victims assert their rights and ensure their dignity was respected. The aim was not to replace legislators or judges but to ensure that the existing body of legislative and judicial supports was effectively applied. It also had the task of recommending new policies and of ensuring restitution to all who had suffered as a result of proven discrimination. In cases where its mediation activities with public authorities remained unsuccessful, the HALDE had the power to refer matters to a court. "We must have an unbreakable political determination to fight discrimination," I declared on its inauguration day. "We must track it down everywhere and for everyone. I ask members of the authority to make the greatest use of the powers of analysis and suggestion conferred on them. I undertake to implement the authority's actions at a national level and on the ground by mobilizing the entire body of public institutions."

HALDE was also entrusted with the mission of ensuring equality of opportunity. Social mobility through education constituted the principal objective of the new law on the future of schools that I asked the government to introduce, and which was adopted in April 2005. I wanted a similar program in the domain of employment and business, where equality of treatment between men and women and diversity in recruitment should be set out in the rules of a new social contract. In this way, our republican pact could be not only safeguarded but also enriched and consolidated in the face of everything that threatened it from various quarters.

On March 28, 2004, the government suffered a serious setback in the regional elections. Twenty-four regions out of twenty-six were won by the left with only Alsace and Corsica escaping the tidal wave. It was the first time since the presidential election of 2002 that the French had been called on to vote, and, after two years of intense reforms, the verdict against the government was severe. It also, of course, reflected on the president. The extent of the repudiation surprised me, even if I realized the reasons for it. For all that, I did not see it as an "April 21 in reverse," in the unjustified words of a serving minister at the time. This vote did not demonstrate— far from it—a breakthrough on the part of the National Front but rather the return in force of the parties of the left that were reaping the fruits of their renewed unity and that had fully recovered their opposition role in a political landscape that had returned to normal. The loss we had just undergone was no less considerable for all that, and my duty was to draw lessons from it.

The reasons for this defeat were first due to the fact that the government team, despite its proactive commitment in many areas, had not yet obtained the expected results of an economic strategy founded on the idea that the only way, or almost the only way, to create employment was via economic growth. This growth had proved weaker than forecast, and the unemployment rate had remained high. To this were added other factors of discontent linked to the reforms that had been carried out. While the opposition demanded a change of policy and of prime minister, a faction of the majority party did not resist the temptation to publicize its own criticisms of government policy and even to cast doubt on the ability of the president to maintain control. I was not taken in by the hidden agendas, which were in fact less and less hidden, that led certain members of the government party to challenge the record of Raffarin or to deplore my supposed indifference to domestic problems. The essential thing in my eyes was to respond to the worry and dissatisfaction of the French people and to take note of the message they had transmitted.

It was for this reason alone that I considered whether I should appoint a new prime minister, as confidants in whom I had great confidence urged me to do. The most forceful of these was the president of the National Assembly, Jean-Louis Debré, whose reservations about the leadership of Raffarin and notably his decentralization policy were no secret. His opinion carried weight with me, partly because he was a friend and partly because he was a member of Parliament solidly anchored in the political world. "We must win back the approval of the French," he said to me, "and for that you need to change the prime minister quickly. Jean-Pierre Raffarin is completely worn out." We reviewed the possible contenders, but none of the most serious among them seemed to him to have the right profile: "Sarkozy's image is too liberal, and that is not what the French want. Because he wants to win over the extreme right in too obvious a way, he will place you in an awkward position. Villepin could bring a breath of fresh air to French politics, but it will be difficult to get him accepted by members of Parliament whom he tends to despise. As for Michèle Alliot-Marie, who is, despite her authoritarian attitude, a good defense minister, she would not be able to rein in Sarkozy or Villepin. . . ." I therefore concluded that Jean-Pierre Raffarin was still the best placed to fill the role.

At the same time, others came to recommend that I appoint Nicolas Sarkozy, who was enjoying a wave of great popularity, to Matignon. One of these was the assistant secretary general of the Élysée, who, knowing my reservations, did not mince his words: "It is in the interest of the country to appoint Nicolas Sarkozy. You need to accelerate the rhythm of your government program, and Sarkozy has the ability and the energy to do that. Of course there are differences of opinion between you, and he does not have, it is true, the deep knowledge of the country that you do. But you can bring him that."

After listening to his arguments, I replied that there could be no more question of it today than yesterday and for the same reasons: "In working with Georges Pompidou, I learned that if Matignon and the Élysée did not get on, everything collapsed. That is inevitably what would happen with Sarkozy. I don't have personal antipathy toward him, quite the contrary. But we do not agree on the essential things. He is an Atlanticist, I am not. He is much more liberal than I am in terms of the economy. He is in favor of positive discrimination and I am radically opposed to it. It could not work."

I was now convinced that nothing justified the departure of the current prime minister. Jean-Pierre Raffarin had devoted himself to the implementation of my presidential project with enthusiasm, steadfastness, and courage and had demonstrated irreproachable loyalty toward me. Keeping him at Matignon meant, however, that his road map needed to be radically changed and his government shuffled so as better to fulfill our compatriots' expectations. The most talked-about changes to his government were the appointment of Nicolas Sarkozy as minister of finance and that of Dominique de Villepin, who succeeded Sarkozy as minister of the interior. This promotion of two men whose dynamism and competence could not be contested was in my view in the country's interests; the fact that it could be interpreted differently was above all due to a political context that had become more strained since the trial and conviction of Alain Juppé on January 30, 2004.

I was in Geneva for a UN meeting on that day when I learned of the verdict against Juppé in an affair involving allegedly fictitious posts within the Rassemblement pour la République: eighteen months suspended prison sentence and banned from entering politics for ten years. Flabbergasted, overwhelmed by a sentence that I immediately felt was severe and unjust, although my position prevented me from commenting publicly on a court case, my first reaction was a long silence. This news plunged me into deep sadness. I thought of what Alain had confided in me some time before: "I don't know how I'll react if I'm sentenced to a loss of civil rights." More than my own trial, it was his that had preoccupied me since he had been indicted six years earlier. A wait that had left his political future uncertain, even if I had not hesitated to offer, in May 2002, that he become my prime minister again. Whatever happened, Alain Juppé would for me remain the best among us. He had declined my offer precisely because of what might happen in his court case. Nonetheless, there was no doubt in my mind that the presidency of the UMP, of which he had been one of the most active founders, was his as by right, in a sense, even though it was decided by vote of the party activists. He obtained almost 80 percent of the votes, for which I immediately congratulated him.

As soon as I got back to Paris, that January 30, 2004, I called Alain to comfort him and reassure him of my affection and my friendship. I felt that he was terribly wounded by what had happened. When I met him on his return from Normandy, where he had gone to rest with Isabelle as soon as the verdict was known, I urged him to keep going and not give up the political fight. But it was no good. Alain thought that because of his conviction, even if he appealed, there could be no question of him keeping the leadership of the UMP. His mind was made up, and I could not get him to change it. He announced his decision to the party activists' meeting in conference on February 8, thereby opening the way to candidates already impatiently setting their sights on his succession. One, above all: Nicolas Sarkozy.

Sarkozy had an undeniable quality: He always made his moves out in the open. His presidential ambitions had rapidly become obvious, almost immediately after arriving at the Ministry of the Interior, even though the elections were not exactly imminent. I had, however, refused to enter into the power play he tried to establish between us, judging that doing so could only damage our institutions. It was not my role, as president, to take part in a sort of competition or rivalry. All that mattered to me was how Sarkozy carried out the ministerial task that had been entrusted to him. Security was one of the priorities of my presidential program; it was not the only one, but it was one of the most important. When I was reelected, considerable funds were put at the disposal of the minister of the interior to carry out his new functions, and I appreciated, as did many of the French, that from 2002 to 2004, he made careful and efficient use of them, in accordance with the country's needs.

In January, I pretended not to realize that I was the target when Sarkozy, during a trip to Hong Kong, saw fit to make ironic comments about fans of sumo wrestling and about Japan, which as he knew were two of my passions. When I heard about it, I simply said to myself that we did not have the same tastes or the same culture. Many of my entourage were surprised that I did not react to all the little provocative phrases shot at me by a serving minister who expressed himself as he saw fit without worrying about sparing the president. But reacting to this, at least in public, could only lead to a clash that, I continued to think, was beneath the dignity of a president of the republic. Should I take a more radical decision in this case, as people advised me to do? After considered reflection, I still concluded that removing him from office would deprive France of a good minister. Nothing in his behavior up to then seemed to warrant it.

This was why I chose, in April 2004, to give Sarkozy a new opportunity to express his talents. On the other hand, eager to maintain both the balance of government and the authority of the prime minister, I thought his ministerial post incompatible with the chairmanship of the presidential party, for which he had decided to run. Having tried in vain to dissuade him, I decided to express publicly, in my address of July 14, 2004, my position on a problem that this time directly concerned the functioning of the state. I began, in response to journalists' questions, by setting the record straight on my recent disagreement with the minister of finance on the defense budget. Sarkozy had thought it too high and had made his opposition known to me whereas for me it was a question of reestablishing our defense provision, within the framework of a new military budget, just as we had done in terms of domestic security. I summed up the reality of the debate in one phrase: "There is no quarrel between the minister of finance and me, for a simple reason, which is that particularly in regard to defense, I decide and he obeys." I added that governmental action was founded on two principles, "collectivity and solidarity," on which I would not accept any dissent, by no matter whom. Then, responding to a question about the probable candidacy of Nicolas Sarkozy for the chairmanship of the UMP, I explained that I would ask the minister of the interior to choose one or the other of his posts: "A minister who is also chairman of the main majority party means in effect that there isn't a prime minister anymore. This touches on the good functioning of institutions and governmental efficacy." I stated that "if any minister is elected chairman of the UMP, he will resign immediately or I will remove him from his post."

I have to confess that in saying that, with all the firmness that was necessary, I thought that Sarkozy would choose to stay in government and serve the national interest. But no. When I saw him again on August 31 to find out his decision, the finance minister confirmed his resolve to make a bid for the chairmanship of the majority party. Not doubting that he would be successful, I confirmed from my side that he would have to give up his ministerial office the day after the UMP conference on November 21. Things were now clear.

24

LAST BATTLES

The last period of my presidential term was extremely full. On the international and European fronts, it saw the culmination, fortunately or unfortunately, of three major struggles on which I had devoted much effort and energy for several years. The first involved the implementation of innovative funding for development and the fight against the great pandemics, particularly AIDS. The second was the withdrawal of Syrian forces from Lebanon, which was finally given its independence. The third was the project of the European constitution to which I was strongly committed but that the French people rejected, with obvious and significant consequences.

"Bashar is like your son and so you should treat him like one," Hafez al-Assad had declared to me shortly before his death in June 2000. The Syrian president—with whom it was important to me to have a good relationship, given the influence of his country in the region and in Lebanon—was clearly anxious to equip his appointed successor, still very inexperienced, with a sort of guardian. During his official visit to Paris the following year, Bashar al-Assad had said to me in his turn: "You know that my father thought that I should be like your son after his death. I would therefore like us to have such a relationship." Unfortunately, this good attitude did not last very long.

It quite quickly became clear to me that I would not have the same type of relationship with Bashar that I had had with his father when we met in Damascus in 1996 and that was confirmed two years later when I had welcomed him to Paris. However inscrutable he was, and in many respects tough and implacable, I had always had the impression that Hafez al-Assad was a man of his word and sincere in his desire for dialogue with France. Attached to the grandeur of his country and to the destiny of the Arab nation, he counted on the support of France to help him put an end, by respecting existing treaties, to half a century of conflict with Israel. Hafez al-Assad had understood that our country had always backed those who sought to establish a just and lasting peace in the Middle East. This could be obtained only if the relevant parties satisfied extremely specific obligations, as I reminded him, as well as the Israeli authorities, whenever I had the opportunity.

There could be a peaceful solution only if the principle, which had been officially acknowledged, of territory in exchange for peace applied to the Golan Heights, which were incontestably Syrian, as well as to the Palestinian territories and to Lebanon, which should regain its independence and its sovereignty. Israel should, in turn, have the right to enjoy full and entire security along its recognized borders. These conditions were inseparable in the eyes of France. In regard to Lebanon, whose fate was particularly close to our heart, France expected from both Syria and Israel an equal respect for its territorial integrity and, consequently, that both cease their military occupation in the country. In short, the withdrawal of Israeli troops from southern Lebanon should go hand in hand with the end of the Syrian guardianship that had been established over the rest of the country since 1989, under the terms of the Taif Agreement.

Hafez al-Assad, who was entirely aware of this demand, had quite cleverly wanted to consult me in December 1998 about the "appointment" of the next Lebanese president. He had asked me to give him the names of five candidates, from whom he would make his choice. I included the name of General Émile Lahoud, who had at that time a good reputation and who was eventually imposed by Damascus. The suggestion quickly proved unfortunate, however. Lahoud was in fact a mediocre figure, without vision or charisma and with no other goal than keeping himself in power so as to maintain a Syrian presence less and less tolerated by the Lebanese people.

In June 2000, I was the sole western head of state present in Damascus to attend the funeral of Hafez al-Assad, a decision primarily inspired by my concern to maintain a relationship with Syria that I hoped would be useful both in terms of peace in the Middle East and in terms of the emancipation of Lebanon. A hope that I shared with my friend Rafic Hariri, the Lebanese leader who embodied more than anyone else his compatriots' aspiration to regain control of their destiny. Having become prime minister again in December 2000, despite the opposition of Émile Lahoud, Hariri relied on the mediation of France and my personal involvement to strengthen his influence with the Syrian government in the attempt to reach a solution to the Lebanese problem. In May 2001, I took advantage of President Lahoud's visit to Paris to insist officially in his presence on the need to make relations between Beirut and Damascus evolve into a "fraternal, open, and progressive approach that takes into account their respective interests." While the Israeli troops had withdrawn from Lebanon several months earlier under Security Council Resolution 425, it seemed as if Syrian forces would remain.

Far from adopting a conciliatory attitude, however, Bashar al-Assad seemed determined to tighten his hold even further over Lebanon, from which he and his clan extracted all sorts of benefits, exploiting an occupation as much political as economic to their advantage. All the hopes for openness and renewal that had been aroused by his coming to power, when he had looked like a young, progressive head of state with a modern wife, had now disappeared. Wrapped up in his system of power and preoccupied only with his personal, family, and community interests, my supposed "son"—whom Hafez al-Assad, probably fearing his inadequacies and his weakness of character, had asked me to guide and advise—had lost no time in listening only to those opinions least likely to upset his plans or to dissuade him from an authoritarian, dominating approach that cut short all hope of development in the Syrian regime.

In vain I tried to convince him to soften his position to enable Syria to be accepted as part of the international community. I succeeded in getting him to support France's position on the invasion of Iraq in the vote on Resolution 1441 in November 2002, but Bashar al-Assad did not, despite my urging in this direction, seize the opportunity afforded by the fall of Saddam Hussein to install Syria as a balancing force in the region. From pride and blindness, he risked taking the opposite path: that of appearing in his turn as a disreputable potentate, unconscious of the changes that had taken place around him and exercising a power for harm at the expense of both his people and his neighbors.

In November 2003, I dispatched Maurice Gourdault-Montagne to advise him, in the name of France but also that of Germany and Russia (after consulting Gerhard Schröder and Vladimir Putin) to take a diplomatic initiative that would allow Syria to assert itself as a state that wanted to work for peace and stability. An initiative that obviously concerned Lebanon as a priority. . . . Bashar merely retorted to my envoy: "Are you speaking on behalf of the Americans?" before virulently denouncing the plans that the latter were hatching to overthrow him. Bashar had not wanted to understand that it was in his interests to get along with France so as to emerge from his isolation and thereby escape the ostracism of those who had already situated his country in the "axis of evil."

Syria was not the only country in the region affected by this problem. Iran was in a similar situation because the regime of the mullahs was very strongly suspected of wanting a nuclear weapons program. Exploiting our good relations with Tehran since the reformers' coming to power in 1997 and the personal dialogue I had then established with President Khatami, France strove to convince the Iranian government to display greater transparency about the real purpose of its nuclear activities and to fully respect its cooperation commitments with the International Atomic Energy Agency. This dialogue, which I initiated, was the beginnings of the negotiations termed "EU 3 + 3," held together with Great Britain, Germany, the United States, Russia, and China to help the Iranians out of the impasse they had created for themselves. This process is still in force today. Although dialogue with the Iranian leaders seemed possible at that time, however, we were confronted with an implacable deafness on the part of the Syrians.

At the beginning of 2004, Hariri and I began talking about calling on the Security Council to vote on a resolution obliging Syria to withdraw its troops, but this could succeed only within the framework of a narrow collaboration with the United States. While we may not have been in agreement about the method of resolving the Iraqi problem, we did share a desire for the countries of the Middle East to move toward democracy and conform to the principles of an international law that some, not least of all Syria, persisted in openly flouting.

The rapprochement that began to be established between Paris and Washington from spring 2004, resolving the issues of contention over Iraq that had temporarily divided us, allowed me to envisage a real possibility of entente involving Lebanon as well as Iran. Even if France had not succeeded, after the end of the military operations and the fall of Saddam Hussein, in getting the White House to agree that the administration of Iraq be entrusted to a UN representative and the occupation troops placed under NATO command, we were nonetheless resolved to meet our commitments and be involved in the economic reconstruction of the country. This was why, with eighteen other countries that all shared my desire to help the Iraqi people, I had responded favorably to the request of the White House— brought to me by the former American secretary of state, James Baker—to cancel most of the debt that Baghdad had contracted with France. The cancellation of this debt took place within the framework and under the rules of the Paris Club, called on to consider the question from April 2003 at the initiative of the G7 finance ministers, culminating in an agreement of all its members in November 2004 for an 80 percent reduction of the Iraqi debt—a debt that none of them in any case expected would ever be repaid.

Informed in February 2004 of the American government's plans for a future "Greater Middle East," I had serious reservations about it; in my view, this global concept could not reflect the reality of such a vast geopolitical space stretching from Rabat to Kabul. I also remained convinced that no collective progress could be made in this area if we did not first succeed in resolving the Israeli–Palestinian conflict. The growing difficulties encountered by the United States and its allies in their pacification operation in Iraq, in the face of increasing terrorist attacks, made this ambition to normalize the internal situation in each of the countries targeted by the United States even more risky in my eyes. I did, however, see the interest in creating a strategic partnership with Washington specifically in regard to Lebanon.

On June 5, the visit to France of George W. Bush for the ceremonies of the sixtieth anniversary of the Normandy landings gave me the opportunity, during the official dinner organized in his honor at the Élysée, to slip this unprogrammed subject into the meetings that had been carefully prepared by our respective diplomatic teams. "In the Middle East," I said to him, "there are two democracies. One, Israel, is powerful. The other, Lebanon, is fragile. We must help it!" Bush seemed surprised, clearly knowing little about this country in which he had never shown much interest. I then explained to him why it was in our interest to support the Lebanese state and of allowing it to regain its independence, as much from Syria as from the Shi'ite Hezbollah that had once more become all-powerful in the south of the country after the withdrawal of Israeli troops. I told him that a presidential election was to take place in Lebanon in October and that if the future president was not, as usual, imposed by Damascus, this would constitute a new departure for the country: "The Syrians will perhaps seek to get the current president, Émile Lahoud, reelected by changing the constitution. I have noted with interest the comments of Colin Powell and Ms. Rice on the need for elections free of all outside interference. I have also seen that one of the conditions for the lifting of American sanctions against Syria is its withdrawal from Lebanon. . . . Let's work together!" President Bush immediately agreed. He proposed that Condoleezza Rice and my own diplomatic advisor—"Gordon Montagne," as Bush called him—start working together as soon as possible to agree on a plan of action.

During that summer of 2004, while my advisors were in constant contact with their American counterparts to work on this planned resolution to demand both the holding of free elections and the unconditional withdrawal of the Syrian army, the takeover bid that Rafic Hariri and I had feared had indeed taken place in Beirut. Bashar al-Assad and his figurehead, Émile Lahoud, had together drawn up a new constitution that allowed the latter, who could not be reelected, to prolong his mandate by three years. Hariri, who as prime minister had immediately denounced this abuse of power, was summoned to Damascus on August 26, several days after having met with Maurice Gourdault-Montagne for a last rereading of the planned resolution.

Hariri related to me exactly what happened that day in Bashar's office in the presence of the Syrian vice president, Abdel Halim Khaddam—who would confirm the content of this conversation to an international commission of inquiry in December 2005.

The Lebanese prime minister had begun by reminding Bashar al-Assad of his commitment not to extend the mandate of Mr. Lahoud. To which Bashar al-Assad had curtly replied that there had been a change of policy and that his decision had already been made. He added that Mr. Lahoud should be considered as his personal representative in Beirut and that opposing him was to oppose Assad himself. He then threatened Rafic Hariri, as well as the Druze leader, Walid Jumblatt, with "physical retaliation" if they both persisted in refusing to recognize the new constitution and thereby accepting that Mr. Lahoud remain in power. "If Chirac wants to get me out of Lebanon," he exclaimed, "I will break Lebanon. Either you do what you are asked, or we will get you, as well as your family, wherever you are!"

Alerted that same evening by Hariri, I began by asking him to pay the greatest attention to his security from then on, to vary the routes he took and to leave his office as little as possible, even to remove himself physically from Lebanon. We also agreed to accelerate the vote on the planned resolution in the Security Council.

Although very preoccupied with the Republican convention being held in New York at that time to prepare for the future American presidential election, Condoleezza Rice, in full agreement with George W. Bush, actively contributed to drawing up the text. She had many telephone conversations on the subject with Gourdault-Montagne, who spoke to her from my office in the Élysée, where I from my side was in permanent contact with Rafic Hariri. At the same time, one of my diplomatic advisors was trying to gather as many votes as possible in support of the resolution within the United Nations while also trying to ensure that the permanent members that had declared themselves opposed to its adoption, China and Russia, did not veto it; my excellent relations with both Vladimir Putin and Hu Jintao naturally came into play in the negotiations. On September 2, Resolution 1559 was adopted by nine votes, with six abstentions, including those of China,

Russia, and Algeria. The text demanded the departure of Syrian forces, the dissolution of all the militia active on the Lebanese territory, and the holding of a presidential election in conformity with "Lebanese constitutional rules drawn up free from all outside interference."

The following day, Bashar al-Assad, who had continued to maneuver right up to the end by delivering multiple promises via the intermediary of the Spanish government in an attempt to impede the vote, decided to totally ignore it and to prolong Émile Lahoud's mandate. Assad's fury was concentrated on Hariri, whom he held to be the principal instigator of the "conspiracy" hatched against him with the complicity of France, which he also accused of having "betrayed" him. From then on, attacks against the declared opponents of Syria began to increase. On October 21, Hariri left his post as prime minister to become head of the opposition. At that time, I decided to dispatch one of my right-hand men to Beirut as the new French ambassador.

Determined to give nothing up, despite the UN injunctions, Assad kept up a threatening pressure on Lebanon. At the start of 2005, he insulted the Norwegian diplomat supervising the implementation of Resolution 1559 on behalf of the UN. When Condoleezza Rice came to the Élysée on February 8, I shared my concern about the hard-line attitude of the Syrian regime, prepared to stop at nothing to ensure the status quo in Lebanon, including giving financial support to terrorist organizations to permanently destabilize the country. "We cannot," I said to her, "let democracy in Lebanon be stifled. Syria must be threatened with financial sanctions—that is the only way to have any effect on the corrupt system that has developed between Damascus and Beirut. We should demand the application of Resolution 1559. This will weaken the tough guys of Damascus. . . . It is in no way in our interests to see a Shi'ite arc in the Middle East, going from Iran to Hezbollah, via Iraq and Syria." The American secretary of state expressed her "total agreement" to the measures I proposed. An unforeseen tragedy—even though it was one that was, unfortunately, foreseeable—would, however, upset the course of Lebanese history.

On February 14, I was holding a meeting at the Élysée when I was informed that Rafic Hariri had been attacked in Beirut; at that moment, it was not known whether he was merely wounded or dead. As I hurried to my office, news arrived that left no more room for hope: Rafic had been killed instantaneously when his vehicle exploded. I was shattered. It was one of the worst shocks of my life, and I experienced Rafic's assassination as if it were my brother who had been killed. A brother whose fate had worried me for several months and whom I had tried several times, in vain, to warn against the threats that weighed on him. Rafic was perfectly well aware of them, but this great gentleman was not someone who let himself be intimidated; indeed, he was quite fatalistic. "I don't have any precise information," I had said to him two weeks earlier, during his last trip to Paris. "But be careful. They are criminals who are capable of anything." Before leaving my office, Rafic had turned to me and had made a gesture that meant "They won't do that to me!" Two days later, haunted by a foreboding that would not leave me, I phoned a mutual friend of ours to tell Rafic again that he should remain extremely vigilant.

Bernadette and I left together for Rafic Hariri's house in Paris to be with his wife, Nazek. When we arrived, other friends were already with her, having also hurried there when they heard the news. I hugged Nazek to me, said a few words to try to comfort her, express my grief, and also assure her that I would not let this crime go unpunished.

Although I was advised not to go to Beirut for security reasons, there was of course no question of my not going to pay respects to the memory of Rafic Hariri and share his compatriots' grief. I would not attend his funeral, however, because I did not want to have to meet the man who bore such a large part of responsibility in this spiral of hate and violence: Émile Lahoud.

When I arrived at Beirut airport on February 16, I made a short statement:

> I have come to Beirut to pay homage to the memory of a personal friend and a head of state with whom I had so many ties, to present my deep condolences to his wife and family in this tragedy that has struck them, and to demonstrate my solidarity, and that of France, with the Lebanese people in the trial they are enduring.
>
> The attack that took the life of M. Rafic Hariri provokes horror and consternation. France has strongly condemned it and asks that light be fully shone on the circumstances of this crime.
>
> M. Hariri gave all his support to the fight for Lebanese democracy, freedom, independence, and sovereignty. That is also the permanent commitment of France, which will always be the friend of Lebanon. With the international community, it will spare no effort in order that this country can freely exercise its choices.

Then Bernadette and I went to join Rafic's family, whom we considered almost our own, in their residence in Qoreitem, where we stayed for many hours to comfort each member of his entourage, his children, and his

closest friends, all paralyzed with horror and grief. At the beginning of
the evening, we went to gather around Rafic's coffin on the esplanade in
the middle of Beirut, surrounded by a huge crowd that had begun to chant
when I arrived, with a mixture of rage and fervor: "Long live Chirac! Long
live France! Syria out!" The coffin was there, covered with flowers and ivy.
An intense silence, heavy with sadness and solemnity, reigned in the square
now plunged in darkness, shot through with the faint light from the candles
held by many Lebanese. It was among them and them alone that I wanted
to pay this last homage to my savagely murdered friend.

Shortly afterward, the Hariri family met to discuss their position and it
was decided, although Rafic had not been in favor of the idea of his children
entering politics, that his son Saad would take up the torch. For her part,
Rafic's wife, Nazek, would look after the Hariri Foundation, which worked
in the fields of teaching and health in Lebanon and for Lebanese throughout the world. In November 2009, four years after the tragedy, Saad Hariri
won the general election and became prime minister of Lebanon in his turn.
He would take on this onerous task with much courage and willingness and
wholly in keeping with his father's political principles of the independence
and sovereignty of Lebanon and intercommunity dialogue.

I had no doubt about Bashar al-Assad's responsibility in the death of
Rafic Hariri, even if I had no absolute proof of it. The day after the assassination, I asked that everything be done to set up an international commission of inquiry as quickly as possible to identify the authors of the attack
and those who had initiated it. As I would say to President Bush in a meeting in Brussels on February 25, 2005, I was convinced that this act could
have been perpetrated only by organized and experienced agents. "For anyone who knows how the Alawai system in power in Damascus functions,"
I added, "there is no possible doubt: The decision was taken by President
Assad. No other hypothesis makes sense."

On March 6, vilified from all sides and conscious of being more than
ever in the firing line of the United States and France, the Syrian president announced the withdrawal of his troops from Lebanon. Rafic Hariri
had had his posthumous victory. A month later, the UN Security Council
agreed to the creation of the international commission of inquiry that I had
wanted. The long work of investigation began, which I watched with the
greatest attention. The report given to Kofi Annan on October 20, 2005, by
the German public prosecutor, Detlev Mehlis, who had chaired the inquiry,
contained many accusations against Syria. In the aftermath, Paris and
Washington strongly supported the official request of the Lebanese government for the creation of an international tribunal for those presumed

responsible for the assassination of Hariri. After extensive negotiations, the Security Council adopted a resolution on this matter on May 30, 2007, several days after I left office as president.

Until the end of my last mandate, I did not cease, as I had always done, concerning myself with the fate of Lebanon and that of the Near and Middle East in general. Since my meeting with Ariel Sharon in Paris on July 27, 2005, I had placed much hope in the possibility of finding a peaceful solution to the Israeli–Palestinian conflict. The decision of the Israeli prime minister to evacuate Israeli settlements in the Gaza Strip constituted an extremely positive sign in this regard. Since the death of Yasser Arafat in Paris in November 2004, Sharon seemed more confident about the chances of a fruitful dialogue with the new Palestinian leadership. Sharon, whom until that time I had seen as very intransigent and whose accusations, direct or insinuated, that France was guilty of anti-Semitism had greatly annoyed me, seemed to me that day very different from the idea I had formed of him. Under his warlike exterior, I discovered a man who displayed the same physical courage and iron will in his quest for peace as he had demonstrated in combat. I had an even more vivid glimpse of his real nature with his lengthy description of his farm, where among other animals he raised Salers cows. For his part, Sharon understood that I was not the enemy of Israel he had always heard about but the representative of a France loyal to its twofold tradition of friendship with both Israel and Arab countries, aims that were not mutually exclusive, who sought only to further the cause of peace. Sharon told me that he had appreciated my efforts to force Syria to leave Lebanon.

In November 2005, shortly before suffering a cerebral hemorrhage and falling into a coma, Sharon asked me to mediate with the Lebanese government to put an end to Hezbollah's provocations toward his country, convinced that this "terrorist organization" had the objective of "kidnapping Israeli soldiers." Which is what effectively took place in July 2006, when two soldiers were kidnapped by Hezbollah.

I was initially in favor of the Israeli military retaliation ordered by Ariel Sharon's successor, Ehud Olmert; seeing it as legitimate self-defense, I signed the common declaration issued by the heads of the state attending the G8 at St. Petersburg denouncing the irresponsible actions of the Shi'ite organization. However, this counterattack of intense bombing of large parts of Lebanon as far as Beirut, destroying much of its infrastructure, was quickly shown to be disproportionate, not to say excessive. Which was why, always eager that the integrity of Lebanese territory should be respected, I proposed that the UN contingent deployed on the border with

Israel be vigorously strengthened. The Security Council unanimously adopted a resolution in this regard on August 11, 2006, and France played a
large role in getting it implemented on the ground—as it had always done
when it is a question not only of arguing for peace but of imposing it.

I have often compared the building of Europe to a mountain path that is
never climbed without difficulty and where there is the ever-present risk of
falling or stumbling across an obstacle. One continually gets up, however,
and starts walking again. I know what I was talking about because since
the 1970s I had been involved, in my successive roles as minister of agriculture, prime minister, and finally president of the republic, with each of the
great steps of this rarely calm and straightforward route that was punctuated with clashes, dramas, and setbacks but also with progress, and that
was always focused on the goal ahead. The journey, which had taken under
half a century, could seem slow and laborious. One needed only to look
back, however, to see the ground that had already been covered in terms of
the creation of a peaceful, united continent capable of taking on the challenges of a world that was itself in the throes of upheaval.

Under my authority and that of my predecessors, France—backed up
by its privileged relationship with Germany—had often been an impetus
for important innovations, such as the creation of the euro. In the speech
I gave to the Berlin Bundestag in June 2000, I was the first head of state
officially to launch the idea of a European constitution. This had become
essential in my eyes, particularly in view of the enlargement of Europe. We
needed to reorganize all the existing treaties to make them more coherent
and comprehensible and make the necessary institutional changes in regard
to the Council, the Commission, and the European Parliament in order
to strengthen the Union's efficiency and democratic control. I wanted this
preparatory study to be conducted in an open fashion, bringing together
governments and citizens through their representatives in the Strasbourg
Assembly and within the national parliaments. A "council of wise persons"
and a convention should be put in place to this end. When they had reached
conclusions, which would probably take some time, the governments and
then the people would be asked to vote on a document that we could then
institute as the first European constitution.

The convention on the future of Europe was created in December 2001.
Composed of five hundred members, it was placed under the chairmanship
of Valéry Giscard d'Estaing, aided by two vice presidents. Together with
Lionel Jospin, I had strongly supported the choice of Giscard to lead it,
given his undisputed competence and authority in this area. The convention

set to work in February 2002, and it presented its proposed European constitution on July 18, 2003, in Rome, where the founding agreement of the Union had been signed forty-six years earlier.

As always, this constitution could not have seen the light of day if there had not been a Franco-German agreement to develop it. Eager to iron out all the differences of opinion that had divided us until the signing of the treaty of Nice in December 2002 and to inject a breath of fresh air into our partnership, Gerhard Schröder and I had begun by agreeing on mutual concessions, obviously in conformity with our respective interests. The first concerned the weighting of votes in the European Council. Germany demanded a greater weighting because of its demographic size, and I eventually agreed to this, obtaining in return the maintenance of the German contribution to the common agricultural policy budget. In September 2003, our two countries also found common ground to improve the functioning of the stability pact, which limited, under the provisions of the Maastricht Treaty, the budgetary deficit of the Eurozone states to 3 percent of their gross national product and together proposed less constricting rules to our partners, aiding employment and growth.

In spring 2004, two major events occurred. First, the enlargement of the Union on May 1 to ten new member states: Estonia, Hungary, Poland, Latvia, Lithuania, Slovakia, Slovenia, and the Czech Republic as well as Cyprus and Malta. The second was the European Council's adoption on June 18 of the constitutional text that then needed to be ratified by each of the states. In my televised address of July 14, I acknowledged these two great reforms, the first allowing democracy and peace in Europe to take even deeper root and the second introducing greater harmony and modernity in the functioning of its institutions. I also announced on that day my decision to hold a referendum on the new constitutional treaty rather than having it ratified by Parliament, as I could have done. Questioned about the political risk of such a procedure, I confessed that I hoped it would be an opportunity for us to give "some impetus to our capacity for dialogue rather than to our culture of opposition." I refused to believe that "a political leader worthy of the name could seriously, unless he or she wanted to put France back fifty years, challenge the positive nature of this treaty." And yet, alas, this was exactly what would happen. . . .

I was not unaware of the risks of all referendums, which most often result in a rejection of what is being proposed or in a very low voter turnout, as we had seen in the referendum on the change to a presidential term of five years. If the "yes" vote had won out in the referendum on the

Maastricht Treaty, at the culmination of a very passionate debate, it was thanks to backing from an opposition party at the time and the support, it must be said, that I had unreservedly given it. Without a sufficiently wide political consensus, failure was virtually inevitable.

It would obviously have been less risky to have the matter decided by the two assemblies, but what convinced me to take the referendum route, other than the fact that I personally found it more democratic to consult the people directly on the great subjects involving their future, was the initiative taken by Tony Blair in May 2004 to hold a referendum in the United Kingdom. By making this abrupt announcement, without first taking the trouble to alert his European partners, the British prime minister created a precedent that was difficult to override for those who, like France, had this procedure available in their constitution.

"I have no choice but to hold a referendum," I told my staff, who had immediately gathered to discuss the matter. "This affair concerns the transfer of sovereignty and involves the organization of public institutions. Given all that is at stake, it seems to me legitimate to ask the French their opinion." This was also the wish of the majority of leading politicians, from both opposition and majority parties—which did not mean, of course, that when it came to it, they would all vote in favor of the proposition.

The first polls were positive on the whole. The "no" vote seemed in the minority within the major political parties. However, ten months would elapse before the vote took place, in May 2005, and this long delay, doubtless too long, allowed plenty of time for the situation to change. I was aware of both the enduring discontent in regard to the government's policies and the feeling, deeply rooted in a great many French people, that Europe was something abstract and complicated, consisting of more disadvantages than advantages. Factors likely to have more and more weight in the debate on the constitution.

At the start of 2005, the document was already the subject of various criticisms, criticisms that would only continue to grow. Other than the fact that it was said to be dense, complex, and unreadable—which was not totally false—various people, chief among whom was Laurent Fabius, accused it of not being socially engaged enough and of neglecting the real concerns of both the French and Europeans as a whole. At the same time, others—including, unfortunately, a large section of the UMP—said that it contained a regrettable flaw and a major disadvantage. The former was that it did not mention Europe's Christian roots in its preamble; this had in fact been my decision, judging that the constitution, like any other judicial text, should be free from all religious references. The major disadvantage, which was not unrelated, was that it left the way open for the eventual membership of Turkey, a country that was Muslim in faith but secular in its administration.

Turkey's entry into Europe is not a recent idea. It had been on the table since the 1960s, benefiting like Greece from the political will of General de Gaulle, among others, from a membership agreement with the European Economic Community in 1963. I was completely in favor of it. Turkey had long played an active role in European culture, and a section of its territory formed part of our continent. Its government had of course to make the necessary effort to conform to the criteria of admission set out at Copenhagen in June 1993 in regard to public freedoms, the respect of human rights, social protection, and the principle of a market economy. The real danger, in my eyes, would be to allow Turkey to remove itself from Europe and its values and then plunge into its Muslim and Asian surroundings, with the possible risks that that involved for our continent.

It had to be acknowledged, however, that these arguments were not sufficient to convince the great majority of French people, who were as hostile to the possible arrival of Turkey as they were fearful of seeing the continued enlargement of Europe to the detriment of their own interests. It was, to say the least, difficult in this context to get the French to see all the benefits that Europe had brought them over nearly half a century—not least of which was the peace that had been so hard won but that was now taken for granted, and the democracy that now existed throughout the continent. Europe also represented a considerable asset in our own economic and commercial development. It was our best response to globalization and was the guarantor of progress in both social legislation and the fight against social problems, as well as in protecting our environment, our cultural identity, the development of scientific research, and the mobility of young people—as I tried to explain to the latter, without great success, in a television debate with them on April 15, 2005, six weeks before the referendum. At the end of this debate I experienced only a sense of mutual incomprehension that, for my part, deeply troubled me.

The doubtless inadequate campaigning of the "yes" camp and the division in the Socialist Party provoked by the position taken by Laurent Fabius, who behaved more like a party politician than a true statesman in the affair, left me little hope as to the outcome of the vote. When I was told that the European constitution had been rejected by 54 percent of the electorate, I was not really surprised. In a short speech, I acknowledged the "sovereign decision" of the French people, but it was with infinite sadness and much bitterness that I also measured the seriousness of the crisis that Europe now faced because of it. France, followed shortly afterward by the Netherlands, had opposed an advance that would be accepted by other member states, including Spain and Luxembourg, and had taken what could only be described as a step backward or at least a preservation of the status quo likely to block all real progress in the construction of Europe for many years to come.

In the short term, however, it was on the domestic front that I had to face the consequences of this defeat.

The team of Jean-Pierre Raffarin had not been able to regain the confidence of the French, as the failure of the referendum demonstrated. The voters had seized this opportunity to express both their distrust of Europe and their discontent with government policy. I had to institute a change of prime minister, as I announced to Raffarin on May 29; he was not surprised. Yet it was a decision I felt forced to take rather than one I wanted.

All that remained was to choose his successor. The possibility of appointing Nicolas Sarkozy was again brought up. President of the majority party and new hope of the right, having earned a good record as minister of the interior, he seemed politically the best placed to take on this responsibility, which he was, in addition, impatient to assume. But that was not the important question. For me, the choice of a prime minister always depends on one and the same criterion, above and beyond the personal qualities and political following of each candidate: the degree of trust and harmony necessary for a peaceful, efficient relationship between the two heads of the executive. Any rivalry between them could only be harmful to the smooth running of our institutions and therefore contrary to the country's interests. Such a risk had become inevitable with Sarkozy from the moment he had openly declared his strategy to win presidential power, which could not be the primary motivation of a prime minister. What is more, his opposition to Turkey's entry to the European Union and his criticisms of the French social model did not bode well for a lasting entente between the Élysée and Matignon.

This did not prevent me from wanting Sarkozy, as I said to him when we met the day after the referendum, to be part of the future leadership team and to take on high-level responsibilities within it. While regretting that he could not obtain more, he agreed in principle to return to his post of minister of the interior, on condition that he could keep the presidency of the UMP. I reminded him of my position on the subject. He replied that for him it was out of the question to abandon something he had only just won. We agreed to speak about it again as soon as the new prime minister was appointed.

I was thinking of appointing Michèle Alliot-Marie when I met, shortly afterward, with Dominique de Villepin. He was among the small number whom I thought fully qualified to fulfill this mission and was in my view the only credible alternative to Michèle Alliot-Marie. As I had often said, Villepin was my "best commando leader." The fact that he was also an amateur poet did not displease me. Everything that marked him out from the traditional political establishment was an argument in his favor, as long as it was not taken to extremes. He had inspiration, enthusiasm, panache, the desire to take on challenges and to act. He had an elevated notion of France and had strived to give the best image of it while at the head of our diplomatic mission. He had also demonstrated, in taking over the Ministry of the Interior, his ability to deal concretely and efficiently with the problems that most directly concerned our compatriots' lives. He was said to be elitist, impetuous, cut off from reality, but he had showed himself to be both an academic and a man of the people. In addition, as everyone knew, Dominique de Villepin had belonged to my "trusted circle" since the presidential campaign of 1995. I had always been able to count on his support in the most difficult moments of cohabitation, and our long collaboration had allowed me to appreciate his qualities, which to me meant that he was destined for the highest positions—although that of prime minister two years away from the presidential election was perhaps not an enviable one. There was a danger for him that he would become too exposed in a task that had seen many a candidate come to grief.

This was what I began by saying to him that May 30, 2005, when we talked about the possibility of his appointment. I had not yet taken my decision. It was claimed after the event that Villepin had forced me to give it to him, which is to misunderstand both me and the relationship between us. He declared himself ready, in the extremely direct manner that was his wont, to tackle alongside me the most pressing challenges of the end of my mandate: reducing unemployment and the government deficit; the creation of a more attractive, dynamic, and competitive economy; and the reinvolvement of France in the construction of Europe. At the end of our meeting, judging that he was probably the only one able to deliver the new impetus, in perfect accord with me, that France needed, I therefore offered Dominique de Villepin the post of prime minister.

We immediately tackled the subject of his governmental team. Dominique realized as I did the need to include Nicolas Sarkozy, although I was not unaware of the rivalry between them—a rivalry that was further exacerbated some time later by what would become the Clearstream affair. In mentioning that, I wish to state here that since my election to the presidency, I had given strong support to the raising of moral standards in international markets, particularly in regard to the signing of large contracts. I had given specific instructions on this to my successive governments and to each minister concerned. It was strictly within this framework that Dominique de Villepin, then minister of foreign affairs, had acted. In regard to the affair itself, I wish to reaffirm that I had never requested any inquiry into any person whatever, political or otherwise, and I am certain that Dominique de Villepin acted similarly.

This problem aside, I saw no obstacle that prevented him and Sarkozy from collaborating, as the general interest dictated. When I saw the latter a little later that day, he eventually agreed to be under the orders of Villepin, on condition that I made it clear that I had offered him his ministerial position on my personal initiative and, of course, if he was allowed to keep the presidency of the UMP. I agreed, judging it to be in the greater interest to do so.

Our first great battle was employment. The new prime minister rightly rejected all fatalism in the fight against unemployment, believing that if many initiatives had been launched, over more than thirty years, to try to resolve this problem, other avenues had probably not yet been explored. I supported his efforts for greater imagination and innovation in this area. The "new position contract" was the first example of this more aggressive policy. While the subsidized contracts that had been implemented by Jean-Louis Borloo in the framework of the social unity plan answered the obvious need for many young people to be integrated into the world of work, the new position contract was designed to facilitate the creation of jobs in economic sectors that had been neglected until then but that, if they were freed from excessive charges and procedures, could turn out to be extremely fruitful. The measure concerned two and half million small businesses with not more than twenty employees, which often were too fragile to take the risk of hiring people on for long-term positions. The new position contract opened up a new possibility for them by making available a long-term contract that could be terminated during a trial period without notice or justification.

This measure, unprecedented in France, led to an undeniable increase in new jobs. At the end of 2006, more than 400,000 employees had been recruited with a new position contract; unfortunately, there were very isolated cases of wrongful termination of contracts, immediately picked up by detractors who used it to vilify such contracts. The new position contract reflected a vision of the economy that was both pragmatic and innovative, introducing greater flexibility by taking the risk of lifting certain taboos. In introducing it, the prime minister had given a concrete demonstration of determination and courage that quickly won him favor in the public eye—his increased popularity also somewhat upset the game plan of those who hoped to succeed me.

My level of activity remained intense during this period of relative sunshine following the change of government. At seventy-two, my rhythm of work remained what it had always been since I had been in office, it never even entering my head that I might need to pace myself. Trips within France or abroad, meetings with ministers and my staff, receptions and welcoming French and international personalities continued to fill my life, totally devoted to the exercise of the presidential mandate that the French had twice entrusted to me. In July 2005, I went to Singapore accompanied by the mayor of Paris to defend—without success, alas!—the bid to host the Olympic games in 2012, before immediately taking another flight on my return to Paris to Gleneagles in Scotland, where the G8 summit was being held, grief-stricken by the terrorist attacks carried out in the London Underground.

Was it the combined effect of fatigue accumulated over the course of these successive trips, the shock experienced over the assassination of Rafic Hariri, and the very rough blow that the failure of the European referendum represented for me? Whatever the case, on September 2, I experienced so-called health issues. I had been lucky enough to be very rarely ill in my life, to the point that I doubtless believed I was indestructible. I had always thought, in fact—as I often said to my family, to their concern—that I would die suddenly like my father, and I had almost accepted the notion.

Back in Paris and about to meet a party of representatives from the principality of Andorra, it had all begun with a violent migraine that was put down to simple tiredness. I then realized that I could no longer read the speech that I was about to give. I called Bernadette, who was outside Paris, to tell her about this persistent vision problem. She immediately advised me to alert the Élysée doctor, Jack Dorol, which I did after greeting my guests and improvising a few words of welcome.

Having trained as an accident and emergency doctor, Dr. Dorol reacted without delay by taking me to the hospital so that I could be examined. En route, I telephoned my daughter Claude to alert her, while reassuring her there was no reason to worry. Then I called Bernadette at the beginning of the evening: The doctors had just diagnosed a "small cerebrovascular accident," identified early enough to be managed. I therefore asked for my appointments over the following few days to be canceled. I had to stay in the hospital several days to rest and undergo further tests. Early the next morning, Claude and Bernadette arrived at the hospital, surprised to find me in good shape, other than the headache, which still had not left. Shortly afterward, I told Dominique about my hospitalization. With the agreement of the secretary general of the Élysée, I wanted the French to know the whole truth about my state of health, and my family insisted on this to the doctors. My cerebrovascular accident proved to be minor, and everything returned to normal. I would simply have to cut back my activities for a time.

Needless to say, the seven days that I was forced to spend in the hospital seemed interminable to me. I busied myself with working and with the visits authorized by the doctors, including those of the secretary general and my diplomatic advisor, Maurice Gourdault-Montagne. I asked Dominique, when he came to meet with me after his return to Paris, to chair the Council of Ministers in my place. As soon as I left hospital on September 9, I went back to my office at the Élysée, where my agenda had been lightened for several weeks. Air flights were forbidden me for the moment, so it was the prime minister who would represent me at a UN summit where I was shortly due to speak.

A cerebrovascular accident often has several repercussions. The only one in my case was a temporary reduction of my field of vision, which meant that the texts I had to read were printed in larger type. But I would now be subject to the scrutiny, rarely benevolent, of those who were watching out for the least sign of tiredness or weariness in me to rush to draw the conclusions that suited them.

At the end of October 2005, France had to face riots in the suburbs on a scale unprecedented in our country. This urban violence had broken out in Clichy-sous-Bois on the twenty-seventh of that month after two young people, who were being chased by the police along with four of their friends, were fatally electrocuted in a substation in which they had taken refuge. A third man had suffered severe burns. The first demonstrations against the forces of order took place in the evening before spreading over the following days to several other housing projects in the Paris region and then to most of the big cities. The riot police were very quickly confronted with rioters armed with Molotov cocktails and others who, in certain places, did not hesitate to shoot at them and at the firefighters with real bullets. Thousands of vehicles were burned, public buildings gutted, and schools and organizations ransacked and vandalized.

I immediately realized the gravity of these events and gave the minister of the interior the instructions necessary to reestablish order. That was the first decision to be taken, even if the problem obviously went beyond security issues. I also requested that the minister of justice organize an inquiry without delay to understand exactly what happened at Clichy-sous-Bois. In addition, I ordered that the procedure for compensating the victims of this violence be speeded up. These were the immediate measures that I decided to implement, together with Villepin. On November 2, I stated in the Council of Ministers that there should be no no-go zones in the republic and warned members of the government against the use of incendiary language, insisting on the fact that "absence of dialogue and the increase of disrespect will lead to a dangerous situation." Then, on November 6, I assembled the Internal Security Council—in other words, the prime minister and the ministers concerned with problems of public order—to further reinforce the actions of the police and the judiciary. Finally, I spoke to the French from the Élysée, delivering the message that the republic would prove stronger than those who wanted to propagate violence.

On November 8, when it became obvious that the situation was worsening despite these measures, the Council of Ministers proceeded to a further step by taking an exceptional decision: proclaiming a state of emergency with a curfew in the towns and areas concerned.

Confronted with this crisis of unprecedented dimensions, we could have only one priority: to act, which is what I did. In such circumstances, one has to beware of proclamations by the media and of categorical or falsely reassuring prescriptions that seek only to stigmatize, intensify hostility, or set one group against another. Obviously, steadfastness and toughness were needed to ensure that people and possessions were protected, but actions alone were needed to express them—acts that did not prevent those entrusted with enforcing them from simultaneously respecting the values of our republic.

This was, primarily, the role of the president. His duty was both to guarantee public order and to safeguard national unity, twin goals that I had continually striven to fulfill since taking office, conscious of the profound malaise, social discord, and identity crisis from which our country had suffered for several decades and eager to locate the causes and mobilize all the forces likely to dispel them. Contrary to what I was hearing from various quarters, this new unrest in the suburbs did not mean that we had failed to implement our successive action plans to help the areas hardest hit by unemployment and social fracture. Important results had been obtained thanks to the creation of urban tax-free zones and to the measures already

taken in the framework of the social unity plan to help the long-term unemployed and hundreds of thousands of young people without qualifications find employment. The measures we had introduced to fight against
social exclusion and discrimination were equally vital. Here, too, progress
had been made, even if much remained to be done. If this package of measures had not been enough to avoid the possible explosion we had feared,
it was doubtless because they had been implemented too late, given the
deep-rootedness of the problems of the suburbs, to have the desired effect.
Which therefore meant that the only solution to the problem was to redou-
ble the efforts that were already under way, not to substitute them with a
demagogic, short-term view that would once more cover up the real causes.

This was the essence of what I wanted to say to the French in my address of November 14, when I stated that what was at stake in this crisis
was both respect for the law and the success of our policy of integration:

*We need to be strict in our application of the rules of family reunification.
We need to intensify our fight against illegal immigration and the trafficking it generates. We need to step up our action against black market
employment rings, that modern form of slavery.*

*But abiding by the law and the values of the Republic necessarily in-
volves justice, fraternity, and generosity. It is in words and looks, with the
heart and in actions, that we express the respect that is everyone's right.
I wish to say to the children of troubled neighborhoods, whatever their
origin, that they are all daughters and sons of the Republic.*

*We can build nothing lasting without respect. We can build nothing
lasting if we allow racism, intolerance, insults, and affronts, wherever they
come from, to increase.*

*We can build nothing lasting if we do not fight the social poison that
is discrimination. We can build nothing lasting if we do not recognize and
assume the diversity of French society. It is written into our history. It is
both a richness and a strength.*

This message helped to calm people down. On November 17, the situation
had returned to normal, which did not mean that it had been resolved.
This was why I felt we had to remain extremely vigilant about anything
that could revive tensions. As I did not hide from him, I did not agree with
the inopportune declarations of the minister of the interior promising, the
previous June 20, to "flush out" the "Cité des 4000" housing estate in
Courneuve and then, on October 25, to rid Argenteuil of this "scum." In
December 2005, I seized the opportunity of a meeting at the Élysée with

fifty or so readers of the daily newspaper *Le Parisien,* who had all witnessed at close hand the riots in the suburbs, to mark my refusal of all "positive discrimination." This concept undermined the essential republican principle of equal access to employment without any distinction other than that related to merit. I equally rejected another concept then in vogue of giving non-European foreigners the right to vote and pointed out, here, too, one of the fundamental principles of our republic, that suffrage and nationality be inseparable.

I welcomed with more interest, however, the project that the prime minister submitted to me in January 2006 of a first jobs contract for young people under twenty-six, designed to facilitate the entry into the jobs market of people who were struggling. At that time, youth unemployment was abnormally high, particularly in the most vulnerable districts. Should this contract, however, be reserved for a single group, at the risk of seeming discriminatory in its turn? I knew from experience just how sensitive a subject all reforms specifically concerning young people could be and how careful one needed to be in making them. However, while warning the prime minister against the danger of a badly understood or badly interpreted measure, I did not oppose it, particularly as it enjoyed the strong support of government members of Parliament, including the most senior leaders of the UMP.

The advantage of the new jobs contract was that it allowed young people confronted with the harsh reality of their first professional experience to have direct access to employment, instead of being offered nothing but work experience or short-term contracts. It also assured them of a salary equivalent to other workers and not a cut-rate minimum wage, as well as individual rights to training and easier access to accommodations. Just as with the new position contract, the employer received in return the right to terminate the contract without justification until an employee was definitively hired and did not have to pay compensation to employees during the first three months.

The first position contract, inserted into the equal opportunities bill, was adopted by the National Assembly on February 9, 2006. Immediately, it met with fierce resistance from the opposition and the trade unions, on the pretext that it would encourage job insecurity—when one out of every four young people was already unemployed—although it was well received by young people in the suburbs, who were well placed to appreciate its usefulness. Over the ensuing weeks, however, it came up against an extremely strong student reaction that was orchestrated by those who, already benefiting from training, were in fact those least concerned by the proposal. Faced with the tide of demonstrations, which inevitably weakened his political situation, the prime minister was then deserted by some in his majority.

On March 31, 2006, I judged it preferable, in agreement with Dominique de Villepin, to announce the withdrawal of the project—without abandoning, of course, the equal opportunities bill. The battle for employment was not, however, lost, as the record of my second term of office clearly shows.

25
RETURN TO ROOTS

The scene took place on the terrace of a hotel in Mauritius one day in the summer of 1990. I was having lunch in the sun, in the company of Bernadette and several friends, when an ascetic-looking man approached our table. I had seen him obviously trying to speak to me for several days without having yet dared approach me. We had simply greeted each other. "M. Mayor," he said to me, "did you know you have one of my books?" I looked at him, not a little astonished, and laughingly replied, so that he would not pursue it: "Listen, my dear sir, I never read books. So I cannot have one of yours." He went on, at the risk of seeming tiresome: "But you do, you do, I even saw it on your desk in *Paris Match*." I explained to him that the only book that was, in fact, placed on my desk at the Paris city hall was a work by Jacques Kerchache on African art. "Well, there you are! I am Jacques Kerchache!" he declared.

And thus began the story of a great friendship and, through it, the adventure of the Quai Branly Museum that I would inaugurate sixteen years later. Jacques Kerchache, whom I immediately had sit down at our table, spoke to me about the manifesto he had just published in the newspaper *Libération* entitled "All Arts Are Born Free and Equal" and about his attempts, thus far unsuccessful, to get masterpieces of primitive art into the Louvre. He had even tried, again without success, to get President Mitterrand interested in the idea. He had regained hope, however, when he had by chance discovered through a photo in a magazine that I was one of his readers. In short, as mayor of Paris, I was his last hope.

Few people at that time knew about my own passion for African and Asian arts, which I had been careful to keep well hidden. It suited me very well to pass for a philistine and, far from trying to undo this reputation that had been conferred on me in certain milieus, I amused myself by stubbornly insisting that I was interested only in westerns and military music. A man in the public eye should be sure to construct an inner world that nobody could enter. It was vital that my little secret garden remain untouched, for I wanted to keep it to myself. Until this meeting with Jacques Kerchache, which would turn out to be such a decisive one for me.

Jacques occupied a very particular place in the world of Parisian gallery owners, where he was seen as an original, and rather volcanic, creature. Product of a middle-class Jewish family, he liked to say that he was the son of a Communist worker. His father had enabled him to open, very young, his first gallery in Paris, already devoted to what would remain his life's passion. But, more than an art trader, Jacques was above all a traveler, an explorer, an indefatigable forager driven by an unwearying curiosity. A sensitive and passionate soul, a free spirit and a very strong personality. A larger-than-life character who approached life with enormous enthusiasm and appetite. He nursed his dreams with incredible obstinacy, overcoming all obstacles and galvanizing all energies to realize them. He spent most of his life wandering the planet drawing up a critical list of world sculpture, from prehistory to contemporary times, in public and private collections, in search of "model forms" of art. Convinced that one could and should bring the same aesthetic consideration to bear on the many stages in the history of creation, through all civilizations and continents, Jacques had a predilection for works that the West considered inferior or marginal. He was a discoverer more than just a simple collector and would hurry to any place he could exhume and save a few neglected treasures. One day, learning that missionaries had thrown a quantity of wooden and metal sculptures into a well in Gabon, he had not hesitated to climb down into the well to save them from permanent loss.

The idea of reaffirming this unjustly neglected and often despised cultural heritage had long obsessed Jacques Kerchache. He believed that the collections of African and Oceanic art that were dispersed through other Parisian museums should not only find their place in the Louvre but also be the subject of a great museological project, both modern and ambitious, and enjoy sufficient funding to be constantly enriched and renewed. This idea was seen as sacrilegious in terms of the existing arrangements, and it above all clashed with the conformities and certitudes, difficult to shake, of certain conservationists for whom the history of art was confined to a given period, outside of which there was only a sort of third or fourth world of creation. I was just as unimpressed as he was by this mentality against which almost no one dared react. Armed with his skills and the resources I had at my disposal, we decided, soon after we first met, to come together to upset this established order by ourselves revealing to the public all that the "specialists" refused to show.

In 1992, the five hundredth anniversary of Christopher Columbus's "discovery" of America gave us an exceptional opportunity to pay homage not to this supposed discoverer but to the peoples and cultures that his intrusion onto this continent had damaged and destroyed. With this, we were right at the heart of the subject that concerned us: the rehabilitation of the oldest civilizations and the irreplaceable artistic legacy they had left to humanity. There was no question, naturally, of the city of Paris playing the smallest role in the official commemorations of an event in which we had no reason to rejoice. When King Juan Carlos telephoned me to express his surprise about this, I simply replied that the expedition of Christopher Columbus did not constitute in my view a great moment of history but rather a calamity that could not justifiably be celebrated. "I intend to organize a large exhibition in the memory of the Native Americans he massacred," I had announced to him. These were the same words that I would use two years later, during the official dinner that followed the inauguration of our exhibition on the Taínos held in the Petit Palais. Offended by my words, the ambassador of Spain and his wife immediately left their table as a mark of protest.

Jacques Kercharche was the creator of this exhibition, which had a great success in 1994. The Taíno people of the Greater Antilles were the first victims of the veritable genocide that had ensued after the arrival of the Spanish troops. More than 80 million Native Americans were exterminated, from Mexico to Tierra del Fuego, in less than half a century. All in the name of the supposed superiority of our religion! Jacques was one of the foremost experts on the Taínos and, thanks to our mutual efforts, the works of this lost civilization were able to live again within the surroundings of the Petit Palais.

This was only a first step in the work of rehabilitation upon which we had embarked. The second was taken the following year, shortly after my election to the presidency. I very quickly decided to set up a commission for the "primitive arts," whose responsibility I entrusted to my very old friend, Jacques Friedman, and for which Claude Lévi-Strauss, on my request, accepted the honorary chairmanship. I had long been one of his readers and admirers. My personal study of the history of civilizations owed much to the author of *Tristes tropiques*, which remained one of my constant bedside books.

In February 1997, despite the reservations of well-known conservationists and professors, the plan to create a "Museum of Arts and Civilizations" was launched, with an initial grant allocation. I was very determined that it should come to fruition. After obtaining the backing of Alain Juppé, I found his successor, Lionel Jospin, immediately favorable to the idea, and his support in this regard never wavered. The site was chosen in July 1998 in agreement with the minister of culture, Catherine Trautmann, who made available to the project an area of about five acres bordering the Seine, on the Quai Branly, belonging to the state. It was on this location, near the Eiffel Tower and virtually opposite the Trocadero, that the museum would be built. In December of that year, the public institution was set up and placed under the chairmanship of Stéphane Martin, a man of rare quality, ingenious and passionate, a former principal private secretary at the Ministry of Culture and very knowledgeable about Africa. He would become a friend. Jospin and I wanted the construction of the museum to be entrusted to one of the great names of contemporary architecture; it was Jean Nouvel who won the competition. When I saw his plans at the end of 1999, I was immediately won over by their beauty and appropriateness.

While work began on this project, in April 2000, I inaugurated rooms in the magnificently designed setting of the Sessions wing of the Louvre containing a hundred or so masterpieces of African, Asian, Oceanic, and American art, thereby fulfilling—not without much effort—Jacques Kerchache's vow. In his manifesto published ten years earlier and signed by three hundred personalities from the artistic, cultural, and scientific worlds, he had declared: "If nothing is done, the France of 1999 will have condoned, with a blindness reminiscent of that justifying colonialism, the exclusion for decades to come of the major works produced by three-quarters of humanity."

It had taken all my authority as president to get the director of the Louvre, Pierre Rosenberg, to agree, fiercely opposed as he initially was to the idea of putting the *Mona Lisa* and the Venus de Milo together with an Aztec statue or a relic from New Guinea. "The man with the red scarf," as I called him, considered this mixing of genres beyond the pale. For him, the history of art consisted of seventeenth- and eighteenth-century French and Italian paintings. Anything else barely merited consideration. He did everything in his power to oppose what he saw as an intrusion into his domain and, if he could not succeed in stopping us, to step up his criticism campaign against us.

One day, I learned that he had ordered the entry tickets for the Sessions wing to be sold separately from those for the Louvre, and by two different agents. My blood boiling, I took him virulently to task during a reception at the Élysée. "One must not mix things," he retorted, with his customarily haughty air. Sickened, I asked him if he had decided to put bones through the noses of the museum attendants at the Sessions wing, and walked away. The day of the opening, the ambassador of Madagascar was rightly shocked when he discovered that a statue originating from his country had been deliberately placed opposite the door of the lavatories.

That April 13, 2000, when tribal art finally entered the Louvre, none-theless constituted a memorable date in the history of contemporary muse-ology. In my speech in the presence of Pierre Rosenberg, I first emphasized that this exhibition constituted a symbolic recognition of the works un-justly omitted until now from the greatest museums in the world and then saluted the huge work accomplished by Jacques Kerchache. Already very weakened that day by the throat cancer from which he had been suffering for several months, Jacques died the following summer during his annual holiday in Cancún. I was deeply saddened by the death of this man of heart for whom I had so much esteem and affection. As soon as I heard the news, I telephoned his wife to help her repatriate the body as quickly as possible, but she replied that Jacques, knowing the end was close, had asked to be cremated there, so that his family could complete their holiday in peace. He was most decidedly a character out of the ordinary.

The defense of indigenous peoples does not consist only of showing all the wealth of their artistic genius. These people still represent 5 percent of the population of the planet, according to United Nations estimates, and their survival also needs to be ensured. They carry the memory of the oldest human experience and through it the secret of our origins. They have the same right to respect and dignity as all other peoples. I had made friends with Chief Raoni, of the Kayopo Indian tribe in the Amazonian rain forest, when I met him on one of his visits to Paris at the beginning of the 1990s, and I intervened with the Brazilian authorities to support his project to cre-ate an institute in the Xingu indigenous lands. This institute would serve to protect the site and allow the ethnic peoples who had never left it to con-tinue to live in their traditional setting. At my initiative, the G8 countries recognized, during the Okinawa summit in 2000, the irreplaceable cultural value and essential role in preserving the ecosystem and biodiversity of these indigenous people, threatened by deforestation and the dramatic re-duction of their ancestral habitat. Most of the great powers—Russia, the United States, Canada, Japan, Great Britain, and France—had members of an indigenous population on their territory. It was therefore a subject of direct interest to the international community.

In the same way I gave all the help I could to the creator of the admi-rable collection "Human Earth," Jean Malaurie, when he mooted the idea of founding a polar academy to ensure the preservation of the indigenous peoples of the Russian Arctic Circle. Vladimir Putin made premises available to this new academy, established in St. Petersburg in 2003, that had the mission of guaranteeing these people an alternative to extinction or assimilation. I engaged in a similar fight alongside Jean Chrétien, the Canadian prime minister, in favor of the Inuits and the autonomy of their territory, the Nunavut. When they eventually obtained it, I went on an official visit, on September 6, 1999, to acknowledge that historic step in the recognition of all indigenous nations but also all those fighting to preserve their identity at a time of globalization. "The most precious thing man has," I declared that day, "is his memory, his history, his roots, his traditions, and the value of his elders—that is, all these intimate landmarks without which he feels frustrated and unhappy."

This permanent combat for recognition of the equality and dignity of all cultures found direct expression in the world Convention on the Promotion and Protection of the Diversity of Cultural Expressions adopted, after years of efforts and negotiation, by UNESCO on October 20, 2005, at the instigation of France. Its goal was to protect us, in all domains of creation, from a twin danger: a uniformity set down by a dominant model and the rise of fundamentalism inspired by intolerant systems of thought. Preserving diversity of cultures did not just involve ensuring the respect and freedom of expression of each one; it was also encouraging exchanges, dialogue, and openness.

It was important to me that France set the example in this regard, both for itself and for other nations. Three major projects, created within the framework of the development of the Louvre, bore testimony to this—facilitated, it has to be said, by the departure of Pierre Rosenberg and the arrival of his successor, Henri Loyrette, who also adhered to a fairly protectionist concept of museology but who displayed a more obvious openness of mind. Actively assisted by two excellent ministers of culture, Jean-Jacques Aillagon and then Renaud Donnedieu de Vabres from 2004, I ensured that the Louvre gave greater expression to its universal mission and exerted its economic power of attraction in places other than just the capital.

In 2003, I proposed the creation of a new department devoted to Islamic arts in order to give greater prominence to a collection of thirteen thousand pieces of an exceptional richness and to highlight the significant contribution of Islamic civilizations to our culture. This wing was planned to open in 2012. In the same vein, after exerting strong pressure, I eventually won agreement for the cooperation arrangement, fiercely contested by some eminent experts, that the emirate of Abu Dhabi had sought with the

Louvre for the creation of its own museum. There was obviously no question of getting rid of our collections, which were transferred on a temporary basis, or of "selling" our national reserves, which were the immediate accusations leveled against us. The negotiations, hammered out by Renaud Donnedieu de Vabres with both the professionals in Paris and the authorities in Abu Dhabi, had the sole goal of arranging a contract of association, signed in March 2007, while also striving in exemplary fashion to create a dialogue between East and West.

It was with the same enthusiasm that I greeted the idea, first put forward by Jean-Jacques Aillagon in 2003, of establishing a branch of the Louvre in a region of France. This was similarly not so as to effect a simple transfer of artwork but in order to implement a specific project of cultural decentralization. My first concern was to enable one of our most underprivileged regions to benefit from the economic fallout. The Nord-Pas-de-Calais was chosen, and it then remained only to choose the town where the new Louvre would be established. Several immediately came forward to bid for it, and after a long debate, made all the more difficult because some were represented by members of the government, I chose the city of Lens, which had been fervently solicited by Renaud Donnedieu de Vabres, together with two representatives of the region, Martine Aubry and Jack Lang, who had directly lobbied me on the subject. I had wanted to allow the former mining valley of Lens to profit from this unexpected new role, thereby giving expression to my goal of making culture, here and elsewhere, a real lesson in humanity.

The inauguration of the Quai Branly Museum on June 20, 2006, was one of the happiest moments of my presidency and one of the greatest joys of my life. Beyond the realization of a personal dream, passionately shared with Jacques Kerchache, it marked the end of a long fight in service of a just cause: the recognition of all that the oldest civilizations on earth had brought to human creation. I arrived early that morning, along with its two architects, Stéphane Martin and Jean Nouvel, to visit this building that had finally reached completion, an enormous vessel made of stone, glass, and plants in which the vestiges of pre-Columbian America rubbed shoulders with those of the great African kingdoms, the islands of Oceania, and distant Asiatic countries.

I had personally drawn up the list of French and foreign guests who would discover the museum alongside me; I knew just how intimately connected some of them had been with the project. I particularly wanted the presence of Rigoberta Menchú Tum, Nobel peace prize winner whom I had met in June 1996 at a reception at the Élysée organized at the end of an international meeting in Paris of Native American communities; United Nations secretary general Kofi Annan; the secretary general of the organization of French-speaking nations, Abdou Diouf; the young prime minister of the autonomous territory of Nunavut, Paul Okalik; Marie-Claude Djibaou, the widow of the nationalist leader of New Caledonia; and many others. All were there, including Claude Lévi-Strauss, whose presence we had thought unlikely because of his age and state of health. As soon as I was told of his arrival and as soon as the guests were all seated, I crossed the room to greet the greatest of our anthropologists, who was sitting in the front row. I had not forgotten the immediate support he had given this project. Without his prestigious backing, perhaps I would never have succeeded in getting it accepted. . . . And I was well aware of how much we all owed, myself first and foremost, to his teaching.

In the speech that I gave, it was above all the greater meaning of our shared engagement that I wanted to express:

> At the heart of our project is the rejection of ethnocentrism, that unreasonable and unacceptable pretension according to which the West carries, entirely alone, the destiny of humanity. There is also the rejection of that false evolutionism that claims that certain people are forever frozen at an earlier stage of human development and that their so-called primitive cultures are worthy of study only by ethnologists or, at best, of serving as a source of inspiration for western art. These are absurd and shocking prejudices that need to be contested. There is no more hierarchy between arts and cultures than there is between peoples. And it is above all that conviction, that of the equal dignity of the cultures of the world, that forms the base of the Quai Branly Museum.

The duty to remember is primarily a duty of justice. This demand for truth and clarity is at the basis of the homage rendered in Quai Branly to people who have so long been ostracized.

It was this same demand that led me in July 1995 to recognize the criminal complicity of the French government in the deportation of Jews. It was also this that inspired my decision in January 2006 to decide to commemorate each May 10 the abolition of slavery and thereby to honor and preserve the memory of the millions of men and women deported from Africa to be used as labor in the colonial plantations of the Antilles archipelago of the United States and South America, notably Brazil.

On June 25, four days after the inauguration of the museum, I went to Douaumont, on the occasion of the eightieth anniversary of the Battle of

Verdun, to celebrate the memory of the 170,000 soldiers from France and overseas territories who were killed in the bloodiest battles of the Great War. I wanted particularly to salute the sacrifice of the 80,000 men from our former colonial empire: Moroccan infantrymen; Senegalese, Algerian, and Tunisian fusiliers; soldiers from Madagascar as well as Indochina, Asia, and Oceania. "These men who fought with such determination were not driven by nationalism or by hatred of the enemy. Their souls were not militarist. Their souls were patriotic. They were republican. . . . Today, still, their sacrifice involves us all."

It was in this spirit that I wanted that year to render justice to the former combatants of the colonies by revaluing their pensions, which had been frozen in 1959 at the time of decolonization. For me this represented an act of solidarity and recognition.

Slavery and the Holocaust were two crimes against humanity; forgetting and indifference were others. A nation could neither forge its identity nor build its unity if it did not have the courage to assume the totality of its history. That was why I refused to allow to continue the official silence that had been deliberately maintained around the least honorable aspects of our collective heritage.

In 2001, France was the first country in the world to inscribe in law the recognition of slavery as a crime against humanity. But I felt it necessary, after discussions with various writers whom I liked and admired, such as Aimé Césaire, Maryse Condé, and Édouard Glissant, to go further; the fate endured by their ancestors should be fully recognized as an integral part of our national memory. From this long procession of suffering and broken lives was born a great culture that now occupied a major place in our literary and artistic heritage. It was a testimony of respect and fraternity that we owed our overseas compatriots, and this was why I decided to take the step of including the history of slavery in the syllabus of our national education program. I had long forged with these men and women of Martinique, Guadeloupe, Guyana, St. Pierre and Miquelon, Mayotte, Polynesia, New Caledonia, and Réunion Island lasting ties of shared trust and friendship. I had always been appreciative of the warmth and naturalness of their welcome. I believed in the future of the French overseas territories within the fold of the republic.

After breaking the silence about its direct involvement in the deportation of the Jews, under my auspices, the French government assumed another responsibility: that of fully recognizing the Shoah and of paying homage, finally, to the French Righteous among the Nations—those French citizens of all origins and backgrounds who had long remained anonymous and who took in and protected, in the most terrible period of the Occupation, the three-quarters of the Jewish community remaining on our soil.

On January 27, 2005, two days after inaugurating the Holocaust Memorial in Paris, I accompanied Simone Veil and several representatives from the Jewish community to Auschwitz for the sixtieth anniversary of the liberation of the camp. The ceremony took place in the freezing cold and an extremely somber atmosphere. It was overwhelming for me to accompany Simone Veil to a place where her own life, at the age of seventeen, and that of her family had suddenly plunged into the horror of the concentration camps. "Let's not talk about it," she had said to me in the past when I had asked her about that period in her life. She refused to speak about the horror that she and her family had endured and preferred to keep silent, as if to stifle the horror in such a way that it could never occur again.

At the end of my address, after having spoken about the "immense and terrible suffering" that Auschwitz and Birkenau forever represented in the history of humanity, I emphasized that "the demands of memorial" should remain, in France and elsewhere, a "demand for truth of responsibility." On my return to Paris, I was deeply touched by the message that I received from Claude Lanzmann, the director of the admirable film *Shoah*. He thanked me for having invited him to accompany me to Auschwitz-Birkenau and did me the honor of recognizing me as one of his people: "our guardian, yes, but also our friend and our brother," he wrote.

On January 18, 2007, a few months before the end of my presidency, I went to the Panthéon cemetery to honor the memory of the 2,725 French Righteous among the Nations who had embodied, at the cost of their lives, our values of fraternity and solidarity. Before unveiling with Simone Veil the plaque in the crypt paying homage to them, I addressed them as the best guardians of our national conscience. One of my first speeches as president of the republic in 1995 recognized the responsibility of the French state in the deportation of the Jews. Symbolically, one of the last speeches of my presidency was devoted to the recognition of this other truth of that dark period in our history. In this way, everything had been said and healing could finally begin. The duty of memory is a political act in the most noble sense of the word.

At the end of summer 2006, the presidential election was planned for the following May. However, I judged that priority should be given, for as long as possible, to the tasks that remained to be accomplished in the interest of the country. I decided to postpone my announcement of my electoral intentions, not to prolong the suspense but to see to the end, with all the required authority, the mission with which the French people had entrusted me. A president is not seen in the same way as soon as it is known that he is preparing to leave power. "We work until the end!" I declared to my team at the beginning of 2007, so that no one would be tempted to diminish their efforts. It was an order that applied to me as much as anyone else.

During the last months of my presidency, my primary concern was to ensure, in permanent collaboration with Villepin and each of the members of his government, the lasting nature of the principal engagements that had marked my two successive mandates. I do not wish in these memoirs to draw up an exhaustive list of the projects that came to fruition during this period, but I would like to mention a few of those that confirmed or amplified the great ambitions that had been mine over the twelve years I spent in the Élysée.

In terms of the economy, my constant goal had been to try to ensure that France remained a great power, dynamic and successful, strongly equipped to take on the challenges of globalization. Throughout the referendum campaign of 2005, I heard the anxieties of French men and women about this planetary phenomenon. Among these worries were those of outsourcing and the threats it posed to employment. People had doubts about the ability of Europe and France to rise to the challenge. One of the conditions of doing so, perhaps the principal one, was for our country to embrace wholeheartedly industrial and scientific innovation; this was a decisive factor of world economic competition and the best guarantee of lasting growth. France possessed considerable assets in this area that we had the duty to bring to the fore.

By setting up in 2006 the Agency for Industrial Innovation and the "pact for research," we both created the tools best adapted to this great national ambition and mobilized considerable financial resources that would allow our country to be more competitive alongside other European and world powers. It was equally imperative to relaunch a policy of great industrial projects along the lines of Airbus, the Ariane rocket, and our nuclear program, thanks to which France had considerably reduced its energy dependence. Massive investment programs were launched in the strategic sectors of information technology, that veritable industrial, social, and cultural revolution, and that of new energy resources. The establishment on our soil of the International Thermonuclear Experimental Reactor at Cadarache—obtained after a hard-fought battle at the international level—was a perfect example of this. I wanted our progress in nuclear energy to be further strengthened by the development of the European pressure reactor on the site of Flamanville. At the same time, the Nuclear Safety Authority was created in order to ensure the regulation and control of such a sensitive sector and to guarantee that the public received reliable and transparent information. This fully independent authority would quickly become a reference and example for the whole world.

In January 2006, I announced an important updating of our policy of nuclear deterrence, as I had already done in June 2001. This update had again been made necessary by the evolution of the international situation in this turbulent and rapidly changing post–cold war period. We needed to go beyond the concept of "weak against strong," overly influenced by the concept of a bipolar world, to adapt it to a period troubled by other threats: those of mass terrorist attacks and nuclear ambitions of countries such as Iran and North Korea, apparently determined to free themselves from international rules concerning their real or imagined nuclear weapons.

Many reforms had been carried out since 1995 to improve and consolidate our social pact, which remained one of the major concerns of my presidency. The French were legitimately attached to what was a choice not of comfort but of justice and solidarity. I therefore wanted to tackle head-on the new problems that needed to be resolved and the imbalances that needed to be corrected. With the decisive step of the rescue of our pension system, we had successfully reduced the deficit of the national health insurance system from nearly 12 billion euros in 2003 to 4 billion euros at the end of my mandate without decreasing the amount spent on health care.

Far from being outmoded, our social model was more than ever an essential element of national unity and identity, but it must also prove its capacity to evolve and modernize. After long experience of public affairs, it seemed to me more and more necessary to establish the rules of a real social dialogue. On October 10, 2006, a decisive step was taken on my initiative with the announcement of a new law forbidding any modification of the labor code without consultation with unions and management, thereby giving our compatriots greater involvement in the preservation of our social pact.

In entering the very last stage of my mandate, I remained extremely concerned about the issue of housing. Several fundamental laws give all our compatriots the right to housing, but in practice the situation of a great number of them had continued to deteriorate, not only for the homeless but for many economically fragile families condemned to live in intolerably insalubrious conditions. The measures I had taken at the beginning of my first mandate, such as the requisition of empty housing, had not been enough to resolve the problem. The government had to go further to guarantee the right to decent, independent housing to everyone of French nationality or living in our country legally and permanently. This was the aim of the law introducing the legally enforceable right to housing, which the government passed, on my request, on March 5, 2007, a measure that was salutary in every respect, even if some people thought it too restrictive, to the point of undermining the right to ownership. Obviously, this law did not magically solve the entire housing issue, but it did enable thousands of families to improve their living conditions and oblige public authorities to find new solutions, particularly in terms of construction.

Another major action in these last months was the writing into the constitution of the abolition of the death penalty, the law that I had proposed on this being adopted by Parliament on February 19, 2007. The abolition of capital punishment, which I had personally supported when it was voted in Parliament twenty-six years earlier, was now recognized as definitive, which meant that it could never be reestablished in our country.

Finally, I strove to preserve the future of the construction of Europe before leaving power. Another way, again, of taking my convictions to the very end. The negative vote of April 25, 2005, had placed France in a difficult position. True, the Netherlands had also rejected the proposed constitution a few days later, while it seemed clear that neither Britain nor Poland would be able to get it accepted as it was. It was also true that it was France, one of the founding members of the European Union, that was the first to take the responsibility of blocking the process that was under way. Faced with this unprecedented situation, I judged that everything should be done to protect the basis of the institutional reforms contained in the defunct constitution. We needed to give ourselves time, which was why I proposed "a period of reflection" to the other European heads of state and of government. Those who wanted to interrupt their ratification process could do so. Even though it was his turn as president of the Union, Tony Blair immediately seized the opportunity to withdraw from the game; Luxembourg, for its part, kept its referendum, brilliantly won by the prime minister, Jean-Claude Juncker, an unflagging pillar of support for European construction.

In April 2006, France had presented to its partners a memorandum containing the few improvements possible in such a restricted framework. They were judged interesting but inadequate. It was clear that only a new treaty could truly give the European Union the institutional means to realize its ambitions. Sooner or later, that seemed vital. In May 2007, people were ready to tackle the debate again on a more solid basis. At the time of my departure from the Élysée, the negotiations with our partners were already well under way to allow an enlarged Europe to equip itself with revived institutions. The Treaty of Lisbon that was subsequently adopted provided for easier decision making, a rebalancing of power between populated and less populated countries, and the introduction of a stable presidency of the European Council and a minister of foreign affairs for the Union.

The failure of the referendum had confirmed to me how difficult it was for Europeans to understand how Europe functioned, probably because we had not been able to explain it to them well enough. This misunderstanding was the cause of the speculations, doubts, and occasional unreasonable fears. I asked our new minister of European affairs, Catherine Colonna, who had strong convictions on the matter but who was pragmatic, to draw up concrete proposals to ensure that Europe was better understood, particularly among young people. Among other measures, this led to the introduction of the subject as part of the "core knowledge" that every student had to master at the end of his or her compulsory schooling—which would enable, I hoped, future generations to have a better grasp of what Europe represented and what it gave them.

During the period of reflection that had led to the signing of a new treaty, another battle had been engaged to establish the European budget for the years 2007 to 2013. As always, this negotiation had been extremely difficult, each country trying to defend its interests and its finances. Agreement was finally reached in December 2005, on a basis that was favorable to France and better balanced. For the first time, the notorious British check, that rebate obtained by Margaret Thatcher in 1984 after she had declared "I want my money back," had been fundamentally revised, economic conditions in Great Britain having greatly changed from the days when it was considered one of the poorest countries of the Union. It was now one of the richest and drew the most benefit from the enlargement to the East. On my insistence and with the support of the new member states, Tony Blair reluctantly accepted in December 2005 that his country should assume its fair share of the solidarity payments given to the most recent members of the European Union.

My other reason for satisfaction was the creation of the tenth European development fund, consisting of 22 billion euros, until 2013. There too I was forced to wage a fierce battle against a certain egotism among our partners. The African countries, which feared they would suffer financially after the enlargement, could thereby count on continuing to receive European aid. In this difficult battle, I benefited from the constant support of the German chancellor, Angela Merkel, who had taken over from Gerhard

Schröder in October 2005. I admired the way in which that woman of great character, originating from the former East Germany, had succeeded in taking over the leadership of her country by eliminating all her rivals. I had met her several times before she came to power, and these early meetings had revealed her keen judgment, her tactical intelligence, and her attachment to the pursuit of the Franco–German alliance. Our all-too-brief collaboration was always friendly, trusting, and warm.

*I*t was on March 11, 2007, after having successfully steered through the last great reforms that seemed to me vital for the future of the country, that I announced to the French people that I would not be trying for a third mandate. At that time, I had reason not to be too unhappy with the record of my presidency, after an intense period of activity to which I had devoted all my energy. This record, the fruit of my personal action as well as that of the governments of Jean-Pierre Raffarin, Dominique de Villepin, and all our teams, was expressed in several numbers that I would like to reproduce here because they are so illuminating. The government deficit was reduced to 2.5 percent of our gross national product and the debt had fallen to 63.8 percent, unemployment had been brought down to 8.1 percent of the active population, while the tax burden was also clearly decreasing. The government of Dominique de Villepin had therefore succeeded in improving the country's situation and the daily life of the French, while also making good use of the end of a presidential term of office that many thought would be devoid of activity.

It was with much emotion that day that I expressed to all my compatriots my pride in the work we had accomplished together, the passion I had felt at serving a France of justice and peace, "a France," I said to them, "that I appreciate as much as I appreciate you." After my reelection in 2002, I had never seriously thought about standing again, even if my deliberate silence on the subject had allowed people to think the opposite and nurse many a calculation. A wise axiom has it that one should "know how to leave power before it leaves you"—even though the heads of state or ordinary leaders who readily accept the axiom and put it into practice are rare. It would be false to pretend that I was an exception to the rule; it took me time to get used to the idea that I would have to give up the political responsibilities that had occupied forty years of my existence. In fact, I do not think I really was prepared for it, even though I believed after careful reflection that there was no other choice and that that was fine.

Whatever they might say, few heads of state truly organize their succession, although that does not stop them having their preferences or possibly expressing them. I was not the only one to think that Alain Juppé possessed all the necessary qualities to assume the office of president. Circumstances, however, decided otherwise. Various other hypotheses opened up, on which it was not my duty to pronounce. Everyone knew the quality of my relationship with Dominique de Villepin, and no one was unaware of the differences of political analysis that had sometimes set me apart from Nicolas Sarkozy, which he himself barely sought to cover up in publicizing his desire to "break free." However, both of them came from the same political group, and it was they alone who had the ability to choose its candidate.

On January 16, 2007, I was informed that Sarkozy had been chosen as the UMP candidate for the presidential election. On March 21, ten days after making my own decision public, I announced on television that I would "naturally give my vote and my support" to his candidacy. I immediately gave the order to the secretary general of the Élysée and all his staff to scrupulously ensure that nothing could occur to hinder, in any way, the campaign of the UMP representative. On March 26, the government was reorganized to ensure that there was no confusion between Nicolas Sarkozy's ministerial status and his position as presidential candidate. I then made the decision, in agreement with Villepin, to appoint François Baroin, a man in whom I had every confidence, as minister of the interior.

It was during the last weeks at the Élysée that I began to reflect on the best way of continuing, when I was no longer in power, my fight for the great international causes that were closest to my heart: development, conflict prevention, the preservation of languages and cultures, and defense of the environment. I very quickly had the idea of creating a foundation. Once its objectives were defined, it remained to establish its organization and funding. There are quite widespread examples of foundations set up by former political leaders. Bill Clinton in the United States and Nelson Mandela in South Africa had effectively continued their public involvement in this manner. It was what I called, as I left the Élysée, "serving differently." In this new life that was coming, a life free of all elected mandate, I wanted to be able still to be useful. I had to invent this new life with this foundation.

On May 6, 2007, Nicolas Sarkozy was elected president of the republic. We gathered at the Élysée that evening with Bernadette, my grandson Martin, and all of my staff, to hear the first statement of the future president. Each of us listened to each word he pronounced with the greatest attention, secretly waiting for the moment when he would mention the name of the man he was preparing to succeed or even thank him for the support the latter had given him. But this moment never came. For my part,

I abstained from displaying the slightest reaction, but deep down I was affected by it and now understood how the land lay.

On May 15, I addressed the French people for the last time, stressing in this last presidential address the need to safeguard in future all that had always been our strength in the most glorious as well as the most tragic moments of our national history:

> A nation is a family. This tie that binds us is our most precious possession. It gathers us, protects us, and allows us to face the future. It gives us the necessary strength to make our mark on the modern world.
>
> Always remain united and supportive of each other. Of course we are deeply diverse and of course we may have differences of perception and view. But we should come together in the essentials, in dialogue and concord. That is how we will continue to make progress. By unifying, as regards our diversity and our values, and by rallying together we can nurture every ambition.
>
> Tonight, I want to describe the strength of the tie that, from the bottom of my heart, unites me to every one of you. This link is one of respect, admiration, and affection for you, for the people of France, and I want to tell you just how much confidence I have in you and just how much confidence I have in France.

The following morning, I thought again with emotion of those forty years spent in serving the French. I was happy and proud of the road we had walked together. I was proud of what I was able to accomplish in the name of a certain notion of humanity and of my country. I also thought of all I had not succeeded in doing. I thought of those people who were suffering and in distress. I thought of the social division that I had tried to reduce but that continually reappeared in new guises. I thought of them. I thought of France. I thought of all the challenges that we still had to take on. History would judge this engagement in the service of my country.

Several hours later, after the transfer of power, Nicolas Sarkozy accompanied me to my car in the courtyard of the Élysée, and I left as serenely, dare I say, as I had arrived twelve years earlier. I did not experience this departure as a brutal wrench or as an event out of the ordinary. It seemed to me simply in the nature of things. There is life after power.

INDEX